CONTEMPORARY MUNICIPAL POLICING

WILLIAM P. McCAMEY

Western Illinois University

GENE L. SCARAMELLA

Lewis University

STEVEN M. COX

Western Illinois University

Boston   New York   San Francisco
Mexico City   Montreal   Toronto   London   Madrid   Munich   Paris
Hong Kong   Singapore   Tokyo   Cape Town   Sydney

Series Editor: *Jennifer Jacobson*
Editorial Assistant: *Elizabeth Lee*
Editorial-Production Administrator: *Joe Sweeney*
Editorial-Production Service: *Denise Botelho, Colophon*
Composition Buyer: *Linda Cox*
Manufacturing Buyer: *JoAnne Sweeney*
Cover Administrator: *Kristina Mose-Libon*
Text Composition: *Galley Graphics, Ltd.*

Between the time Website information is gathered and then published, it is not unusual for some sites to have closed. Also, the transcription of URLs can result in unintended typographical errors. The publisher would appreciate notification where these errors occur so that they may be corrected in subsequent editions.

Library of Congress Cataloging-in-Publication Data
McCamey, William
   Contemporary municipal policing / William P. McCamey, Gene L. Scaramella, Steven M. Cox
      p. cm.
Includes bibliographical references and index.
ISBN 0-205-34105-5 (alk. paper)
   1. Police administration—United States.   I. Scaramella, Gene L.   II. Cox, Steven M.   III. Title.
HV7991 .M335 2003
363.2′0973—dc21
                                                                                                   2002071213

Printed in the United States of America

10 9 8 7 6 5 4 3 2 1   VHG 07 06 05 04 03 02

CONTENTS

CHAPTER THREE
Police Operations   56

CHAPTER SIX

Women and Minorities in Policing   140

CHAPTER SEVEN

The Police Subculture and the Personal Costs of Police Work   164

CHAPTER EIGHT

Policing in a Multicultural Setting   196

CHAPTER NINE

Ethical Practice and the Use of Discretion in Policing   223

CHAPTER TWELVE

**The Future of Policing in the United States:
Changing Images, Technology, and Terrorism   301**

APPENDIX
Public Information Policy: River Forest Police Department   333

PREFACE

Municipal police in the United States operate in a climate of constant change. As we enter the twenty-first century, we expect them to continue to perform traditional tasks related to law enforcement and order maintenance, and, at the same time, to become problem solvers, community organizers, and terrorism preventers. Further, perhaps more than ever before, we expect them to perform these diverse tasks by exercising discretion wisely within an ethical framework. As the police intervene in our daily lives, many of us are suspicious of their motives and uneasy in their presence. On one hand, we recognize their role in an orderly society; on the other, we would prefer that they intervene in our lives only if and when we need them. It is our belief that much of the current criticism of the police and dissatisfaction among the police results from confusion over the appropriate role of the police and the misleading and sometimes unreasonable expectations that arise as a result. In this book, we present a realistic, practical view of the police as they interact with other citizens, as they organize for such interactions, and as they hire and train officers to engage in these interactions.

Sir Robert Peel developed and promoted a model for municipal police that has often been ignored in our society, but many of the basic tenets of that model have been resurrected recently in the form of community policing. Thus, we have come to realize once again that a basic requirement for an effective, efficient, civil police is a meaningful partnership between the police and other citizens. Only when such a partnership exists can the police perform their tasks as problem solvers, service providers, and occasional law enforcers, because only then will the public provide the support and resources necessary for the successful performance of these tasks. This partnership must be based on open, two-way communication between the police and other citizens in the joint venture of order maintenance and law enforcement.

Although we discuss police discretion, functions, organization, recruitment, training, and a variety of other topics separately, it is important to recognize that they are all interrelated and must be considered as part of the network of policing. Stresses and strains in any one area will have repercussions in others, and the relationships between the various parts must be considered if policing is to make sense.

It is also important to note from the outset that the terms *policing* and *law enforcement* are not synonymous. The latter constitutes only a small, though critical, part of the former. The basic task of the police in any society is not law enforcement, but problem solving (sometimes referred to as order maintenance), which may or may not include, in any given encounter, law enforcement.

A good deal of what follows is based on our observations and interactions with municipal police officers over the past thirty-five years.

ACKNOWLEDGMENTS

We acknowledge the assistance of the many police officers who contributed to our graduate-level classes and those who allowed us to observe them in action over the years. Specifically, we would like to thank Chiefs Jerry Bratcher, O. J. Clark, Don Cundiff, John Harris, Bill Hedeen, Mike Holub, Mark Fleischhauer, Ron Moser, and Superintendent Terry Hillard for their insights. Others in the police community who deserve special mention are Jerry Friend, Norma Venzon, and Sharon Anderson.

For their academic insights, we thank Drs. John P. Clark, Norm Denzin, Jack Fitzgerald, Giri Raj Gupta, Michael Hazlett, Dick Ward, Robert Fischer, and Sandy Yeh.

A word of thanks to those who reviewed the original manuscript and made valuable suggestions is also in order. Thanks to Lori Guevara, University of Texas at Arlington; Michael Holm, Northern Michigan University; Miriam Sealock, Towson University; and Arvind Verma, Indiana University—Bloomington.

Finally, for offering encouragement and support along the way, thanks to Ann, Jody, and Robin.

W.P.M.
G.L.S.
S.M.C.

CHAPTER ONE

HISTORICAL DEVELOPMENT OF AMERICAN MUNICIPAL POLICE

INTRODUCTION

American police are employed at the international, national, state, county, and municipal levels in both public and private agencies. Some 800,000 sworn police personnel are employed in nearly 19,000 public agencies, ranging in size from one officer to 37,000 in New York City (Reaves & Goldberg, 1998). The seventy-six largest police departments, which represent less than 1 percent of all agencies, employ 39 percent of all police

1

officers (Walker, 1999, p. 50). However, over 2,200 police departments have just one full-time officer, and almost 1,200 departments rely entirely on part-time police officers (Reaves & Goldberg, 1998, p. 2). Some police departments utilize the most modern technological equipment; some have difficulty even obtaining good radios. Some officers are well trained; others receive very little training. Some routinely intervene in the daily lives of their fellow citizens; others do not. Some are held in high regard by their fellow citizens; others are not (see Highlight 1.1). Any attempt to discuss this heterogeneous group as a whole is likely to be confusing or inaccurate, or both.

To avoid such confusion and inaccuracy, we will focus on municipal police in this text. A great deal of what we say also applies to county police, some to state police, and somewhat less to federal and international police. We do not attempt to deal with private police in detail here, although their relationship with municipal police is discussed in several places. As you read this book, then, please keep in mind that we are discussing municipal police unless otherwise noted. Before turning our attention to municipal policing, a very brief look at the composition of state and federal police is helpful in order to distinguish them from local police.

State and Federal Police

Prior to 1900, federal and state governments played very limited roles in policing. In fact, only two states, Texas (1835) and Massachusetts (1865), had some type of state police at the turn of the century (Johnson, 1981; Roberg & Kuykendall, 1993). The Pennsylvania State Police was established in 1905 to deal with ethnic and labor disputes, but its duties eventually expanded to include general police functions throughout the state. Over the next twenty years, numerous other states adopted the Pennsylvania model of state police (Champion, 1998, p. 89).

As the number of highways increased, state police agencies took on the responsibility for traffic enforcement on these thoroughfares, particularly in areas outside corporate limits of cities and towns. Eventually, a bifurcation occurred, with some agencies (twenty-five states) focusing almost exclusively on traffic control (highway patrol departments) and others (twenty-four states) maintaining more general enforcement powers (state police departments) (Barker, Hunter, & Rush, 1994, p. 70). Currently, there are twenty-six highway patrols and twenty-three state police agencies. The state police are empowered to provide law enforcement service anywhere in the state, while highway patrols have limited authority based on type of offense, jurisdiction, or assignment to specific duties (Gaines, Kappeler, & Vaughn, 1999). All states except Hawaii have some type of state police agency. In addition to their basic tasks, many of these agencies provide statewide communications and computer systems, assist in crime scene analysis and multijurisdictional investigations, provide training for other police agencies, and collect, analyze, and disseminate information on crime patterns in the state. In addition, many state police agencies have expanded their goals to include aircraft support, underwater search and rescue, and K-9 assistance. Many state police agencies also are responsible for state park security (park police or rangers), security of state property and state officials, and regulation of liquor and gambling-related activi-

■ ■ ■ ■ ■ ▬▬▬▬▬▬▬▬▬▬▬▬▬▬▬▬▬▬▬▬▬▬▬▬▬

HIGHLIGHT 1.1
SMALL-TOWN POLICE OFTEN OUTGUNNED

The Associated Press

The rookie police officer in Minatare, Nebraska, had good reason to worry.

A madman headed toward his village had wounded two officers in a shootout and killed a farmer who stumbled upon him in hiding.

Officer Matt Rockwell was already outgunned. He was without a bulletproof vest. His only protection was a 10-year-old handgun he bought himself. "I was a little nervous about it," said Rockwell, 27. "I hadn't even been to the academy yet or had much training."

The wanted man, Charles Lannis Moses, Jr., passed through town unnoticed. Moses broke into a house six miles out of Minatare before crossing into Wyoming, where he was caught the next day.

In many small Nebraska towns like Minatare, population 800, the officers required to protect the public often cannot properly protect themselves.

Many wear outdated bulletproof vests or don't have any at all. Sheriffs in Arthur and Blaine Counties must drive their own cars while on duty. Many police cars are without video camera, a technology that has helped protect officers and the public.

Other equipment problems exist, but some officers are reluctant to talk about them for fear of showing their hand to criminals.

Even in the state's largest city of Omaha, officers sometimes are outgunned. Officer Jimmy Wilson Jr. was fatally shot during a routine traffic stop in 1995. The weapon used to kill the 24-year-old officer was an automatic assault rifle commonly used by the military.

His father, retired officer Jimmy Wilson Sr., started a foundation in Wilson's name to provide bulletproof vests, video cameras and other equipment needed to protect officers in Nebraska and Iowa.

"I get at least half a dozen calls a week from departments saying, 'We need anything we can get,'" said Kim Van Brunt with the Wilson Foundation. "I've got people literally begging for money."

The foundation recently bought prisoner cages for Nebraska State Patrol cruisers. Until the donation, those patrol cars had no inside barrier between state troopers and the suspects they arrested.

The cages are vital to officer safety, Wilson said.

"Especially when there's 40 miles between some trooper and his backup," he said.

The foundation keeps raising money and fields a seemingly endless list of requests for help for police agencies ranging from one-officer operations to the Omaha Police Department.

Most local law enforcement agencies face a constant budget battle to update what equipment they do have, mostly when it comes to weapons, Blair Police Chief Marvin Doeden said.

Where criminals used to carry revolvers, they now sometimes have a cache of automatic weapons. Blair police officers recently recovered an assault rifle during a methamphetamine raid.

"We used to carry the old wheel guns. I can't imagine carrying that today," Doeden said. "You simply need the firepower."

The problem for police seems to get worse father away from the state's largest cities, where departments are typically better funded and have a nearby State Patrol station available for backup.

"It's bad, it's really bad out here," said Duane Pavel, a former Boyd County sheriff who spends much of his time visiting police agencies in the western part of the state as an employee of the Nebraska Sheriff's Association.

Money is the biggest challenge to properly equipping rural officers. County, city or village boards sometimes are reluctant to provide the funds needed for law enforcement, Pavel said. He said the problem is especially serious in western

(continued)

HIGHLIGHT 1.1 Continued

Nebraska, where many officers must rely on hand-me-down tools or buy their own weapons.

Brown County Sheriff Greg McBride in Ainsworth said a lot of resources have gone to equip his department to a secure level, but it is not what he would prefer.

Bulletproof vests should be replaced every three to five years, but McBride said his department can't afford replacements. Three of the department's six cars don't have video cameras.

With only two weapons purchased by Brown County for the six-man sheriff's department, officers must buy their own guns. Most have Ruger Mini-14 rifles, a semiautomatic with a 20-round clip that is also used by the State Patrol and cost $500 to $700 each.

McBride spent nearly $900 on his H&K handgun, highly modified so he feels safe.

"We've got to be ready to go to war at a moment's notice, or less," he said. "You never know what you might be facing."

What McBride finds most frustrating is that many citizens don't think officers need to be so well-armed.

"They seem to think we ought to be able to handle a dog call, chase cows off the road, handle an accident, maybe write a ticket now and then," McBride says.

ties. The forty-nine state law enforcement agencies employ about 54,600 sworn police officers, and the number of sworn state police increased by 9.1 percent from 1992 to 1996 (Reaves & Goldberg, 1998, p. 3).

United States Marshals were the first federal police, established in 1789 for the purpose of enforcing directives of the federal courts. There are currently over sixty federal agencies that exercise police powers. The Department of Justice and the Department of the Treasury contain the most well known law enforcement divisions: the Drug Enforcement Administration (DEA); the Federal Bureau of Investigation (FBI); the U.S. Marshals Service; the Bureau of Alcohol, Tobacco and Firearms (ATF); the Internal Revenue Service (IRS); the U.S. Customs Service; and the U.S. Secret Service. Other federal agencies employing law enforcement officers include Amtrak, the U.S. Supreme Court, the Environmental Protection Agency (EPA), and the Library of Congress. These agencies employ a total of 83,143 full-time sworn personnel (Bureau of Justice Statistics, 2000). The largest employers of federal law enforcement officers (61% of the total) are the Immigration and Naturalization Service (16,552), the Bureau of Prisons (12,587), the FBI (11,285), and the U.S. Customs Service (10,539). While each agency has a set of specific duties, there is a good deal of overlap and duplication among them. They do not, for the most part, engage in those activities normally provided by local and county police agencies, such as patrol, provision of services, and maintenance of order (Langworthy & Travis, 1999). Relatively few federal officers, usually referred to as "agents," are uniformed, and their primary duties involve investigation and control of federal crimes, such as bank robberies and crimes involving the crossing of state lines. They also are responsible for protecting federal property and federal officials. Finally, federal agencies provide training and logistical support for state and local police, and the FBI collects and disseminates national crime statistics.

Municipal Police

Municipal policing is a relatively recent phenomenon. In the Western world, municipal policing began, for all practical purposes, in 1829 in London as a result of the efforts of Sir Robert Peel, who was then Home Secretary. Peel believed that the police should be organized along military lines, under government control. He also thought police officers should be men of quiet demeanor and good appearance, and be familiar with the neighborhoods in which they were to police. In addition, he supported a territorial strategy of policing in which officers would walk prescribed beats in order to prevent or deal with crime. By 1870, Peel's territorial strategy, at least, had spread to every major city in America (Lane, 1992, pp. 6–7; Barlow, 2000, p. 166). Ultimately, Peelian reform served as a model for modern police management.

Municipal police in the United States have provided and continue to provide an extremely wide range of services, many of which, as we shall see, have little to do with crime or law enforcement. Each municipal department exists in its own context. Policing in a large metropolitan area may be considerably different from that in a small rural community in terms of the frequency of certain types of activities and the degree of specialization within the department, though the types of services provided are basically the same. Within any given police agency, each officer has considerable discretion with respect to the way in which she provides services. The diversity in American municipal police organizations makes them unique and is often confusing to foreign visitors familiar with more centralized police services.

What are the origins of municipal police? Why and how did we decide that it is necessary to specially designate certain individuals to provide the services associated with the police? What are these services? What are the special characteristics of municipal police? We will illustrate the development of police, beginning with the early English settlers. As you will discover, historical analysis reveals the roots of many current issues in policing, such as corruption, brutality, discretion, professionalism, and inefficiency.

THE CONCEPT OF POLICE

In early human groups, norms were largely informal, and various means of responding to violations of norms were developed to hold the groups together. These informal social control mechanisms consisted of providing rewards for conforming behavior and punishments for failing to conform, and they remain powerful influences on our behavior today. In small, homogeneous groups, behavior was controlled informally through the use of group pressure, and violations of customs, traditions, or moral standards were punished in a variety of ways, ranging from gossip to excommunication (Cox & Fitzgerald, 1996).

The expectations of those around us continue to play a more powerful role than the formal norms (laws) that are enforced by specially designated individuals (police officers). These formal norms may have arisen as farming and herding replaced hunting and gathering as subsistence modes (Cox & Fitzgerald, 1996). As communities grew, different groups or segments within the communities pursued their own ends, and community consensus no longer existed to the same extent as in smaller, more homogeneous groups. Kinship ties were replaced by more centralized community leadership (government). Communities became increasingly diverse, and government (the state) emerged as a means of providing order and security. To ensure a degree of order and security, certain individuals were designated to exercise civic or collective authority. These individuals (the police, from *polise*, the Greek word for "city") served as an arm of government to mediate and sometimes arbitrate disputes arising from the numerous rules and regulations (laws) developed to ensure order. These specially designated persons were also charged with apprehending offending parties and bringing them before other specially designated persons (prosecutors, judges), who had further authority to sanction undesirable behavior. Of course, in a democratic society, conflicting demands of various groups must be accommodated (at least to the point of being heard), and it is virtually guaranteed that not all parties to a dispute can be satisfied at the same time. Those responsible for policing democratic societies, then, occupy inherently problematic positions.

HISTORICAL DEVELOPMENT OF AMERICAN MUNICIPAL POLICE: THE EARLY YEARS

To understand the complexities and variations in policing today, it is useful to revisit the historical traditions that eventually led to contemporary police operations. The origins of policing date back to ancient empires around the world. Greeks, Romans, Egyptians, Spartans, ancient Israelis, and civilizations throughout Medieval times to the present have had forms of policing to enforce laws and maintain order. Gradually, over time, policing became formalized.

English settlers (about 90% of all early settlers) in America brought with them a night watch system that required able-bodied men to donate their time to help protect the cities. As was the case in England, some of those who could afford to, hired others to serve in their place and those substitutes hired to serve were not particularly effective. During this period, citizens often resolved disputes among themselves. Such resolution involved intergenerational blood feuds, eye gouging, gunfights, and duels (Miller, 2000). As cities grew larger and more heterogeneous, voluntary citizen participation in law enforcement and order maintenance became increasingly less effective, and something was needed to replace it. In 1749, residents of Philadelphia convinced legislators to pass a law creating the position of warden. Each warden was authorized to hire as many watchmen as needed, the powers of the watchmen were increased, and they were paid from taxes. Others cities soon adopted similar plans (Johnson, 1981, p. 7). The wardens served warrants and acted as detectives, often recovering stolen items in cooperation with the thieves themselves (Miller, 2000). They also patrolled the streets, but they were

FIGURE 1.1 The Sheriff of Nottingham The Sheriff of Nottingham, famous for his quest to arrest Robin Hood, was a police agent of the King of England.

not widely respected. In fact, as Walker (1999, p. 22) indicates, "Colonial law enforcement was inefficient, corrupt, and subject to political interference."

By the 1800s, with the rapid growth of cities, crime and mob violence had become problems in both British and American cities. In England, Sir Robert Peel was finally successful in establishing the London Metropolitan Police in 1829. Shortly thereafter, day-watch systems were established in America (Philadelphia, 1833; Boston, 1838; New

York, 1844; San Francisco, 1850; Los Angeles, 1851). By the 1850s, day- and night-watch systems were consolidated to provide twenty-four-hour protection to city dwellers (Berg, 1992, p. 31; Barlow, 2000, pp. 165–166).

By the middle of the nineteenth century, the main structural elements of American municipal policing had emerged. Watch and ward systems had been replaced, in the cities at least, by centralized, government supported police agencies whose tasks included crime prevention, provision of a wide variety of services to the public, enforcement of morality, and the apprehension of criminals. A large force of uniformed police walked regular beats, had the power to arrest without a warrant, and began to carry revolvers in the late 1850s (Miller, 2000). The original concept of "preventative policing had been modified to include maintenance of order functions which included finding lost children, moderating quarrels, and helping at fire scenes. Municipal police performed these tasks and were supplemented by county sheriffs in rural areas. Over time, these police agencies were further supplemented by the development of state and federal agencies" (Sweatman & Cross, 1989, p. 12).

Although they adopted a good many practices from their British counterparts, American police lacked the central authority of the crown to establish a legitimate mandate for their actions. Small departments acted independently within their jurisdictions. Large departments were divided into precincts that often operated more as small individual departments than as branches of the same organization (Kelling & Moore, 1988, p. 3). Colonists feared government intervention into their daily lives and thus disliked the idea of a centralized police force. Police officers represented the local political party in power rather than the legal system (Roberg & Kuykendall, 1993, p. 59; Conser & Russell, 2000, p. 167).

As a result of the political heterogeneity, officers were often required to enforce unpopular laws in immigrant ethnic neighborhoods and, because of their intimacy with the neighborhoods, were vulnerable to bribes for lax enforcement or non-enforcement (Kelling & Moore, 1988, p. 4; Conser & Russell, 2000, p. 168). In addition, the police found themselves in frequent conflict with rioters, union workers and their management counterparts, looters, and others.

> Expectations that the police would be disinterested public servants . . . ran afoul of the realities of urban social and political life. Heterogeneity made it more difficult to determine what was acceptable and what was deviant behavior. Moreover, urban diversity encouraged a political life based upon racial and ethnic cleavages as well as clashes of economic interests. Democratic control of police assured that heterogeneous cities would have constant conflicts over police organization and shifts of emphasis depending upon which groups controlled the political machinery at any one time. (Richardson, 1974, pp. 33–34)

In some cities, such as New York, political corruption and manipulation were built into policing. New York police officers in the 1830s were hired by elected officials who expected those they hired to support them politically, and they fired those who did not. "The late nineteenth century policeman had a difficult job. He had to maintain order, cope with vice and crime, provide service to people in trouble, and keep his nose clean politically" (Richardson, 1974, p. 47). The police became involved in party politics, including, granting immunity from arrest to those in power (Lane, 1992, p. 12; Conser & Russell, 2000, p. 168). Corruption and extortion became traditions in many departments, and discipline and professional pride were largely absent from many departments. Police spent most of their time providing services to local supporters, maintaining a reasonable level of social order necessary for the city and local businesses to operate smoothly, and seeking out every opportunity to make money (Barlow & Barlow, 2000).

According to Johnson (1981, p. i), America's brand of local self-government gives both citizens and professional politicians considerable influence in policing: "The need to respond to the diverse, often conflicting demands of various constituencies has given American policing a unique character which effects its efficiency as well as its reputation. However one views the police today, it is essential to understand how the theory and practice of politics influenced the nature, successes, and problems of law enforcement."

POLICING DURING THE NINETEENTH AND EARLY TWENTIETH CENTURIES

Attempts at reform, including the Pendleton Act (1883), which extended civil service protection to first federal and later state and local employees, led to some improvement, but old traditions and perceptions died hard and, in some cases, not at all. An excellent illustration of the complex intermingling of politics and policing is the office of sheriff. The sheriff was and remains a political figure charged with police duties. In America, rural policing was, almost from the beginning (Virginia, 1634), in the hands of the sheriff.

By the middle of the nineteenth century, as a result of the not infrequent killing of unarmed officers by armed offenders, many American police officers had purchased and carried their own firearms.

> However unhappy the critics of an armed police might be, they had to face one unavoidable fact. Americans, unlike the British, had a long tradition that every citizen had the right, even the duty, to own firearms. Guns were part of the American culture. . . . Beginning in the 1840s, people in cities began to use firearms against one another systematically for the first time. The problem facing the police had now become critical. Patrolmen never could be sure when a rowdy might have a gun, yet the officer knew he had to intervene in disorder quickly or risk having a small dispute between a small number of people grow into a serious problem. . . . The public accepted an armed police because there appeared to be no other alternative at the time. (Johnson, 1981, pp. 29–30)

In America, many citizens were opposed to the idea of a centralized police force because they feared that such forces might become instruments of government repression. The desire to protect individual rights was strong, yet the need to ensure some degree of order in the society was also apparent. To both maintain order and enforce the law, municipal police had to be granted the right to intervene in the daily affairs of private citizens. Regulation of morals, enforcement of traffic laws, mediation of domestic disputes, dealing with juveniles, and other activities required such intervention. Yet many of the early settlers in America had immigrated precisely because they did not want government intervention in and regulation of their daily activities. Predictably, then, police intervention in areas that citizens generally regarded as private generated suspicion and hostility toward the police. Nonetheless, then, as now, with increasing demands for public order come increasing intolerance of criminality, violence, and riotous behavior. Citizens want the police to address their concerns and to solve the problems they have brought to the attention of the police, but otherwise to leave them to their own pursuits (Toch & Grant, 1991, p. 3).

This was certainly the case in America beginning in the late 1800s and early 1900s when technological advances such as the invention and use of the call box, telephone, two-way radio, and patrol car led the police to believe that they could make great strides in eliminating urban crime and to inform the public of this belief. Promises to cut response time, apprehend more criminals, and prevent more crimes led to an increasing number of requests from citizens to produce such results (Reiss, 1992, p. 53; Alpert & Dunham, 1997, p. 31). Police activity varied depending on the local government and the political group in power. Standards for officer selection, training procedures, rules and regulations, level of enforcement of laws, and police-citizen interactions varied across the United States.

As the police continued to be involved in areas having little to do with law enforcement or crime, the public came to expect the police to respond to almost any request for assistance and, particularly during the hours between 5 P.M. and 8 A.M., did not hesitate to call them for assistance normally provided by some other agency. Fighting crime and enforcing laws were duties of the police, but the proportion of time devoted to these other activities was, and remains, very small in comparison to the proportion of time spent providing other services.

Throughout most of the nineteenth and into the twentieth century, the basic qualification for becoming a police officer was a political connection (Roberg & Kuykendall, 1993, pp. 61–66; Barlow, 2000, p. 167). The ability to read and write and good physical health were not among the necessary prerequisites (Richardson, 1974, p. 27), though sheer physical size was often a consideration. Men who had no education, long criminal records, and serious health problems were readily hired as police officers (Walker, 1999). Training was practically nonexistent, with most new officers being handed equipment and an assignment. Officers were expected to "handle" whatever problems they encountered while patrolling their beats, not simply enforce the law. The lack of strong central administration, the influence of politicians, and the neighborhood ties between the police and the people ensured a partisan process of policing (Langworthy & Travis, 1999). The degree of decentralization facilitated fragmented police services. This encouraged a close relationship with the citizens, but the lack of a central command led to inconsistency, confusion, and eventually, a call for reform. "For the patrolman, unless he was exceptionally stubborn or a notoriously slow learner, the moral was clear: if you want to get along, go along" (Richardson, 1974, p. 57).

To be promoted to the rank of captain or above in many big-city departments, an officer needed political support and, in some cases, a great deal of money. The police were a part of the political machinery; and politicians were seldom interested in impartial justice. The police became a mechanism that permitted politicians to solidify their power by controlling political adversaries and assisting friends and allies (Gaines, Kappeler, & Vaughn, 1999). Arrests were of little importance; the primary mission of the police was to provide services to citizens and garner votes for the politicians. The police provided a range of services, including babysitting at the police station, helping people find employment, feeding the homeless, and basic medical care. The recruitment of neighborhood residents as police, coupled with the level of decentralization of police services, ensured that the police reflected community values in their law enforcement and order-maintenance decisions (Langworthy & Travis, 1999). However, without accountability for the politicians and police, corruption, graft, and bribery reached a new level. At one point, police promotions and assignments were auctioned to the highest bidder, and illegal operations, including gambling and prostitution, made monthly contributions to police officers. According to Walker (1999, p. 25), "Police patrol was hopelessly inefficient. . . . Officers easily evaded duty and spent much of their time in saloons and barbershops."

Beginning in the 1870s, attempts emerged to reform the government generally and the police specifically. Examinations were recommended for those seeking public employment or promotion in an attempt to remove direct political influence and to recruit qualified personnel. Although some improvements resulted, political motivations continued to plague the selection of both officers and chiefs: "Too many chiefs were simply fifty-five-year-old patrolmen" (Richardson, 1974, p. 70). Additionally, although reformers made police corruption a major issue, their efforts were generally unsuccessful (Walker, 1999, p. 26).

This tradition continued into the twentieth century and is still deeply rooted in policing. The hiring and firing of police chiefs that accompanies changes in the political leadership of communities continues today, as do attempts on behalf of politicians to influence the daily activity of police officers and chiefs (Barlow, 2000, p. 167; Jackson, 2000).

Although the mixture of politics and policing has created numerous problems for the police, there is another side to this issue. In a democratic society, how are the police to be controlled? If the police are to be accountable and responsive to the citizens they serve, through what procedures are the needs and desires of the citizens to be made known to the police? According to Goldstein, "The suggestion that police agencies be directly supervised by elected municipal executives conjures up the image of police administrators beholden to various interests—including criminal elements—on whose continued support the elected mayor, their boss, may depend. . . . Is this not one of the costs of operating under our system of government?" (Goldstein, 1977, pp. 151–152).

In short, our system operates with elected representatives, and although their representation may not always satisfy us, we depend on them to convey our needs and desires to the institutions over which they preside. In our society, politics and policing are inevitably interwoven, and while we must be constantly alert to potential problems that result from this relationship, it is both necessary and desirable in a democratic society.

In the early 1930s, movements to professionalize the police began to materialize (although police professionalization was recognized as an important issue by August

Vollmer, chief of police in Berkeley, California, from 1905 to 1932 and the father of modern police management systems, at least as early as 1909). In part because of the Great Depression, policing became more attractive to young men who, in better times, might have sought other employment, thus making it possible to recruit and select qualified police officers. August Vollmer, Arthur Neiderhoffer, William Parker, and O. W. Wilson, among others, promoted professionalism and higher education for police officers, which, coupled with the impact of various reform movements, began to show positive results. O. W. Wilson's text, *Police Administration*, was adopted by administrators as the authority on structuring and organizing a police department.

As reformers attempted to define policing as a profession, the service role of police changed to more of a crime-fighting role. The passage of the Eighteenth Amendment in 1920 and the onset of the Great Depression in 1929 placed the police under a new public mandate for crime control and public safety (Lyman, 1999). As a result, police no longer provided the wide range of service activities mentioned previously (e.g., assisting the homeless, babysitting, and helping people locate employment). Reformers began to centralize command and control and remove the politicians from the police department (Walker, 1999). In addition, reformers adopted military customs and created specialized units, including vice, juvenile, and traffic divisions.

The task of police reform was to centralize police administration, improve the quality of police personnel, and destroy the power of the political bosses (Langworthy & Travis, 1999). However, the historical development of large, bureaucratically organized police departments can in part be attributed to a larger movement by government to obtain legitimacy for their agencies by adopting the rational–legal formal structure, which placed more emphasis on impersonal rules, laws, and discipline (Barlow & Barlow, 2000). Reformers rapidly infused science into policing through improved record keeping, fingerprinting, serology, and criminal investigation. The reform movement involved radical reorganization, including strong, centralized administrative bureaucracy; highly specialized units; and substantial increases in the number of officers.

Concern about the police reached a national level with the appointment by President Hoover of the Wickersham Commission (1931). The Commission was formed to investigate rising crime rates and directed police away from the service role, challenging them to become law enforcers and reduce the crime rate. The onset of World War II and the Korean War made recruitment of well-qualified officers more difficult during the 1940s and 1950s, respectively, and the riots and civil disorders of the late 1960s and early 1970s made policing less attractive to some. During this period, observers of the police, and sometimes the police themselves, seemed to equate technological advances and improved administration with professionalism.

While technological advances did occur, changes in standards; development of ethical codes, education, and training provided by those outside policing; and other indicators of professionalism were basically lacking. Still, some important changes had occurred. Reformers had identified inappropriate political involvement as a major problem in American policing. Civil service successfully removed some of the patronage and ward influences on police officers. Laws and professionalism were established as the bases of police legitimacy. Under these circumstances, policing became a legal and technical matter left to the discretion of professional police executives: "Political influence of any kind on a police department came to be seen as not merely a failure of police leadership but as corruption in policing"(Kelling & Moore, 1988, p. 5).

CONTEMPORARY POLICING

The 1960s was the most challenging era in American history for the police. During the 1960s, the crime rate per 100,000 persons doubled, the civil rights movement began, and antiwar sentiment and urban riots brought police to the center of the maelstrom (Dunham & Alpert, 1997). Also during this era, the nation experienced great turbulence as a result of the assassination of President John F. Kennedy (1963), Robert Kennedy (1968), and Martin Luther King Jr. (1968). Furthermore, during the 1960s, the U.S. Supreme Court exerted tremendous influence on police behaviors in *Chimel v. California* (1969), *Terry v. Ohio* (1968), *Spinelli v. the United States* (1969), *Escobedo v. Illinois* (1964), *Katz v. the United States* (1967), and *Miranda v. Arizona* (1966).

It was apparent that the police were not adequately prepared to address the civil unrest and the rapidly rising crime rate. The social disorder of this period produced fear among the public, as it appeared that families, religion, and the police were losing their grip on society (Barlow & Barlow, 2000). Legislators began to pass laws that provided substantial resources to police agencies. In the 1960s and into the 1970s, there was a rapid development of two- and four-year college degree programs in law enforcement and an increased emphasis on training. These changes were in large part due to the 1967 report of the President's Commission on Law Enforcement and Administration of Justice, which was, in part, responsible for Congress passing the Omnibus Crime Control and Safe Streets Act of 1968. This act established the Law Enforcement Assistance Administration (LEAA) and provided a billion dollars a year to improve and strengthen criminal justice agencies.

With funding available, social scientists began to test the traditional methods of police deployment, employee selection, and training, and to question the appearance of racial discrimination in arrests and the use of deadly force (Dunham & Alpert, 1997). Federal and state funding was available to police officers seeking to further their educations, and potential police officers began to see some advantage in taking at least some college-level courses. Although there were vast differences in the quality of these programs, they did create a pool of relatively well qualified applicants for both supervisory and entry-level positions. Many programs resulting from federal and state funding were targeted toward the development of community relations programs. These programs established many innovative approaches, including "officer-friendly" programs and school classroom presentations by police (Lyman, 1999).

These developments, coupled with improvements in police training, salaries, benefits, and equipment, helped create a more professional image of the police. At the same time, however, police came under increasing scrutiny as a result of their role in the urban disorders of the late 1960s and early 1970s. In addition, there had been consistent increases in crime, despite the movements toward professionalizing the police. The initial reaction of the police to the failure to control crime and disorder was to increase professionalism and militarization (Barlow & Barlow, 2000). Challenges to

When civilian police cannot maintain order, the military may be called to assist the police.

both authority and procedure were common, and criticism from the outside continued into the 1980s. The police were seen as partially responsible for continued high crime rates and civil unrest, and the number of complaints and civil actions brought against the police skyrocketed. As America entered the 1990s, Bouza (1990, pp. 270–271) noted:

> It is becoming ever clearer that underlying social and economic conditions are spawning crime and that society's unwillingness to do anything meaningful about them has really sealed the fate of the police effort to cope with the symptoms. Society wants to fight crime with more cops, tougher judges, and bigger jails, not through such scorned 'liberal' schemes as social welfare programs. . . . Police executives believe that today's unattended problems, concentrated in our urban centers, will only get worse, eventually resulting in riots and heightened violence.

There is clearly a discrepancy between what the public assumes the police can accomplish (based on media presentations, etc.) and what the police can actually accomplish. While the expectation may be that more police will solve the problems referred to by Bouza, the reality is that no increase in the numbers of police officers, in and of itself, will produce the desired result. The discrepancy is highly problematic, impacting not only on police administrators' decisions concerning operations, but also on the type of personnel who apply for police positions and the type of preparation for the job they receive. At the same time, collective bargaining and unionization in police departments have changed considerably the complexion of relationships between police administrators and rank and file officers. While police unions have undoubtedly helped improve police salaries and working conditions, they remain controversial because of their emphasis on seniority and perceived opposition to reform.

A noteworthy development in policing occurred in 1979. In response to repeated calls for police professionalism, the Commission on Accreditation for Law Enforcement Agencies was established. The Commission was formed through the efforts of the International Chiefs of Police Association, the National Organization of Black Law Enforcement Executives, the National Sheriffs Association, and the Police Executive Research Forum. The Commission became operational in 1983 and since that time has been accepting applications for accreditation, conducting evaluations based on specific standards for law enforcement agencies, and granting accreditation. By 2000, over four hundred agencies had been accredited, with another five hundred or so awaiting accreditation. In fact, many agencies originally accredited have now been through the reaccreditation process.

The amount and quality of research on the police improved drastically beginning in the 1960s. The 1967 Presidential Commission on Law Enforcement and the Administration of Justice, The National Advisory Commission on Civil Disorders in the same year, and the 1973 National Advisory Commission on Criminal Justice Standards and Goals represented major efforts to better understand styles of policing, police community relations, and police selection and training (Alpert & Dunham, 1997). Many other private and government-funded research projects contributed to current knowledge in these and other areas relating to the police. Yet today, municipal police reflect 150 years of conflict and attempts at reform. Most chiefs continue to be selected against a backdrop of party politics, which may be good or bad for the agency, as we have seen. There has been some consolidation and standardization of services, but not a great deal. The police appear to have become more concerned about social responsibility, but they still have difficulties interacting with some segments of society. Diversity remains the key characteristic of municipal police, and local control the key to such diversity.

Progress in policing has been made on many fronts. Progressive police chiefs, concerned academics, and other involved citizens have helped pushed the boundaries of traditional policing and shared their thoughts and findings at both national and international levels by publishing, teaching and training, and promoting exchange programs. Research on and by the police has increased dramatically in the past several years. As Petersilia (1993, p. 220) points out, ". . . police leaders have been under considerable pressure to manage personnel and operations as efficiently as possible. This pressure may help explain why police administrators have apparently been even more willing than leadership in other criminal justice areas to question traditional assumptions and methods, to entertain the conclusions of research, and to test research recommendations." Conser and Russell (2000, p. 197) conclude, "Essentially, what the [police] literature describes about the policing role in the United States is that it is unsettled, subject to ongoing societal change, and continually evolving."

The Community Policing Era

Throughout the history of American policing, community control of the police has been a major concern. When police administrators attempted to maximize the advantages of speed and mobility through the use of patrol cars, and when they turned to a more professional model of policing, they created social distance between the officers and the other citizens they served. Many citizens preferred to have police officers walking the beat, and research on foot patrol suggested that it contributed to city life, reduced fear, increased citizen satisfaction with the police, improved police attitudes toward citizens, and increased the morale and job satisfaction of police officers (Kelling & Moore, 1988, p. 10). Many of the community relations programs developed in the 1960s were the initial experiments into a radical revolution in policing: "Speaking at community centers and in schools was one of the first attempts to improve community relations. These programs eventually expanded to include neighborhood storefront offices, ride-along programs, fear reduction programs, police academies for citizens, cultural diversity training, police–community athletic programs, and Drug Abuse Resistance Education (DARE)" (Barlow & Barlow, 2000, p. 43). Beginning in the late 1970s, there was a movement away from the crime-fighting model to toward a community policing model. It was believed that in their pursuit of professionalism through enhanced technology and paramilitary organization style, the police had lost touch with the citizenry they were sworn to serve and protect (Lyman, 1999).

Unfortunately, the promised advantages of speed and mobility had little positive effect on crime. As police departments became more technologically sophisticated, citizens' expectations increased, and, using traditional means, the police were unable to meet these expectations. By the mid-1980s, it was clear that the police, by themselves, were unable to deal with increasing crime and violence. Recognizing that only with public cooperation could their performance in the areas of crime control and order maintenance improve, progressive police administrators turned to community-oriented or community-based policing as a possible solution to their problems. (See Chapter 3 for a detailed discussion of community policing.)

At the same time, problem-oriented policing was the subject of research in several communities. This approach to policing emphasizes the interrelationships among what might otherwise appear to be disparate events. For example, in one major city, for any given year, 60 percent of the calls for police assistance originated from 10 percent of the households calling the police (Pierce et al., 1987). Rather than dealing with all of these calls as separate incidents to be "handled" before clearing the calls and going on to other calls, problem-oriented policing focuses attention on the underlying difficulties that create patterns of incidents (Goldstein, 1979). It allows officers to take a holistic approach, working with other citizens and other agency representatives to find more permanent solutions to a variety of police problems (see Highlight 1.2).

Both community-oriented and problem-oriented policing emphasize the importance of the police–community relationship so clearly recognized by Peel over 150 years ago. Further, they recognize that police work is largely order maintenance performed through the use of negotiations (discussed in subsequent chapters). Some time ago, Sherman (1978, p. 4), proposing changes to improve education for future police officers, recommended that in addition to familiarizing students with the criminal justice system, all police education programs should emphasize the consideration of value choices and ethical dilemmas in policing and should "include comprehensive treatment of the most commonly performed police work, which falls outside of the criminal justice system."

HIGHLIGHT 1.2

CITIZEN ACADEMY PROVING POLICEWORK NOT LIKE TV

Ames Boykin Daily Herald Staff Writer

They won't get a badge, but Elk Grove Village residents will soon have a chance to attend a police academy.

The first class of the Citizens Police Academy has begun meeting this week, for 10 weeks of instruction on law enforcement and details only privy to police until now. For those who believe police work is just like it's portrayed on TV, think again.

"(On TV) They make an arrest, but they never do any paperwork. They never go to trial. They never go to jail," said Sgt. Dave Naumann. "That's not fun. That's not good TV."

The class will get a tour of the police department, a briefing on traffic laws and how an accident site is reconstructed for the investigation, and a look at how an evidence technician dissects a crime scene, Naumann said.

Students also will get to see a police dog demonstration, take aim at the shooting range and learn how officers determine when to use force, sometimes deadly, in crisis situations.

Some of the information that will be discussed has been reserved for legitimate graduates of the police academy, Naumann said. None of the information given away is so critical that it would somehow inhibit the job of police, he added.

The mock academy is not meant to serve as a recruiting tool for the department but rather as a way to increase citizen participation in the law.

Naumann said the more knowledge residents have, the more they will "become better eyes and ears" for the community because those attending the class will be better versed on the day-to-day activities of police.

People too often hesitate before they call police, or never call them at all because they don't feel comfortable. "This may help people feel better about calling the police," Naumann said.

The history of policing demonstrates the various roles assumed in the pursuit of law and order. Whether it was an English king appointing a sheriff to protect his country from invasion, or a Tamanny Hall politician hiring and promoting police officials to do his bidding, one thing is clear: Many variables have traditionally affected police practice in both positive and negative ways. Policing, in ancient and modern times, has been, first and foremost, a response for order maintenance. From the local fiefdoms of medieval times to the huge metroplexes of today, policing has been a necessary and primary function of all societies. Police authority has consistently inspired responses ranging from fear of the office to dependency on the office in times of crisis. Positions of authority, such as those occupied by police, run the risk of corruption, unethical behavior, and abuse of power, actions that have followed policing since its beginnings and that continue to capture headlines when exposed.

A lesson from the police archives is that changing times demand changing police methods and strategies. Just as the inception of motorized vehicles and radios dramatically altered police practice and public expectation in the early twentieth century, the

Bicycle patrol is sometimes used in place of motorized patrol to bring the police closer to the public.

explosion in technological resources in the late twentieth and early twenty-first centuries has again demanded equivalent acceleration in police tactics and capabilities. In addition to technology, police have had to react to crimes unheard of during most of the twentieth century, including computer crime, environmental crime, and various new forms of financial fraud. Some crimes have not changed (murder, arson, robbery, assault, and theft), but police intervention and investigative techniques have again adapted to crime solving by utilizing available resources such as DNA and other genetic based detection devices.

The world has become a global village where the possibility exists to travel literally anywhere within a matter of hours. And the ability to communicate has become instantaneous. In simpler times, law enforcement personnel could be recruited from almost any walk of life because the nature of crime did not generally require great technical expertise. In the twenty-first century, however, successful policing demands that the expertise of personnel be consistent with the advances in the field. Although it is difficult to generalize about the future of the police in the United States because of their diversity, Alpert and Dunham (1997) pinpointed several continuing dilemmas for the police, each of which has its roots in the historical issues discussed earlier. These issues include the need to bring greater numbers of qualified minorities and women into policing at all ranks. The use of force by the police, including the regulation of police pursuits, also must be addressed. Finally, the issues of police liability and lawsuits against the police remain important.

Bayley (1998, p. 5) concluded that the future of American policing will be shaped most profoundly by privatization; restructuring of government; group violence stemming from the inequities of race, gender, and ethnicity; and growth in the destructiveness of criminal violence.

Finally, Meadows (1998, p. 145) concludes, "Policing in the twenty-first century will be a more demanding and delicate process. The police and the community will share in the crime control function. . . The police will be given more legal freedom mandates, but will continually be held accountable for mistakes. These trends signal a need for the police to be better trained in the total crime prevention process and functions associated with community service."

The historical context of policing is important to understanding its present and its future. Policing is, and will remain, a big business. History has shown us that policing has evolved and adapted over time as the result of attempts to meet the needs of society. In the remainder of this book, we explore the issues raised here, along with the variety of ways in which American police attempt to define and fulfill their obligations and responsibilities (realistic and unrealistic) and the consequences of their attempts.

DISCUSSION QUESTIONS

1. Why is it so difficult to discuss and generalize about the police in the United States?

2. Briefly discuss the history of American police and the problems they currently face that are part of this history.

3. How, in the conduct of human affairs, did the need for police arise?

4. What problems confronting the police are inherent in democratic societies?

5. What are the positive and negative effects of the interaction between politics and the police in our society?

REFERENCES

Alpert, G. P., & Dunham, R. G. (1997). *Policing urban America*, 3rd ed. Prospect Heights, IL: Waveland.

Barker, T., Hunter, R. D., & Rush, J. P. (1994). *Police systems & practices*. Englewood Cliffs, NJ: Prentice-Hall.

Barlow, H. D. (2000). *Criminal justice in America*. Upper Saddle River, NJ: Prentice-Hall.

Barlow, D. E., & Barlow, M. H. (2000). *Policing in a multicultural society: An American story*. Prospect Heights, IL: Waveland.

Bayley, D. H. (1998). Policing in America: Assessment and prospects. In *Ideas in American policing*. Washington, DC: Police Foundation.

Berg, B. L. (1992). *Law enforcement: An introduction to police in society*. Boston: Allyn & Bacon.

Bouza, A. V. (1990). *The police mystique*. New York: Plenum.

Bureau of Justice Statistics. (2000). *Federal law enforcement statistics*. Washington, DC: U.S. Department of Justice.

Champion, D. (1998). *Criminal justice in the United States*, 2nd ed. Chicago: Nelson-Hall.

Conser, J. A., & Russell, G. D. (2000). *Law enforcement in the United States*. Gaithersburg, MD: Aspen.

Cox, S. M., & Fitzgerald, J. D. (1996). *Police in community relations: Critical issues.* Madison, WI: Brown & Benchmark.

Dunham, R. G., & Alpert, G. P. (1997). *Critical issues in policing: Contemporary readings,* 3rd ed. Prospect Heights, IL: Waveland.

Gaines, L. K., Kappeler, V. E., & Vaughn. J. B. (1999). *Policing in America,* 3rd ed. Cincinnati, OH: Anderson.

Goldstein, H. (1977). *Policing a free society.* Cambridge, MA: Ballinger.

Goldstein, H. (1979). Improving policing: A problem-oriented approach. *Crime and Delinquency, 25,* 236–258.

Jackson, D. (2000, October 22). Sordid ties tarnishing city police. *Chicago Tribune,* p. A1.

Johnson, D. R. (1981). *American law enforcement: A History.* St. Louis: Forum Press.

Kelling, G. L., & Moore, M. H. (1988, November). The evolving strategy of policing. In *Perspectives on policing.* Washington, DC: U.S. Government Printing Office.

Lane, R. (1992). Urban police and crime. In Tonry, M., & Morris, N. (eds.), *Modern policing* (pp. 1–50). Chicago: University of Chicago Press.

Langworthy, R. H., & Travis, L. F. III. (1999). *Policing in America: A balance of forces.* Englewood Cliffs, NJ: Prentice-Hall.

Lyman, M. D. (1999). *The police: An introduction.* Upper Saddle River, NJ: Prentice-Hall.

Maguire, K., Pastore, A. L., & Flanagan, T. J. (1993). *Sourcebook of criminal justice statistics—1992.* Washington, DC: U.S. Government Printing Office.

Meadows, R. J. (1998). Legal issues in policing. In Muraskin, R., & Roberts, A. R. (eds.), *Visions for change: Crime and justice in the twenty-first century.* Upper Saddle River, NJ: Prentice-Hall.

Miller, W. (2000, August). The good, the bad & the ugly: Policing America. Available at *History Today:* http://www.findarticles.com.

Petersilia, J. (1993). Influence of research on policing. In Dunham, R. G., & Alpert, G. P. (eds.). *Critical issues in policing: Contemporary readings.* Prospect Heights, IL: Waveland.

Pierce, G. et al. (1987). *Evaluation of an experiment in proactive police intervention in the field of domestic violence using repeat call analysis.* Boston: The Boston Fenway Project.

Reaves, B. A., & Goldberg, A. (1998). *Census of state and local law enforcement agencies, 1996.* Washington, DC: U.S. Department of Justice.

Reiss. A. J. Jr. (1992). Police organization in the twentieth century. In Tonry, M., & Morris, N. (eds.), *Modern policing* (pp. 437–474). Chicago: University of Chicago Press.

Richardson, J. F. (1974). *Urban police in the United States.* Port Washington, NY: Kennikat Press.

Roberg, R. R., & Kuykendall, J. (1993). *Police in society.* Belmont, CA: Wadsworth.

Sherman, L. W. (1978). *The quality of police education.* San Francisco: Jossey-Bass.

Sweatman, B., & Cross, A. (1989). The police in the United States. *Criminal Justice International, 5,* 11–18.

Toch, H., & Grant, J. D. (1991). *Police as problem solvers.* New York: Plenum.

Walker, S. (1999). *The police in America.* Boston: McGraw-Hill.

CHAPTER TWO

POLICE ORGANIZATION AND ADMINISTRATION

Organizations are among the more rational, efficient forms of grouping people. They have existed in one form or another for centuries, and the best of them are both effective and efficient. Effective organizations accomplish their goals, while efficient organizations make optimum use of resources.

One way of looking at organizations is to view them as arenas in which tasks are performed. The dynamic nature of organizations can easily be seen in a comparison with a sports arena in which the major focus of attention is on the playing field, in which people are constantly changing positions (entering and leaving), in which some spectators and participants are happy while others are unhappy, and in which a large number of secondary activities are occurring at any given time (concession stand sales, souvenir sales, business conversations, etc.). All of these activities in the arena (organization) require planning, organizing, staffing, directing, and controlling, and these activities are performed in varying degrees by personnel occupying positions at different levels within the organization.

Early in the twentieth century, police management adopted Luther Gulick's (1937) research on the seven tasks performed by organization administrators. The acronym POSDCORB is still included in many police management courses:

Planning—a broad outline of what the organization needs to accomplish

Organizing—establishment of a formal structure for the purpose of accomplishing the organization's mission

Staffing—the personnel functions, including recruitment, selection, and training of employees

Directing—the decision-making process involving the development of rules, policies, and procedures

COordinating—a process of ensuring that groups work together toward a common mission

Reporting—record-keeping and communication process

Budgeting—fiscal planning and management of organization resources

Planning and organizing are tasks that involve more time on the part of upper level management, while those at lower levels spend more time directing and coordinating everyday activities. In terms of police organizations, the chief of police and his immediate staff are likely to be involved in budgeting and policy making, while the shift and field supervisors are more concerned with day-to-day operations (directing and controlling personnel). Of course, the time spent in these various functions is also influenced by the size of the organization (Roberg & Kuykendall, 1997, p.11). The chief of a small police agency may complete all the functions associated with planning, coordinating, reporting, and direct supervision of employees. In short, we can analyze organizations in terms of the tasks (functions) they perform, recognizing that organizations are in a constant state of change brought about by both internal (e.g., number, quality, dedication of personnel) and external (e.g., legal, political, financial) factors.

POSDCORB is evident in the structure in all police agencies. Through the years, police have explored other forms of organizational structure, but today all police organizations are accurately described as *hierarchies*. Most hierarchies appear as a pyramid structure, with many employees at the bottom of the pyramid and few management personnel at the top. The personnel pyramid in policing, except for small police forces, has a very flat, extended base that quickly tapers to an elongated top (Bayley, 1994, p. 61). The top of the pyramid is reserved for administrators who possess broad responsibilities related to the organization's mission, including, at the very top, a vision for future activities of the organization. Upper-level administrators are defined by the rank of chief, director, deputy chief, or assistant chief. An organization with many levels of administration results in a tall hierarchy. Communications in such organizations often follow a rigid chain of command that presents a number of problems to personnel. Top administrators communicate explicit orders and directives downward, but there are few provisions for upward communications from lower ranks. Bayley (1994, p. 64) concluded that the command-and-control system of police management is paradoxical: It seeks to regulate in minute ways the behavior of individuals who are required by the nature of their work to make instant and complex decisions in unpredictable circumstances. Accordingly, many departments are moving toward flattening the organizational structure or reducing the number of traditional ranks, a movement sure to be met by resistance, because there will be less opportunity for upward mobility to fill the many ranks of taller structures (Swanson, Territo, & Taylor, 2001, p. 188). Because rank promotions are often directly tied to increases in pay, recognition, and responsibility, police administrators will need to develop alternative incentives for the traditional rank structures.

The middle of the police hierarchy includes the ranks of captain, commander, lieutenant, and sergeant, and these individuals have the responsibility of commanding or administering special units within the organization (Gaines, Kappeler, & Vaughn, 1999, p. 160). Examples of middle managers include a lieutenant in charge of an investigations unit or a night-shift patrol commander. The bottom levels of the hierarchy consist of those who do the actual police work in the organization: the patrol officers and investigators. In most organizations, positions in the hierarchy dictate the level of responsibility of the person occupying the rank. Thus, chief executives have greater responsibility than middle managers, who have greater responsibility than lower level employees. However, in policing, the status of police officers is inversely proportional to their responsibilities (Bayley, 1994, p. 72). In other words, police officers on the street have more policing responsibilities than administrators but occupy lower ranking positions.

Another way of describing the positions in the hierarchy involves examining the structural arrangement of positions. The term *line personnel* refers to those directly involved in performing the basic mission of the organization and, in policing, includes patrol officers and investigators (LaGrange, 1998, p. 319). However, as organization complexity increases, additional personnel are needed to allow line personnel to complete the basic work of the organization. Staff personnel are added to support line functions and, in policing, include training officers, community relations personnel, and lab technicians, among others.

ORGANIZATIONAL STRUCTURES

It is obvious that the types of functions police officers perform depend to a considerable extent on the type of organization in which they are employed and the position they occupy within the organization. The organizational structures of police departments vary considerably depending on the style of policing involved, the size of the community and the police force, the resources available, and so on, and these variables are, of course, interdependent. Organizational structures range from the small, single-person department in which the officer (chief, marshal, constable) performs all functions related to the police to those involving thousands of police personnel and dozens of specializations. The way in which an organization is structured helps to determine productivity, the manner in which goals are achieved, and the influence of individual variations on the organization. Organizational structures are the settings in which decisions are made and within which operations are carried out (Hall, 1999, p. 48).

Research has shown that structural differences exist between work units, departments, and divisions within organizations, and that differences exist according to the level in the hierarchy (Hall, 1999, p. 48). Even though most police organizations share some common characteristics, within a police department, hierarchical differences exist. For example, the employees who work in the evidence room are guided by strict rules and regulations. Police officers assigned to the investigations unit typically operate under broader guidelines and enjoy more discretion.

The Paramilitary Structure

Early police management theorists were influenced by classical managerial approaches such as those of Frederick Taylor (scientific management, stressing increased efficiency), Max Weber (bureaucracy, emphasizing hierarchical authority and control), and by some so-called universal principles developed by administrative theorists (Roberg & Kuykendall, 1997, p. 29). Police management theorists hoped, through the adoption of these classical principles, to create more professional police organizations. The result was a highly bureaucratic structure, managed and organized along classical military lines, that closely controlled police behaviors (Roberg & Kuykendall, 1997, p. 29). The intent of the structure was to improve efficiency of operations, provide fast response to emergency situations, use retrospective criminal investigation to achieve organizational objectives, and attempt to ensure the fair and impartial enforcement of the law (Engelson, 1999, p. 64). The typical characteristics associated with this paramilitary model include the following:

1. Central command structure
2. Rigid differences among ranks
3. Terminology similar to that of the military
4. Frequent use of commands and orders
5. Strong enforcement of rules, regulations, and discipline
6. Discouragement of individual creativity
7. Resistance of system to challenge (LaGrange, 1998, p. 318)

Although police organizations have traditionally employed paramilitary structures, such organizational structures are typically resistant to change and are poorly suited to meet the rapidly changing needs of a public service agency. They often fail to promote communication horizontally and from the bottom up, and they frequently fail to encourage employee commitment through participation. To be sure, there are times in policing when a highly centralized, authoritarian command structure is an advantage. There is little time to call a committee meeting to decide what to do when riotous protesters are threatening the police station, or what should be done when a police officer responds to a 911 armed robbery call. But as officers become increasingly well educated and trained, the demand for explanations of, and participation in, decision making in less trying circumstances increases as well.

Many police organizations have adopted the paramilitary model in highly specialized police units, called *police paramilitary units* or PPUs (Roberg, Crank & Kuykendall, 2000, p. 118). PPUs include such units as SWAT (special weapons and tactics), SRTs (special response teams), and ERUs (emergency response units). Such police units are structured much like military units because of the perception that a "war" is being waged against crime and military units are clearly established and trained to fight wars (Engelson, 1999, p. 64). For example, Walker (1999, p. 356) concluded that police resemble the military in that they wear uniforms, use military rank designations and a hierarchical command structure, carry weapons, and have the legal authority to use deadly force and deprive individuals of certain rights. Most police work, however, is not of this nature. There is minimal research into the effects of the paramilitary model on police operations; however, Peak (1997, p. 114) found that the quasi-military organizational structure places restrictions of personal freedoms; is characterized by communications blockages, and demonstrates lack of flexibility and narrowness of job descriptions. Some authors (Gaines & Swanson, 1997, pp. 364–367) question the capacity of the quasi-military organizational model to meet today's policing needs. We discuss these issues and proposed organizational changes in the remainder of this chapter.

There are a number of different designs for police departments. We examine three of them: functional design, place design, and time design.

Functional Design

A functional design involves the creation of positions and departments on the basis of specialized activities (Hellriegel, Slocum, & Woodman, 2001, p. 487). The functional design is one of the most widely used methods of organizing police agencies and involves identifying and consolidating common tasks (functions) and areas of work. The functional method of organizing is based on a consideration of the tasks performed by all police departments, but it recognizes differences based on size. In large departments, it can be efficient and cost effective to establish a specific unit for a specific task. For example, in a very large department, the operations function could be divided into patrol, traffic, burglary, narcotics, juvenile, vice, and many other specialized areas. One advantage to this type of organization is that responsibility and accountability for the completion of work is clearly understood by employees assigned to each unit. A disadvantage is that the functional method fosters a limited point of view in which employees often lose sight of the functions of the organization as a whole (Hellriegel, Slocum, & Woodman, 2001, p. 489). In addition, the functional organization design has minimal application to small police departments, in which officers are expected to possess multiple skills and broad knowledge concerning the police role. For example, in one incident, a small-town officer may be handling a traffic problem, in the next, a juvenile issue, and then the officer may be called on to handle a major burglary, which requires crime scene search skills (Turner, 2000, p. 50). Realizing that no one officer can readily accumulate all the sophisticated skills associated with all of the functions performed by police officers, numerous small departments have developed alternatives. Many agencies have begun to contract for specialized services with other law enforcement agencies, created mutual aid agreements, or consolidated services in regional crime laboratories (Turner, 2000, p. 50).

Most departments with a sufficient number of personnel tend to organize by function by creating at least two divisions with distinct, if somewhat overlapping responsibilities. These divisions are Operations and Administrative/Staff Services. Each of these typically includes several subdivisions, and as the number of subdivisions grows, problems with coordinating the functions of the various subdivisions arise. In an attempt to prevent loss of control and ensure uniformity among subdivisions, most organizations create extensive rules, policies, and procedures, and police organizations are no exception.

Operations Division

Patrol. Patrol operations have long been regarded as the backbone of the police organization. Patrol is typically the largest division in a police department, often accounting for 60 percent of the department's personnel (Berg, 1992, p. 58). The patrol division is responsible for providing continuous police service and some degree of visibility. In the past, patrol operations were assumed to deter crime, and many police administrators believe that patrol serves a deterrent function and enhances citizen satisfaction. In spite of the fact that a number of patrol studies suggest that routine patrol does not perform either of these functions (Kelling et al., 1974; Skolnick & Bayley, 1986; Toch & Grant, 1991), many police administrators continue to operate as if it did. In any case, there is little doubt that the impact of patrol officers on other citizens is considerable. Patrol officers respond to calls for service in their zones, beats, or districts, and they patrol the streets in their assigned areas when they are not responding to calls or completing the reports that inevitably accompany calls for service. The majority of patrol work is reactive, although, occasionally, patrol officers do come on a crime in progress. They also often use patrol to initiate contact based on traffic violations. In addition, patrol officers are generally responsible for securing crime scenes and conducting preliminary investigations as first responders. Once a crime scene has been secured, patrol officers often turn further responsibilities over to the investigative or detective division, although in some departments, patrol officers maintain responsibility for such investigations. In addition to their involvement in crime control, patrol officers also are responsible, in smaller departments, for traffic control and investigating traffic accidents. Larger departments are likely to have separate traffic and accident investigation units within the operations division.

An increasing number of police administrators, recognizing that routine patrol may not pay good dividends, are experimenting with other types of patrol. These include, among others, *directed* or *targeted* patrol, in which cars and officers are assigned to areas based on crime analysis in the hopes of catching, deterring, or moving offenders; *split* patrol, in which part of the force is involved in directed or targeted patrol while the remainder of the patrol officers answer calls for service; *saturation* patrol, in which officers flood a particular area in hopes of deterring, apprehending, or moving offenders;

offender-based patrol, in which officers target known offenders; and *foot* patrol, often used in congested areas, in which the intention is to increase citizen contact as well as deter and prevent crime. The latter has become increasingly common with the growth of community policing.

In some departments, boat, air, bicycle, and canine-assisted patrols are employed, and in others, volunteers are used to patrol specific areas under the supervision of police officers (Wrobleski & Hess, 1990; Berg, 1992; Parsons, 2000; Domash, 2000).

Directed patrol strategies appear to make far more sense than routine patrol, in which officers are simply sent out at the beginning of their shifts with little or no direction. In many cases, these officers do little more than drive around waiting for a call for service, with no apparent goal other than to be seen. When this occurs, the net result may be a loss of person hours, which could be used far more wisely, and wear and tear on the vehicles involved.

Over the years, working in the patrol division for a prolonged period takes on negative connotations. In the words of one young patrol officer, "Everyone knows you have to get out of patrol if you want to go anywhere in the police world" (personal interview). In fact, patrol officers with 25 years of service are often held in low regard by those hoping to "go somewhere" in policing. This view fails to recognize that some police officers like working the streets and the type of interaction this suggests. Many have a wealth of experience to share about the beats and/or communities they patrol, but much of this experience is lost when they retire. To some extent, community policing

Some police officers prefer to work the street.

has returned respectability to patrol work by emphasizing the importance of mutual recognition and understanding between police officers and the citizens they serve. Still, many young officers seek their police fortunes elsewhere, often in the investigations bureau.

Investigations.   The investigations bureau is a subdivision of the operations division and is basically responsible for obtaining and processing evidence and making arrests based on such evidence. The evidence involved may be tangible (physical evidence collected at a crime scene or at the residence of a suspect) or intangible (accounts from witnesses or informants). While this division is often regarded as the "glamour division" because it is thought to involve "real" police work, the evidence indicates that investigators are not particularly likely to solve crimes unless a witness steps forward to identify the offender (Greenwood, Chaiken, & Petersilia, 1977; Bouza, 1990).

Nonetheless, investigators spend a good deal of time photographing and sketching crime scenes, interviewing and interrogating suspects and witnesses, collecting and analyzing fingerprints, and sifting through records, reports, and other materials that may contain leads relevant to specific crimes. In some instances, evidence is processed in the departmental crime laboratory; in others, such evidence is sent to state crime laboratories for processing. Once evidence has been obtained, investigators are responsible for establishing a custody chain that governs storage and protection of the evidence. Case preparation and testifying in court are additional responsibilities of investigators. Investigators also are responsible for conducting undercover operations and developing informants (though many patrol officers also have informants), often in connection with investigations related to vice or drugs.

Juvenile or youth officers are frequently found in the investigations bureau as well. Among these officers are specialists in gang intelligence, physical and sexual abuse of children, and crime prevention among youth. Others specialize as school liaison/resource officers and serve as counselors, facilitators, and coordinators for youth and as representatives of other service agencies and schools. Included in this latter category are DARE (Drug Abuse Resistance Education) officers who teach in the school system. In an increasing number of states, youth officers must be specially trained or certified because they deal with laws relating to juvenile or family court acts, which are often considerably different from criminal statutes in terms of procedural requirements.

Administrative/Staff Services Division.   The administrative services division may include several subdivisions (Thibault, Lynch, & McBride, 2001):

1. Personnel
2. Research and planning
3. Budgeting
4. Data collection/crime analysis/computer section
5. Training
6. Counseling services
7. Maintenance
8. Communications/records
9. Civilian employees

10. Legal advisors
11. Internal affairs

Personnel employed in this division are often specialists, as you can see from the preceding list. They are not typically in the chain of command, although the rank structure in the division may be the same as in other divisions. These staff personnel provide information and advice to the chief and other supervisors concerning a wide variety of topics and process the mass of information that is characteristic of police organizations.

A typical functional design organizational chart for a small police department would look something like the one shown in Figure 2.1. In larger police organizations, the number of specializations within each division increases, leading to an organizational structure such as the one shown in Figure 2.2. In departments of the size and complexity illustrated in Figure 2.2, officers may not even know all the officers who work on their shifts or in their divisions. Further, only designated officers may be permitted to handle cases in their specialization. That is, an officer working in burglary may not handle a robbery or some other type of theft. Officers may become so specialized that they handle only one particular type of crime (e.g., computer theft). Patrol personnel may be limited by departmental policy as to their involvement in investigations, in part because they lack the specialized training required to handle certain types of investigations.

In some departments, for instance, patrol officers responding to a crime scene are only to secure the scene and complete a preliminary report, which is then given to the investigative division for follow-up. In many instances, the patrol officer never learns the outcome of the case she initiated. As might be expected, this sometimes leads to intradepartmental rivalries and occasionally to open hostility between divisions in the same department. It is not uncommon to find investigators and patrol officers working for the same agency who seldom speak to one another or share information. This is also true when looking at the broader picture: cooperation among different police agencies working on the same case. This lack of communication, often based on territorial jealousy, seriously impairs the ability of the police organization in performing its functions and has been a major problem in contemporary policing.

The organizational charts shown in Figures 2.1 and 2.2 illustrate that police departments employ both sworn and nonsworn (civilian) personnel. One of the major trends accompanying community policing in the past decade has been to increase the number of civilians employed.

People-Processing Organizations. As noted, organizations may be viewed as interpersonal networks that focus on the performance of certain tasks or functions. Police organizations are people-processing networks in which the raw material processed (people) is non-uniform (Perrow, 1967). In such organizations, individual staff members are responsible for the actions of other people and, in general, have a great deal of personal responsibility (discretion) for the effectiveness (success in achieving goals) and efficiency (judicious use of resources) of the organization. Effective organizations of this type consistently foster in their employees a strong sense of organizational values, self-respect, responsibility, and freedom to deliver services according to their own judgment (Holden, 1994, p. 154). The importance of formal and informal, horizontal and vertical,

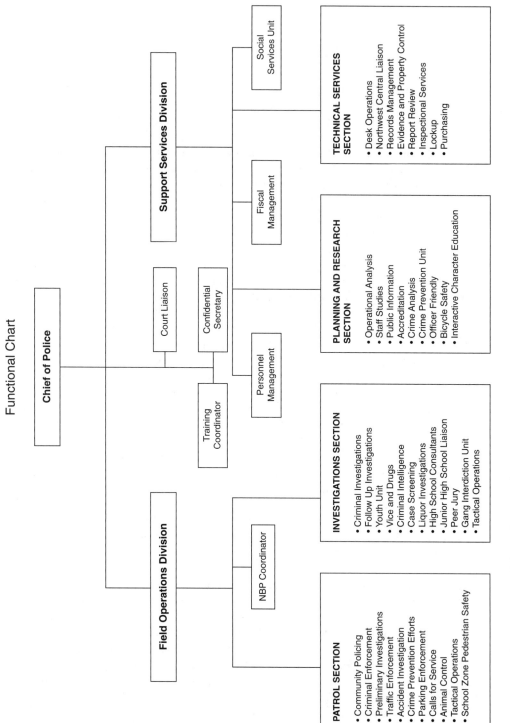

FIGURE 2.1 Organization of the Palatine Police Department

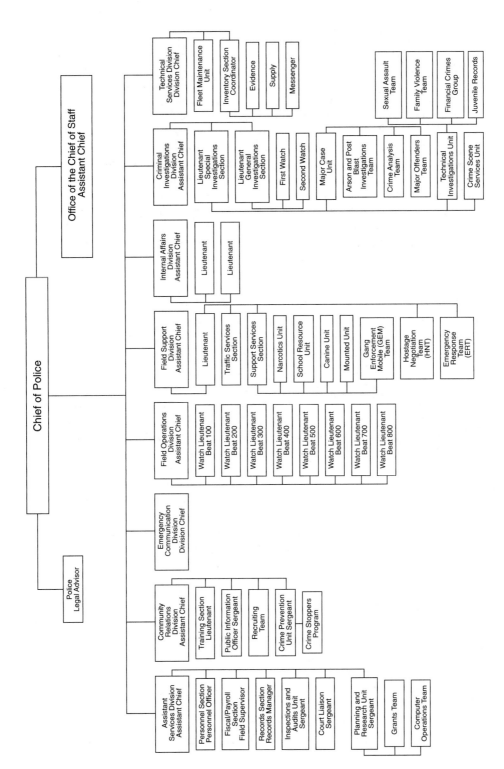

FIGURE 2.2 Chicago Police Department Organization for Command

and internal and external lines of communication is emphasized in such organizations. So, too, is the importance of specialized personnel with expertise in handling various types of non-uniform raw material (clients, suspects, offenders). For example, it may be difficult for the same person to deal expertly with patrol, investigations, juveniles, the elderly, the mentally ill, hardened criminals, those involved in domestic disputes, and so on. Regardless of the difficulty, however, police personnel in small agencies must attempt to provide all types of services to all types of clientele. Thus, the same person may answer the phone, respond to a crime scene, conduct an investigation, prepare charge sheets and written reports, secure evidence, interrogate suspects, interview witnesses, and appear in court to testify. In larger departments, many of these tasks are performed by different divisions and personnel.

Officers in small departments are often expected to be jacks of all trades. Except in very small departments, however, there is typically some attempt to designate certain officers as specialists in investigations, while others are viewed as performing basic patrol, supervisory, or administrative functions.

Place Design

Place design involves establishing an organization's primary units geographically while retaining significant aspects of functional design (Hellriegel, Slocum, & Woodman, 2001, p. 489). For example, patrol divisions are responsible for all geographic areas within the limits of the municipality. The city is typically divided into *beats*, *zones*, or *areas*, with each having coverage on eight-, ten-, or twelve-hour shifts. Patrol officers perform their basic functions within the assigned geographic areas, but sometimes leave the beat to assist officers in other beats. In large cities, beats may be combined to form *sectors*, which are administered by a sergeant or a lieutenant, or both. In the largest cities, sectors maybe combined to form *precincts*. Precinct houses are distributed geographically, and each may be viewed, to some extent, as a separate department with ties to central headquarters. For example, the New York Police Department, which serves eight million people with almost 40,000 police officers, has seventy-six police precincts spread throughout the five boroughs of New York (Dempsey, 1999, p. 71). As with the functional design, the place design can increase coordination problems, depending on the number of beats, zones, areas, sectors, and precincts.

Time Design

The final organization design found in police agencies involves organization by time. The patrol division is typically divided into three *watches*, *tours*, or *shifts* to provide twenty-four-hour coverage. The day shift often operates from 8 A.M. to 4 P.M., the afternoon or evening shift from 4 P.M. to 12 midnight, and the night shift from 12 midnight until 8 A.M. Some department employ *power shifts*, which typically involve assigning additional personnel to cover part of the evening and part of the night shift (e.g., adding additional personnel who work from 8 P.M. until 4 A.M.).

Officers have traditionally worked eight-hour shifts five days per week, with two days off, but some departments schedule officers for ten-hour shifts for four days, with the following three days off (Moore & Morrow, 1987). Other agencies divide the twenty-four-hour required coverage into twelve-hour shifts. Often, this involves dividing the patrol division into four shifts: two morning shifts and two evening shifts. The shifts usually work two, three, or four days; then the other patrol shifts work two, three, or four days, depending on the type of twelve-hour shift schedule (Chapiesky, 1999, p. 3). Using the traditional three-tour system, it takes three officers to cover each day: one on the night tour, one on the day tour, and one on the evening tour. When regular days off, vacation time, personal days, and sick leave are factored into the three-tour system, approximately five officers are required to cover each beat twenty-four hours a day, seven days a week, 365 days a year (Dempsey, 1999, p. 72). However, Bayley (1994, p. 52) argued that in order to increase the street presence of the police by one additional officer, it would be necessary to hire as many as ten additional police officers. He concluded that only 60 to 70 percent of all police are assigned to patrol, leaving approximately 17.5 percent on the street at any given moment, due to the need to cover four shifts. Furthermore, Bayley (1994, p. 53) found that sick days, leave, training, administrative tasks, and numerous other activities further reduced the number of patrol officers on the street.

Future Organizational Designs

Based on limitations in the previous designs and the need for an organizational structure to be able to adapt to a changing environment, many police agencies are experimenting with more decentralized structures. As police departments attempt to move toward community policing, which includes the decentralization of operations and decision making, becoming less specialized, and flattening the hierarchy, the effectiveness of the paramilitary design is increasingly being questioned (Roberg, Crank, & Kuykendall, 2000, p. 117). As a result, police organizations have modified the traditional paramilitary style of policing. The principles associated with the traditional model tend to stifle innovation and creativity, and promote alienation and loss of individual self-worth (Swanson, Territo, & Taylor, 2001, p. 201). More citizen-police interactions, better educated police officers, and budgetary constraints are forcing police organizations to reexamine the manner in which they provide service to the community (Dantzker, 1999, p. 29).

If the traits of the paramilitary model were ever conducive to effective police work, they are considerably less so with the transition to better educated, better trained officers. While some police chiefs reflect on the "good ole days" when officers simply did what they were told by an officer of superior rank and seldom questioned the orders and directives they received, most realize that current conditions require officers who can think on their feet; question, understand, and explain the rationale for the directives they follow; and exercise discretion wisely. Proactive police work in contemporary society calls for organizations that achieve the following:

1. Support the exercise of initiative and discretion at all levels
2. Exert control through the use of guidance and techniques, coaching, and counseling

3. Are characterized by communications that flow both vertically and horizontally in both directions
4. Use positive reinforcement as opposed to punishment to motivate personnel
5. Promote flexibility in operations
6. Are more decentralized
7. Encourage decision making at the lowest possible level
8. Emphasize participative management
9. View change as an indicator of organizational health
10. Develop and distribute guidelines delineating organizational expectations and evaluate personnel in terms of these guidelines (Skolnick & Bayley, 1986; Sparrow, Moore, & Kennedy, 1990; Toch & Grant, 1991; Cox & Fitzgerald, 1996)

Policing in the new millennium requires innovative organizational designs. Necessarily, such designs will be less formalized, less specialized, and less bureaucratic (rule oriented), with direction from the organization emphasizing shared values, participatory decision making, and a collegial atmosphere (Swanson, Territo, & Taylor, 2001, p. 202). Of course, as previously discussed, the application of these organizational design characteristics cannot be generalized to every situation. In police work, certain emergency situations demand an immediate response that can best be achieved by adhering to the paramilitary model. When such situations arise, there is often little or no time for debate. Nonetheless, debriefings following such situations afford the opportunity for input from all parties involved, and lessons that may lead to a more effective response in future similar incidents are often learned.

Major structural changes (e.g., flattening the structure by significantly reducing levels and command ranks) are difficult to effect and are time consuming (Roberg, Crank, & Kuykendall, 2000, p. 116). Problems often arise as police departments attempt to make the transition from traditional to community policing. For example, Roberg, Crank, and Kuykendall (2000, p. 152) found that successful implementation of community policing requires decentralization of the organization, participatory management, higher educational standards, redefining the police role (including training, reward, and promotions), and citizen involvement. These are major changes for traditional police organizations, and they are not adopted easily. Such structural changes and role modifications require a substantial paradigm shift for police.

The matrix structure design, for example, challenges some classical organizational design principles. A *matrix structure* is based on multiple support systems and authority relationships whereby some employees report to two superiors rather than one, a clear violation of the principle of chain of command adhered to in the paramilitary structure (Hellriegel, Slocum, & Woodman, 2001, p. 495). The essence of a matrix structure is in the assignment of members from different functional areas (e.g., patrol, detectives, and support services) to specific projects (e.g., task forces and crime-specific programs) (Swanson, Territo, & Taylor, 2001, p. 195). The formation of a drug task force is an example of a matrix organization. The drug task force has a supervisor who directs task force operations, but officers assigned to the task force (selected based on their expertise and their ability to contribute to the group) may still be required to report to the supervisors of the units or departments from which they were selected. This can cause confusion for the officers involved and can also lead to hard feelings between the supervisor of the task force and the supervisor of the unit or department. Nonetheless, because a task force assignment is often temporary, the personnel involved eventually return to their regular duties and regular supervisors after a specific length of time or after the task force has completed its goal.

Staffing in Police Organizations

In spite of the current experimentation discussed in the previous section, most police departments maintain a common organizational structure in terms of personnel positions. A chief of police who is responsible to city administrators for organizing and distributing police resources is in charge of the agency. The chief's job is basically administrative and he also serves as a figurehead for the agency. Some departments assign a deputy chief to assist the chief in his duties, but this is perhaps less popular today than in the past. Typically, the functional divisions of the department are headed by officers with the rank of commander or captain who are responsible for ensuring that their units function in accordance with the goals established by the chief in consultation with city administrators. These positions, too, are basically administrative. Watch commanders, usually lieutenants, are responsible for providing police services for the chronological periods of the day in which their watches or shifts operate.

Other lieutenants may occupy staff positions supervising specific programs or areas of operation within the department (e.g., research and planning). Sergeants typically serve as field-level supervisors, responsible for supervising specific groups of personnel while acting as liaisons with the shift commander. This position includes some administrative work, but often requires working the streets or handling calls as well. Those with the rank of sergeant also may serve in staff functions such as those described for staff lieutenants.

Police Organizations in Context

It is important to note that police organizations do not exist in a vacuum, nor are police functions determined totally or even largely by the police themselves. The police always operate in a political arena under public scrutiny (though a good many try to minimize such scrutiny). The police chief heads the police department, but is responsible to a city manager, mayor, police commissioner, and city council. In many instances, in which city government regards the separate public service agencies as consumer oriented, chief executive officers are viewed as part of a cooperative team, with responsibilities to one another as well. Thus, the chief of police may request new equipment monies one year but defer to the fire chief the next. Further, in the vast majority of police agencies, hiring, disciplining (beyond a limited amount), termination, award of benefits, and so on, is governed not by the police chief, but by fire and police commissions or civil service boards.

As is the case with all organizations, police departments exist in environments from which they draw resources and in which they provide services. The extent to which these resources are allocated and the manner and type of services provided are largely controlled by external sources. Finally, police departments are only one component of the justice network that sets parameters within which the police must operate.

The courts, for example, have indicated clearly that they are willing to intervene in police practices ranging from search and seizure, to interrogation, to hiring and promotion.

Change in Police Organizations

The way in which an organization deals with change tells us a great deal about its effectiveness and efficiency. As indicated earlier, change is a given in all organizations. Personnel retire, resign, are injured, are recruited, and are promoted. Resources fluctuate with the state of the economy and the political power of the organization. Realistically, police personnel must be willing to accept change as a normal part of their occupational world, and police supervisors must be prepared to administer change. Change, whether in personnel, legal requirements, technology, distribution and types of crime, or requests for service represents a constant challenge. Many of us resist change because we have become comfortable with the status quo. When sudden or drastic change imposed from above occurs, reactions are likely to be negative. As Bobinsky (1994, p. 17) notes, the change from traditional to community-oriented policing is not always smooth: "While I expected a degree of community skepticism regarding the ambitious program, the negative sentiments expressed by some of my fellow officers represented a more formidable obstacle. These comments, whether directed to one another or to local residents, were difficult to deal with, both on a personal and professional level."

Still, change can be accomplished if employees are involved in the decision-making process, are knowledgeable about the consequences of the change, and feel as though a need has been fulfilled by the change (More, Wegener, & Miller, 1999, p. 262). Similarly, when change occurs in organizations that are flexible, encourage initiative, and allow for the exercise of discretion in implementing change, the results can be favorable. The tendency among police personnel to resist change results from the fact that they operate in a reactive, paramilitary setting for the most part. As Gaines, Southerland, and Angell (1991, p. 106) note, "Innovation is stifled in the traditional organization; members of traditional organizations tend to resist changes which challenge the old ways of operating. . . . Members of traditional organizations are also exposed to a conflicting set of expectations—one moment they must make on-the-spot life-and-death decisions, and the next they are treated like children who are not permitted to decide which uniform to wear when the weather changes."

As police administrators adopt less rigid, less hierarchical structures and encourage more participation on the part of personnel at all levels, the police will come to act and think in terms of change rather than to react to change as a crisis.

POLICE LEADERSHIP

The quality of leadership in police organizations varies greatly. Some organizations carefully select entry-level personnel, carefully evaluate their potential for promotion, promote based on merit, and prepare those who are to be promoted by sending them to appropriate training and/or educational programs. Other organizations do none of these things. Many, perhaps most, departments have a difficult time deciding what types of leaders or supervisors they want. Should leadership positions be offered to personnel with exceptional communication and supervisory skills? Should positions be offered only to personnel with extensive street experience? Are policing skills or management skills more important? Answers to these questions are crucial in determining the criteria for promotion to leadership positions. The issue is further complicated by the fact that, at the level of the chief at least, an understanding of city politics and the ability to cooperate as an agency representative with respect to other public service agencies sometimes conflict with expectations of agency personnel.

Field supervisors, typically holding the rank of sergeant, are selected based on years of experience (a minimum of two to three may be required in order to test for the position), performance evaluations based on patrol and/or investigative work, written examinations, and oral interviews. Unfortunately, neither years of service nor performance in investigative or patrol functions necessarily indicates ability to succeed as a supervisor.

Assessment centers may help considerably in this regard, but they are far from perfect. Mistakes made in promotions at this level are likely to be perpetuated because those promoted to the rank of shift supervisor (typically lieutenants) are generally selected from a pool of sergeants with a specified minimum level of experience. Similarly, division commanders (captains) are selected from the ranks of shift commanders based on the criteria mentioned previously. Lateral entry at any of these levels is rare, although exempt rank positions, particularly at the upper ranks, are becoming more popular. Exempt rank personnel serve at the pleasure of the chief, although they may have continued employment rights (civil service rank) if demoted from their exempt positions. Individuals occupying exempt rank positions are not always well received by other police personnel because they have "jumped" rank and because they sometimes come from outside of the ranks of the police.

Police Chiefs

Those occupying the position of police chief run the gamut from "good old boys" who have worked their way through the ranks of the department to become chief to those who are highly skilled, trained or educated professional managers. While the prevalent path to chief is the "insider" path, "outsiders" with police experience and advanced education are increasingly in demand in progressive agencies. Outside promotion encourages the infusion of new ideas by a person unshackled by existing personnel cliques or political struggles (LaGrange, 1998, p. 355). "Complete outsiders," those who come from outside the realm of policing, are rare (Bouza, 1990, pp. 40–42).

Goldstein (1977, pp. 228, 230) indicates that the record of providing qualified police chiefs is poor. He notes that as early as 1920, Raymond Fosdick, an early police researcher, found police leadership to be mediocre, and that in 1931, the Wickersham Commission pointed to incompetent leadership as a major problem in policing. In conclusion, Goldstein indicated the following:

> The costs of having made inadequate provision for police leadership are plainly apparent as one views the overall status of policing in the United States. Many police agencies tend

to drift from day to day. They respond excessively to outside pressures; they resort to temporary expedients; they take comfort in technical achievements over substantive accomplishments; their internal procedures become stagnant, cumbersome, and inefficient; and they seem incapable of responding innovatively to new demands and new requirements.

Contributing to these problems is that most police chiefs have very little job security. The average length of tenure for police chiefs is five years (LaGrange, 1998, p. 355). Chiefs, in many cases, serve at the pleasure of the city council, mayor, or city manager. Without job security, the ability of a chief to implement broad changes in the department is in question. According to LaGrange, "If chiefs are constantly 'looking over their shoulders' to see who is offended by their leadership, they are not acting from a position of strength" (LaGrange, 1998, p. 356).

Lee Brown (1985), former chief of the Houston and New York City police departments, called for a new type of police leadership that recognizes that the police are basically problem solvers and multiservice providers dependent on the community for understanding, support, and cooperation. Brown believes that police executives have not been in the forefront of government and business efforts to encourage joint efforts, and that they have not accepted the fact that one of their primary responsibilities is educating the public with respect to their law enforcement and crime-control obligations. Police executives, according to Brown, need to view themselves as "major municipal policymakers" involved in actions that determine the quality of life of community residents. Finally, these executives need to regard themselves as members of public service teams and give up the idea of building empires of their own. Fortunately, more and more police executives have come to agree with Brown's assessment. Witham states, "It is widely recognized that the most critical ingredient in the success of an organization is the quality of its leadership. Although police leaders alone, cannot upgrade law enforcement, there is no other single group as important to the process" (1987, p. 6).

Since the mid-1980s, substantial changes in police leadership have been evident. According to Whisenand (2001, p. 128), police leadership today is composed of a "group of people with shared responsibilities and clear accountabilities strategizing together, reaching decisions by consensus, coordinating implementation, and generally performing many, if not all the functions previously performed by a police chief." Policing in the 2000s "will belong to passionate, driven team leaders—those people who not only have enormous amounts of energy, but also those who can energize those whom they lead" (Whisenand, 2001, p. 127).

Couper and Lobitz (1993) list what they consider to be the seven essential factors that police leaders must consider when improving and changing police operations:

1. Leaders must create and nurture a vision (about what the department will look like after change has occurred).
2. Leaders must live their values and share them with others.
3. Leaders must listen to their employees and communities.

4. Leaders must hire for tomorrow and to reflect the communities in which they serve.

5. Leaders need to be more concerned about coordinating neighborhoods than manning shifts.

6. Leaders must realize that perceptions are as important as reality.

7. Leaders must practice quality improvement.

Couper and Lobitz view all of these concerns as compatible with community policing.

The International Association of Chiefs of Police recommended several courses of action to satisfy the leadership demands of the early years of the twenty-first century (*Police Chief*, 1999, p. 57). The Association recommended that twenty-first-century police leaders bring passion to the job, begin by understanding themselves and their personal visions, consider customer satisfaction a priority, and provide leadership for change. Such police leaders should create an environment of partnerships, continually evaluate the forces of change, foster debate and innovation, and concentrate on leadership development. Ideally, these chiefs would allow others to be recognized and would master the vital art of communication.

Dobbs and Field (1993) point out that commitment to organizational success requires shedding traditions that inhibit or are counterproductive to change. They note that many police administrators cling to tradition because they perceive this approach as one carrying low risk. They are often unable to admit that there is more than one way to run the organization and that subordinates may have worthwhile suggestions. Unlike their predecessors, today's police executives must assume circumstance-specific, multidimensional leadership roles, and empower and motivate subordinates who are much more qualified than their predecessors (Breen, 1999, p. 63). Breen concluded that this challenge to police leaders is "complicated by collapsing organizational hierarchies, matrix organization implementation, heavier caseloads, a broadening mission, shrinking resources, rapidly evolving administrative and managerial technologies, changing citizen and employee demographics and increasing reliance upon interagency response to multi-agency issues" (Breen, 1999, p. 63).

Simonsen and Arnold (1993) note that among the alternative strategies for running police organizations is total quality management (TQM). TQM involves four basic elements that might be incorporated in a new model of policing: client identification and feedback; tracking of performance by simple, valid methods; continuous improvement; and employee participation in all change processes. This approach requires police leaders to identify their many clients or customers; to determine the needs of each; and to work, along with other police personnel, toward meeting these needs. The authors conclude that if police leaders fail to meet this challenge in a time in which public service agencies are required to do more with what they have, they will soon find themselves trying to do more with less as a result of client dissatisfaction.

Another alternative strategy available to twenty-first-century leaders is reengineering. Compared to TQM, reengineering involves a radical review of the entire organizational structure, while TQM programs exist within the framework of existing organizational structures (Thibault, Lynch, & McBride, 2001, p. 94). These authors illustrated the use of reengineering in the reorganization of the New York Police Department (p. 96):

1. The hierarchy was flattened.
2. Focus groups created better information flow.
3. Decision-making authority was distributed to lower levels.
4. There was extensive use of crime-mapping techniques.
5. Quality-of-life issues in neighborhoods were addressed.

A final alternative strategy available to police leaders is the concept of servant leadership. According to Spears (1998, p. 1), the following are elements of servant leadership:

1. Listening receptively to others
2. Acceptance of others
3. Foresight and intuition
4. Awareness and perception
5. Having highly developed powers of persuasion
6. An ability to conceptualize and to communicate concepts
7. An ability to exert a healing influence
8. Building community within the workplace
9. Practicing the art of contemplation
10. Recognition that servant leadership begins with the desire to change one's self

McGee-Cooper (1999, p. 1) concluded that the first defining quality of a servant leader is "a deep belief in the unlimited potential of each person and that it is the leader's role to invite, develop and encourage this valuable resource."

POLICE UNIONS, PROFESSIONALISM, AND ACCREDITATION

Police Unions

Unionization and collective bargaining in police agencies have received a good deal of attention over the past three decades, although the history of police labor disputes dates back to the 1800s (Gaines, Southerland, & Angell, 1991). Generally speaking, public-sector unionization has lagged behind that of the private sector by at least twenty-five to thirty years. There are several reasons for this slow development in the public sector. First, the government had legal mechanisms with which to squelch labor movements that were not available to the private sector (Holden, 1994, p. 237). Second, public opinion opposed strikes by police and firefighters, whose duties were to protect people and property. Thus, unionization of police personnel did not become an issue of major importance until the 1960s and 1970s, at which time the increasing complexity of policing was recognized and police officers demanded compensation commensurate with the task and more comparable to that of the private sector (Sapp, 1985). Today, with the exception of teachers and firefighters, police are the most organized of public-sector employees, with perhaps 75 percent belonging to one union or another. The unions or bargaining agents of choice include the American Federation of State, County, and Municipal Employees (AFSCME); the American Federation of Government Employees (AFGE); the International Brotherhood of Teamsters, Chauffeurs, Warehousemen, and Helpers of America (IBT); the International Brotherhood of Police Officers (IBPO); the International Conference of Police Associations (ICPA); the International Union of Police Associations (IUPA); and the Fraternal Order of Police (FOP) (LaGrange, 1998, p. 372). Highlight 2.1 is an example of a current issue facing public-sector labor and management.

The unionization of police employees proceeded slowly for several reasons. Among the more important was public and legislative reaction to the Boston police strike in 1919, following which, looting, robberies, and general disorder occurred until the state guard was called in to reestablish order. Some 1,100 police officers were fired by Governor Calvin Coolidge and never regained their jobs. Some observers feel that the impact of the Boston disaster was sufficient to force unionization of police personnel into dormancy for the next 50 years (Thibault, Lynch, & McBride, 2001, p. 411). The perceived vulnerability of communities to criminal activities during work stoppages has resulted in a generalized rejection of police strikes by the public. Many police officers share this public rejection of any police work stoppage. When strikes have occasionally occurred, there is little evidence to support the belief that crime rates rise rapidly (Gaines, Southerland, & Angell, 1991, p. 328; Stone & DeLuca, 1994, p. 458). Nonetheless, some police employees continue to view collective action as self-defeating because it may result in hostility on the part of the public, the police chief, or others in positions of power.

By 1987, thirty states had enacted legislation authorizing collective bargaining in public-sector agencies, including police departments (Sandver, 1987, p. 397). Collective bargaining is a process by which employee representatives meet with management representatives to establish a written contract that sets forth working conditions for a specific time, usually one to three years (Bennett & Hess, 2001, p. 227). In response to the legislation, in many departments, police employees petitioned state labor boards for recognition of exclusive bargaining agents. A petition of this type is typically followed by an election, in which it is determined whether the majority of employees wants union representation and, if so, which union. Those eligible to vote in police organizations differ from jurisdiction to jurisdiction but generally include those with a mutuality of job interests. Thus, rank-and-file employees are likely to be members of one union, but supervisors at different levels may belong to another union or may have separate unions of their own. Regardless of the specific union involved, it appears that police officers have joined unions in increasing numbers in order to gain a stronger voice in the governance of the agency, to protect their constitutional rights, to establish communications with management, and, perhaps, to improve their public image (Bouza, 1990; Alpert & Dunham, 1997; Gaines, Kappeler, & Vaughn, 1999; Langworthy & Travis, 1999).

Among the major concerns of police unions in negotiating with management are salary, insurance, vacation and sick days, pensions, longevity pay, compensatory time or

■ ■ ■ ■ ■ ▬▬▬▬▬▬▬▬▬▬▬▬▬▬▬▬▬▬▬▬▬

HIGHLIGHT 2.1

OFFICER SUES WHEATON, SAYS HIS FREE SPEECH WAS VIOLATED

Christy Gutowski, *Daily Herald* Legal Affairs Writer

When asked what he thought of a new emergency response policy, Wheaton police Officer Larry Smith publicly criticized the department procedure.

Those comments, published in the *Daily Herald* in February, prompted his supervisor to write Smith a memo, reminding him of another policy barring officers from speaking to the news media.

In a lawsuit filed Friday, Smith contends the restriction violates his right to free speech. He and the police union are asking a Du Page County judge to prohibit the police department from continuing the gag order—a rule also in place at many other suburban police agencies. Police administrators said Tuesday they hadn't seen the lawsuit and could not comment. But City Manager Donald Rose called the suit "silly," because officials last spring suspended the ban and began researching a less-restrictive alternative.

"It needs to be, in all likelihood, modified," Rose said. "There is a fine line when it starts to deal with issues of safety or public concern. But, I don't know where you draw that line. We're leaving it up to our attorneys to decide."

Smith's attorney, Stanley Jakala, said the union decided to file the suit Friday because a policy still is not in place months after the issue first arose.

"I just wanted to be sure the officers are protected, that someone is going to do something," Jakala said.

Smith, the union president, was quoted as criticizing a new policy on how many police officers respond to an emergency call with their squad

lights ablaze, sirens blaring and at a high rate of speed.

In the past, at least two squad cards were dispatched in emergency mode to calls of potential robberies, assaults, home invasions, shootings and other urgent situations.

Under the new policy, only one squad car responds at full speed, unless a supervisor determines others are needed more quickly.

The change, which took effect Feb. 1, was designed to put fewer officers and other motorists at risk of getting into a high-speed crash. Authorities say as many squads as needed still are dispatched at full speed to handle life-threatening situations.

Smith told the Daily Herald the change could cause delays while an officer waits for his or her backup to arrive. The policy also forgets about the people who are calling for police help, he said.

"When I call 911 and I'm scared, I want them to send at least two cars, if not more," he said in the article.

The suit contends the issue is one of public concern and that police officers should be able to discuss it publicly.

Still, Rose said the lawsuit is not necessary. The department, for example, has directed one of its police commanders, Joe Eversole, to research federal laws and how other departments are handling the issue of free speech while he attends the FBI training academy.

"The whole thing is silly and a waste of the court system's time," Rose said. "It's absurd."

Smith could not be reached for additional comment Tuesday.

pay, hiring standards, assignment policies, discipline and grievance procedures, promotions, layoffs, productivity, and procedural rights of officers. In short, initial concerns cover the entire range of working conditions, not simply economic factors. In addition, many union and management conflicts are concerned with different perceptions of management rights. According to Bennett and Hess (2001, p. 230) management rights include "determining staffing and staffing levels; determining work schedules, patrol areas, and work assignments; controlling police operations; establishing standards of conduct on and off duty; establishing hiring, promoting, transferring, firing, and disciplinary procedures; setting work performance standards; establishing department goals, objectives, policies and procedures; and establishing training programs." Thus, if negotiations fail to lead to improvement in any or all of these areas, the possibility of a work stoppage exists in unionized police departments. While police strikes are, for the most part, prohibited by law, police occasionally use job actions. These alterations of normal duties often take the form of "blue flu," work slowdowns, or work speedups.

The blue flu sometimes, surprisingly, affects large numbers of police officers working for the same department at the same time, creating difficulties in providing police coverage. Speedups involve writing considerably more citations than are normally written, so that the public complains to the chief or city council members, who will presumably pay more attention to the desires of the officers as a result. Traditionally, the public has been strongly opposed to the use of work stoppages by the police, and the courts have generally been willing to issue injunctions to bring them to a halt in a relatively short time. Further, many police managers, recognizing the possibility of work stoppages, have prepared contingency plans to guarantee the continuation of police services. When implemented, these plans have generally shown that a community can survive without its regular police force, and such plans have cut short police strikes, concluding them without meeting union demands.

Collective bargaining involves an adversarial relationship between union and management. Management offers certain incentives for the coming contract period. The union presents management with a list of the demands of its members. Management responds by stating either that it will meet these demands or that it cannot meet them. The demands of the union are supported by evidence gathered for that purpose; the response of management is typically explained using evidence gathered for that purpose. Bargaining sessions are then scheduled to attempt to convince the opposing side of the validity of the arguments presented and/or to reach a compromise acceptable to both parties.

Such bargaining (negotiating) is to be done in good faith by representatives of both sides in an attempt to reach a reasonable solution in a reasonable period of time. The powers of the two parties are articulated in a labor relations or public employment relations act, as are the rights of the two parties, the procedures to be followed, and the scope of the negotiations. When negotiations, properly conducted in terms of the applicable regulations, fail to lead to an acceptable compromise, an impasse results. Procedures for resolving the impasse are also found in labor relations law. Such procedures typically involve fact finding, mediation, and, if these approaches fail, some form of arbitration (voluntary, binding, final offer).

As a result of an impasse or stalemate between the union and management, either side can claim an unfair labor practice (ULP). A ULP (also known as an IP, or improper labor practice) occurs when management does one or more of the following:

1. Interferes with, restrains, or coerces employees in regard to forming or joining a labor union.
2. Dominates or interferes with the formation or administration of a labor union.
3. Discriminates against employees for the purpose of encouraging or discouraging membership or activity in the union.
4. Refuses to negotiate in good faith with the recognized or state-certified representatives of the employee union.
5. Assigns work performed by union employees to nonunion employees. (Thibault, Lynch, & McBride, 2001, p. 423)

The final product of collective-bargaining negotiations is a contract that covers specific areas of employer–employee relations and which binds both parties legally and morally to abide by its provisions during a specified time period.

What factors have been responsible for the growing interest in police unions? First and, in many ways, most important has been the problem of unenlightened managers. Because many police leaders came up through the ranks of paramilitary organizations, they learned how to issue orders and to expect that such orders will be obeyed. Some also learned the importance of listening to subordinates and explaining the reasons for orders issued, but many did not. Some felt they should be followed because they were in leadership positions, rather than because their arguments made sense or because they were good leaders. Some felt that policing was a unique enterprise and that the principles and procedures that worked in other types of organizations did not apply in theirs. Others were less concerned about the well-being of their officers than about the trappings of professionalism, in the form of new technologies and hardware. Some simply became so far removed from the streets and those who police them that their perceptions of the requirements of the occupation/profession were no longer realistic. Still others apparently felt that fraternizing with subordinates diminished their authority or importance. And, to some extent, these problems continue to plague police managers and those they supervise. To the extent that such problems continue, they create environments in which union organizers are likely to be successful.

There are a number of other reasons for the increasing unionization of police personnel. In the 1960s and 1970s, union representatives began to recognize that further organizing in the private sector was likely to become increasingly difficult because of saturation and increasingly enlightened management. They realized the tremendous potential for growth in the expanding public sector and began to explore this new market. At the same time, many of the legal restrictions on collective bargaining among public-sector employees were relaxed (Swanson, Territo, & Taylor, 2001, p. 392). Coupled with police dissatisfaction with wages, working conditions, and level of public support, these changes resulted in a wave of union activities in police agencies. Further, the police had seen the results of well-organized, concerted action among other groups. The protests of the 1960s and early 1970s often resulted in grievances being redressed or at least looked into. If such actions could succeed elsewhere, why not among police officers?

Bouza (1990, pp. 266–268) and Murphy and Caplan (1993, pp. 309–310) observe that many police unions and associations are not content to deal with wages and working conditions; they also make their views known on minority hiring, department reorganization or reform, and other issues. Many police unions have become powerful forces in the operation of their departments, and police executives must note this development and be prepared to deal with unions or they are likely to find themselves embroiled in controversy. Consequently, police unions have had a profound influence on salaries, supplemental pay, and benefits; working conditions; allocation and assignment of personnel; discipline; evaluation; and policy (More, Wegener, & Miller, 1999, p. 356).

The bottom line in assessing the impact of police unions is whether they have improved the quality of police services. Some (Bouza, 1990, p. 267; Murphy & Caplan, 1993, p. 309) believe that unions have often been great obstacles to reform of corrupt departments. Unions also may fragment the chain of command, contribute to racial tensions, emphasize seniority over merit, and produce inefficiency (Swanson, Territo, & Taylor, 2001, pp. 392–398; Stone & DeLuca, 1994, p. 457). However, police unions have improved morale by achieving better salaries, fairer procedures, and better lines of communication (Swanson, Territo, & Taylor, 2001, pp. 392–398; Gaines, Southerland, & Angell, 1991, pp. 312–313; More & Wegener, 1992, pp. 507–511).

Police Professionalism

Police professionalism was a focal point for police reformers during the past century. However, ambiguity concerning the police role has seriously hampered efforts to professionalize the police, because deciding on the proper role of the police is a necessary precursor to outlining and assessing steps towards professionalism. In addition, *police professionalism* means different things in different places and at different times, making consensus about the requirements for a professional police force unlikely. Finally, it is important to note that *professionalism* may refer to police organizations or to police officers, or both. Some police administrators refer to tangible improvements such as computers, the latest weaponry or communications, or advances in crime lab equipment as signs of professionalism. In fact, a department may have all of these tangible indicators but still be unprofessional if officers fail to meet some of the requirements of professionals discussed in this section. That is, the assumption that changes of this sort will automatically increase professionalism among officers is not necessarily valid. *Professionalization* has been described as the process of legitimation an occupation goes through as it endeavors to improve its social status. *Professionalism* involves the adoption of a set of values and attitudes by members of an occupation that are consistent with a professional ideology (Vollmer & Mills, 1966).

While we generally use these terms interchangeably, it must be recognized that the former does not always lead to the latter. For example, as police agencies become more bureaucratic, rely more on civil services rules and regulations, and become more unionized, officer discretion tends to be more restricted. That is, officer autonomy is increasingly curtailed, yet autonomy is highly valued by most professionals. The distinguishing feature of professional work is the freedom to make decisions according to professional norms of conduct without having to temper every decision by bureaucratic constraint (Caplow, 1983). Thus, it is possible that as organizations become more "professional" in terms of standardized rules and regulations, "professionalization" of employees may become more difficult. To some extent, this has been the case with the police, as we shall see.

Characteristics of a profession include the following (Swanson, Territo, & Taylor, 2001, p. 3; Roberg & Kuykendall, 1993, pp. 127–129; Barker, Hunter, & Rush, 1994, pp. 205–207):

1. A body of professional literature
2. Research
3. A code of ethics
4. Membership in professional associations
5. Dedication to self-improvement
6. The existence of a unique, identifiable academic field of knowledge attainable through higher education

To what extent do the police currently meet these requirements of a profession? With respect to the first two criteria, there clearly is a growing body of professional literature on the police. Journals such as *Police Studies* and the *American Journal of the Police* contain reports of police research (the second criterion). Periodicals such as *Police Chief*, the *FBI Law Enforcement Bulletin*, and a rapidly expanding number of government reports and texts on the police contribute additional information on police operations, organizations, and programs. In addition, there are literally hundreds of master's theses and doctoral dissertations concerning the police. Much of the information contained in these publications has been collected using legitimate research techniques, and the body of literature based on police research has expanded dramatically in recent years as grant monies from a variety of sources has become available.

A code of ethics (and conduct) for the police has been developed and modified by the International Association of Chiefs of Police. It is difficult to determine the extent to which police officers are familiar with these documents (Highlights 2.2 and 2.3), but our observations indicate that many officers know a code exists but are unfamiliar with its contents. Gaines, Kappeler, and Vaughn, (1999, p. 343) concluded that the IACP's Code of Conduct offers little control over police officers and provides only the external trappings of professionalism, because there exists no professional standards committee that reviews and sanctions police for the violation of their own code.

There are a number of professional police associations, mostly for chief executive officers. Organizations such as the Fraternal Order of the Police are oriented toward rank-and-file officers as well, but they have typically served more as either social organizations or, more recently, as collective-bargaining agents. Associations for staff personnel and field supervisors are far less common, making creating and sharing a professional body of knowledge among those occupying such positions difficult. In recent years, there has been some expansion of professional organizations among police planners, investigators, and those assigned to the accreditation process.

■ ■ ■ ■ ■

HIGHLIGHT 2.2
ORIGINAL LAW ENFORCEMENT CODE OF ETHICS

AS A LAW ENFORCEMENT OFFICER my fundamental duty is to serve mankind; to safeguard lives and property; to protect the innocent against deception, the weak against oppression or intimidation, and the peaceful against violence or disorder; and to respect the Constitutional rights of all men to liberty, equality and justice.

I WILL keep my private life unsullied as an example to all; maintain courageous calm in the face of danger, scorn, or ridicule; develop self-restraint; and be constantly mindful of the welfare of others. Honest in thought and deed in both my personal and official life, I will be exemplary in obeying the laws of the land and the regulations of my department. Whatever I see or hear of a confidential nature or that is confided to me in my official capacity will be kept secret unless revelation is necessary in the performance of my duty.

I WILL never act officiously or permit personal feelings, prejudices, animosities or friendships to influence my decisions. With no compromise for crime and with relentless prosecution of criminals, I will enforce the law courteously and appropriately without fear or favor, malice or ill will, never employing unnecessary force or violence and never accepting gratuities.

I RECOGNIZE the badge of my office as a symbol of public faith, and I accept it as a public trust to be held so long as I am true to the ethics of the police service. I will constantly strive to achieve these objectives and ideals, dedicating myself before God to my chosen profession . . . law enforcement.

(International Association of Chiefs of Police, 1992)

The evidence is mixed when it comes to dedication to self-improvement. There are currently no national minimum standards for either departments or police personnel. Many states do not even mandate training on a recurring basis after completion of the basic-training program. Concurrently, among more progressive police personnel, there is an increasing interest in establishing police officer standards and in accreditation.

A unique, identifiable field of study in police science has emerged. As we have seen, there are hundreds of college-level academic programs in policing and criminal justice. The quality of these programs varies tremendously but, generally speaking, seems to have improved over the past decade. While there is no consensus on precisely what topics are to be included in these programs, there is enough agreement to argue that the field is unique and identifiable in general terms at least. Further, an increasing number of officers are earning both undergraduate and graduate degrees in police science, law enforcement, and criminal justice programs. These achievements notwithstanding, police professionalism remains an elusive goal for a variety of reasons. Dedication to the attainment of professional standards exists among some police executives, is given lip service by some others, and is totally lacking among some.

A key determinant of such dedication appears to be the background, particularly the educational level, of the police chief executive. According to Crank and colleagues (1987, p. 5), "The most salient background characteristic of chiefs is their level of

POLICE CODE OF CONDUCT

All law enforcement officers must be fully aware of the ethical responsibilities of their position and must strive constantly to live up to the highest possible standards of professional policing.

The International Association of Chiefs of Police believes it important that police officers have clear advice and counsel available to assist them in performing their duties consistent with these standards, and has adopted the following ethical mandates as guidelines to meet these ends.

PRIMARY RESPONSIBILITIES OF A POLICE OFFICER

A police officer acts as an official representative of government who is required and trusted to work within the law. The officer's powers and duties are conferred by statute. The fundamental duties of a police officer include serving the community, safeguarding lives and property, protecting the innocent, keeping the peace and ensuring the rights of all to liberty, equality and justice.

PERFORMANCE OF THE DUTIES OF A POLICE OFFICER

A police officer shall perform all duties impartially, without favor or affection or ill will and without regard to status, sex, race, religion, political belief or aspiration. All citizens will be treated equally with courtesy, consideration and dignity.

Officers will never allow personal feelings, animosities or friendships to influence official conduct. Laws will be enforced appropriately and courteously and, in carrying out their responsibilities, officers will strive to obtain maximum cooperation from the public. They will conduct themselves in appearance and deportment in such a manner as to inspire confidence and respect for the position of public trust they hold.

DISCRETION

A police officer will use responsibly the discretion vested in his position and exercise it within the law. The principle of reasonableness will guide the officer's determinations, and the officer will consider all surrounding circumstances in determining whether any legal action shall be taken.

Consistent and wise use of discretion, based on professional policing competence, will do much to preserve good relationships and retain the confidence of the public. There can be difficulty in choosing between conflicting courses of action. It is important to remember that a timely word of advice rather than arrest—which may be correct in appropriate circumstances—can be a more effective means of achieving a desired end.

USE OF FORCE

A police officer will never employ unnecessary force or violence and will use only such force in the discharge of duty as is reasonable in all circumstances.

The use of force should be used only with the greatest restraint and only after discussion, negotiation and persuasion have been found to be inappropriate or ineffective. While the use of force is occasionally unavoidable, every police officer will refrain from unnecessary infliction of pain or suffering and will never engage in cruel, degrading or inhuman treatment of any person.

CONFIDENTIALITY

Whatever a police officer sees, hears, or learns of that is of a confidential nature will be kept secret unless the performance of duty or legal provision requires otherwise.

Members of the public have a right to security and privacy, and information obtained about them must not be improperly divulged.

INTEGRITY

A police officer will not engage in acts of corruption or bribery, nor will an officer condone such acts by other police officers.

The public demands that the integrity of police officers be above reproach. Police officers must, therefore, avoid any conduct that might compromise integrity and thus undercut the public confidence in a law enforcement agency. Others will refuse to accept any gifts, presents, subscriptions, favors, gratuities or promises that could be interpreted as seeking to cause the officer to refrain from performing official responsibilities honestly and within the law. Police officers must not receive private or special advantages from their official status. Respect from the public cannot be bought; it can only be earned and cultivated.

COOPERATION WITH OTHER POLICE OFFICERS AND AGENCIES

Police officers will cooperate with all legally authorized agencies and their representatives in the pursuit of justice.

An officer or agency may be one among many organizations that may provide law enforcement services to a jurisdiction. It is imperative that a police officer assist colleagues fully and completely with respect and consideration at all times.

(International Association of Chiefs of Police, 1990)

PERSONAL-PROFESSIONAL CAPABILITIES

Police officers will be responsible for their own standard of professional performance and will take every reasonable opportunity to enhance and improve their level of knowledge and competence.

Through study and experience, a police officer can acquire the high level of knowledge and competence that is essential for the efficient and effective performance of duty. The acquisition of knowledge is a never-ending process of personal and professional development that should be pursued constantly.

PRIVATE LIFE

Police officers will behave in a manner that does not bring discredit to their agencies or themselves.

A police officer's character and conduct while off duty must always be exemplary, thus maintaining a position of respect in the community in which he or she lives and serves. The officer's personal behavior must be beyond reproach.

formal education. Education has been described as the centerpiece of professionalization. Professionalized police agencies place proportionally more emphasis on formal education. . . ."

Another factor involved in the pursuit of professionalism is resistance on behalf of both rank-and-file and middle-management personnel. To the extent that these personnel view their jobs as blue-collar shift work involving little need for advanced education, dedication to self-improvement may be minimized. To some extent, of course, this view is encouraged by both the paramilitary nature of police organizations and the police subculture, which often regards police work as piecework—a certain number of moving citations, nonmoving citations, responses to service requests, and arrests equals a good day's work. To be sure, some police administrations encourage this view as well. Finally, unionization of police officers may inhibit progress toward professionalism. This relationship is complex and deserves a closer look.

Police Unions and Professionalism

Some authors have concluded that unions frequently frustrate attempts at professionalization by taking negative positions on issues such as advanced education, lateral transfer, and changes in recruiting standards (Broderick, 1987; Bouza, 1990). In addition, collective bargaining typically results in highly formalized rules indicating the rights and obligations of both parties. The more formalized these rules become, the less autonomy exists and the more difficult it becomes to bend the rules, even though both parties may be willing. In clarifying the relationships between police administrators and line officers in a union contract, negotiators may go overboard and tie the hands of one or both sides when it comes to the exercise of discretion. For example, a contract that limits the amount of overtime an officer may be required to work may prevent an officer who is willing to work, and is needed on a particular shift, from working. Contracts that specify that every contribution officers make to the organization should be reimbursed in some way (pay, compensatory time, etc.) may limit contributions that officers would willingly make, but for which there is no money to pay them.

There is little doubt that the protection offered by unions in terms of salaries, working conditions, and governance is required in some police organizations. In such organizations, administrative personnel appear to be more concerned about productivity than people, and the rights of employees need to be protected. Unfortunately, some employees are unwilling or unable to contribute their fair share to the organization but are protected by unions. And the principle of rewards based on merit is most often compromised in the process of unionization, so that those who perform best can be rewarded no more than those who fail to perform.

It has been argued that unions promote mediocrity by requiring only minimal performance levels and by failing to allow rewards for those who exceed these levels. Those who are self-motivated, dedicated, and interested in advancing their careers and the organization are not encouraged to do so, and those who contribute little to the organization are protected. Additionally, unions tend to take on lives of their own, and union leaders sometimes represent their own interests, or those of the larger union, rather than those of the officers immediately involved. Union representatives may come to see these positions as more important than their positions as police officers, and police administrators may come to view union representatives as adversaries rather than employees. Unions and management need not be adversaries. Both can work toward the betterment of the organization and its employees; this sometimes happens in the case of the police. More frequently, however, unions and managers do see each other as adversaries and, even though compromises may be worked out, come to distrust one another. Thus, in some departments, there are different unions representing different groups, based on rank or race or some other factor (e.g., National Organization of Black Law Enforcement Officers [NOBLE], Latino Police Officers' Association). This differentiation creates divisiveness within a department, so that middle-management personnel turn to their unions to promote their welfare, field supervisors turn to their union, whites to theirs, and blacks to theirs, and so on. Professional standards are very likely to get caught in the shuffle.

While it is our observation that unions and professionalization, as we have discussed them here, are basically incompatible, unions in policing are here to stay. This being the case, it behooves police administrators to become, or to hire, good negotiators and to negotiate, to the extent possible, contracts that are compatible with professional growth. Contracts that provide reimbursement for improving one's education are good examples, as are those that require open, honest evaluations and disciplinary proceedings. Contracts that are viewed in terms of victories or losses are seldom of these types. Contracts that are viewed as representing legitimate efforts on behalf of both parties to improve the organization and the welfare of those employed may achieve this goal. An alternative is enlightened management that seeks to promote the interests of both employees and the organization without the need for third-party intervention.

Accreditation

Through the combined efforts of the International Association of Chiefs of Police, the National Organization for Black Law Enforcement Executives, the National Sheriff's Association, and the Police Executive Research Forum, the Commission for Accreditation of Law Enforcement Agencies was established in 1979. The Commission is a "private, nonprofit corporation working to promote, recognize and maintain professional excellence in law enforcement through accreditation" (Commission on Accreditation for Law Enforcement Agencies, 2000, p. 1). The Commission developed a voluntary accreditation process through which law enforcement agencies at the state, county, and municipal levels were evaluated in terms of more than nine hundred standards. However, the last edition of the process (January 1999) was reduced to 439 standards organized into forty chapters, which cover the following areas:

1. Role and responsibilities of law enforcement agencies and relationships with other agencies
2. Organization, management, and administration
3. Personnel structure
4. Personnel process
5. Operations
6. Operational support
7. Traffic operations
8. Prisoner and court-related activities
9. Auxiliary and technical services

These standards are intended to assist police agencies to do the following:

1. Strengthen crime prevention and control capabilities
2. Formalize essential management procedures
3. Establish fair and nondiscriminatory personnel practices
4. Improve service delivery
5. Solidify interagency cooperation and coordination
6. Boost citizen and staff confidence in the agency

To become accredited, the agency first files an application and receives a questionnaire designed to allow agency personnel to conduct a self-evaluation of the agency's current status with respect to applicable standards. Nearly all of the accreditation

■ ■ ■ ■ ■ ▬▬▬▬▬▬▬▬▬▬▬▬▬▬▬▬▬▬▬▬▬▬▬▬▬▬▬▬▬▬▬▬▬▬▬▬▬▬

HIGHLIGHT 2.4
POLICE ACCREDITATION IS A PROUD MOMENT

National accreditation of a police force is comparatively rare, even in states considerably more populous than Nebraska. So it is an honor that such recognition has been given to the Omaha Police Department, and not just as pleasant professional praise.

Such accreditation isn't just a reflection of the fact that board members of a national commission like what they see. It's a firm indicator that a police agency has met stringent standards. In most cases, and Omaha is no exception, it means that weak spots have been strengthened—often after considerable effort and some expense. Omaha's police department joins that of Lincoln and the Nebraska State Patrol as the only three accredited law enforcement agencies in the state. In order to do that, it had to effect three important changes:

It's doing a better job of distributing its officers. This means better response times, along with added ability to anticipate times and locations of greatest need.

Police pursuits are now being reviewed monthly and comprehensively, which implies fewer accidents and greater public safety without appreciably sacrificing effectiveness.

The police are now logging and reviewing incidents in which officers felt obliged to use force. Before, this meant weapons only. Now it has been expanded to include subduing suspects by hand. The hope here, said Chief Don Carey, is to point to specific training when needed. This may help officers know better how to avert such situations.

The accreditation was two years and $19,000 in the making, and comparable outlays will be needed every three years in the future for re-accreditation. This strikes us as something that will pay for itself many times over. It not only means the better use of available resources but also makes the department more professional, more effective. It may well save lives, on both sides of the badge.

Meeting such professional standards helps police officers do a better and fairer job than ever before and makes it possible for the community at large to perceive them in that light. Chief Carey and the whole department are richly entitled to be proud of the accomplishment.

standards require only that a formal policy or procedure be established or that records be maintained (Roberg, Crank, & Kuykendall, 2000, p. 382). There is no formal monitoring to determine the extent to which the policies and procedures are followed. Highlight 2.4 illustrates several important issues in the accreditation and re-accreditation process.

Once the self-evaluation is completed, the agency may either determine that it is not yet ready for accreditation and work towards that goal or request an on-site assessment. In the latter case, the Commission appoints a team of impartial assessors who conduct an on-site assessment. These assessors write a report on their findings, and the Commission on Accreditation renders a decision. Costs vary, depending on the size of the agency involved. Internal preparation costs are relatively high, because it often takes a year to eighteen months for the designated coordinator to prepare for the assessment. Nonetheless, more than six hundred agencies have been accredited, and several hundred more are in the process of preparing for accreditation. To remain accredited, agencies must apply for re-accreditation after five years, and a number of agencies are currently involved in that process.

Several unanticipated consequences of the accreditation process have emerged. A number of states have formed coalitions to assist police agencies in the process of accreditation, thereby improving interagency cooperation. Some departments report decreased insurance costs as a result of accreditation. Doerner and Dantzker (2000, pp. 195–197) reported that the most often cited advantages to accreditation include recognition as a leader in law enforcement, reduction in legal liability costs, and enhanced employee development. Individuals who serve as assessors are currently updated with respect to the latest developments in policing and can share their experiences with others in the field, thereby promoting both dedication to and attainment of professionalism.

In summary, while professionalism has proved an elusive goal for the police, and while there are still pockets of resistance to meeting the requirements of a profession, a growing number of police personnel appear to be committed to that goal. The role of unions in this process remains unclear, but it is likely that enlightened police administrators will negotiate with unions to convince them to participate as partners in the search for professionalism.

DISCUSSION QUESTIONS

1. Describe the current state of police organizations.

2. What are the relationships among police discretion, police organization, and police functions?

3. Describe the traditional police organizational structure. Discuss its strengths and weaknesses.

4. Compare and contrast the advantages of small (fewer than ten personnel) and large police agencies from the perspective of the public, the officers involved, and the chief executive officer.

5. Compare and contrast the function, place, and time organizational designs.

6. Discuss the context in which police organizations operate and the importance of the environment to the police.

7. Assess the current state of police leadership in your community, using whatever sources are available (interviews with police supervisors, the media, etc.).

8. Discuss some of the factors that have made the police search for professionalism so difficult.

9. What are the characteristics of a profession? To what extent are these characteristics currently found among police personnel?

10. Why were police unions so slow to emerge? What are some of the reasons for the rapid increase in the number of police unions in the past two decades?

11. Are police unions and police professionalism compatible? Why or why not?

12. What are the relationships between police professionalism and accreditation? What is the rationale behind police accreditation?

13. Are the police currently professionals? If not, will they become professionals?

REFERENCES

Alpert, G. P., & Dunham, R. C. (1997). *Policing urban America*, 3rd ed. Prospect Heights, IL: Waveland.

Barker, T., Hunter, R. D., & Rush, J. P. (1994). *Police systems and practices: An introduction*. Englewood Cliffs, NJ: Prentice-Hall.

Bayley, D. H. (1994). *Police for the future*. New York: Oxford University Press.

Bennett, W. W., & Hess, K. M. (2001). *Management and supervision in law enforcement*, 3rd ed. Belmont, CA: Wadsworth.

Berg, B. L. (1992). *Law enforcement: An introduction to police in society*. Boston: Allyn & Bacon.

Bobinsky, R. (1994). Reflections on community-oriented policing. *FBI Law Enforcement Bulletin, 63*, 15–19.

Bouza, A. V. (1990). *The police mystique*. New York: Plenum.

Breen, M. D. (1999). Today's leadership challenge for police executives. *Police Chief, 66*, 61–63.

Broderick, J. J. (1987). *Police in a time of change*, 2nd ed. Prospect Heights, IL: Waveland.

Brown, L. (1985). Police-community power sharing. In Geller, W. (ed.), *Police leadership in America: Crisis and opportunity*. New York: Praeger.

Caplow, T. (1983). *Managing an organization*. New York: Holt, Rinehart and Winston.

Chapiesky, M. (1999) *The twelve hour shift*. Master's thesis. Macomb, IL: Western Illinois University.

Commission for Accreditation for Law Enforcement Agencies. (2000). *Standards for law enforcement agencies*. Fairfax, VA: CALEA.

Couper, D., & Lobitz, S. (1993). Leadership for change: A national agenda. *Police Chief, 60*, 15–19.

Cox, S. M., & Fitzgerald, J. D. (1996). *Police in community relations: Critical issues*, 3rd ed. Madison, WI: Brown & Benchmark.

Crank, J. P., Regoli, R. M., Culbertson, R. G., & Poole, E. D. (1987, March). Linkages between professionalization and professionalism among police chiefs. Paper presented at the Academy of Criminal Justice Sciences Annual Meeting, St. Louis, MO.

Dantzker, M. L. (1999). *Police organization and management*. Boston: Butterworth-Heinemann.

Dempsey, J. S. (1999). *Policing: An introduction to law enforcement*, 2nd ed. St. Paul, MN: West.

Dobbs, C., & Field, M. W. (1993). Rational risk: Leadership success or failure? *Police Chief, 60*, 64–66.

Doerner, W. G., & Dantzker, M. L.(2000). *Contemporary police organization and management*. Boston: Butterworth-Heineman.

Domash, S. F. (2000). Marine Bureau fires up its jets. *Police, 24*, 40–43.

Engelson, W. (1999). Leadership challenges in the information age. *Police Chief, 66*, 64–66.

Gaines, L. K., Kappeler, V. E., & Vaughn, J. B. (1999). *Policing in America*, 3rd ed. Cincinnati, OH: Anderson.

Gaines, L. K., Southerland, M. D., & Angell, J. E. (1991). *Police administration*. New York: McGraw-Hill.

Gaines, L. K., & Swanson, C. R. (1997). Empowering police officers: A tarnished silver bullet? In Gaines, L. K., & Cordner, G. W. (1999). *Policing perspectives: An anthology* (pp. 363–371). Los Angeles: Roxbury.

Goldstein, H. (1977). *Policing a free society*. Cambridge, MA: Ballinger.

Greenwood, P. W., Chaiken, J., & Petersilia, J. R. (1977). *The criminal investigation process* (chaps. 14, 15). Lexington, MA: D.C. Heath.

Gulick, L. (1937). Notes on the theory of organizations. In Gulick, L., & Urwick, L. (eds.), *Papers on the science of administration* (pp. 3–13). New York: Institute of Public Administration.

Hall, R. H. (1999). *Organizations*, 7th ed. Upper Saddle River, NJ: Prentice-Hall.

Hellriegel, D., Slocum, J. W., & Woodman, R. W. (2001). *Organizational behavior,* 9th ed. Cinncinnati, OH: South-Western College Publishing.

Holden, R. N. (1994). *Modern police management,* 2nd ed. Englewood Cliffs, NJ: Prentice-Hall.

Kelling, G. L., Pate, T., Dieckman, D., & Brown, C. E. (1974). *The Kansas City preventive patrol experiment: A summary report.* Washington, DC: Police Foundation.

LaGrange, R. L. (1998). *Policing American society,* 2nd ed. Chicago: Nelson-Hall.

Langworthy, R. H., & Travis, L. F. (1999). *Policing in America: A balance of forces,* 2nd ed. New York: Macmillan.

McGee-Cooper, A. (1999). Servant leadership. *Fluid Power Journal.* Available online at: http://www.fluidpower journal.com.

Moore, D. T., & Morrow, J. G. (1987). Evaluation of the four/ten schedule in three Illinois Department of State Police districts. *Journal of Police Science and Administration, 15,* 105–109.

More, H. W., & Wegener, F. W. (1992). *Behavioral police management.* New York: Macmillan.

More, H. W., Wegener, F. W., & Miller, L. S. (1999). *Effective police supervision,* 3rd ed. Cincinnati, OH: Anderson.

Murphy, P. V., & Caplan, D. G. (1993). Fostering integrity. In Dunham, R. G., & Alpert, G. P. (eds.), *Critical issues in policing: Contemporary issues* (pp. 304–324). Prospect Heights, IL: Waveland.

Parsons, G. (2000). K-9s put through their paces in heartland. *Police, 24,* 12.

Peak, K. J. (1997). *Policing America,* 2nd ed. Upper Saddle River, NJ: Prentice-Hall.

Perrow, C. (1967). A framework for comparative organizational analysis. *American Sociological Review, 32,* 194–208.

Police leadership for the 21st century. (1999). *Police Chief, 66,* 57–60.

Roberg, R. R., Crank, J., & Kuykendall, J. (2000). *Police and society,* 2nd ed. Belmont, CA: Wadsworth.

Roberg, R. R., & Kuykendall, J. (1993). *Police management,* 2nd ed. Los Angeles: Roxbury.

Sandver, M. (1987). *Labor relations: Process and outcomes.* Boston: Little, Brown.

Sapp, A. D. (1985). Police unionism as a developmental process. In Blumberg, A. S., & Niederhoffer, E. (eds.), *The ambivalent force: Perspectives on the police,* 3rd ed. (pp. 412–419), New York: Holt, Rinehart and Winston.

Simonsen, C. E., & Arnold, D. (1993). TQM: Is it right for law enforcement? *Police Chief, 60,* 20–22.

Skolnick, J. H., & Bayley, D. H. (1986). *The new blue line: Police innovation in six American cities.* New York: Free Press.

Sparrow, M. K., Moore, M. H., & Kennedy, D. M. (1990). *Beyond 911: A new era for policing.* New York: Basic Books.

Spears, L. C. (1998). Greenleaf Center for Servant-Leadership. In Mulherin, T. (ed.), *Servant leadership: Ancient concept, emerging concept.* National Association of Mutual Insurance Companies. Available online at: http://www.namic.org/n/pb/pc/070898/servant.htm.

Stone, A. R., & DeLuca, S. M. (1994). *Police administration: An introduction,* 2nd ed. Englewood Cliffs, NJ: Prentice-Hall.

Swanson, C. R., Territo, L., & Taylor, R. W. (2001). *Police administration,* 5th ed. New York: Macmillan.

Thibault, E. A., Lynch, L. M., & McBride, R. B. (2001). *Proactive police management,* 5th ed. Englewood Cliffs, NJ: Prentice-Hall.

Toch, H., & Grant, J. D. (1991). *Police as problem solvers.* New York: Plenum.

Turner, Y. C. (2000). Decentralizing the specialized unit functions in small police agencies. *Police Chief, 77,* 50–51.

Vollmer, H. M., & Mills, D. L. (1966). *Professionalization.* Englewood Cliffs, NJ: Prentice-Hall.

Walker, S. (1999). *The police in America,* 3rd ed. Boston: McGraw-Hill.

Whisenand, P. M. (2001). *Supervising police personnel,* 4th ed. Upper Saddle River, NJ: Prentice-Hall.

Witham, D. C. (1987, December). Transformational police leadership. *FBI Law Enforcement Bulletin, 56,* 2–6.

Wrobleski, H. M., & Hess, K. M. (1990). *Introduction to law enforcement and criminal justice,* 3rd ed. St. Paul, MN: West.

CHAPTER THREE

POLICE OPERATIONS

The functions of the American police are extremely diverse, as is the manner in which such functions are performed. American officers are expected to police public manners and morals, prevent crime through territorial patrol, apprehend criminals, recover stolen property, bring an end to domestic disputes, and accomplish dozens of additional tasks. Police performance in these and other areas is generally governed by the federal Constitution, related statutes, and court decisions, which outline the federal powers, duties, and limitations of police officers. Their performance is further governed by state constitutions and related statutes and court decisions, which outline the state powers, duties, and limitation of police officers. Municipal charters and ordinances govern their operations at the municipal level.

At the state level, for example, the *Illinois Complied Statutes* (2000) state that the corporate authorities of each municipality may pass and enforce all necessary police ordinances and prescribe the duties and powers of all police officers (65 ILCS 5/11-1-1). Police officers are described as "conservators of the peace" with powers to

(1) arrest or cause to be arrested, with or without process, all persons who break the peace, or are found violating any municipal ordinance or any criminal law of the state; (2) to

commit arrested persons for examination; (3) if necessary, to detain arrested persons in custody overnight or Sunday in any safe place, or until they can be brought before the proper court; (4) to exercise all other powers as conservators of the peace that the corporate authorities may prescribe. (65 ILCS 11-1-2)

Further,

It shall be the duty of every sheriff, coroner, and every marshal, policeman, or other officer of any incorporated city, town, or village, having the power of a sheriff, when any criminal offense or breach is committed or attempted in his or her presence, forthwith to apprehend the offender and bring him or her before a judge, to be dealt with according to law; to suppress all riots and unlawful assemblies; and to keep the peace, and without delay to serve and execute all warrants and other process to him or her lawfully directed. (65 ILCS 5/3.1-15-25)

Other states, of course, have similar statutes, like those previously cited, that serve to indicate some of the specific functions of the police (e.g., serving warrants, detaining persons) as well as some of the general ones (e.g., keeping the peace). In addition, the Bill of Rights and civil rights legislation restrict police behavior by establishing, defining, and guaranteeing certain freedoms for all American citizens. Basically, this means that police powers and actions cannot conflict with the rights of the individual to freedom of speech, religion, press, assembly, and security from unreasonable searches and seizures.

American police, as we note throughout this text, are primarily public servants whose foremost duty is to maintain order; whose powers are established and defined by federal, state, and local laws and court decisions; and whose actions are tailored to and by the communities in which they police.

BASIC POLICE FUNCTIONS

The cover of a major news magazine shows two police officers reaching for their guns as they burst through the doors of an apartment in a housing project. In the background is a police car with flashing red lights. A less dramatic scene on another page shows a policewoman talking to a grateful mother whose lost child was returned. Which of these illustrations most accurately describes the police role? How frequently do the events depicted by these illustrations occur? What percentage of police activity is violent and dangerous? What do police officers really do?

The answer to the question, "What do police officers really do?" is that they spend a good deal of their time on routine matters, including coffee breaks, meals, taking reports, running errands, and attending court. Traffic, social service, police-initiated events, and crimes against property account for most of the rest of a patrol officer's time. Only a small percentage of the officer's time is spent on "serious" crime.

Police officers give advice on repossession, insurance matters, commercial fraud, and how to help children with school problems. They spend part of their time helping to protect drunks from being "rolled" and helping citizens find shelter for the mentally ill and the retarded (Bittner, 1967; Toch & Grant, 1991; Bowker, 1994). A study of police officers' responsibilities revealed the following rankings of tasks by frequency: patrol, investigation, traffic enforcement, community relations, warrant service, evidence and property control, civil process, dispatching, identification, bail/court duties, vice investigation, narcotics investigation, and other duties (Michigan Law Enforcement Officers Training Council, 1997). Langworthy and Travis (1999) indicate that the police, like welfare and health departments, are responsible for the general safety and security of the community. And Bouza (1990) describes police functions that include dealing with "the human animal's dark underside," consisting of people who are out of control, nasty, and generally in trouble or disarray.

Of course, the way in which the police view their role helps determine the nature of the functions they perform and, as we shall see, the manner in which they organize to perform these functions. Thus, it is apparent that any list of police functions must be arbitrary and incomplete, but the following police functions have been suggested in the literature (American Bar Association, 1974; Goldstein, 1977; Sparrow, Moore, & Kennedy, 1990; Cox and Fitzgerald, 1996):

1. Prevent and control serious crime that threatens life and/or property
2. Assist individuals in danger of physical harm
3. Protect constitutional guarantees
4. Facilitate pedestrian and vehicle traffic
5. Assist those who cannot care for themselves
6. Resolve conflict
7. Prevent problem situations from escalating
8. Distribute situational justified, nonnegotiable force when necessary to accomplish any of the other functions
9. Generate feelings of security among citizens

Arriving at a formal definition of the role of the police, one that is universally acceptable, is difficult. Most authorities recognize the existence of a law enforcement role and an order maintenance component of policing. However, many believe that the functions of American police are so complex that they are not adequately described by the term *order maintenance*. Fyfe (1986) concluded that police tasks often have little to do with crime or law, little to do with threats of public order, and that many involve no coercion or threat or use of force.

Jurkanin et al. (2001, p. 45) believed that the phrase *order maintenance* should be described as "temporal order maintenance." The concept of temporal order maintenance involves the police maintaining the status quo, or, in other words, keeping society stable and functioning by acceptable rules, by using interventions with short-term effects. Goldstein (1977, p. 41) proposed a similar definition for the broad nature of policing: "The police function, if viewed in its broadest context, consists of making a diagnostic decision of sorts as to which alternative might be most appropriate in a given case. In this respect the total role of the police differs little from their role in administering first aid to the sick and injured persons."

Temporal order maintenance has three strategic objectives: public service/public safety, conflict management, and law enforcement (Jurkanin et al., 2001, p. 45). In prior research, Brooks (2001) recognized that the distinction between law enforcement and order maintenance for certain activities (such as a domestic violence arrest) was not clear. Jurkanin et al. (2001, p. 46) believed that the on-scene objectives of the police and their preferred intervention techniques are best represented as a continuum of responses, not separate categories. For example, a theft involving acquaintances is often conflict management, while a lost child, which appears to be a public service/public safety problem, may evolve into a law enforcement issue (e.g., kidnapping, rape, and/or murder). Hence, the police often respond to a given situation with an assumed on-scene objective and with a preferred intervention technique, but both very often change as further information is obtained (Jurkanin et al., 2001, p. 47). In other words, clear, mutually exclusive categories of police objective and accompanying intervention techniques do not exist. At best, a continuum of objectives and techniques are intermingled, although patterns of association are definable (Jurkanin et al., 2001, p. 47).

As an example of the complexity of the police role, Bittner (1990, p. 55) summarized the nature of police discretion and the situational interventions often found on skid row:

> The basic routine of keeping the peace on skid row involves a process of matching the resources of control with situational exigencies. . . . Precisely because patrolmen see legal reasons for coercive action much more widely distributed on skid row than could ever be matched by interventions, they intervene not in the interest of law enforcement but in the interest of producing relative tranquility and order on the street.

Related to this is the fact that the police often assume sole responsibility for dealing with mentally ill persons whose behavior warrants some form of intervention. Research has shown that developmentally disabled persons are approximately seven times more likely to come into contact with the police than are others (Curry, Posluszny, & Kraska, 1993) and to require police intervention because they are often unable to protect themselves (Debbaudt & Rothman, 2001). Public inebriates also often become the responsibility of the police, because limited bed space and selective admission practices at detoxification centers hinder police attempts to find shelter and care for those who are drunk in public. At the same time, of course, the use of jails to house public inebriates is deemed inappropriate, placing further restrictions on the alternatives available to the police. The police also are frequently called to remove the homeless from streets and parks because these persons have a negative impact on business, create an appearance of community neglect, and are often a danger to themselves (especially in cold weather). But what options are available to the police? Shelter facilities have limited space, and many refuse to admit those who are mentally ill or alcoholic. Thus, finding a suitable alternative for the homeless often becomes a difficult task for the police.

In recent years, the police have been called on to enter the public school setting as a result of violence therein. The Department of Justice's Office of Community Oriented Policing Services (COPS) recently expanded its services to include a new "Cops in Schools" program. This expansion included granting nearly $75 million to hire new police officers to work in the nation's schools. Officers are expected to serve as role models and mentors in addition to providing school security (Schmidt, 2000).

Another important function of the police is the investigation of crimes, complaints, and calls for service. Almost all calls to the police involve some type of investigation.

INVESTIGATIONS

The investigation unit is responsible for obtaining and processing evidence and effecting arrest. Bayley (1998, p. 71) concluded that about 15 percent of all police personnel are assigned to investigation, a much smaller number than the 60 percent assigned to patrol. Job duties associated with the investigation unit include, but are not limited to, the following: preparing and testifying in court to present facts surrounding any civil, criminal, or departmental action; conducting background and criminal investigations of persons and organizations; operating undercover to secure evidence and information; maintaining surveillance; and preparing written reports to accurately reflect the information gathered in the course of an investigation (Iowa Department of Public Safety, 2001).

Previous research by the Rand Corporation and the Police Executive Forum examined the efficiency of the criminal investigation process. The Rand Study concluded that a substantial amount of an investigator's time is spent in nonproductive work and that investigators' expertise has little impact on the solution of cases. Furthermore, this study concluded that more that half of all serious crimes receive no more than superficial attention from investigators, and that half of all investigators could be eliminated without negatively influencing the crime clearance rate (Greenwood & Petersilia, 1975; Gilbert, 2001).

Police investigate all types of incidents, from simple vandalism to homicide. In some departments, cases are assigned by specialization depending on the nature of the case (Gilbert, 2001, p. 46). This allows investigators to develop an expertise in specific areas and often enhances success through the grouping of crimes with common elements. For example, many investigative units recently expanded their functions to include the following law violations: Medicaid fraud, state lottery fraud, odometer fraud, and complex financial crimes. In addition, many investigative agencies have special programs, such as the Sexual and Violent Crime Offender Registry, arson detection teams, and marijuana eradication programs (Montana Department of Justice, 2001). Many criminal investigative units have established cybercrime units, given the popularity and potential for criminal violations on the Internet. The Virginia State Police (2000) established a special unit to investigate the following violations, many of which involve recently enacted laws:

Child pornography
Computer fraud
Computer trespass
Computer invasion of privacy

Theft of computer services
Personal trespass by computer
Cellular phone cloning

Nonetheless, not all police officers perform advanced investigative functions. In large departments, it has been customary for the police officer assigned to the district where the crime occurs to respond to every call and then to call in specialists for all but the "routine" nontraffic and noncriminal calls (Adams, 2001, p. 280). In other words, most patrol officers are instructed to render aid to the victims, establish control of the crime scene, and make an arrest only if the perpetrator is at the scene and the crime is in progress. Most department regulations require the patrol officer to not take any actions until the investigators arrive. However, the actions of the patrol officers are extremely important if the criminal investigation is to be successful. Often, the single most important determinant of whether a case will be solved is the information the victim supplies to the responding patrol officer (Greenwood & Petersilia, 1975). Greenwood and Petersilia believe that if information that uniquely identifies a perpetrator is not available when the crime is reported, the perpetrator often is not identified.

The computer has modernized investigative techniques.

The adoption of a community policing philosophy by many police departments has influenced investigative unit functions. Many departments are reexamining the traditional method of only permitting specialists to conduct criminal investigations. Many departments have trained patrol officers as generalists and permit them to conduct follow-up investigations. In this form of investigation, there is little consideration as to the type of crime committed. Many have also eliminated the practice of conducting an extensive follow-up investigation of every reported crime, focusing instead on the more serious offenses and on cases that can be solved (Cordner, 1999, p. 49). In areas where serious crimes occur frequently, investigators often assign levels of priority to each investigation. The large volume of cases assigned to each investigator, the limited number of personnel, and the relative seriousness of each offense make priority ranking necessary (Gilbert, 2001, p. 46). Furthermore, police departments are trying to have investigators expand their case-by-case orientation to include problem solving and crime-prevention activities.

Several initiatives are being refined to further the capabilities of criminal investigators. These include the cold case squad (using new technology to solve past unsolved cases), multiagency investigative units, major offense bureaus (identification of career criminals), and specialized evidence processing (Gilbert, 2001, pp. 559–573).

All police functions are performed through the processes of arrest and detention, investigation, and police community relations programs. To help ensure that these processes are carried out successfully, the police must recruit, select, train, educate, evaluate, and promote officers capable of fulfilling these functions. Even though the selection and training procedures employed by the police result in the hiring of officers capable of performing the functions listed, using the processes outlined, there is tremendous variation in the manner in which these officers perform their tasks, even on the same shift, in the same division, and in the same department. As we have seen, the exercise of discretion by police officers plays an important role in their encounters with other citizens. So, too, does the manner in which the police organize to perform their tasks.

STYLES OF POLICING

James Q. Wilson (1968) identified three relatively distinct types of policing. The first type, referred to as the *watchman style*, involves police organizations in which the principal function is order maintenance rather than law enforcement in cases that do not involve serious crime. The police use the law more as a means of maintaining order than regulating conduct, and judge the seriousness of infractions less by what the law says about them than by their immediate and personal consequences. In other words, circumstances of person and situation are taken into account. Police officers are encouraged to follow the path of least resistance in carrying out their daily duties. "Little stuff" is to be ignored, but officers are to be "tough" when serious matters arise. This style of policing often occurs in departments with low-level educational requirements (high school education or less), relatively low wages, little formal training, considerable on-the-job training, and few formal policies. Such departments have few specialized personnel; thus, departmental transfers are rare. Officers are encouraged to take personal differences into account both when enforcing the law and when addressing citizens. Other than in serious cases, who the citizen is, is as important as what she has done (Wilson, 1968, pp. 140–171).

The second style of policing is the *legalistic style*. In such police organizations, officers are encouraged to handle commonplace situations as if they were matters of law enforcement as opposed to order maintenance. Traffic tickets are frequently issued, juveniles are often detained and arrested, misdemeanor arrests are common, and the police take action against illicit enterprises on a regular basis. Patrol officers are under pressure to "produce" arrests and tickets and are expected to simply "do their jobs," as defined by an administration that views a high volume of traffic and other stops as simply a means of discovering more serious crimes. Technical efficiency is highly valued, and promotions are based on such efficiency. Middle-class officers with high school educations are recruited, and professional image (new buildings and equipment) is viewed as important. The law is used to punish those perceived as deserving of punishment. Orders are issued by supervisory personnel and are followed, regardless of whether officers deem them appropriate (Wilson, 1968, pp. 172–199).

The third policing style is the *service style*. Service-style police officers intervene frequently but not formally, take seriously all requests for service, and frequently find alternatives to arrest and other formal sanctions. Officers are encouraged to be consumer-oriented and to produce a product that meets community needs. Officers are expected to be neat, courteous, and professional. Authority is less centralized, and community relations and public education are viewed as important aspects of policing. College education is valued, salaries are reasonably good, and specialized expertise is encouraged (Wilson, 1968, pp. 200–226).

While most police organizations have characteristics of all three styles of policing, tendencies to emphasize one style over the others are often easily discernible. In fact, particular communities sometimes become known for their emphasis on a specific style of policing ("Don't speed in that town; they ticket everybody"; "The town lives off income from traffic citations"; or "You can get anything you want in that town as long as you don't rock the boat"). While many watchman and legalistic departments exist, service-style organizations appear to represent the current trend in policing. Given the emphasis on community policing and cooperation between the police and other citizens in maintaining order and enforcing the law, this trend is not surprising. New trends with an emphasis on community policing have required police administrators to reexamine the abilities of available personnel to accomplish these new initiatives. In the next section, we discuss how administrators determine the number of personnel needed for the various styles of policing.

PATROL STRENGTH AND ALLOCATION

Police administrators have often asked, "How many patrol officers do we need?" There is no exact standard for the required number of police. Two cities with very similar populations may have different numbers of patrol officers on the same shift. However, population is only one factor that determines the number of police officers needed to answer service requests. Additional factors to be considered include the types of service provided (bomb disposal, underwater recovery, school-crossing services, search and rescue), whether the department has a community policing plan, available resources, and other variables. First, we examine the methods use to determine the number of police officers needed for patrol. Then, we discuss the methods of need-based allocation or the assignment of patrol officers to areas with prioritized needs.

Before beginning the process of determining the required number of patrol officers and how they are allocated, we must define the expected outcomes of patrol. Alpert and Dunham (1997, p. 166) state that patrol can be divided into three related, expected outcomes. First the presence of patrol officers may frighten the offender away or influence him to not commit a violation until the police leave the area. There is enough evidence to conclude that these actions do not actually prevent crime, but simply displace or move the criminal activity to another location lacking in police patrols. Second, patrol provides police an opportunity to determine the probabilities of criminal behavior and, through preventive strategies, reduce or eliminate those probabilities (Alpert & Dunham, 1997, p. 167). Finally, Alpert and Dunham found that patrol provides police the opportunity to respond or react to calls for assistance in a timely manner. But how do we determine the number of patrol officers needed in a community?

There are at least three ways to determine the appropriate number of police personnel for any given jurisdiction: intuitively, comparatively, and by workload (Roberg & Kuykendall, 1993, p. 313). According to Roberg and Kuykendall, the intuitive approach involves little more than an educated guess and is often based on tradition (personnel numbers from previous years). However, this approach is in part based on the number of crimes cleared or total number of arrests. In other words, many administrators demand more police officers be hired as crime rates increase. However, Bayley (1994, p. 4) concluded that differences in crime rates should not be attributed to variations in the number of police. He found that since World War II, increases in the number of police have closely paralleled increases in crime rates. Communities hire more police when crime rate rise, but this is a desperate game of catch-up that has no effect on the rate of increase in crime (Bayley, 1994, p. 4).

The comparative approach involves comparing one or more cities, using the ratio of police officers per one thousand population units; if the comparison city has a higher ratio of police to population, it is assumed that an increase in personnel is justified to at least the level of the comparison city (Roberg & Kuykendall, 1993, p. 314). On average, larger municipal police departments employ twenty-three full-time officers per ten thousand residents. Larger county police and sheriff's departments employ an average of fourteen and thirteen officers per ten thousand residents, respectively. State law enforcement agencies employ an average of two officers per ten thousand residents (Reaves & Hart, 1999). The exclusive use of this method to compute police personnel needs is not recommended. Communities possess unique characteristics concerning the size of the area served, mile of roads, crime rate, number of juveniles, economic strength, employment rates, size of the elderly population, and special tourist attractions, which could have a substantial impact on the number of personnel required to fulfill service requests. In other words, there is no universal number that will accurately reflect the police personnel needs of all jurisdictions.

The final approach, workload, requires an elaborate information system, standards of expected performance, well-defined community expectations, and the prioritization of police activities (Roberg & Kuykendall, 1993, p. 315). The workload analysis of patrol often involves the following (Cordner & Sheehan, 1999, p. 442):

1. Documenting the total amount of patrol workload that occurs
2. Determining the time it takes to handle that workload
3. Translating the workload data into the number of patrol officers required to handle it
4. Determining how many patrol officers are needed at different times of the day (allocation)
5. Determining how many patrol officers are needed on different days of the week (scheduling)
6. Determining how best to assign patrol officers to geographic areas (deployment)

Ammann and Hey (1986) believe that the measurement of demands for police services is based on "work generating" variables, including citizen calls for police services, investigative caseload practices, and service delivery policy and procedures established by local government and community expectations (tradition). Of course, the actual computation of patrol workload is complicated by the issue of uncommitted time. O'Boyle (1991, p. 92) states that a patrol officer should be observing or being observed (uncommitted time) between 40 and 60 percent of the shift. Even though the workload analysis has been demonstrated to be methodologically sound, few jurisdictions use this form. Most administrators cite the cost, complexity of the formula, and extensive data collection as the reasons for not using a workload formula.

Once the police administrator has used the intuitive, comparative, or workload approach to compute the number of police personnel required, she must determine the appropriate method for the allocation of personnel. Allocation involves taking the total number of police personnel and assigning them to a specific area or special task. The unique problems found in all communities prohibit the equal assignment of personnel across all districts, beats, or zones. The effective allocation of personnel involves a variety of factors, some of which are unique to different jurisdictions. For example, Adams (2001, pp. 28–29) recommends that administrators consider the following in the assignment or deployment of police personnel: resident and transient populations; number, type, and location of crimes; traffic patterns; location of hazards; disproportionate concentration of population; socioeconomic factors; geography and topography; recreational facilities, and other factors. The Illinois State Police (1999) use the following factors to allocate sworn personnel to state police districts: density (population, square mile), demand, law enforcement coverage (number of local police), general crime, nonlethality of crime, personal crime, and traffic need. Of course, the issue of how to effectively allocate personnel to community policing initiatives raises some concerns. And the involvement of police personnel in problem solving, improving quality of life, and generally interacting with people makes allocation even more challenging. The Illinois State Police (1999, p. 4) conclude that, "under the guiding philosophy of community policing, there is no exact science to allocate personnel."

Once the number of patrol officers has been determined, the administrator must decide how to most effectively and efficiently accomplish the functions of patrol. Next, we describe the most common types of police patrol. Then, we explore the research on patrol and the various alternative patrol strategies.

Types of Patrol

Police use a variety of techniques to achieve the tasks associated with patrol. Often, these variations depend on the size and individual needs of the local jurisdiction. The Law Enforcement Management and Administrative Statistics (LEMAS) report (Reaves & Hart, 1999) found that 100 percent of the reporting police agencies use automobiles as a patrol unit on a routine basis. In addition, the report concluded that 67 percent of the police use motorcycle patrols; 62 percent, foot patrols; 79 percent, bicycle patrols; 19 percent, horse patrols; and 28 percent, some form of marine patrol. A substantial increase in the number of departments routinely using foot and bicycle patrols is noted in comparison with statistics in previous LEMAS reports.

Foot patrol is the original form of patrol. Although it confines police to small areas and limits the scope of certain types of activities, foot patrol is still among the most effective of the various forms of patrol (Adams, 2001, p. 126). While many agencies report that they routinely use foot patrol, a number employ this strategy for special occasions, such as festivals, concerts, sporting events, and parades. Moving foot patrol is used where there is considerable foot traffic, as in business and shopping centers, bars and taverns, high-crime areas, special hazard areas, and streets where there are many multiple-family dwellings (Adams, 2001, p. 126).

Significant research studies on the evaluation of foot patrol were conducted in Newark, New Jersey, and Flint, Michigan. In Newark, foot patrol officers were assigned patrol beats in one of eight neighborhoods (Pelfrey, 2000). The results of these studies suggested that increased foot patrol by police officers is not associated with reduced levels of crime, but it was noticed by citizens and appeared to reduce fear of crime and increase public satisfaction with the police (Moore, 1992). Wilson and Kelling (1999a, p. 154) concluded from the Newark study that citizens felt more secure and had a more favorable opinion of the police, compared with those residing in other areas. Directed foot patrol (assigning the officer to a specific area) is the most popular form of foot patrol and is utilized in areas that allow the police to interact easily with large numbers of people. Another form of foot patrol involves the "Park, Walk, and Talk" initiative, in which police are required to exit their patrol cars and conduct thirty-minute foot patrols twice a shift (Young, 2000, p. 315). This form of foot patrol is not directed at a specific area or crime problem. The intent of this program is to encourage communication between the police and the residents of the areas they patrol. Parks et al. (1999) indicated that foot patrol officers, who are typically less burdened by dispatched assignments than motor officers, have greater discretion to select the citizens they will contact.

Bicycle patrol is extremely popular in many departments. Bicycles have the advantage of low cost compared with automobiles, but bicycle patrols do require additional training and special equipment. The benefits of bicycle patrols include the following: Officers are accessible to the public; officers can silently approach a situation on specially designed bicycles; much more area can be covered compared with foot patrol; and bicycles can travel where automobiles are unable to patrol (Metro Nashville Police Department, 2000). Highlight 3.1 illustrates the diverse areas in which police can deploy bicycle patrols.

Another form of patrol involves air support units consisting of fixed-wing aircraft and helicopters. Air support units often assist ground units with fleeing felons, high-speed pursuits, missing person searches, drug suppression activities, and general crime prevention. While there is little question about its effectiveness, air support is by far the most expensive type of police patrol. However, studies claim that helicopters have fifteen times the surveillance capacity of a ground unit and that one helicopter can be as effective as twenty-three ground officers in terms of observation ability (Denver Police Department, 2000).

Mounted patrols are popular in larger departments with unique patrol requirements, including parks and lakefronts. Mounted patrols are involved in crime prevention, community interaction, and crowd control. The Chicago Police Department (1998) estimates that one mounted police officer has the effect of ten to twenty police officers on foot. However, with the addition of bicycles, more foot patrols, and all-terrain vehicles (ATVs), the number of mounted patrol units has been declining.

Patrol Strategies

Although the patrol division involves the largest assignment of personnel in a police department, little research into the effectiveness of this strategy was completed until 1960. Prior to this, the patrol officers provided a wide range of services, solving almost any problem presented to them, with minimal accountability to administrators, the public, or the courts. Parks et al. (1999) described the duties of patrol as "911 policing." This involves allocation of resources in a case-by-case fashion (incident-driven basis) as citizens demand them (reactively). According to Parks et al. (1999, p. 484), "Under 911 policing, departments have invested in increasingly sophisticated systems to receive citizens' calls for service, to locate calls spatially, and to designate a patrol unit for rapid response." However, the concept of 911 policing has recently been modified by the adoption of community policing. As we discuss in Chapter 9, community policing involves the reorientation of police patrol to increase citizen interaction and, to a great extent, turns traditional police practices upside down.

Various reform efforts and tensions between the police and citizens led to the examination of several aspects of policing, including patrol. Experiments included Operation 25 by the New York Police Department, the British Beat Patrol Experiments, the Los Angeles Police Department survey, the Rand Corporation research, and Albert Reiss's study of police patrol operations in high-crime neighborhoods (Peak, 1997, pp. 151–153; Fyfe et al., 1997, pp. 194–196).

■ ■ ■ ■ ■ ▬▬▬▬▬▬▬▬▬▬▬▬▬▬▬▬▬▬▬▬▬▬▬▬▬▬▬▬▬▬

HIGHLIGHT 3.1

HORSEPOWER PLUS LEG POWER: NEW ELECTRIC BICYCLE GIVES GURNEE POLICE A CHARGE

Bob Susnjara Daily Herald Staff Writer

Gurnee police bicycle patrol officers now have the ability to get a little extra juice to help them on the job.

Through a donation from ComEd, Gurnee and several other Lake County police departments have bicycles equipped with an electric motor that allows the officers to travel up to 18 mph without even pedaling—and can go much faster in combination with foot power.

Gurnee received its bicycle earlier this month. Make no mistake, officers will not be taking the lazy way out with the new-fangled bikes that run about $1,500.

"It's a pedal-assist bike," said Gurnee police bicycle patrol officer Aaron Tokarz, a two-year veteran of two-wheelers. "It's not meant to be primarily the electric. You're supposed to start off on your own riding and then use the electric. If you're going uphill or you're getting tired, it's meant to assist you."

Tokarz, 26, said the electricity kicks in with a simple push of a button on the handlebar. A battery power pack is situated below the seat and a motor is toward the rear, which adds an additional 15 pounds to the special bicycles.

Gurnee's police officers cover several areas of the village on bicycles until 10:30 p.m. They roam through residential subdivisions, village parks, Six Flags Great America's lot, outside Gurnee Mills and the Des Plaines River trail.

Police Chief Robert Jones said the village has three bicycles, including the one that gets a jolt of electricity. Jones said there are reasons why it would not be practical to have all of the bicycles with electric power capability.

Electric bikes would not have worked to patrol areas during this year's flooding in the older part of the village east of the Des Plaines River, said Jones, because the power packs would have gotten waterlogged. He said traditional bikes were an invaluable tool to navigate floodwater.

"I think we'll keep our fleet diversified," Jones said.

Jones, without elaborating, said Gurnee police have conducted "some interesting patrols" on village bicycle paths. Bike officers even have been aiming radar at drivers on main village streets, alerting a cop in a squad car when someone is speeding.

Beyond reaching areas not easily accessible for vehicles and conducting traffic surveillance, Jones and Tokarz said the bikes are a useful tool for police to come into closer contact with residents. Tokarz said it's common for adults and children to approach him while he works the street on his bike.

"From my standpoint, it's really going to assist us in our community-policing efforts," said Jones.

Weather determines when the bicycle officers can hit the streets. Tokarz said the electric-assist bicycles will not give police a greater ability to work in snow or other nasty weather.

Gurnee police could be in for a razzing if ComEd experiences a slew of power outages as it did last year. ComEd's logo is noticeable on the bike's power pack.

"Their only requirement with us is that we keep the logo on the battery. And that's it. We can take it anywhere we want," said Deputy Police Chief Henry Schwarz.

The Kansas City preventative patrol experiment was one of the most comprehensive assessments of the effectiveness of random police patrol. The experiment analyzed variations in the level of routine preventive patrol within Kansas City. In the reactive beats, routine preventive patrol was eliminated and police officers responded only to calls for service. In the control beats, routine preventive patrol was maintained at its usual level. In the proactive beats, routine preventive patrol was intensified by two to three times its usual level through the assignment of additional patrol cars and the frequent presence of cars from the reactive beats. The experiment concluded that decreasing or increasing routine preventive patrol in the areas tested had no effect on crime, citizen fear of crime, community attitudes toward the police on the delivery of patrol services, police response time, or traffic accidents. (Kelling et al., 1974).

The results of the Kansas City study had minimal effect on the primary strategy of police. Today, thirty years since the Kansas City experiment in 1972, random mobile, uniformed patrol is still the primary strategy used by police. Bayley (1998, p. 27) concluded that the Kansas City preventive patrol research results "are generally accepted as being true; its research strategy is considered to be seriously flawed; it has never been replicated; it has not lessened appreciably the reliance of the police on random patrolling; but it has encouraged a rethinking of police purposes and methods." Since the results of the Kansas City study, many police departments have returned to strategies of the past or have combined ideas practiced in earlier years with newer ones to improve the effectiveness and efficiency of patrol (Alpert & Dunham, 1997, p. 168).

Crank (1998, p. 45) believes that the phrase *random preventive patrol* is self-contradictory, without meaning. He suggests that random preventive patrol permits many opportunities for proactive activity on the part of individual officers. Random preventive patrol is a way of doing police work that allows police officers to control their territories. As Crank states, "Officers have the discretion to do what they want where they want it, guided by the cultural stipulation that they must control what goes on in their territory" (1998, p. 46). Let's briefly examine what police do while on random preventive patrol.

A study by Greene and Klockars (1991, pp. 273–284) concluded that police spend 26 percent of their work time on criminal matters, 9 percent on order maintenance assignments, 4 percent on service-related functions, 11 percent on traffic matters, 2 percent on medical assistance and 12 percent on administrative matters. Using the data from this study, Dempsey (1999, p. 135) found that when the percentage of time involved in unavailable, administrative, and clear time is excluded from the data, the data indicate that the police spend approximately 50 percent of their time on criminal matters, 16 percent on order maintenance, 8 percent on service, 21 percent on traffic, and 4 percent on medical assistance. Thus, he concluded that 47 percent of a police officer's time was not spent on actual assignments. This is a reasonable amount of uncommitted time, because most service organizations in reality have limited numbers of contacts with their clients. The results of these studies challenged police to examine their patrol operations and to develop alternative strategies for random mobile patrol. We now discuss some of these alternative strategies.

Directed Patrol.   To improve the effectiveness and efficiency of random patrol officers, many departments began to use a form of goal setting. Goal setting involves specifying the desired outcomes toward which individuals, teams, departments, and organizations should work (Hellriegel, Slocum, & Woodman, 2001, p. 164). Highlight 3.2 illustrates the implementation of a successful goal-setting process by police.

Directed patrol involves the reduction of uncommitted patrol time (i.e., no call assignment is pending) through the assignment of certain activities. Hess and Wrobleski (1993, p. 231) believe that "if a department's goals are clear, and if the department has kept accurate records on calls for service and on crimes committed in the community, then based on this data, patrol time should be effectively structured to provide the best service and protection possible." For example, the Chicago Police Department (1998a) uses Information Collection for Automated Mapping (ICAM), a computerized mapping program, to generate maps of timely, accurate crime data for beats, sectors, and districts. ICAM allows patrol officers to identify the ten most frequent crimes occurring on their beats over the previous week, month, or year. Using this information, Chicago police can set priorities and direct patrol officers to targeted hot spots of criminal activity. The following is an example of the implementation of directed patrol by Chicago police.

> When sector Sergeant Dennis Porter recently visited a senior citizen housing complex on the 3900 block of South Calumet Avenue, he learned from residents about the fears over extensive drug trafficking in the immediate neighborhood. Sergeant Porter immediately directed beat and rapid response cars on a *directed patrol mission* in the area, and he gave residents direct phone numbers to the 2nd District Station they could use to report crimes.
>
> Police quickly made several arrests in the area, but dealers quickly set up shop at a nearby location. Undaunted, Sergeant Porter encouraged residents to continue calling the police, and officers from the Tenth Sector adjusted their patrol mission to target the new location, once again resulting in several arrests.
>
> When residents attending beat meetings on Beat 211and 212 reported that the drug operation had moved once again, officers and citizens adjusted their efforts as well, resulting in even more arrests. While residents now report that drug trafficking in the area has greatly diminished, police and residents remain vigilant in their monitoring of the situation. (Chicago Police Department, 1998c)

Differential Response.   Differential response involves rejecting the idea of dispatching each request for assistance or service in the order the call is received. Police have consistently responded to one radio call and returned to the vehicle to answer the next call. Police would resolve an assault in progress and then immediately drive to a residence to a take a theft report that had occurred three weeks prior. Many began to question the effectiveness and efficiency of an immediate response to every type of call received by the dispatcher.

Walker (1999, p. 88) states that differential response programs classify calls by their seriousness: (1) an immediate response by a sworn officer, (2) a delayed response by a sworn officer, or (3) no police response, with reports taken over the telephone, by

■ ■ ■ ■ ■

HIGHLIGHT 3.2
PUBLIC OUTCRY LEADS TO MORE GARY POLICE PATROLS

GARY—When Lt. Roger Smith and his police caravan cruise the streets, residents respond in two ways. Many wave and call greetings. Others run and hide.

Smith, the commander of Gary's narcotics and vice unit, wants it that way. "We want to give this community back to the good people. The bad should hide or, better yet, leave," he said.

Since the beginning of June, Smith and his narcotics detectives have been working with officers from Community Orienting Policing Services in the eastern portion of the Aetna area, similar to a project earlier this year in the Glen Park section.

The COPS officers are talking to residents about many neighborhood problems, while the drug investigators are looking specifically for dealers.

"We go where the people want us," Smith told the Gary *Post-Tribune*.

"The Glen Park project was in response to complaints by residents who were tired of hearing gunshots and seeing drug sales conducted in the open," he said. "I've had several people out here calling our office with information, so we moved out here to hit some of these spots. We want to help the residents who want our help."

The COPS officers look for abandoned cars, mini-dumps and other community eyesores. They visit with residents in an effort to introduce them to the COPS concept, based on communication. The drug unit seeks out activity at vacant houses and makes undercover buys, followed by arrests.

"When you see six or seven able-bodied young men just standing around, you know what they're doing," Smith said. "What they're doing is keeping the good people inside. That's not right. Young mothers ought to be able to take their children outside without worrying every second."

Several probationary officers who recently graduated from the police academy are with the COPS officers as they approach Aetna residents to learn what the police can do to help improve the neighborhood.

"We're here for the community," said Sgt. Dave Marek, a supervisor. "And when we serve them, they can serve us by helping target the trouble and troublemakers."

The COPS officers who gathered on 13th Place in Aetna last week were enthusiastic about the joint program.

"This is what police work should be all the time," patrolman Gregory Davis said.

The concentration in one neighborhood by the 15 COPS officers, rookies and drug investigators brings good results, the officers say. The officers' enthusiasm matches the positive response from residents.

"It's a lot better since the police have been present," longtime resident Ozzie Robinson said.

Robinson recalled when his neighbor was hospitalized for a few days with a chronic illness.

"Everyone saw the ambulance take him away, and that night they were here taking his gutters and screen door off his house. I heard the noise and thought, 'Who works on their house at 2 a.m.? What kind of people do that?'" he said.

Robinson's house is next door to a vacant lot where a house once stood. The cement slab remains, piled high with branches and trash. Marek said overgrown lots filled with garbage send the wrong message. When people see that, they think they can do anything, he said.

"How a neighborhood looks sets the tone for how people will act in that area," he said.

mail, or by having the person come to a police station in person. Some departments support their own web page and allow the submission of certain types of information on forms that can be downloaded from the web page or transmitted by fax or e-mail directly to the department. Worden (1996, p. 148) found that differential police response was equitable and efficient and that citizens were not dissatisfied with delayed responses, even if the response time was an hour or more.

Often, police departments utilize a community service officer (CSO) to enhance differential patrol strategies. CSOs are nonsworn employees who perform duties not requiring a police officer (unlock a vehicle, file insurance reports, document minor traffic accidents). CSOs are distinguished from police officers by different uniforms and patches and by different vehicles. Some departments have implemented Social Service Units and Police Assistant programs composed of civilians who help relieve police officers of routine duties, including directing traffic and taking theft reports (Palatine Police Department, 2000). Bryan Police recently added a police assistant resident volunteer program that requires training in criminal law, municipal ordinances, preliminary investigations and report writing (Creel, 1999). The Palatine Police Department's Social Service Unit provides the following services through referrals by police officers: crisis intervention, clinical assessments, short-term counseling, information and referral, court advocacy with victims, consultation to local professionals, and public awareness presentations.

Saturation Patrol and Crackdowns.   Saturation patrol involves adding patrol officers, thus increasing police visibility. Crackdowns involve more planning than mere saturation. Crackdowns refer to a sudden increase in the number of police, with the objective of aggressive patrolling and elevated numbers of arrests for a specific violation or crime (Cordner, Gaines, & Kappeler, 1996, p. 125). The intent of both of these strategies is to prevent criminal activities, increase police presence to reduce citizen's fears, and increase voluntary compliance with laws within the patrol area. Sherman and Weisburd (1995) introduced the idea of "hot spots of crime," or identifying locations that produce the highest number of police requests for service. He concluded that concentrating resources on these locations and conducting crackdowns in which police concentrate forces on crime may help reduce criminal activity. Most believe that saturation patrol and crackdowns produce positive effects. For example, crackdowns may have a residual deterrence effect (some crime reduction, even after the crackdown is ended) and an announcement effect (publicity causes some people to alter their behavior) (Roberg, Crank, & Kuykendall, 2000, p. 235). However, Roberg, Crank, and Kuykendall concluded that these behaviors often return to normal after the publicity subsides.

The following is an example of a New York City crackdown strategy, known as the Model Block Program.

> The police temporarily take control of the streets to keep the criminals out. They put up barricades with 24-hour patrols to monitor foot and vehicle traffic. The police might stop pedestrians and vehicles at checkpoints for identification. They may padlock apartments used for illegal activities and later recycle them to legitimate families. Of course, an elderly

woman asked the question on everybody's mind: How long would the cops remain in place? (Maas, 1998, p. 5)

Other examples of saturation patrols and crackdowns include Operation ABC Mobilization (crackdown on impaired drivers and drivers who fail to buckle up children and themselves), Click It or Ticket (zero-tolerance approach to the use of seat belts) and Operation C.A.R.E. (Combined Accident Reduction Effort) (Illinois State Police, 1999–2001).

Compstat. The New York Police Department's Crime Control Model (Compstat) is a multifaceted system used to administer police operations. The model is a comprehensive, continuous analysis of results for improvement and achievement of prescribed outcomes (McDonald, 2002, p. 7). Compstat was created to provide police agencies with preliminary crime statistics that would permit tactical planning and deployment of police resources. Today about one-third of the nation's larger police departments (those with more than one hundred sworn officers) have implemented some form of Compstat, and another quarter say they are planning to do so (Anderson, 2001, p. 1). According to McDonald (2002, p. 8), Compstat is composed of five basic principles: specific objectives, timely and accurate intelligence, effective strategies and tactics, rapid deployment of personnel and resources, and relentless follow-up and assessment. For example, the "effective strategies and tactics" objective involves dealing with the hot spots of serious crimes and detailed crime and other problems, such as quality-of-life offenses that were identified through the collection, analysis, and mapping of data (Philadelphia Police Department, 2001). Guiliani and Safir (1998, p. 5) believe that possible police tactics include saturation of an area with uniformed and plainclothes officers, checkpoints, "buy and bust operations," surveillance, sting operations, regular vertical patrols in buildings, and enforcement plans for specific holidays. Many skeptics have noted that the declines in crime in cities that adopted Compstat were part of a broader trend. However, one New York Police Department official supports the accomplishments of Compstat. He stated, "During the two year decline in crime, social conditions have not radically changed, we have the same police department with the same number of officers. Nothing has changed but how we deploy and utilize police officers" (Anderson, 2001, p. 2).

The evaluation of these various policing strategies has produced mixed results. In the next section, we discuss the evaluation of police performance. We explore the methods used for evaluation and the concerns surrounding which aspects of policing to measure.

EVALUATION OF POLICE PERFORMANCE

The evaluation of performance and the measurement of employee performance are closely related to the delivery of services by an organization. According to Cordner and Sheehan (1999, p. 349), "Without such measurement devices, we will not know when the organization needs improvement; we will not know what aspects of the organization need improvement the most; and, following the implementation of changes, we will not know whether improvements have been achieved." However, any evaluation of performance can have an affect on employees and strongly influence their completion of daily activities. For example, if the number of bicycle tickets written is an important part of the department's evaluation instrument, many police officers will seek to increase their number of bicycle citations they issue. Depending on the perceived weight or importance of the evaluation, some officers will ignore other citations and focus only on bicycle violations. Cordner and Sheehan (1999, p. 354) found that "performance criteria originally selected because of the ease of their measurement may become, in effect, the goals of the police department and the objectives of its individual officers." However, if properly administered, this form of evaluation permits advancement of organizational objectives and accomplishment of certain career goals. The administrator would have to continually assess the evaluation criteria and ensure that the evaluation process is fair for all police personnel. For example, an officer assigned to the "power shift" from 8 P.M. to 4 A.M. would be less likely to encounter as many bicycle violations as would a day-shift officer.

As discussed in previous sections, the role of modern police is often difficult to define using terms that permit easy measurement and evaluation. It is difficult to apply quantifiable measures to many of the tasks performed by the police. For example, consider the New York Police Department's (2000) mission statement:

> To protect life and property, reduce crime, and improve the quality of life while dealing with the citizens of this city with courtesy, professionalism, and respect.
>
> Direct, coordinate, and control the efforts of seven patrol boroughs and the Special Operations Division.
>
> Provide sufficient uniformed patrol officers to respond to emergencies, minimize harm, and maximize public safety.
>
> Deploy resources to effectively combat crime and respond to community needs for police services.
>
> Observe and evaluate performance, equipment, and training of field personnel.

Police have consistently used a set of conventional indicators of police performance that involve the counting of certain desirable law enforcement activities: the number of field reports submitted, number of tickets written, number of referrals made to other agencies, and number of arrests or number of felony arrests (LaGrange, 1998, p. 365). However, the number of arrests and reports only represents the quantitative measures of police performance. According to Roberg and Kuykendall (1997, p. 163) because it was more difficult to assess the qualitative measures of policing (order maintenance, community service, and problem solving), the quantitative law enforcement activities became the most important, prestigious, and rewarded. And besides only representing a portion of the role of the police, quantitative measures are subject to misinterpretation. As Dantzker (1999, p. 251) concluded, "Reporting a low crime rate may not actually indicate that the police department is doing a great job, only that crime reporting is low." Dantzker further suggested, "One could argue that citizens do not report crimes to police agencies they do not trust or they believe to be ineffective, while they report crimes when they believe that the local police agency is honest, responsive, and effective" (Dantzker, 1999, p. 251). In other words, according to this logic, crime rate measures could be an inverse measure of police performance.

It is important to note that a substantial part of the New York Police Department's mission statement focuses on quality of life, professionalism, respect, and the public safety accomplishments of New York police officers. Thibault, Lynch, and McBride (2001, p. 57) found that qualitative measures of police performance could be accomplished through "community leadership meetings and discussions with questionnaires, focus groups from the community where the services were delivered, and community attitude surveys." They concluded that surveys should include questions about the courtesy of police officers, police brutality, level of citizen fear, and general questions concerning how well the police are performing in the community.

The value of measuring police performance subjectively increased during the 1980s, when researchers discovered that the public perceptions had behavioral consequences that affect the quality of life (Bayley, 1994, p. 98). For example, fear of crime can produce sickness and cause absenteeism and truancy; suspicion of the police reduces the willingness of people to provide essential information to the police, thereby decreasing the chances that crimes will be solved; fear of victimization can raise distrust among neighbors, undermining the ability of communities to undertake cooperative crime-prevention action; and the fear of crime may contribute to the decline of neighborhoods as people stop maintaining their property, avoid local businesses and places of recreation, and move to safer, more desirable communities (Bayley, 1994, p. 98; Wilson & Kelling, 1999).

Of course, as with almost any service organization, the measurement of quantitative and even qualitative tasks is a challenge because few consistent work tasks exist. For example, how many cases should a juvenile officer handle in a month? How many traffic tickets should a traffic officer write per month? How many drug arrests should a narcotics officer complete per month? These answers depend on "how serious the crime problem is to begin with, the wishes of the community, the department's resources, and the department's mission" (LaGrange, 1998, p. 368). The evaluation of police personnel may be even more challenging with the implementation of community policing. For example, "How does a supervisor rate an officer who no longer is making arrests because there is not as great a need? How do you quantify interaction with citizens that simply garners good will?" (Dantzker,1999, p. 252). Fyfe et al. (1997, p. 378) found that communities that have implemented community policing could evaluate traffic safety productivity by measuring traffic congestion and accident reductions instead of by counting the number of traffic tickets issued by police officers.

POLICE AND THE MEDIA

No discussion of police operations would be complete without considering the media. The media play a very important role in shaping the public's attitudes and images of the police and of relations between the police and the community. According to Surette

Keeping the media informed is an important part of contemporary policing.

(1992, p. ix), "Most people interact with the mass media as passive consumers rather than as thoughtful, critical users. We have been conditioned to receive the entertainment and knowledge the media provided without considering where this entertainment and knowledge comes from, what effect they have on our attitudes and perceptions, and how they affect society." And as Walker (1999, p. 5) states,

> The myth of the crime fighter endures for many reasons. The entertainment media play a major role in popularizing it. Movies and television police shows feature crime-related stories because they offer drama, fast-paced action, and violence. . . . The news media are equally guilty of overemphasizing police crime fighting. . . . A serious crime is a newsworthy event. There is a victim who engages our sympathies, a story, and then an arrest that offers dramatic visuals of a suspect in custody. A typical night's work for a patrol officers, by way of contrast, does not offer much in the way of dramatic news.

For most people not directly involved in crime events, the images and impressions of the participants in police encounters, of the issues involved, and of police procedures are shaped by the media. Because press, radio, and television to some degree select the events, the people, and the issues to be covered, and because these are the principal sources of information about what is happening in a community or in the nation as a whole, the media are recognized as very powerful forces. They reach large numbers of people on a regular, frequent, and continuing basis, and no police department can long maintain a favorable image without their support (Cox & Fitzgerald, 1996, p. 65).

The media affect and sometimes determine police community relations. Content analysis research has documented media negativity toward the police, and survey data have confirmed increasingly negative perceptions of the police associated with television tabloids and television entertainment talk shows (Moy, Pfau, & Kahlor, 1999).

An excellent example of the power of the media is the recent attention given to racial profiling by the police. Hundreds if not thousands of articles in newspapers and interviews on television have built a library of anecdotal information concerning police persecution of minority (racial and ethnic) drivers. Yet at least one observer has challenged this anecdotal information, claiming that if crime statistics implicate disproportionate rates of crime among minorities, overrepresentation of minorities in traffic stops is to be expected, whether or not race and ethnicity are overriding factors. According to MacDonald (2001, p. 25),

> One way to make sure that nasty confrontations with the facts about crime don't happen again is to stop publishing those facts. And so, New Jersey State Police no longer distribute a typical felony-offender profile to their officers, because such profiles may contribute, in the attorney general's words, to "inappropriate stereotypes" about criminals. Never mind that in law enforcement, with its deadly risk, more information is always better than less. Expect calls for the barring of racial information from crime analysis to spread nationally.

At the same time, however, there is no denying the police brutality involved in the Rodney King incident (several officers beating King), in the Abner Louima incident (Louima hospitalized as a result of rectal injuries suffered at the hands of the police), or in the Amadou Diallo incident (shot numerous times by the police while holding a wallet), all of which attracted national media attention (Locy, 2001; Rashbaum, 2001).

It may be useful to distinguish between two different functions of the media in their coverage of police–community conflicts. On one hand, when covering the police in action, the media have a responsibility to the community they serve: to observe with as much objectivity and to report with as much neutrality as possible. To fulfill this responsibility, the media actively seek to discover what is going on and why, then to inform their readers, viewers, and listeners about their observations. In this aspect of their role, the media may provide background information, including the opportunity for those involved to explain their positions, air their views, and account for their behavior. It is essential that the police are aware of this aspect of the media's role. When appropriate, a department spokesperson should be available to furnish information about the role, obligations, and conduct of the police in the situations being discussed. On the other hand, those involved in disputes with the police, being fully aware of the power of the media to shape public opinion, may view reporters as forces to be manipulated to their own ends. In this phase, the media become the objects of other people's actions. In certain cases, groups deliberately stage events in order to attract the attention of the press or television cameras. In some of these instances, calculated attempts are made to provoke extreme, inappropriate responses from the police so as to undermine their reputation and authority. In this way, groups may seek to engage the sympathy of media audiences for themselves and for the cause they espouse. When the police are deceived by such provocations and respond by using excessive force, these reactions seriously impair police–community relations. In addition, there is the physical harm inflicted on those who are objects of such treatment. Pictures of uniformed officers wielding nightsticks on crouched or prone civilians are vivid in the memories of many American citizens. It is precisely when the temptation is greatest for the police officer to retaliate in a very personal, violent way that it is essential to respond with minimum necessary force. This is characteristic of a well-trained and disciplined professional police officer.

The police should regard difficult situations as valuable opportunities to demonstrate their ability to keep their cool, to function well under stressful conditions. They should take advantage of such opportunities to display the professional care and skill with which they discharge their obligations. Thus, they can keep the public informed about police behavior during such events.

This has not always, of course, been the case, and the relationship between the media and the police has often been antagonistic. To avoid embarrassment to the department, police officials are sometimes reluctant to have certain matters reported to the general public. This reluctance may conflict with media representatives' responsibilities to keep the public informed. On occasion, this may lead to the temptation to deceive the media or to withhold information that the public has a right to know (Brooks, 1999). The media, too, may make the relationship more difficult by reporting inappropriate information gleaned from questionable sources within or without the department. And, the media can be fickle. What is news one day is not the next, and editorial opinion often fluctuates. For example, for eighteen months in 1999 and 2000, the New York media waged war on the New York Police Department (NYPD), characterizing its members as racist and brutal. Then, when the Puerto Rican Day Parade in June 2000 deteriorated into a situation in which dozens of women were fondled, stripped, and robbed, the New York media opportunistically chastised the NYPD for being too soft on crime and being unassertive. MacDonald (2000, p. 17) argued that the media's prior campaign was in part to blame for the police failure to take aggressive action and that the media's response to the attacks on women showed the partisan nature of media coverage.

Former commissioner of the London Police Department, Sir Robert Mark (1977, pp. 50–51) put it in these terms: "We had always adhered to the principle 'Tell them [the media] only what you must.' After consultation with most of the principle editors in London, we reversed this to 'Withhold only what you must' and we delegated to station level the authority to disclose matters of fact not subject to judicial privacy or policies within the sphere of the home office." Playing things too close to the vest only exacerbates images of secrecy and self-protection among police personnel (Cox & Fitzgerald, 1996, p. 67).

The media can and should be viewed as police allies, rather than as critics of policing. The primary goal of the media is to observe life conditions and objectively report these events to the public. The positive influence of the media is often overlooked by the police because of the perceived adversarial nature of their relationship. Media attention is a powerful tool, and a continuing relationship with media representatives (i.e., phone calls, personal visits) will establish a pattern of repeated coverage. Not all coverage will be completely sympathetic to the police cause, but establishing solid professional relationships will create a foundation of honesty and mutual respect (Scaramella & Newman, 1999).

Media Relations Programs

That the media quickly pick up on any negative behavior on behalf of the police is widely known. Corruption, brutality, discrimination, and other forms of misconduct are frequently lead topics on television and radio news as well as in the headlines of newspapers. Prime time television shows also frequently develop plots based on such negative behavior shortly after the behavior is revealed to the public. Staszak states, "The overwhelming search for news should warn law enforcement that the media will get their story one way or another" (2001, p. 11). Convincing the media to cover routine or positive encounters between the police and other citizens in order to provide balanced coverage is the task before the police. To accomplish this task, police administrators need to develop and implement media relations programs. Such programs are beneficial to the extent that they involve open, honest, timely communication between representatives of the media and the police (Davis, 1978; Sullivan, 1998).

A media relations policy based on the public's right to know about the workings of government agencies (with certain important exceptions), and the media's obligation to keep the public informed is important to every police agency. Although various state laws and departmental policies restrict the release of certain information from the police (e.g., information concerning ongoing or anticipated investigations), police personnel should be willing to explain why such information is withheld. The goal of police departments is to develop a cooperative relationship with the media in which information may be provided that does not hamper police operations or violate constitutional rights. (See the Appendix for an example of a media relations policy.)

Some police agencies appoint a public information officer (PIO) to represent the agency in all contacts with the media. This officer typically reports directly to the chief and is responsible for informing and educating the public on matters of public safety. The chief of police also is typically available to address issues of mutual concern, to release information concerning the department, and to provide news releases concerning major crimes and investigations. Funneling all information through these two individuals is done to avoid the confusion that sometimes results from having several different individuals provide information. According to Stascak, "Recognizing that the reporter may not know the difference between subpoenas, indictments, or summonses, proactive PIOs should assist the reporter in learning about and understanding the law enforcement profession" (2001, p. 11).

Other agencies allow any officer with relevant information (except that which is protected, as indicated previously) to discuss police operations. Such agencies allow media ride-alongs so that reporters can see first-hand encounters involving the police and other citizens. To avoid officer and departmental liability, policies concerning ride-alongs should be drafted so that they limit the involvement of third parties in law enforcement activities (Crawford, 2000). Ed Davis (1978, p. 201), former Los Angeles police chief, pointed out that "it is very important that a police agency have an open media policy. A media policy should permit anyone in the department who has adequate knowledge of relevant information, from the lowest to the highest ranking person, to talk to the press."

One context in which the media are especially significant is their treatment of encounters between the police and protestors. Heavy media coverage can help transform a neighborhood disturbance or protest into a citywide or national phenomenon and, in the process, escalate a local neighborhood issue into a citywide crisis. Decisions by media executives not to cover or to discontinue coverage of a demonstration severely restrict the extent to which others may become aware of or involved in the event, and raise serious questions about the proper role of the press in society.

In the final analysis, in spite of accusations of bias in coverage and the potential of the media for abusing the public's trust, the presence of the media in the various arenas of community conflict appears to be in the best interests of both the police and the public. Besides functioning as reporters of community events, the fact that media observers are present, that they have the ability to communicate their observations quickly to many others, in most circumstances tends to discourage extreme behavior in all parties to a conflict. Furthermore, in a democracy, exposure to public scrutiny is a salutary experience for all-powerful forces, including the police.

DISCUSSION QUESTIONS

1. What are the functions of the police?

2. Describe the investigative function of today's police.

3. Describe Wilson's three styles of policing.

4. What are the expected outcomes of police patrol?

5. Is random police patrol an effective technique?

6. Describe the methods for determining the appropriate number of police personnel. Discuss the strengths and weaknesses of each method.

7. Discuss the factors used in the allocation of police personnel.

8. Describe the various forms of police patrol.

9. Compare and contrast the relationship between the strategies of directed patrol, differential response, and saturation patrol and crackdowns.

10. How can we evaluate police performance?

11. Why are police media relations so important to the police? The public?

REFERENCES

Adams, T. F. (2001). *Police field operations*, 5th ed. Upper Saddle River, NJ: Prentice-Hall.
Alpert, G. P., & Dunham, R. G. (1997). *Policing urban America*, 3rd ed. Prospect Heights, IL: Waveland.
American Bar Association (1974). *The urban police functions*. New York: American Bar Association.

Ammann, E. P., & Hey, J. (1986). Establishing agency personnel levels. *FBI Law Enforcement Bulletin*, *55*, 16–20.

Anderson, D. C. (2001) Policing by the numbers. *Chiefly Speaking*, *8*, 1–3.

Bayley, D. H. (1994). *Police for the future*. New York: Oxford University Press.

Bayley, D. H. (1998). *What works in policing*. New York: Oxford University Press.

Bittner, E. (1967). The police on skidrow: A study of peace-keeping. *American Sociological Review*, *32*, 699–715.

Bittner, E. (1990). *Aspects of police work*. Boston: Northwestern University Press.

Bowker, A. L. (1994). Handle with care: Dealing with offenders who are mentally retarded. *FBI Law Enforcement Bulletin*, *63*, 12–16.

Bouza, A. V. (1990). *The police mystique*. New York: Plenum.

Brooks, L. W. (2001). Police discretionary behavior. In Dunham, R. G., & Alpert, G. P. (eds.), *Critical issues in policing*, 4th ed. Prospect Heights, IL: Waveland.

Brooks, M. E. (1999). The ethics of intentionally deceiving the media. *FBI Law Enforcement Bulletin*, *68*, 22–26.

Chicago Police Department. (1998a). Information collection for automated mapping (ICAM). Available online at: http://w5.ci.chi.il.us/CAPS/ToDelete/NewTech/ICAM.html.

Chicago Police Department. (1998b). Mounted patrol unit. Available online at: http://www.ci.chi.il.us/communitypolicing/DistrictHome/SpecialFunctions/Mounted.html.

Chicago Police Department. (1998c). Senior's persistence pays off in moving drug dealers on. Available online at: http://w5.ci.chi.il.us/cp/AboutCAPS/SuccessStories/Dist02.95.06.html.

Cordner, G. W. (1999). Community policing. In Alpert, G. P., & Piquero, A. R. (eds.), *Community policing contemporary readings*, 2nd ed. (pp. 45–62). Prospect Heights, IL: Waveland.

Cordner, G. W., Gaines, L. K., & Kappeler, V. E. (1996). *Police operations*. Cincinnati, OH: Anderson.

Cordner, G., & Sheehan, R. (1999). *Police administration*, 4th ed. Cincinnati, OH: Anderson.

Cox, S. M., & Fitzgerald, J. M. (1996). *Police in community relations: Critical issues*, 3rd ed. Dubuque, IA: Wm. C. Brown.

Crank, J. P. (1998). *Understanding police culture*. Cincinnati, OH: Anderson.

Crawford, K. A. (2000). Media ride-alongs: Fourth Amendment constraints. *FBI Law Enforcement Bulletin*, *69*, 26–30.

Creel, B. (1999). Citizens on patrol. The Battalion. Available online at: http://batweb.tamu.edu/archives/99c/9-7/state1.html.

Curry, K., Posluszny, M., & Kraska, S. (1993, Winter). Training criminal justice personnel to recognize offenders with disabilities. *News in Print*. Washington, DC: U.S. Government Printing Office.

Dantzker, M. L. (1999). *Police organization and management*. Boston: Butterworth-Heinemann.

Davis, E. (1978). *Staff one: A perspective on effective police management*. Englewood Cliffs, NJ: Prentice-Hall.

Debbaudt, D., & Rothman, D. (2001). Contact with individuals with autism: Effective resolutions. *FBI Law Enforcement Bulletin*, *70*, 20–24.

Dempsey, J. S. (1999). *Policing*, 2nd ed. St. Paul, MN: West.

Denver Police Department. (2000). *Air support unit*. Available online at: http://www.denvergov.org/content/template2922.asp.

Fyfe, J. J. (1986). The split-second syndrome and other determinants of police violence. In Dunham, R. G., & Alpert, G. P. (eds.), *Critical issues in policing*, 4th ed. Prospect Heights, IL: Waveland.

Fyfe, J. J., Green, J. R., Walsh, W. F., Wilson, O. W., & McLaren, R. C. (1997). *Police administration*, 5th ed. New York: McGraw-Hill.

Gilbert, J. N. (2001). *Criminal investigation*, 5th ed. Upper Saddle River, NJ: Prentice-Hall.

Goldstein, H. (1977). *Policing a free society*. Cambridge, MA: Ballinger.

Greene, J. R., & Klockars, C. B. (1991). What police do. In Klockars, C. B., & Mastrofski, S. D. (eds.), *Thinking about police: Contemporary readings*, 2nd ed. (pp. 273–284). New York: McGraw-Hill.

Greenwood, P. W., & Petersilia, J. (1975). *The criminal investigation process: Volume I: Summary and policy recommendations*. Santa Monica, CA: Rand.

Guiliani, R., & Safir, H. (1998). *Compstat-leadership in action*. New York: New York Police Department.

Hellriegel, D., Slocum, J. W., & Woodman, R. W. (2001). *Organizational behavior*, 9th ed. Cincinnati, OH: South-Western College Publishing.

Hess, K. H., & Wrobleski, H. M. (1993). *Police operations.* St. Paul, MN: West.

Illinois Compiled Statutes. (2000). Chapter 65.

Illinois State Police. (1999). *Combined need-based allocation and community policing: Forcing a square peg in a round hole.* Springfield, IL: Illinois State Police.

Illinois State Police. (2001). Homepage. Springfield, IL: Illinois State Police. Available online at: http://www.state.il.us/isp.

Iowa Department of Public Safety. (2001). *Special agent job description.* Available oneline at: http://www.state.ia.us/government/dps/jobs/dcisa.htm.

Jurkanin, T., Hoover, L., Dowling, J., & Ahmad, J. (2001). *Enduring, surviving, and thriving as a law enforcement executive.* Springfield, IL: Charles C. Thomas.

Kelling, G. L., Pate, T., Diekman, D., & Brown, C. E. (1974). *The Kansas City patrol preventive patrol experiment: A summary report.* Washington, DC: Police Foundation.

LaGrange, R. L. (1998). *Policing American society,* 2nd ed. Chicago: Nelson-Hall.

Langworthy, R. H., & Travis, L. F. (1999). *Policing in America: A balance of forces,* 2nd ed. Upper Saddle River, NJ: Prentice-Hall.

Locy, T. (2001, April 17). Problems with police not new: What is new is the reporting, investigating of misconduct. *USA Today,* p. 3A.

Maas, P. (1998, May 10). What we're learning from New York City. *Parade.* New York: Parade Publications, pp. 4–5.

MacDonald, H. (2001). The myth of racial profiling. *City Journal, 11,* 14–27.

MacDonald, H. (2000). N.Y. press to NYPD: Drop dead: The police are too aggressive, except when they're not aggressive enough. *American Enterprise, 11,* 16–17.

Mark, R. (1977). *Policing a perplexed society.* London: Allen & Unwin.

McDonald, P. P. (2002). *Managing police operations.* Belmont, CA: Wadsworth/Thomson.

Metro Nashville Police Department. (2000). Bicycle patrol. Available online at: http://www.nashville.net/~police/citizen/bicycle_patrol.htm.

Michigan Law Enforcement Officers Training Council. (1997). Report for large cities, villages, and townships: Statewide job analysis of the patrol officer position. Lansing: Michigan Law Enforcement Officers Training Council.

Montana Department of Justice. (2000). Investigations bureau. Available online at: http://www.doj.state.mt.us/les/dci_inv.htm.

Moore, M. H. (1992). Problem-solving and community policing. In Alpert, G., & Piquero, A. (eds.), *Community policing,* 2nd ed. Prospect Heights, IL: Waveland.

Moy, P., Pfau, M., & Kahlor, L. (1999). Media use and public confidence in democratic institutions. *Journal of Broadcasting & Electronic Media, 43,* 137–158.

New York Police Department. (2000). Mission statement. Available online at: http://www.ci.nyc.ny.us/html/nypd/html/pct/psb_mission.html.

O'Boyle, E. H. (1991). Manpower. *Law and Order, 39,* 88–93.

Palatine Police Department. (2000). Police assistant program. Available online at: http://www.palatine.il.us.

Parks, R. B., Mastrofski, S. D., Dejong, C., & Gray, M. K. (1999). How officers spend their time with the community. *Justice Quarterly, 16,* 484–518.

Peak, K. J. (1997). *Policing America,* 2nd ed. Upper Saddle River, NJ: Prentice-Hall.

Pelfrey, W. (2000). Precipitating factors of paradigmatic shift in policing. In Alpert, G., & Piquero, A. (eds.), *Community policing.* Prospect Heights, IL: Waveland.

Philadelphia Police Department. (2001). The compstat process. Available online at: http://www.ppdonline.org/ppd_compstat.htm.

Rashbaum, W. K. (2001, May 30). Quietly, police give protestors a night in jail. *New York Times,* p. 1B.

Reaves, B. A., & Hart, T. C. (1999). *Law enforcement management and administrative statistics, 1999: Data for individual state and local agencies with 100 or more officers.* Washington, DC: U.S. Department of Justice.

Roberg, R. R., Crank, J., & Kuykendall, J. (2000). *Police and society,* 2nd ed. Los Angeles: Roxbury.

Roberg, R. R., & Kuykendall, J. (1997). *Police management,* 2nd ed. Los Angeles: Roxbury.

———. (1993). *Police and society.* Belmont, CA: Wadsworth.

Scaramella, E., & Newman, A. (1999). Community education and the media: A partnership for effective crime control. *Crime and Justice International, 15,* 9–10, 12.

Schmidt, A. (2000). COPS office brings community policing into school with new program. *Police, 24,* 8.

Senna, J., & Siegel, L. (1999). *Introduction to criminal justice,* 8th ed. Belmont, CA: West/Wadsworth.

Sherman, L., & Weisburd, D. (1995). General deterrent effects of police patrol in crime "Hot Spots: A randomized study." *Justice Quarterly, 12,* 625.

Sparrow, M. K., Moore, M. H., & Kennedy, D. M. (1990). *Beyond 911: A new era for policing.* New York: Basic Books.

Staszak, D. (2001). Media trends and the public information officer. *FBI Law Enforcement Bulletin, 70,* 10–13.

Sullivan, M. J. (1998, January). Managing major case investigations: Suggestions for supervisors. *FBI Law Enforcement Bulletin, 67,* 1–5.

Surette, R. (1992). *Media, crime & justice: Images and realities.* Pacific Grove, CA: Brooks/Cole.

Thibault, E. A., Lynch, L. M., & McBride, R. B. (2001). *Proactive police management,* 5th ed. Upper Saddle River, NJ: Prentice-Hall.

Toch, H., & Grant, D. (1991). *Police as problem solvers.* New York: Plenum.

Virginia State Police. (2000). Computer crimes. Available online at: http://www.vsp.state.va.us/bci_gid_cyber.htm.

Walker, S. (1999). *The police in America,* 3rd ed. Boston: McGraw-Hill.

Wilson, J. (1968). *Varieties of police behavior: The management of law and order in eight communities.* Cambridge, MA: Harvard University Press.

Wilson, J. Q., & Kelling, G. L. (1999). Broken windows. In Kappeler, V. E. (ed.), *The police and society,* 2nd ed. (pp. 154–167). Prospect Heights, IL: Waveland.

Worden, R. E. (1996). Toward equity and efficiency in law enforcement: Differential police response. In Cordner, G. W., Gaines, L. K., & Kappeler, V. E. (eds.), *Police operations* (pp. 131–156). Cincinnati, OH: Anderson.

Young, J. (2000). Community policing in Savannah, Georgia. In Alpert, G., & Piquero, A. (eds.), *Community policing,* 2nd ed. (pp. 305–323). Prospect Heights, IL: Waveland.

CHAPTER FOUR

POLICE RECRUITMENT AND SELECTION

Every police department is faced with the necessity of recruiting and selecting personnel to fill the complex role discussed in the preceding chapters. Personnel must be recruited and selected to fill positions at three different levels: the entry level, the supervisory level, and the chief's level. Current evidence indicates that police officer applicant numbers may be decreasing in many areas (Swope, 1999; Flynn, 2000; Ferkenhoff, 2001), with some departments reporting that the number of entry-level candidates has fallen by half since 1995 (*Crime Control Digest*, 2001, p. 1). Because recruitment and selection are critical to the success of any agency, and because virtually all promotions within police agencies are internal, the inability to attract sufficient numbers of qualified recruits presents major problems for police administrators. This is particularly true with respect to women and minorities, an issue that is addressed in detail in Chapter 6. As we begin this chapter, several questions come to mind: Is there a group of traits that characterize the "ideal" police officer? Have these traits been identified? Can this group of traits be developed in recruits?

THE IMPORTANCE OF RECRUITMENT AND SELECTION

The importance of productive recruitment and selection procedures cannot be overemphasized, regardless of the level involved. Poor recruitment and selection procedures result in hiring or promoting personnel who cannot or will not communicate effectively with diverse populations, exercise discretion properly, or perform the multitude of functions required of the police. Following is a list of the traits necessary to be an effective police officer (adapted from Nowicki, 1999):

Enthusiasm
Good communications skills
Good judgement
Sense of humor
Creativity
Self-motivation
Knowledge of the job and the system
Ego (positive image of themselves)
Courage
Understanding of discretion
Tenacity
Thirst for knowledge

Recognizing the need for candidates with such traits, most departments expend considerable time and money in the process. The New York City Police Department, for example, estimates that the costs associated with each new officer, from recruitment through the end of probation, are in the area of $500,000 (Decicco, 2000). The extent to which such recruitment efforts are successful largely determines the effectiveness and efficiency of any department. Highlight 4.1 discusses the decline in police candidates and the future recruitment challenges facing police chiefs.

It must be pointed out that the process of recruiting and selecting officers and chiefs and promoting supervisors is, in many cases, done in large part by those outside of policing. That is, police and fire commissioners, personnel departments, or civil service board members often determine who will be eligible for hiring and promotion, and assessment teams, city managers, mayors, and council members typically determine who will fill the position of chief. To be sure, in the former case, police officials may select the officers they choose from among those on the eligibility list and, in the case of promotions, have a good deal of input, as we shall see later. Still, much of the

■ ■ ■ ■ ■

HIGHLIGHT 4.1

POLICE CHIEFS TRY MANY RECRUITING STRATEGIES TO BOOST APPLICANT POOL

The competition to fill law enforcement positions is presenting unprecedented challenges to police chiefs, some of whom have seen the number of officer candidates fall by half since 1995.

With private businesses offering better pay and significantly less risk and controversy, police departments are increasingly seeking new ways to attract recruits, including the Internet and raids on other agencies.

The International Association of Chiefs of Police traces the beginning of the decline to the mid-1990s when "dot.coms" swept the country.

IACO says many departments have reported a 50 percent plunge in the number of applications.

For example, Louisville, Ky., tested 662 applicants in 1995 and only 310 in 2000.

IACO says salary has been a key issue. The starting salary in Louisville is $29,043.20. After 20 weeks of training and 32 weeks of riding with a veteran officer, officers can expect an increase plus $3,000 in supplemental pay each year after completing training at an accredited recruit academy.

Besides higher pay, police have widened their searches beyond local communities.

The Los Angeles Police Department has recruited in Chicago. The Chicago Police Department has recruited in Wisconsin.

The New York City Police Department relaxed its age and education requirements, lowering the minimum age to 21 from 22 and allowing some applicants to substitute work experience for college credits. Minnesota is considering a similar route.

Where did aspiring police officers go? With a tight labor market, many are attracted to safer, less stressful jobs. Even veteran officers get lured to higher-paying jobs in private security or federal agencies such as the FBI.

The Kentucky State Police now have application forms on the Web where they can be easily downloaded, according to chief recruiter Capt. Jerry Nauert.

The Kentucky State Police will be able to accept applications online by the end of the year, Nauert says.

Police in California, New York and Indiana also put information about openings on the Internet.

The Indianapolis Police Department allocated $27,000 to an advertising campaign that involved painting a bus to look like a patrol car complete with a toll-free telephone number offering information on career opportunities with the police. In addition, the agency is advertising on billboards and in movie theaters.

recruitment and selection of police personnel is done by civilians with varying degrees of input from police administrators.

It is important to note that recruitment and selection are ongoing processes that recur throughout the career of an officer. Once selected for an entry-level position by a specific department, the officer is likely to be involved in selection procedures involving appointment to different assignments (detective, juvenile officer, crime technician, patrol officer, etc.), to different ranks (promotional examinations), to different schools or training programs, and so on. For some, the process ends with their selection as chief; for others, the process continues as they seek the position of chief in other agencies; and for some, the process begins and ends at the rank of patrol officer.

Nonetheless, even for the latter, the process is repeated over and over throughout their careers, even though they may choose not to participate directly. That is, some officers make a conscious choice to remain patrol officers and not to seek opportunities for training. These officers, too, are important in understanding the recruitment and selection process involved in promotions, because they may become perceived as outside of the pool of candidates to be recruited for such advancement or training. In addition, those who are selected for such assignments must be prepared to deal with career patrol persons, just as these patrol persons must be prepared to deal with those promoted. An examination of the various requirements and strategies employed in the recruitment process reveals some of the difficulties involved in selecting personnel who will both fill the official vacancy and meet the situation-specific needs of various departments. However, before we turn our attention to recruitment and selection at the various levels, we need to understand the legal context in which such processes occur.

Equal Employment Opportunity and Affirmative Action

For most of our history, American employers, both public and private, have felt relatively free to hire and promote employees according to whatever criteria they established and, similarly, to exclude from employment and promotion those they deemed, for whatever reason, to be unfit. This was true even though the U.S. Constitution, in the First, Fifth, and Fourteenth Amendments, prohibits deprivation of employment rights without due process of law. Further, the Civil Rights Acts of 1866, 1870, and 1871 (based on the Thirteenth and Fourteenth Amendments) prohibited racial discrimination in hiring and placement as well as deprivation of equal employment rights under the cover of state law (Bell, 1992).

Still, it wasn't until 1964 and the passage of the Civil Rights Act of that year, and specifically Title VII of the act, that many employers began to take equal employment rights seriously. The act prohibited discrimination in employment based on race, color, and national origin and applied to all employers receiving federal financial assistance. Title VII of the 1964 Civil Rights Act, as amended in 1972, extended the prohibition of discrimination in hiring to religion, sex, and national origin, and applied to federal, state, and local governments, among others. This act, the Equal Employment Opportunity Act (EEOA), established a commission (EEOC) to investigate complaints of discrimination. Following these changes in federal law, states also began passing such laws in the form of fair employment statutes (Bell, 1992).

In general terms, these laws hold that discrimination occurs when requirements for hiring and promotion are not bona fide (i.e., they are not actually related to the job) and when a disparate impact occurs to members of a minority group. Federal legislation requires that all employers with more than fifteen employees refrain from policies and procedures that discriminate against specified categories of individuals (Brooks, 2001, p. 26). The burden of demonstrating that requirements are job-related falls on the employer, while the burden of showing a disparate impact falls on the complainant. For an employer to be successfully sued in this regard, both conditions must be met. That is, it is possible to have job requirements that have a disparate impact but are nonetheless valid. For example, if it could be demonstrated that police officers routinely have to remove accident victims from vehicles in order to avoid the possibility of further injury due to fire or explosion, and if this job requirement also eliminated from policing women and/or other categories of applicants, the requirement would not be discriminatory under the law. If, however, these actions are seldom if ever required of police officers, the requirement would be discriminatory. We will have more to say about such requirements later in this chapter, but it is important to understand here the context within which charges of discrimination are filed and decided.

The combined impact of equal employment opportunity laws and executive orders eventually came to be realized by government agencies, among them the police. Prior to the early 1970s, most police departments had employed predominantly white men, a practice that came to be the focus of numerous legal challenges. These challenges came in the form of both court actions and complaints to the EOC alleging discrimination on the part of employers.

During the same period, the concept of affirmative action gained prominence. Affirmative action programs have two goals. First, they are intended to prevent discrimination in current hiring and promotional practices. Second, they may be used to help remedy past discrimination in hiring and promotion.

Equal employment opportunity and affirmative action programs may be implemented in a number of different ways. First, some employers voluntarily establish affirmative action programs because they recognize the importance of hiring without regard to race, creed, or ethnicity. Second, some employers implement such programs when threatened with legal action based on alleged discrimination. Third, some employers fight charges of discrimination in the courts and are found to be in violation. When this occurs, such employers are in danger of losing federal financial support and agree to develop and implement affirmative action programs in order to prevent this loss of federal monies. This typically occurs through the use of a consent decree in which the employer agrees to strive to achieve some sort of balance in terms of race/ethnicity and/or gender in the workforce. In other cases, the courts impose plans and time tables on employers and can impose severe sanctions in the form of fines if the goals of the plans are not met within the specified time period.

The use of consent decrees has led to a good deal of confusion and widespread ill feelings on behalf of employers and white, male employees. On one hand, the EOA prohibits discrimination based on race, creed, religion, sex, or national origin and states that employers will not be forced to hire less well qualified employees over more well qualified employees. On the other hand, the courts have reached agreements with employers that would seem to discriminate against white male employees and have, although the EEOA prohibits the use of quotas to achieve racial balance, imposed quota systems on some employers (Berg, 1992).

For example, in 1987, the U.S. Supreme Court upheld promotional quotas that required that the Alabama State Police promote one black officer for each white officer until blacks held at least 25 percent of the top ranks in the department (Gest, 1987). More importantly, perhaps, this decision protected over a hundred affirmative action cases that included quotas (Sullivan, 1989, p. 337).

A number of police administrators have complained that they have been forced to hire minority employees who do not meet the standards they have established to improve police services, and thousands of white, male applicants for police positions complain that, although they are better qualified than minority candidates in terms of test results, the latter have been hired or promoted. Both of these complaints are, in individual instances, justified, but they must be viewed in light of the goals of affirmative action, especially the goal of remedying past discrimination.

In essence, white men applying for police positions or promotions in some areas are suffering the same fate their black and Hispanic counterparts have suffered over the past three centuries in American society. Now that the "shoe is on the other foot," it pinches. In some cases, white, male applicants have filed suits claiming discrimination and have prevailed. The shift from discriminatory employment practices in policing, as well as in many other areas, has been slow and sometimes painful, yet it is necessary in order to maximize the number of qualified applicants and to make police agencies representative of the communities they serve. As Cox and Fitzgerald (1996) note, the police will not be viewed as understanding community problems unless they have members who can view them from the community's perspective.

Unfortunately, in spite of the fact that the International Association of Chiefs of Police unanimously adopted a resolution in 1975 supporting minority recruitment (Broderick, 1987, p. 214), in many cases, police agencies and the municipalities in which they operate have chosen to continue discriminatory hiring and/or promotional practices until and unless someone files legal action to force change. Others, though perhaps a minority, made and are making deliberate attempts to hire and promote minority group members for the obvious advantages that result. In either case, it is clear that certain requirements must be met to avoid charges of discrimination in employment (Sullivan, 1989, p. 337):

1. Requirements must be job-related.
2. Requirements must be validated.
3. Requirements must be free of "inherent bias."
4. Requirements must be properly administered.
5. Candidates must be properly graded.

As a result of numerous claims of reverse discrimination by white men, the Supreme Court considered the issue in 1989 (it had previously done so to some extent in 1987 in the case of *Baake v. California*). The Court's decision indicated that statistical comparisons of populations alone are insufficient to show discrimination and that cases of overt discrimination are the only cases covered by Title VII (Gaines, Kappeler, & Vaughn, 1994, p. 73). The Court recognized in a number of cases the concept of reverse discrimination and, in a case involving firefighters in the city of Birmingham, Alabama, found that well-qualified whites who are passed over for promotion in order to promote less well-qualified blacks have a cause of action against the city (and, presumably, across the country). This means that municipalities operating under consent decrees, in which agreement has been reached to preferentially hire minorities, may be, by adhering to the conditions of the decree, opening themselves up to lawsuit in the name of reverse discrimination.

In 1992, President Bush signed legislation intended to clarify issues arising from what appeared to be conflicting Supreme Court decisions. As a result of that legislation, "statistical and other adjustments that would give minorities an advantage over majority candidates in the selection process" were prohibited. "Such things as adding points, using dual lists, or using quotas became prohibited." In addition "the act re-introduced disparate impact as a method of determining whether discrimination existed" (Gaines, Kappeler, & Vaughn, 1994, p. 73).

The Americans with Disabilities Act

In 1990, the Americans with Disabilities Act (ADA) was enacted. While the impact of the act on policing is not yet entirely clear, at least a brief description of the ADA is in order, because there is little doubt that many police agencies will be involved in litigation as a result of the act.

The ADA makes it illegal to discriminate against persons with certain categories of disabilities, limits blanket exclusions, and requires that the selection process deal with individuals on a case-by-case basis. To be protected under the ADA, the individual must have a disability or impairment (physical or mental), or must have a record of such disability, or must be regarded as having such a disability, and must be otherwise qualified for the position in question. *Otherwise qualified* means that the applicant must be able to perform the essential elements of the job with or without reasonable accommodation. *Reasonable accommodation* refers to new construction, modifying existing facilities, work schedules, or equipment, as long as such modification does not cause the agency undue hardship (significant expense or difficulty). Examples of disabilities covered by the ADA include vision, hearing, breathing, and learning problems, as well as AIDS and HIV infection (Rubin, 1993). Examples of accommodation include building ramps to provide access to buildings or work sites, designating parking spaces for those with disabilities, installing elevators, and redesigning work stations and restrooms.

The ADA places considerable emphasis on job-task analysis to determine the essential functions of positions and, of course, requires that job requirements be bona fide (Schneid & Gaines, 1991; Colbridge, 2000). It does not, however, create a statutory preference for people with disabilities (Colbridge, 2000, p. 29). Thus, a person with a disability that kept him from meeting state-mandated police certification requirements does not have to be considered by the police (Colbridge, 2000, p. 29).

The ADA divides the employment process into three phases: the application/interview phase, the postconditional offer stage, and the working stage (Colbridge, 2001). During phase 1, the ADA limits inquiries to nondisability qualifications of applicants. Employers may not ask about prior drug addiction, for example, because that is covered under ADA. They may ask about current illegal drug use, because that is not covered under ADA. Similarly, applicants may be asked how they would perform job-related functions, as long as all applicants are asked the same question. Applicants indicating they would need reasonable accommodation to perform job-related tasks must be provided such accommodation unless doing so would create an undue hardship for the employer (Colbridge, 2001, p. 25).

The psychological examination may be viewed as part of the medical examination if it is used to uncover recognized mental disorders, and therefore violates the ADA because the ADA protects those with mental impairments who are otherwise job-qualified. In such cases, the psychological test, like the medical examination, should be delayed until after an employment offer is made. Psychological tests dealing with honesty, tastes, or habits of the applicant are not considered medical examinations and may be used at the application/interview stage (Colbridge, 2001, p. 26).

Once a conditional offer of employment has been made, employers may ask about disabilities in order to determine whether reasonable accommodation is necessary and feasible. If it is necessary and reasonable, such accommodation must generally be provided. Medical examinations also may be required during the postconditional phase, and again reasonable accommodation for disabilities must be provided (Colbridge, 2001). Following employment, the ADA requires that disability-related inquiries be made only if they are job related, and reasonable accommodation is again required.

The EEOC is charged with enforcing the ADA. If the Commission determines that discrimination does not exist, the claim is dismissed (although the complainant still has the right to sue the employer). When the Commission determines that there is reasonable cause to believe discrimination has occurred, it will seek a negotiated settlement or bring a civil action against the employer (Colbridge, 2000).

Let us now turn our attention to the entry-level requirements that have been established for police officers and the recruitment and selection process at this level.

ENTRY-LEVEL RECRUITMENT AND SELECTION

According to Alpert and Dunham (1997, p. 40), "It is difficult to emphasize sufficiently the importance of recruitment, selection and training. After all, a police agency is no better than those who perform the day-to-day tasks. Police work is a labor-intensive service industry, in which roughly 85 percent of the agencies' budgets are devoted to these personnel costs . . . the most significant investment police departments make is in the recruiting, selection and training of their personnel."

One important personnel cost for any organization is that associated with attracting qualified applicants to fill vacancies. This is certainly true in policing, which, as indicated previously, is labor-intensive. The costs of recruitment begin with the advertising process and, hopefully, end with the successful completion of the probationary period. In other words, the objective of the recruitment process is to select potential police officers who can not only meet entry level requirements, but also successfully complete training academy requirements and the probationary period. While recruit qualifications vary tremendously in different departments, some general requirements and concerns can be discussed. Highlight 4.2 focuses on the recruitment problems experienced by small police departments.

The objective in advertising is to attract from the total pool of potential applicants for police work those, and only those, who are both qualified and seriously interested in becoming police officers. The more applicants attracted who do not meet both of these requirements, the more expensive the recruiting process. Let us assume, hypo-

---

HIGHLIGHT 4.2

SMALLER POLICE DEPARTMENTS STRUGGLE TO MAINTAIN OFFICERS

PEORIA—Faced with officers leaving his ranks for city jobs, Peoria County Sheriff Chuck Schofield is forced to recruit from a labor force that undoubtedly includes officers from surrounding small-town departments.

And as the job market for police officers tightens, that domino effect which drives leapfrogging from one local department to the next is bound to grow more intense, he said Wednesday.

"If the rumors hold true, then I'm going to lose five to six officers to the city of Peoria in the very near future," Schofield said. "I have an eligibility list. Naturally, the first ones I'd look at are the ones that are already certified (and trained)."

Hiring officers from smaller departments is not ideal, but the alternative is hiring a rookie who would require nearly a year's worth of training to be ready to hit the streets.

"This is not something that is our choice, but it's just a hard, cold fact of life," Schofield said. "The city of Peoria needs people, so they're taking people from us. It's part of the game. There's no ill feelings for that."

The county is now even considering "buying out" officers' contracts with other departments—in other words, paying another municipality for training if an officer leaves before their contractual commitment ends.

"It's not a desirable situation to find yourself in. It's not something that I really approve of.

But it's a situation where you're looking at the dollars," Schofield said.

The county also is exploring the idea of implementing contracts for their own offices, requiring a certain tenure. A decision is expected to come soon.

The Peoria Heights Village Board raised wages for officers in recent years and enforced residency requirements, in an effort to stop major turnover.

Village officials complained about footing the bill for training rookie officers—which can range upwards of $10,000—and being used as a stepping stone, without a return on their investment.

"We're always going to have a couple of officers who fulfill their contracts here and want to get into a bigger department," said Peoria Heights Police Chief Dustin Sutton.

He says he's all for people bettering themselves and moving on, as long as they fulfill a 30-month contractual commitment. Recently, he had an officer leave for a county job after just a year's time.

County Board member Mike Phelan said he wants to make sure the county isn't trying to lure small-town officers away from obligations with smaller departments.

Klopfenstein, S. (2001, August 30). Smaller police departments struggle to maintain officers. *Journal Star*, p. A05.

thetically, that the cost of processing one police recruit from application to placement on the eligibility list is $1,000. Suppose the agency attracts fifty applicants for the one vacancy available. And suppose that forty of the fifty applicants pass all the tests given in the early stages of the selection process. When the agency conducts background investigations of those who have successfully completed the tests, however, it is discovered that ten of the applicants have prior felony convictions. In essence, the municipality has wasted the money spent on hiring these individuals because, in most jurisdictions, they could not be hired as police officers regardless of their performance on the tests. Again, suppose that ten more applicants really have no interest in police work once they discover something about its nature and would not accept a police position if it were offered. The time and money spent on these individuals is also wasted. Now there are thirty applicants remaining, but the agency has only one vacancy. As you can see, the cost of recruiting the one individual who is selected is quite high.

To some extent, these difficulties are inherent in the recruitment/selection process, and to some extent they may be offset by the establishment of an eligibility list (if there are other vacancies within a relatively short period of time). That is, those involved in the hiring process probably cannot determine at the outset who will and will not decide to accept the position if it is offered, and if several of the people who qualify are hired, the costs may be reduced. Costs also may be reduced, however, by developing an advertising campaign that clearly states the requirements of the position and that, to the extent possible, accurately describes the duties to be performed. Thus, a statement that those with prior felony convictions need not apply might be part of the advertisement. While this does not guarantee that such persons will not apply, it at least indicates to them that they have no chance of being hired if discovered and probably prevents many with prior convictions from applying. The point is that the more accurately the qualities sought are described, the less likely it is that large numbers of unqualified people will apply, thus helping to keep recruiting costs as low as possible. At the same time, however, advertisements must be designed to attract as many qualified applicants as possible. This includes not only describing the benefits associated with the position available, but also indicating that the police department is an equal opportunity employer and that women and minorities are invited to apply. Including these statements is especially necessary in police recruitment, because police departments, for reasons detailed previously, have traditionally been viewed by both minorities and women as basically white, male domains. Advertising campaigns must take this fact into account, and advertisements should be placed in magazines likely to be read by women and minorities as well as in the more traditional professional journals and newspapers.

Further recruiting efforts may be directed at college campuses, high schools, and minority neighborhoods. Conducting orientation sessions that provide a realistic picture of police work in the department in question for applicants is another valuable tool in "selecting out" those who find they have no interest in such work. More and more police departments are using the Internet to advertise vacancies, and some allow application over the Internet. Those seeking jobs as police officers can also use the Web to learn how to take entry-level tests (Brandon & Lippman, 2000). Although those responsible for recruiting police personnel have made strides in these areas in recent years, there is still much to be done. The bottom line is that if those charged with hiring police officers want to have representative police departments in order to provide the best services available to the communities served, they must attract the best qualified candidates.

When the application deadline indicated in the advertisements has been reached, the applications that have been filed must be analyzed. The better the application form, the easier the analysis. The form might request information on prior experience in policing, prior criminal convictions, educational background, reasons for the interest in police work, prior drug and alcohol use, and other information considered pertinent by specific departments. It should also provide some indication of the applicant's ability to express herself in writing. Some departments have found that charging a nominal fee for the application eliminates some applicants who might simply be "testing the waters," and detailed application forms requesting specific information probably also eliminate some who are using narcotics, some who have prior felony convictions, and so on. The more of these types applicants eliminated at this stage, the less costly the recruiting process. However, in today's tight market, charging an application fee, especially when not all agencies do so, may not be in the department's best interests.

As we have seen, standards of selection for police officers were virtually nonexistent in the early days of American policing. When standards did begin to emerge, they often required little more than allegiance to a particular politician or political party. The past two decades have seen an increase in the concern with establishing minimum entry-level requirements for police officers, and only in the past ten to fifteen years has what has been called the "Multiple-Hurdle Procedure" become common (Stone & DeLuca, 1985; Decicco, 2000). The term refers to a battery of tests or hurdles that must be successfully completed before the recruit can become a police officer. In the following sections, we critically analyze each of these tests, which may be generally divided into the following categories:

1. Status tests
2. Physical tests
3. Mental tests
4. Tests of morality
5. Tests of ability to communicate

It should be pointed out that the different types of tests sometimes overlap, but we discuss each independently.

Status Tests

Status tests have to do with areas such as citizenship, possession or ability to obtain a driver's license, residency, service in the military, educational level, and age. Police officers are virtually always required to be citizens, though some court challenges to this requirement are being made. Is citizenship a bona fide job requirement? Can one who is a citizen perform police functions better than one who is, for example, a permanent resident who has passed a test covering the U.S. and state constitutions? This is an issue that will eventually be decided by the courts, but for the time being, it is safe to say that citizen status is typically required. The requirement that the applicant have or be able to obtain a driver's license seems likely to be upheld for obvious reasons. Some municipalities and states require that newly hired personnel be residents, or be willing to become residents, of the jurisdiction involved. This requirement, too, has been and continues to be subject to court battles, and a majority of jurisdictions have modified the requirement (Gaines, Kappeler, & Vaughn, 1994, p. 78). Many suburban police departments, for example, simply require that officers live no more than twenty or thirty minutes from their place of duty.

Questions concerning prior military service arise because bonus points (veterans' preference points) may be added to the test scores of applicants if they have such prior service, thus affecting the final eligibility list. Most departments have minimum educational standards, typically, possession of a high school diploma or its equivalent, which must be met by applicants, and these standards have been upheld by the courts.

Finally, the vast majority of departments require that applicants be adults (the age of majority) at the time of employment and not be more than thirty-six to forty years of age at the time of initial employment in policing. The minimum age requirement makes sense in terms of maturity and meeting statutory requirements for entering certain types of establishments. The upper age limit has been called into question as a result of the Age Discrimination Act of 1990, which prohibits age discrimination with respect to those over age forty. Whether the applicant meets the status requirements can be determined largely from the application form.

Physical Tests

Physical tests include physical agility tests, height/weight proportionate tests, vision tests, and medical examinations.

Physical Agility Tests. Physical agility tests are used by about 80 percent of police agencies to determine whether applicants are agile enough, in good enough condition, strong enough, and have enough endurance to perform police work (Ash, Slora, & Britton, 1990; Decicco, 2000). These tests must be job-related, and many have fallen by the wayside as the result of court challenges. Tests of coordination and actual agility can typically be shown to be job-related, whereas tests based on sheer strength are more difficult to validate. Many departments at one time required that applicants be able to complete a specified number of pull-ups or push-ups in a specified time period. It is difficult to justify such tests on the basis of job-relatedness, however. How often does a police officer have to do pull-ups in the performance of his duty? A more realistic test is the wall test in which the applicant must clear a wall of a certain height. One can at least envision the possibility of this type of activity in the performance of police duties.

It may be that the basis for such strength tests was a desire to eliminate female applicants from police employment, or it may be that police administrators sincerely believed that strength was an important requirement for police officers. Whatever the case, the requirement that such tests be validated has led to a number of changes in the types of physical tests now employed, and a wide variety of testing strategies characterizes different police departments. One study by Booth and Hornick (1984, p. 40)

Physical fitness is a critical part of policing.

concluded that the ability to react quickly is the most critical and frequently required physical attribute of police officers, while brute force and long-term endurance are the least frequently performed and least critical of the physical activities performed by police personnel. The current situation seems to be that only those standards that relate to business necessities and that can be met by individuals already occupying police positions are likely to be upheld by the courts (Decicco, 2000).

Height/Weight Proportionate Tests. Height/weight proportionate tests have replaced traditional height requirements, which eliminated most women and many minority group members from policing. Such tests make sense in the context of police work and the previously discussed agility requirements. As originally employed, these tests seemed largely superfluous because few departments required that proportionate height and weight be maintained after initial employment, but many, if not most, departments now test for proportionate height and weight on a regular basis. This requirement makes the initial employment requirement more meaningful, because it seems apparent that if the requirement is important for young officers, it is doubly important for those with several years of service whose age may make them more vulnerable to problems related to disproportionate height and weight (McCormack, 1994).

Vision Requirements. Vision requirements vary greatly among departments and are the subject of controversy. When such requirements are for uncorrected vision, they are especially controversial. Most departments have established corrected vision requirements that may be justified on the basis of driving ability, ability to identify license plates or persons, or weapons qualification (Holden & Gammeltoft, 1991). While it is certainly possible that an officer may have her glasses broken or lose a contact lens in an altercation, we know of no strong evidence to indicate that these happenings occur frequently enough to be problematic or to justify stringent, uncorrected vision requirements.

Medical Examinations. The medical examination is a critical part of the testing process from the point of view of the department. This is so because an officer who becomes disabled as a result of injury or illness is often eligible for life-long disability payments. To detect conditions that may lead to such illnesses or injuries, virtually all police agencies require a medical examination, which is intended to detect problems of the heart, back, legs, and feet, among others. These conditions may be aggravated by police work, and the department would prefer to eliminate from consideration applicants with such problems. Due consideration must be given to the requirements of the Americans with Disabilities Act, of course.

Mental Tests

Mental tests may be divided into two categories: those designed to measure intelligence, knowledge, or aptitude and those designed to evaluate psychological fitness.

Tests of Intelligence, Knowledge, or Aptitude. Written tests are used as an early screening device by the vast majority of police agencies (Ash, Slora, & Britton, 1990). These paper-and-pencil tests come in a variety of forms and are intended to measure a variety of things. To be of value, the tests must deal with job-related issues and must have predictive value; that is, they should be able to predict whether an applicant has the ability to perform police work well. Such prediction is attempted despite the fact that there is no accepted definition of a competent police officer, or of what qualities are required for or are likely to increase competence (Burbeck & Furnham, 1985, pp. 64–65).

In addition, these written tests have historically eliminated most minority group members. Millions of dollars have been spent in attempts to develop "culture fair" tests to avoid this bias, but with, at best, only moderate success (Winters, 1992). And, perhaps for lack of a better screening device, the vast majority of departments continue to use written tests in spite of their obvious inadequacies. In most departments where such tests are used, they are scored on a point system, and the score obtained becomes a part of the overall point total used to determine the eligibility list. Differences of one or two points might, therefore, make the difference between hiring one applicant and another, even though differences of five to ten points probably indicate little difference between candidates. Although a score of 70 is often established as the cutoff point for passing, this score may be raised or lowered, depending on the candidate pool, indicating that there is nothing magical about the score itself. The very fact that there are many different tests and forms of tests available implies that there is no consensus about a best test or best form.

While there are some difficulties involved in conducting the research necessary to evaluate written entry-level tests, such research is essential if we are to develop a test with predictive power. Such research would require that a department hire applicants regardless of their scores on the test (including those who failed), keep the test results secret from those who evaluate the officers' performance over a period of time (preferably at least eighteen months to two years), and then compare performance evaluations over the time period with initial test scores. If those who scored high on the written test were also the best performers on the job, the validity of the test would be demonstrated, all other factors being equal (which they seldom are). Although the research required is relatively simple, questions of liability exist for a department choosing to participate in such research. What happens, for instance, if an applicant who failed the test is hired and performs so badly that someone is injured or killed as a result? In addition, the time period involved is quite long, and many agencies and test constructors are unwilling to wait the required time to obtain meaningful results.

Some research has been done that suggests that situational tests, which place the potential officer in situations designed to test whether he possesses the necessary skills to perform police work, recognizes when such skills are required, and demonstrates the motivation or willingness to apply these skills, appear to be indicative of job performance over the first two years of employment (Pugh, 1985; Pynes & Bernardin, 1992; Decicco, 2000). It may be that tests of this type, actually a form of the assessment center (to be discussed) as it relates to promotions, prove to be more valuable than paper-and-pencil tests. About 58 percent of police agencies use some type of situational testing, including mock crime scenes, shoot/don't shoot exercises, and role-playing sessions (Decicco, 2000).

Still, most police agencies continue to use written entry-level tests as screening devices in spite of their obvious shortcomings. Despite the intensive effort to improve written tests, there is little convincing evidence that test scores can predict what officer performance will be over any extensive period of time.

Psychological Tests. Psychological tests present even more difficulties than written tests of intelligence, aptitude, or knowledge. Psychological tests have been used increasingly over the past thirty years, and the President's Commission in 1967 recommended they be used by all police departments to determine emotional stability (Meier, Farmer, & Maxwell, 1987). In spite of the many weaknesses discussed here, psychological tests continue to be employed both because of the liability that may result from hiring police officers without the use of such tests and because many police administrators believe that they at least screen out those applicants who are clearly suffering from emotional disorders: "Over one hundred books and articles have been published on the subject of psychological assessment in police selection in the past twenty years. Some of this activity has no doubt been stimulated by court decisions in which police departments have been held liable for dangerous behavior of employees, both on and off duty, when no adequate screening for psychological stability was performed" (Pendergrass, 1987, p. 8).

Meier, Farmer, and Maxwell (1987, p. 215) note in their review of psychological screening as it relates to police officers that there may be other reasons for the continuation of the practice. They list the defense against negligent hiring and retention as one motivating factor, and note that equally relevant is the social responsibility of protecting the public and the responsibility to assist officers who face serious problems.

The task of predicting psychological stability—for short time periods, let alone the career of a police officer—is a formidable one. This is especially true because the psychological characteristics of the ideal police officer have not been, and perhaps cannot be, identified. The very diversity in American policing discussed in the first two chapters of this book, in combination with the complexity of the police role, make obtaining a consensus about the characteristics of the ideal officer highly unlikely. Pugh (1985, p. 176), for example, suggests that policing makes varying demands on police officers and that the personality qualities required early in an officer's career may differ from those required later.

Benner (1989, p. 83) discusses the extent to which psychological tests can select out police applicants who are either unstable or unsuitable (or both) and concludes, "It matters little that the field of psychology is only marginally capable of predicting 'bad' officer candidates. Psychologists and psychiatrists are expected, not only, to screen out the 'bad' but be able to screen in the 'good.' Unfortunately, consensus definitions of 'good' or 'suitable' have not been developed either among the professionals or members of the lay public."

Tests commonly used to help determine suitability and stability of prospective police officers include the Minnesota Multiphasic Personality Inventory (MMPI), the California Personality Inventory (CPI), the Fundamental Interpersonal Relations Orientation-B (FIRO-B), and the Inwald Personality Inventory (IPI), among others (Decicco, 2000). These tests are sometimes used in combination with others to form test batteries, which are thought to be more comprehensive than individual tests (Pendergrass, 1987; Ash, Slora, & Britton, 1990). In addition, personal interviews with psychologists or psychiatrists frequently supplement the paper-and-pencil tests.

According to Pendergrass (1987, pp. 25–29) and Hiatt and Hargrave (1988, p. 125), there are several studies indicating that the use of psychological tests for screening entry-level police officers has led to the recognition of certain characteristics, including level of cognitive functioning, personal history, and possibly, work interests, which may help predict success.

Burbeck and Furnham (1985, p. 68) concluded that psychological testing may select out people suffering from some mental abnormality. The tests, however, are not infallible because subjects can successfully fake results, and the tests are "expensive to administer for a very small return of aberrant scores."

Pendergrass (1987, p. 29) indicates that psychological tests can make a contribution to the selection process but should not "replace other methods nor are the results of psychological assessment without error in prediction of success of candidates . . . selection based entirely upon psychological testing is likely to eliminate a number of good candidates and retain some poor candidates in error."

While the literature on psychological testing of police recruits is confusing, at best, it appears certain that such testing, unless used to supplement the other procedures discussed here, is of limited value. Meier, Farmer, and Maxwell (1987, p. 213) conclude that there is no convincing evidence for the use of psychological instruments to predict long-term successful employment in policing, although they believe research in this area should continue, because there is some consensus that the techniques can identify applicants who may represent a real risk to the public.

Dwyer, Prien, and Bernard (1990) and Wright, Doerner, and Speir (1990) conclude that psychological tests are of unknown validity and that the available research does not support their use. Still, about two-thirds of all police departments continue to use psychological tests in the selection process (Ash, Slora, & Britton, 1990), perhaps more because they believe in the value of the tests as a defense against litigation than because they believe in their value as a tool in predicting success as a police officer. Still, there is a question as to whether psychological testing done only at the time of application can ever be an accurate predictor of police officer behavior, because psychological problems may result from serving as a police officer even though they may not have existed at the time of hiring (Alpert & Dunham, 1997, p. 55).

Tests of Morality

Tests of morality include background investigations, drug tests, and polygraph examinations. We refer to these requirements as tests of morality because they are used to evaluate the moral character of police applicants. Certainly drug testing also constitutes a physical test, but it is typically the use of drugs rather than the impact of the drugs on the physical well-being of the applicant that is of primary concern.

Background Investigations.   The importance of background investigations is clearly demonstrated in an example cited by Ferguson (1987, p. 6). In a community in the Southwest, a new police chief was appointed based on the favorable impression he made during his visit and on the references listed on his application. He then hired his own officers. The city failed to check the references listed by the chief or those of the new officers. Eventually, reporters did check these references and found that the chief's were phony and that one of the officers he had hired and promoted to the rank of sergeant was a wanted felon in another state. Even the most precursory background investigation could have saved the city the embarrassment that ensued.

Background investigations are used by almost all police agencies, but the extent and intensiveness of these investigations vary considerably. In some cases, listed references are simply checked by phone, while in other cases, a good deal of time and money are expended to verify the character of the applicant. In cases of the latter type, the investigation normally includes the following:

1. A check of education and training accomplishments listed on the application
2. A check of former employers
3. A neighborhood investigation
4. An investigation of the circumstances surrounding separation from the military in appropriate cases
5. An investigation of financial history
6. A check on the place of residence

7. A check with state and national crime information centers to determine prior criminal history (Swanson, Territo, & Taylor, 1988; Roberg & Kuykendall, 1990; Decicco, 2000)

In short, a major purpose of the background investigation is to determine the honesty of the applicant as reflected by the information she provided on the application form and in subsequent communications with those in charge of recruiting and selecting. Background investigations may exclude, or highlight for further inquiry, applicants with prior felony convictions or who are currently wanted; those with a history of serious employment, family, or financial problems; those who have been dishonorably discharged from the military; and those who have failed to tell the truth during the application process. In addition, prior and current use of alcohol and/or other drugs is typically explored in the context of making reference contacts. The rationale for excluding or further investigating applicants with problems in these areas is relatively clear. It makes little sense to hire as a police officer an individual who has serious drug-related problems; in virtually all jurisdictions, those with prior felony convictions are excluded from policing by statute. Those with histories of domestic violence or bankruptcy also present problems, because they may be corruptible or prone to the use of force in their positions as police officers. In short, the background investigation represents an attempt to select into policing only those with what is defined as good moral character.

Drug Tests. The possession, manufacture, distribution, and sale of illegal drugs are all serious problems in our society, and applicants for police work are not immune to these problems. One study of police applicants found that one of every three police candidates was rejected because of drug use (Van, 1986). A survey of thirty-three major police departments found that twenty-four had drug-testing programs, that virtually all had written policies and procedures relating to drug testing, and that twenty-four indicated that treatment as opposed to dismissal would be appropriate for some officers using drugs (McEwen, Manili, & Connors, 1986). About a quarter of all municipal police departments require drug testing of all applicants, and the percentage requiring such testing increases with the size of the department (U.S. Department of Justice, 1992). Increasingly, police departments are finding large numbers of applicants reporting drug use that would make them unacceptable for police employment (Gaines, Kappeler, & Vaughn, 1994, p. 83). However, as Baxley (2000, p. 371) indicates, due to increasing difficulties in recruiting, there is a "growing tendency to tolerate some history of drug use or criminal activity by recruit candidates. . . . Many agencies now take into consideration the type and amount of drugs used, the length of time since the last use, and the nature of the offense. Those who have merely 'experimented during high school or college' are often allowed to join the force."

The International Association of Chiefs of Police has developed a model drug-testing policy that calls for testing of all recruits prior to employment, testing of current employees under certain circumstances, and periodic testing of officers assigned to narcotics units (McEwen, Manili, & Connors, 1986). Although the issue of drug testing, usually accomplished through urinalysis, has led to a great deal of litigation, it appears that when such testing is done according to a schedule (as opposed to random testing) and when it is done in reasonable fashion and on reasonable grounds, the courts will allow the testing as it relates to policing. This appears to be so because of police departments' interests in protecting the safety of the public and of other employees. The possibility of a drug-impaired police officer injuring a colleague or another person as the result of a vehicle accident, firearm discharge, or use of excessive force clearly exists. Thus, drug testing is likely to become even more prevalent among police agencies than it is now, as the legal requirements for such testing are more clearly elaborated by court decisions and revision of statutes.

Polygraph Examinations.   Polygraph examinations are employed by about half of the municipal police agencies in the United States (Ash, Slora, & Britton, 1990; Decicco, 2000), although changes in federal legislation have already greatly restricted their use in the private sector and may eventually have the same impact of the public sector. The rationale behind the use of the polygraph for recruitment and selection appears to be twofold. First, the results of the examination are used as one indicator of the honesty of the job applicant. Second, the results are used to eliminate applicants whose responses are not acceptable to the police agency in question, regardless of the honesty of the applicant. Either or both of these purposes may be justified, but there is, and always has been, considerable controversy over the accuracy of polygraph tests, raising the issue of rejecting some qualified applicants while accepting others who are deceitful (Decicco, 2000). While supporters of the polygraph test claim accuracy in the 85 to 90 percent category, opponents claim results are little more reliable than guessing who is being deceitful and argue that a margin of error of 10 to 15 percent is unacceptably large.

The problem with polygraph tests does not lie with the machine, which simply measures heart rate, rate of breathing, and galvanic skin response (changes in electrical resistance in the skin) over time. The interpretation of the results and the way in which the test is administered depend on the polygrapher. Training, skills, and competence of polygraphers vary widely, and the conditions (anxiety and nervousness on behalf of applicants) under which employment and promotional polygraph interviews are conducted are less than ideal for ensuring accurate results. According to Horvath (1989, p. 509), "(another) use of polygraph testing is in preemployment screening of applicants for police work. The use of the polygraph for this purpose is very controversial and is, in fact, illegal in some jurisdictions." The American Polygraph Association and the International Association of Chiefs of Police have both published model policies dealing with polygraph use in law enforcement hiring (Eller, 1999). If the tests have any value in recruitment and selection, it would appear to be as one small part of the overall process.

Tests of Ability to Communicate

As indicated earlier, many of the recruitment and selection procedures used with respect to the police overlap. This interdependence of procedures is perhaps best illustrated by tests of ability to communicate. Properly conceived, these tests include the application form and the written tests taken by applicants and the oral interview typically required of potential police officers. Because we have already discussed the application and written tests, we concentrate here on the oral interview, or oral "board" as it is often called. Let us simply note that it is both possible and desirable to evaluate the written communications skills of applicants by requiring them to write a job history or autobiographical statement as a part of the application form, because a large measure of police work involves writing reports that require accuracy and comprehensiveness. While a misspelled word or two is probably no cause for concern, serious defects in the ability to communicate in writing indicate, at the very minimum, the need for some remedial work in this area.

The Oral Board.   Oral interviews of police applicants are used by most agencies. These interviews, or "boards," are typically conducted by members of the fire and police or civil service commission, or by the personnel department in larger police agencies, often in conjunction with representatives of the police agency. In some cases, the latter actually participate in the interview, while in others, they simply observe. The number of interviewers varies, but three to five is typical.

The expressed purpose of the oral board is to select a suitable applicant to fill the existing police vacancy. There is, however, often a second goal in these interviews: that of selecting a certain kind of person to fill the vacancy. In addition to demonstrating the skills necessary to fill the formal organizational position, the applicant's loyalty to the department, trustworthiness with respect to other police officers, and, although legally and formally forbidden, race, gender, and general presentation of self may be considered (Gray, 1975; Cox & Fitzgerald, 1996). While it is undoubtedly true that efforts to reduce the amount of subjectivity in oral interviews have been made in the form of standardized questions and independent evaluation by the raters, it is equally true that the way we look (dress, skin color, gender, etc.) and act (eye contact, handshake, degree of self-confidence expressed) affects our daily interactions and, despite attempts to minimize the impact of these variables on the scoring of the interview, also affect the interviewers (Falkenberg, Gaines, & Cox, 1990). Having served on oral boards periodically over the past twenty years, it is the authors' definite impression from conversations with other board members that factors that are expressly forbidden from consideration, in terms of equal employment opportunity guidelines, for example, do affect the judgment of interviewers in subtle, if not obvious, ways.

The interview format varies a good deal. In most cases, general questions about the applicant's background, experiences, education, prior training, and interest in police work in general and in the specific department in question are asked. These may be followed by a series of questions to test the applicant's knowledge of some legal, moral, and ethical issues relating to police work. For example, the applicant may be asked how she would respond to the apparent corruption of another officer or what response would be appropriate if a traffic violator turned out to be the mayor, or how much force is justified in a certain type of incident.

These questions may be asked slowly, with follow-up questions, or they may be asked and followed up in such a fashion that they create stress for the interviewee (see, e.g., Holloway, 2000). The responses to the questions are evaluated by each of the raters independently and, should major differences in evaluation occur, may be discussed among the raters in an attempt to reach some consensus about the applicant's worthiness. The final scores for the oral board are then added to the scores from the other portions of the testing procedure to establish an eligibility list from which the chief of police or personnel department may select candidates to fill existing and future vacancies.

There is a definite irony here that needs to be pointed out. Although the selection process today is conducted under the guise of objectivity, including having the written tests sent elsewhere for scoring, scoring by identification numbers as opposed to names, rating interviewees independently, and calculating scores to the nearest point (or, in some cases, tenth of a point), when the process is completed, the final rank order based on the complex scoring system may be ignored by the chief or personnel department. That is, the applicant who scored third highest overall may be selected to fill the vacancy instead of the applicant who scored highest. Although there is perhaps nothing wrong with giving the chief some input at this stage of the selection process, it tends to call into question the value of all the apparent objectivity surrounding the process, particularly during the promotion process, to which we shall soon turn our attention.

In the past, many police recruits have come from families with a history of involvement in policing or from military backgrounds (Baxley, 2000). This is perhaps less true today than at any time in the recent past. As we enter the new millennium, recruits are most likely to be interested in a good salary and a good benefits package. They also may assess the state of departmental technology, opportunities for advancement, and equipment available before making a career choice. And such choices are increasingly made with the assistance of the Internet. Thus, police agencies must be attuned to the goals of potential recruits in order to establish recruitment practices that meet the needs of recruits.

The recruitment and selection process does not end with the establishment of the eligibility list. Rather, it continues as those selected for hiring go to the training academy, as they return to the department to serve their probationary period, and as they proceed through their careers in policing.

SUPERVISORY RECRUITMENT AND SELECTION

As indicated earlier, the recruitment and selection process does not end with initial employment, but continues as some individuals are promoted to supervisory positions and special assignments. If it is important to select prospective police officers carefully, it is equally important to promote carefully to ensure that those who supervise new recruits are well prepared to do so. As Baxley (2000, p. 371) indicates, "Too often we promote persons to supervisory positions on the basis of their longevity with the department. A long-term employee does not always make a good supervisor. . . . Well-trained supervisors who make good decisions earn the respect of both their troops and their community. They also create an environment where the troops enjoy working—and happy troops are a department's best recruiting tool."

The same equal employment and affirmative action rules discussed previously apply when selecting and recruiting police supervisors, including chiefs. The vast majority of police supervisors are promoted from within the ranks of the department (with the exception of police chiefs, about whom we shall have more to say in the following section), because lateral entry is the exception rather than the rule in American policing.

As Bouza (1990, pp. 40–41) notes, there are two ways of shaping supervisory talent: formal education and on-the-job training. For the latter to produce a highly skilled supervisor, a wide variety of experiences should be included (a variety of different assignments). Because the police culture largely downplays the importance of theories of management and liberal arts education, on-the-job training is critical. However, it often fails to provide the breadth of training necessary, because the skills of the up-and-coming officer may be so valuable to the chief that he comes to rely almost totally on that officer for certain kinds of information or input. Thus, the about-to-be promoted may remain in the same positions for most of their prepromotional careers. This narrow focus makes it difficult for those promoted to understand the broader police picture and leads to scorn on behalf of line officers. Further, the testing procedure itself is almost always suspect from the perspective of both those applying for advancement and those who will be effected by having new supervisors. Basically, observers tend to believe that it is "who you know" rather than "what you know" that leads to promotion.

Advertisements typically consist of position vacancy announcements posted within the police agency. Outside advertisement, although it may sometimes occur, is greatly limited (e.g., to other agencies that employ city workers).

Because most police departments retain paramilitary structures, promotional opportunities exist at the level of the field supervisor (typically at the rank of sergeant), shift or watch commander (typically at the rank of lieutenant or commander), division commander (typically with the rank of captain or above), and for a host of specializations in larger departments (juvenile, burglary, fraud, vice, and so on). As is the case at the entry level, the vacancy announcements should clearly state the qualifications for the positions and indicate how interested parties may go about applying. Individuals applying for these positions are required to pass status tests similar to those discussed for entry-level employees, with the additional stipulation that they have served a specified number of years in policing or at the level immediately below the one for which they are applying. In other words, to become a lieutenant, an officer would have to meet the basic status requirements of the department and, in addition, might be required to have served three years at the rank of sergeant.

Typically, physical tests are not employed in the selection of supervisors. The assumption may be that they have already passed such tests as the department requires or that the position to which they aspire does not require the same degree of physical agility required of line officers. Neither of these assumptions is entirely justified, however, and some measures of physical fitness appear to be appropriate. At a minimum, a thorough medical examination should be required, and proportionate height and weight requirements would appear to be reasonable.

Paper-and-pencil tests are often part of the supervisory selection process, though they have not been demonstrated to be any more successful in predicting success as a supervisor than as an entry-level officer (Bennett & Hess, 2001, p. 344). Because this is the case, another technique, known as the assessment center, has been used increasingly in recent years.

Assessment Centers

The assessment center had its origins in the 1920s and was used by the military in World War II. The concept was furthered in the 1950s in private industry (Cosner & Baumgart, 2000). As O'Leary (1989, p. 28) indicates, prior to the 1970s, many police departments promoted people because they had "influential contacts, or did well in objective paper-and-pencil tests, or impressed a civil-service board made up of a variety of people from law-enforcement in neighboring departments, state highway patrol, private-sector managers, and perhaps representatives of the local department of human resources." Such promotions often resulted in ineffective supervisors, because the interviewers had an inaccurate picture of the duties and responsibilities accompanying the position. The interview, as a predictive tool, proved to be only marginally effective. Paper-and-pencil tests also turned out to be poor indicators of supervisory performance.

Pynes and Bernardin (1992) found that assessment centers for entry-level police officers predicted training academy and on-the-job performance, the latter better than paper-and-pencil tests. They also found that assessment centers had less disparate impact on blacks and Hispanics than did cognitive paper-and-pencil tests. The assessment center may prove to have these same benefits at the supervisory level.

To use the assessment center, there must first be a comprehensive, accurate job description of the position advertised. Second, a group of trained observers, usually three to five, must observe the candidates for the position as they go through a number of job-related activities. Such activities might include an oral presentation; dealing with incoming memos, mail, and phone calls; handling a grievance; fielding questions at a press conference; and so on. The assessors rate the applicants individually on each of the tasks assigned over a one- or two-day period.

In some cases, the applicants' performances are videotaped and may be reviewed by the assessors at their convenience. Then the candidates are interviewed by the assessors, using a standardized format that provides latitude for assessors to raise questions concerning issues brought to light by the various exercises in which the candidates have engaged.

Finally, the assessors, usually under the direction of a team leader, meet to discuss their scores and impressions of the applicants. Each assessor must be prepared to defend his scores, and discrepant scores often become topics of heated debate. In the ideal case, differences can be resolved through discussion, and the applicants are then listed in order of the assessors' preferences. Final selection is accomplished by the personnel department, police chief, city manager, mayor or council, or some combination of these.

While the costs of the assessment center are high, success in predicting good performance has been equally high, and, when measured against the costs of making a bad appointment, the costs are less imposing than they might seem. According to Lynch (1995, p. 251), "History has shown that the assessment center approach may help to pinpoint quality candidates and, more importantly, lend a sense of fairness to the promotional process. . . . Although assessment centers may not be the final answer, they are certainly helpful in identifying the assets and liabilities that a candidate may bring to a new position."

Polygraph, drug, and psychological tests, as well as an updated background investigation also may be required for promotion. Tests of ability to communicate are incorporated into the assessment center when it is employed, or may be evaluated by an oral board in a fashion similar to that discussed for entry-level personnel.

Evaluations based on past performance also are frequently used when considering applicants for promotion. The usefulness of these measures remains to be established, because they are typically based on behaviors relevant to the current position of the applicant that may or may not be related to the position for which she is applying. That is, excellent performance as a street officer may be totally unrelated to performance as a supervisor. Nonetheless, in many departments, these evaluations account for 20 to 30 percent of the total score considered for promotion.

RECRUITING AND SELECTING POLICE CHIEFS

The skills required of a police chief are, in many instances, significantly different from those required of new recruits or lower ranking supervisors. The chief not only maintains general control over the department, but also is its representative in dealing with other municipal agencies, other police agencies, and elected officials. In some very small departments, the police chief must perform patrol and investigative functions and has few supervisory responsibilities. In police agencies with more than four or five employees, however, administrative and supervisory responsibilities become more important than street work.

Advertising for police chiefs is generally done through professional police publications as well as through the use of area newspapers and bulletins (see Highlight 4.3 for an excellent example). Recruitment for the position of chief may involve going outside the department, staying within the department, or a combination of the two (Kroecker, 2000). Thus, lateral entry, while seldom a possibility at other police ranks, is possible at the level of chief. Chiefs recruited from outside appear to be better educated, to be more likely to have held a variety of administrative positions, and to have shorter careers than those recruited from inside (Enter, 1986).

The status requirements discussed with respect to other supervisory personnel typically apply, with the number of years service required and the level of police experience required varying greatly across communities. Hiring is done primarily by the mayor or city manager in conjunction with the city council or a committee (police and/or personnel) of the council (Bennett & Hess, 2001, p. 44). As is the case with other supervisory personnel, written tests related to administrative and supervisory tasks are often employed, and, in addition, attempts may be made to assess the extent to which the candidates view themselves as part of a management team. Educational and training requirements also vary considerably, ranging from high school graduation and basic police training to possession of a master's degree and attendance at one of the more prestigious police management schools (such as the FBI Academy or the Southern Police Institute).

■ ■ ■ ■ ■

HIGHLIGHT 4.3   **Advertisement for a Chief of Police**

Position: Chief of Police

Deadline: July 02, 2001

Agency: Palatine Police Department

Location: Palatine, IL USA

Salary: low $90s

Qualifications: The ideal candidate is a seasoned, decisive, results-oriented leader, experienced in all aspects of professional policing, with a minimum of 10 years at the command level. In addition, candidates should have a proven commitment to community policing, a track record of improving service delivery, and demonstrated ability to build and maintain strong relationships with the community, elected officials, employees, village leadership and other law enforcement agencies. A bachelor's degree is required; a master's degree is preferred. The candidate must also have completed executive-level training such as the FBI Academy, Southern Police Institute A.O.C., or Senior Management Institute for Police. An unblemished record of ethical and professional conduct that can withstand intense public scrutiny is essential.

Responsibilities: Palatine is located in the northwest suburbs of Chicago in Cook County (approximately 28 miles from the Chicago Loop) and has a population of 65,400. The police department operates with 111 sworn officers and 33 full-time civilian employees and an annual budget of 10.3 million. The Palatine Police Department is a professional, progressive, and innovative law enforcement agency seeking a leader who will take the vision of community policing to the next level, while maintaining the strong tradition of providing unusually high levels of service to the citizens of Palatine.

The department received CALEA accreditation in 1986 and has been re-accredited three times since. In 1996, Good Housekeeping rated the Palatine Police Department one of the eight best suburban police departments in the United States. With a strong council/manager form of government, the village enjoys a very stable administration. The police chief is appointed by and reports to the village manager.

Special Conditions: The beginning salary for this position is in the low 90s, with a comprehensive fringe benefit package.

Website: http://www.palatine.il.us

How To Apply: To apply, send a one-page cover letter, four professional references, and a resume summarizing your qualifications by Monday, July 2, 2001, to Human Resources Consultant, 200 East Wood Street, Palatine, IL 60067.

Used with permission.

While many chiefs are hired based on interviews with officials of city government, performance on written tests, and background investigations, more and more are being processed through assessment centers designed to test their administrative skills.

The vast majority of police chiefs come from the police ranks, and hiring those without prior police experience, though it does occasionally occur, is the exception. Unlike other police personnel, chiefs are seldom required to attend training schools after being hired, although the political and public relations skills required to be successful indicate the need for further training in many, if not most, cases.

Goldstein (1977, p. 230) and others indicate that the record of providing qualified police leadership at the chief's level in the United States is unenviable:

> The costs of having made inadequate provision for police leadership are plainly apparent when one views the overall status of policing in the United States. Many police agencies tend to drift from day to day. They respond excessively to outside pressures; they resort to temporary expedients; they take comfort in technical achievements over substantive accomplishments; their internal procedures become stagnant, cumbersome and inefficient; and they seem incapable of responding innovatively to new demands and new requirements.

Garner (1993, p. 1) notes some of the same deficiencies: "Many police administrators become so preoccupied with current problems that they fail to plan for the future. Some do not believe that strategic planning is worth the effort. Others lack the imagination and creativity required to project in the abstract." Such imagination and creativity are clearly required for the transition from traditional policing to community policing, for empowerment of police officers and the public, and for meeting budgetary and other challenges.

Bouza (1990, p. 41) perhaps best sums up the difficulties in selecting a police chief: "A chief's selection by the mayor probably accommodates some narrow and probably temporary political objective, which undoubtedly did not include considerations of competence. It is no small wonder that two former chiefs dubbed these chief executives 'fifty-year-old cops' and 'pet rocks.'"

While some improvement has occurred in this area, promotion to rank of chief from within undoubtedly contributes to continuing resistance to change in a good many police agencies. Some chiefs are basically contract chiefs, serving for a specified period of time, with periodic reviews. Others are essentially given tenure when hired, though most all serve at the pleasure of the head of city government and the council, and job security is often a major concern (Frankel, 1992). When the chief reports directly to the mayor or council, political considerations are often extremely important. The city manager form of government provides some insulation from direct political ties and, from the perspective of promoting a professional, somewhat apolitical department, the latter arrangement is probably superior.

DISCUSSION QUESTIONS

1. Why are the costs of recruitment of police personnel so high? How can such costs reasonably be reduced?

2. Can you locate any Web sites dealing with police recruitment? What are they, and what kinds of information do they contain? Do any allow you to apply online?

3. Why is recruitment of qualified personnel so important to police agencies?

4. Discuss some of the changes in the selection of police officers that have occurred as a result of equal employment opportunity laws and affirmative action programs. What are some of the positive and negative consequences of EEOC and affirmative action programs?

5. List and discuss the five basic types of police officer selection requirements. How do such requirements apply to promotions?

6. What is an assessment center, why are such centers being used increasingly, and what, if any, disadvantages do they have?

7. What are the backgrounds of most police chiefs, and what implications do these backgrounds have for policing as a profession?

8. How do the provisions of the Americans with Disabilities Act affect the police? How do you feel about ADA requirements?

9. What types of information are available from the Web site www.LearnaTest.com?

REFERENCES

Alpert, G. P., & Dunham, R. G. (1997). *Policing urban America*, 3rd ed. Prospect Heights, IL: Waveland.

Ash, P., Slora, K. B., & Britton, C. F. (1990). Police agency officer selection practices. *Journal of Police Science and Administration, 17,* 258–269.

Baxley, N. (2000). Recruiting police officers in the new millenium. *Law and Order, 48,* 371.

Bell, D. (1992). *Race, racism and American law*, 3rd ed. Boston: Little, Brown.

Benner, A. W. (1989). Psychological screening of police applicants. In Dunham, R. G., & Alpert, G. P. (eds.), *Critical issues in policing: Contemporary readings* (pp. 72–86). Prospect Heights, IL: Waveland.

Bennett, W. W., & Hess, K. M. (2001). *Management and supervision in law enforcement.* Belmont, CA: Wadsworth.

Berg, B. L. (1992). *Law enforcement: An introduction to police in society.* Boston: Allyn & Bacon.

Booth, W. S., & Hornick, C. W. (1984, January). Physical ability testing for police officers. *Police Chief, 1,* 39–41.

Bouza, A. V. (1990). *The police mystique: An insider's look at cops, crime, and the criminal justice system.* New York: Plenum.

Brandon, H., & Lippman, B. (2000). Using the Web to improve recruitment. *Police Chief, 67,* 37–41.

Broderick, J. J. (1987). *Police in a time of change*, 2nd ed. Prospect Heights, IL: Waveland.

Brooks, M. E. (2001). Title VII of the Civil Rights Act of 1964 and 1991 may prohibit employers from creating discriminatory physical fitness standards. *FBI Law Enforcement Bulletin, 70,* 26–31.

Burbeck, E., & Furnham, A. (1985). Police officer selection: A critical review of the literature. *Journal of Police Science and Administration, 13,* 58–69.

Colbridge, T. D. (2001). The Americans with Disabilities Act: A practical guide for police departments. *FBI Law Enforcement Bulletin, 70,* 23–32.

———. (2000). The Americans with Disabilities Act. *FBI Law Enforcement Bulletin, 69,* 26–31.

Cosner, T. L., & Baumgart, W. C. (2000). An effective assessment center program: Essential components. *FBI Law Enforcement Bulletin, 69,* 1–5.

Cox, S. M., & Fitzgerald, J. D. (1996). *Police in community relations: Critical issues*, 3rd ed. Dubuque, IA: Brown & Benchmark.

Crime Control Digest. (2001, February 2). Police chiefs try many recruiting strategies to boost applicant pool, 1–2.

Decicco, D. A. (2000). Police officer candidate assessment and selection. *FBI Law Enforcement Bulletin*, *69*, 1–6.

Dwyer, W. O., Prien, E. R., & Bernard, J. L. (1990). Psychological screening of law enforcement officers: A case for job relatedness. *Journal of Police Science and Administration, 17*, 176–182.

Eller, M. A. (1999). Standardization of pre-employment police applicant screening test results. *Polygraph, 28*, 304–309.

Enter, J. E. (1986). The rise to the top: An analysis of police chief career patterns. *Journal of Police Science and Administration, 14*, 334–346.

Falkenberg, S., Gaines, L. K., & Cox, T. C. (1990). The oral interview board: What does it measure? *Journal of Police Science and Administration, 17*, 32–39.

Ferguson, R. (1987). Pre-screening of police applicants. *Police Chief, 2*, 6.

Ferkenhoff, E. (2001, January 4). City works to win more recruits for police force. *Chicago Tribune*, p. 1A.

Flynn, K. (2000, September 23). City short of police recruits as job loses luster. *New York Times*, p. 1A.

Frankel, B. (1992, November 19). Police chiefs worry about job security. *USA Today*, p. 10A.

Gaines, L. K., Kappeler, V. E., & Vaughn, J. B. (1994). *Policing in America*. Cincinnati, OH: Anderson.

Garner, R. (1993). Leadership in the nineties. *FBI Law Enforcement Bulletin, 62*, 1–4.

Gest. T. (1987, March). A one-white, one-black quota for promotions. *U.S. News and World Report*, p. 8.

Goldstein, H. (1977). *Policing a free society*. Cambridge, MA: Ballinger.

Gray, T. C. (1975). Selecting for a police subculture. In Skolnick, J., & Gray, T. C. (eds.), *Police in America* (pp. 46–54). Boston: Little, Brown.

Hiatt, D., & Hargrave, G. E. (1988). Predicting job performance problems with psychological screening. *Journal of Police Science and Administration, 16*, 122–125.

Holden, R. N., & Gammeltoft, L. L. (1991). *Toonen v. Brown County:* The legality of police vision standards. *American Journal of Police, 10*, 59–66.

Holloway, J. (2000). Oh, those oral board blues. *Women Police, 34*, 3, 14.

Horvath, F. (1989). Polygraph. In Bailey, W. G., (ed.), *The encyclopedia of police science* (pp. 507–511). New York: Garland.

Kroecker, T. (2000). Developing future leaders: Making the link to the promotional process. *Police Chief, 67*, 64–69.

Lynch, R. G. (1995). *The police manager,* 4th ed. Cincinnati, OH: Anderson.

McCormack, W. U. (1994). Grooming and weight standards for law enforcement: The legal issues. *FBI Law Enforcement Bulletin, 63*, 27–31.

McEwen, J. T., Manili, B., & Connors, J. (1986, October). Employee drug testing policies in police departments. In *Research in brief*, National Institute of Justice. Washington, DC: U.S. Government Printing Office.

Meier, R. D., Farmer, R. E., & Maxwell, D. (1987). Psychological screening of police candidates: Current perspectives. *Journal of Police Science and Administration, 15*, 210–215.

Nowicki, E. (1999). 12 traits of highly effective police officers. *Law & Order, 47*, 45–46.

O'Leary, L. R. (1989). Assessment centers. In Bailey, W. G. (ed.), *The encyclopedia of police science* (pp. 28–30). New York: Garland.

Pendergrass, V. E. (1987). Psychological assessment of police for entry-level selection. *Police Chief, 11*, 8–14.

Pugh, G. (1985). Situation tests and police selection. *Journal of Police Science and Administration, 13*, 30–35.

Pynes, J., & Bernardin, H. J. (1992). Entry-level police selection: The assessment center as an alternative. *Journal of Criminal Justice, 20*, 41–56.

Roberg, R. R., & Kuykendall, J. (1990). *Police organization and management*. Pacific Grove, CA: Brooks/Cole.

Rubin, P. N. (1993, September). The Americans with Disabilities Act and criminal justice: An overview. In *Research in Action*, National Institute of Justice. Washington, DC: U.S. Government Printing Office.

Schneid, T. D., & Gaines, L. K. (1991). The Americans with Disabilities Act: Implications for police administrators. *American Journal of Police, 10,* 47–58.

Stone, A., & DeLuca, S. (1985). *Police administration.* New York: Wiley.

Sullivan, P. S. (1989). Minority officers: Current issues. In Dunham, R. G., & Alpert, G. P. (eds.), *Critical issues in policing: Contemporary readings* (pp. 331–345). Prospect Heights, IL: Waveland.

Swanson, C. R., Territo, L., & Taylor, R. W. (1988). *Police administration,* 2nd ed. New York: Macmillan.

Swope, C. (1999, November). The short blue line. *Governing,* 32–33.

U.S. Department of Justice. (1992, May). Drug enforcement by police and sheriff's departments, 1990. In *Bureau of Justice Statistics Bulletin.* Washington, DC: U.S. Government Printing Office.

Van, J. (1986, February 17). 1 in 3 police candidates found to use drugs. *Chicago Tribune,* pp. 1, 5.

Winters, C. A. (1992). Socio-economic status, test bias, and the selection of police. *Police Journal, 65,* 125–135.

Wright, B. S., Doerner, W. K., & Speir, J. C. (1990). Pre-employment psychological testing as a predictor of police performance during an FTO program. *American Journal of Police, 9,* 65–84.

CHAPTER FIVE

POLICE TRAINING AND EDUCATION

The extent and nature of police training and education have been controversial issues since at least 1908, when August Vollmer began formal training for police officers. Although the two issues are intimately interrelated, they are distinct, and we address them separately in this chapter.

One of the most frequently debated issues concerning the police revolves around the distinction between training and education. While there is clearly a good deal of overlap, training may be regarded as the provision of basic skills necessary to do the job, and education may be viewed as providing familiarity with the concepts and principles underlying the training. From this perspective, training is more concrete and practical, and education more abstract and theoretical. The discussion that follows is based on these distinctions, though the reader should note that there is no absolute agreement concerning the distinctions made. Baro and Burlingame (1999), for example, argue that a good deal of contemporary police training (cultural diversity, communications, interpersonal skills) is based on scholarly theory and research; thus, the lines between education and training are blurred.

POLICE TRAINING

Policing is a difficult and complex career. The police officer is called on to play psychiatrist, doctor, lawyer, judge, jury, priest, counselor, fighter, and dogcatcher. The training requirements to become a police officer have been long neglected, however. According to Nowicki,

> Police officers must be experts in interpersonal communications, possess intimate knowledge of counseling and crisis intervention strategies, and be able to defuse potentially volatile domestic disturbances. Yet the time allotted to these topics in my police academy is a paltry seven hours total. . . . Police officers . . . can and do make decisions to arrest and restrict a person's freedom, and the power of life and death is literally at their fingertips, but on the average they receive less than one-quarter of the training required to give someone a haircut. (1990a, p. 4).

Since 1989, however, both the duration and variety of topics covered in police training centers throughout the United States have increased, although there are significant differences across state boundaries.

Police administrators and the governmental bodies they represent spend millions of dollars on training personnel. There is no longer any debate that initial, basic training for police officers is mandatory, both to improve their performance and as protection against any liability that may result from failure to train (Phillips, 1988). Inadequate or inappropriate training can lead to poor decision making, too much or too little self-confidence, and inaccurate assessments of situations (Graves, 1991, p. 62). But, how much training should be done? Who should do it? What should the content of the training be? What form should it take? How can training best be used to benefit officers and the citizens they serve? How effective is the training received? Answers to these questions are not always easy to come by, but they are essential if our goal is to develop highly trained, competent police officers. Highlight 5.1 discusses the expense of police training and the costs to small departments that continually recruit and train police officers.

How Much Training Is Enough?

Simply put, police officers can never have enough training, and training is, therefore, a career-long commitment. This observation is based on the assumption that the world is constantly changing and that police officers must constantly respond to that changing world. So much is happening so rapidly that no one of us can possibly keep up with the changes in technology and theory. Only proper training and education (as we shall see later in this chapter) can keep police officers current. This is indicated by the increase in the use of computers for communications, forensics, crime analysis, and so on. The need for training pervades all levels of police agencies. Unfortunately, many police administrators fail to take advantage of training opportunities as a result of busy schedules, lack of interest, or the mistaken belief that they already know all there is to know. A frequently heard comment in training sessions is, "I wish the chief could hear

■ ■ ■ ■ ■

HIGHLIGHT 5.1
SHERIFF'S DEPARTMENTS SHOULDER BURDEN

David Bakke, Staff Writer

Confronted with rising costs and a high turnover rate within their police forces, some village officials are looking for new and cheaper ways to provide law enforcement for their towns.

Among the options being attempted in Illinois are contracting with the sheriff's department for coverage, hiring off-duty officers to patrol the town or merging police forces with a nearby town.

A recent study, "Small Town Policing in the New Millennium: Strategies, Options and Alternate Methods," examined the problem. The Illinois Law Enforcement Training and Standards Board and the Illinois Institute for Rural Affairs at Western Illinois University sponsored the study. Robin Johnson, director of the Illinois Center for Competitive Government, located at the Institute for Rural Affairs, wrote the report. The report found that most people are unaware of the evolution that is taking place. The changes are not only in how the police forces are composed, but also in the type of work that they do.

Village police operations are facing nontraditional types of crime. The National Center for Rural Law Enforcement reports that gang activity and drug crimes are on the increase in rural areas. The manufacture of methamphetamines, which involves fertilizer—widely available in rural areas—has exploded. Illinois has experienced more than 100 meth lab seizures in the past three years.

"Decision makers in small towns throughout the state will need to be creative and innovative in order to adapt to meet the changing needs of their individual communities," the report states.

"What we tried to do," Johnson says, "is put the report into useful language for local officials. We're saying, 'Here's what other areas are doing—why don't you consider this?'"

Much of the burden of protecting small towns has fallen on sheriff's departments. Several Christian County towns have no police forces, relying totally on the sheriff's departments. Sheriff Bob Kindermann asked the Christian County

Board for another deputy to handle the heavier load. His request was denied. As a result, the sheriff made a tour this summer of village board meetings to talk to them about alternatives, including "community policing."

"We are attempting to meet their needs as far as providing them with law enforcement," Kindermann says. "We have the same staff covering a wider area. It's important for citizens to know that even in the communities with law enforcement officers, when they're not on duty, oftentimes we are called out. When they aren't available, the burden falls back on the sheriff's office."

Menard County Sheriff Larry Smith has seen the number of calls to his office rise substantially, despite a decline in the crime rate. In many small towns, a call to the local police is answered by a recorded message directing the caller to contact the sheriff's department.

"Just because the crime rate is down doesn't mean the number of calls aren't up," says Smith. "Our calls for service have been up and continue to go up."

A federal grant is paying for a new deputy in Menard County, but the additional deputy won't help handle the increase in calls. That's because that deputy is assigned full-time to Petersburg PORTA High School.

"We contracted with Tallula four years ago to provide service," says Smith. "Then we got a federal grant for two part-time officers working 18 hours each. One works the west side of the county, and the other works Tallula, where there is no police force, and also Oakford, where they have no police force."

The increased workload has a ripple effect, says Greg Sullivan, director of the Illinois Sheriffs Association: As sheriff's offices work on more cases, it also means more work for crime labs and state's attorney's offices.

"Lots of small towns here don't have a police force, which is more work for the sheriff's

(continued)

HIGHLIGHT 5.1   Continued

department," says Macoupin County Sheriff Gary Wheeler. "We've talked about having the sheriff's department take care of everything in the county. I'm not big on that idea."

The groups behind the report on small town police have distributed a survey to sheriffs across the state to learn, in part, how they cope with increased work loads. The results will be presented at the state sheriff's association meeting in January.

Police protection is one of the most costly services provided by local governments.

Squad cars are a major police-related expense. So is communication equipment. Then there are personnel costs, such as salaries, equipment and benefits for officers. It becomes tempting for villages to throw in the towel and just let the sheriff's department cover the town.

Linda Shaw, village manager in Rochester, estimates that it costs $70,000 to $80,000 to train a police officer. What often happens is that an officer in a small town will complete the required 400 hours of training, get some field experience and then leave for more money in a bigger town. The resulting turnover means the village has to continually recruit and train new officers.

Rochester, as do other small communities, has a clause in its employment contract that says if an officer leaves within three years, he must repay the village for the cost of his training. The amount to be repaid decreases the closer the officer gets to the three-year mark.

Rochester aggressively recruits officers, sending people to other states to perform background investigations on candidates and track down leads on others. That costs money. Putting

in the extra effort makes it more frustrating when young officers quickly leave for a job in a larger town.

"There's quite a school of thought within law enforcement," says Shaw, "that the Generation X concept is at work in police departments, as it is in other fields. Young people are not interested in security and building a life in a community. They're looking for salary and benefits, and they move on to get them."

Edinburg Police Chief Dennis Greenwalt has been on the job for 11 years.

"With a new guy on the block," says Greenwalt, "it's hard for people to have confidence in him. I go out to people's back yards and have tea or cake and cookies. I stop at the coffee shop and joke, kid and shoot the bull with everybody.

"They came up with this phrase 'community policing' in the last few years. We've been doing that in small towns for years."

In his 11 years in Edinburg, Greenwalt says, he has seen three officers come and go in the neighboring town of Stonington and another four come and go in nearby Kincaid.

In Chatham, so many officers left that a few years ago the village board raised the pay of Chatham officers to 90 percent of what Springfield officers make. Chatham Chief Roy Barnett says the move has slowed down turnover.

"Our biggest problem here was that we were losing officers to the county, Springfield and the state police," Barnett said. "They all said they loved working here and loved the town, but it was a matter of economics. I look at what we did as 'catch up.' It took a long time to get there."

this." A police administrator who wants a well-trained department must send the message that training is important in a variety of ways, including at least his own occasional attendance at training sessions.

Before proceeding to an in-depth analysis of the many issues surrounding training and education, it is important to note here that a number of states now mandate training both at the entry level and on a continuing basis. Peace Officer Standards and Training commissions now operate in all states prescribing and supervising training for police officers.

TYPES OF TRAINING

Basic Recruit Training

Most new police recruits attend police training institutes or academies. Such training is referred to as *basic* or *recruit training* and comprises (roughly in order of the amount of time spent on each) patrol techniques and criminal investigation, force and weaponry, legal issues, administration, communications, criminal justice systems, and human relations. A 1986 survey of state and municipal police agencies (in cities with at least 50,000 population) indicated that the mean (average) length of basic training was 13.5 weeks or 541.5 hours (Sapp, 1986, p. 62). A similar study conducted by the U.S. Department of Justice (DOJ) in 1997 showed dramatic increases in this regard. According to the DOJ study, "The typical new officer recruit was required to complete 1100 hours of training in local police departments and 900 hours in sheriff's offices." While this nearly 100 percent increase in the amount of training looks extremely promising at a glance, what must be emphasized is that in almost none of these academies does the amount of time spent on human or community relations and ethical decision making exceed 10 percent, although the vast majority of a police officer's time is spent in encounters and duties requiring skills in these areas. The paradox in the current state of police training is that the majority of training is designed to teach police officers what they will be doing during a small percentage of their on-duty time (Birzer, 1999, p. 17). This must change if police officers are to perform their duties competently and ethically in the journey along the continuum of professionalization. Birzer (1999) concluded that as policing evolves into community-oriented strategies, academies should include more than the mechanical aspects of policing in their curriculums.

Field Training

Although the information provided in basic training academies is crucial, there is often a considerable gap between what is taught and what actually occurs on the streets. In a very real sense, academy training is simply a preparatory step to on-the-job or field training. The first opportunity to practice what the recruit has been taught comes during the first year to eighteen months of service, often referred to as the *probationary period*. During this period, new officers are, or should be, involved in field training under the supervision of field training officers (FTOs) who have been selected and trained to direct, evaluate, and correct the performance of recruits. Such programs have become widespread since their inception in San Jose, California, in 1972. They provide the daily evaluation of recruits' performance by two or more FTOs as well as weekly or monthly evaluations by other supervisory personnel. The programs are typically divided into introductory, training, and evaluation phases. If the recruit successfully completes these phases, she becomes a full-fledged police officer at the end of the probationary period.

If remedial training is required, that is provided. If remedial training fails to produce the desired results, FTO evaluations may serve as a basis for terminating undesirable or ineffective personnel. Herein lies much of the problem, for when FTOs and supervisory personnel determine or recommend that a recruit be terminated for unsatisfactory performance, most police executives remain reluctant to terminate the individual(s) in question because of the significant costs associated with the hiring process. This economic short-sightedness, however, generally ends up costing the agency much more through the years, in terms of civil liability and strained community relations, than the cost of training. Thus, we stand firm in our claim that when the need arises, probationary officers who do not satisfy the demands placed on them by their field training should be terminated.

This issue aside, formalized field training programs make it easier for both the FTOs and the recruits to assess progress. Since each recruit has two or more FTOs during the course of the training, the possibility of personality conflicts or bias leading to unfair judgments is reduced (McCambell, 1986). As Nowicki (1990b, p. 34) indicates, FTOs are no longer "macho" types, although certain physical and survival skills remain important. Good FTOs teach their trainees how to recognize and deal effectively with problems in ways other than the use of physical force. Trained FTOs know that an officer's verbalizations should be used to avoid problems rather than create them. This claim is bolstered by Johnson's (1998) work, entitled "Citizen Complaints: What the Police Should Know." He found that in the municipal agencies included in his study, more than 50 percent of all citizen complaints against police pertained to officers' verbiage and demeanor—perhaps an indication that increased training in the area of human relations and communication skills is desperately needed.

In-Service Training

Also referred to as *continuing professional education* (CPE), most police personnel receive periodic in-service training provided either by department personnel or by training consultants hired by the department or by regional or local training boards. While most departments offer occasional in-service training, many conduct it on a hit-and-miss basis, with no real plan or program in mind. Further, it is sometimes viewed as a necessary evil by both those conducting it and those being trained rather than as a valuable means of keeping current in the field. Perhaps Ilsley and Young (1997) describe this dilemma in police training best:

> Education and training can transform the current police culture into one that values interdepartmental communication . . . community involvement, and the power of learning. Paramount in any organizational transformation is the role continuing education and training will play. Continuing criminal justice education will not be transformative until some basic issues are addressed. For one thing, there is no reason why training cannot be more relevant and interesting, as opposed to dry and even punitive. There is every reason for continuing professional criminal justice education to be cutting edge, high interest, and even enjoyable. But first there must be a stronger reason to attend other than orders. As for new skills necessary for effective policing as we enter the 21st century,

they are numerous. New equipment, procedures, and operations top the list of new things to learn. Computers will play a much bigger part than they do now. We should see an increase in simulation training, competency-based education and performance-based training, as a result of such things. (pp. 5–6)

The question is, does participation in CPE activities keep one current in the field? An even more appropriate question is, do police personnel in this country participate in these activities? If they do, are they forced into participating? Would they participate if they were not forced to? To answer these questions requires an analysis of the literature pertaining to professional education. Highlight 5.2 illustrates the use of simulation in police training.

The purpose and benefits of CPE and whether participation should be mandatory for professionals took centerstage in the relevant literature for nearly two decades, from the mid- to late 1970s to the early 1990s. During the past three decades, there has been a growing concern by consumer groups, various governmental agencies, and professional regulatory boards regarding the competency of practitioners in many of the professions. Dramatic advances in technology and the accompanying information explosion have caused many to question whether initial licensure or certification ensures competency throughout the span of one's career.

In response to this public concern, either through direct government regulation of licensure laws or through indirect regulation via employer and professional organization membership requirements, the vast majority of professions across the United States require professionals to participate in a prescribed amount of educational activities to maintain their licenses. For example, in Illinois, the Department of Professional Regulation (IDPR) is responsible for the licensing, testing, and certification of more than 151 different types of licenses encompassing forty-one professions. The mandate of the IDPR is to "ensure the protection of the public health, safety, and welfare by licensing qualified individuals" (IDPR, 1994). Following is a list of the broad categories covering the various professions:

Architecture	Land sales
Athletics	Land surveying
Athletic training	Landscape architecture
Barbering	Marriage and family therapy
Chiropractic	Medical
Collection agency	Medical corporation
Controlled substances	Nail technology
Cosmetology	Naprapathy
Dentistry	Nursing
Detection, alarm, and security	Nursing home administration
Dietetics and nutrition	Occupational therapy
Environmental health	Optometry
Esthetics	Pharmacy
Funeral directing and embalming	Physical therapy
Interior design	Physician assistant

■ ■ ■ ■ ■ ▬▬▬▬▬▬▬▬▬▬▬▬▬▬▬▬▬▬▬▬▬▬▬▬▬▬▬▬▬▬▬▬

HIGHLIGHT 5.2
VETERAN COPS GO BACK TO SCHOOL
Frank Main

"Sesame Street" was blaring on the TV when the plainclothes officers burst into a West Side home screaming, "Search warrant! Freeze! Get down on the floor!"

The veteran officers handcuffed five angry residents and ordered them to kneel next to a wall while they searched for drugs and guns.

They found a kilogram of cocaine, several pistols and an armed man hiding in a bathroom closet. But they missed a gun that one of the handcuffed women was hiding in her clothes, and they didn't show the tenant their search warrant, even though he asked several times. The recent raid was part of the Chicago Police Department's new training for veteran officers. All 13,500 officers will receive $2\frac{1}{2}$ days of instruction in shooting, street safety skills, handling domestic violence calls and ethics.

"I can't put a price tag on it," said Sgt. Robert Wheeler, who led a team of plainclothes officers through one of the simulated drug raids. "We made a few mistakes, but we'll learn from them. This may save our lives."

Gary Schenkel, a former Marine hired to take over the Police Academy last year, said he has heard similar testimonials from grizzled officers and thinks they're genuine.

One reason: The officers doing the training also have been puffed from the streets for their experience and are highly respected among their peers, Schenkel said. Cops have been offering suggestions for other training they think they need.

"We're already designing the program for next year," Schenkel said. "The more you can set the stage and stress them here, they'll be better out there."

Street safety skills training began Jan. 29, and the shooting training started April 1. The program was launched after the Federal Law Enforcement Training Center in Georgia last year recommended in-service training for the department after several controversial police shootings of citizens here.

In the past, officers could voluntarily receive training at the academy, but it wasn't mandatory until this year. "Approximately 9,200 people will go through our in-service training in the next five months," Schenkel said. "That's more than we've had cumulatively over the past 10 years."

New computerized firearms ranges are in place at the city's five detective headquarters. Virtual criminals fire back with small plastic balls.

The department is considering taking the weapons training a step further with "simunitions." Cartridges filled with colored detergent can be loaded into officers' 9mm pistols, allowing them to exchange gunfire with role players in training scenarios, Cmdr. Sam Christian said.

Narcotics officer Brian Luce, who was training his fellow officers last month, said he was looking forward to simunitions, which would make the program even more realistic. In one of the training sessions, the man hiding in the bathroom came down the stairs and shot half of the officers in the living room to death. Live fire would drive the lessons home even more, Luce said.

"We're trying to give them little tips to get them home safely every night," he said. "A lot of young officers come up and say, 'I'll never walk past a door without checking it.' If they take that one lesson from here, it's worth it."

Podiatry
Professional counseling
Professional engineering
Professional service corporation
Psychology
Public accounting
Real estate
Real estate appraisal

Roofing
Shorthand reporting
Social work
Speech pathology and audiology
Structural engineering
Veterinary medicine
Wholesale drug distribution

Noticeably absent from this rather lengthy list of professions that require participation in CPE activities as a condition of re-licensure is the field of policing. As cited in Scaramella's (1997) review of the literature, researchers point to a variety of benefits associated with a policy of mandatory continuing education (MCE), including the following:

- MCE serves to either eliminate the laggards from the ranks of the profession or revive their interest in learning (Phillips, 1987).
- By virtue of its very existence, the quantity and quality of programs tends to increase (Frye, 1990).
- Participation in MCE is viewed as being more acceptable to professionals than periodic reexamination for license renewal (Rockhill, 1983).
- MCE promotes lifelong learning habits and increases professional interchange (Maple, 1987).
- It protects the public from those who are unwilling to keep up with current developments in their field, thus increasing public confidence (Maple, 1987).

It must be emphasized at this point that among the professions and their related literature, participation in MCE is no longer an issue; rather, it has become accepted practice. As such, since the early 1990s, very little, if any, literature pertaining to this issue can be found.

Unfortunately, the field of policing has not incorporated this educational philosophy into its practice. For the most part, participation in CPE endeavors is left entirely up to individuals and their respective agencies. Even the minuscule amount of in-service training that is mandated for American police officers normally pertains to areas associated with civil liability, such as the use of firearms, physical force, and high-speed vehicle pursuits. Moreover, because liability is almost always directed toward employers, such training efforts are usually only offered because of court orders and/or malpractice insurance requirements. Thus, as Schwartz and Yonkers (1991) point out, "Unlike many other American professions, or unlike policing in some other countries, such as Germany, there are often no continuing education requirements for American police officers" (p. 50).

In addition, most of the other in-service training efforts seem to have fallen victim to many of the early criticisms of MCE in other professions. For example, vendors supplying the majority of police training programs fail to incorporate principles of adult

The emphasis on training and education starts with the chief of police.

learning in their dissemination of information. As a matter of fact, researchers estimate that approximately 95 percent of those vendors have no formal training in education (Cervero, 1988). Also, research is rarely used to identify training needs and link new knowledge and skills with practice. Perhaps more providers of police in-service training should follow the British philosophy, in which "teaching methods include facilitated learning in small groups to encourage depth of understanding; didactic teaching is usually reserved for those occasions when the principal aim is to impart knowledge" (Bunyard, 1991, p. 13).

To help remedy some of the problems associated with in-service training, some states have developed mobile training units responsible for planning and providing training within specified geographic areas on a regular basis. These units frequently arrange training at different locales within their territories to make it easier for police personnel from rural areas and small towns to attend. Unfortunately, budgetary cutbacks and, in some instances, union contracts have made it increasingly difficult for departments to release personnel to attend such training.

To offset the high costs associated with training, a number of additional strategies have been implemented and actually show quite a bit of promise in this regard. A good example is the Public Safety Council Consortium of Lake County, Indiana. It is composed of twenty-two agencies from northwest Indiana that have pooled their money to provide training opportunities for their personnel. The many advantages to such an operation include the following (Marsh & Grosskopf, 1991):

- It is centrally located.
- The center operates on a year-round basis.
- The curriculum covers a wide array of contemporary topics.
- It keeps the cost down to a minimum—only $50 per year per officer.
- It allows personnel from smaller departments the opportunity to attend training activities they might not otherwise be able to experience.
- The instruction is facilitated by professional educators, normally drawn from the ranks of regional universities.

A similar and equally promising in-service training innovation was developed by the Columbus, Ohio, Police Department and has been appropriately named the Entrepreneurial Training Program. As stated by its program administrator, "The idea is simple: Instead of always sending officers to training seminars in other cities, the program brings trainers to Columbus for some of those sessions. Then other law enforcement agencies are invited to attend for a fee. The money saved in transportation coupled with money brought in through fees helps the program nearly pay for itself" (Narciso, 2001, p. 2B).

A similar innovation was developed by the Suffolk County, New York, Police Department. In addition to keeping training costs down, their new training program for more than five hundred Detective Division personnel addressed more logistical impediments to in-service training efforts, such as maintaining full coverage of work schedules, days off, overtime, and funding to facilitate the training sessions. As Kiley (1998, p. 18) concludes from his work on "The Advanced Criminal Investigation Course: An Innovative Approach to Detective In-Service Training,"

> Using experts within the department as instructors, coordinating efforts among all levels of supervision, and incorporating flexibility into the planning of the program, the department succeeded in developing a training program that keeps its detectives on the job and its overtime budget minimally affected. Other law enforcement agencies may benefit from implementing such an in-service . . . course.

In an era of increased fiscal accountability, police executives are well advised to follow the lead of their counterparts from Indiana, Ohio, and New York.

Other Types of Training

Selected police personnel have the opportunity to participate in longer term, more intensive training offered by a variety of training institutes around the country. Among the more popular of these training groups are the Northwestern Traffic Institute, the Southern Police Institute, and the FBI National Academy, all of which offer courses lasting a week to several months. Courses offered by these institutions cover topics ranging from traffic investigation to executive management. At California's Command College, future concerns of police officers and agencies are addressed. The college began operation in 1984 and covers topics such as "Defining the Future," "Human Resource Management," and "Handling Conflict." Controversial topics and ideas are discussed and alternatives to traditional policing are outlined (Lieberman, 1990).

"Operation Bootstrap," begun in 1985, arranges tuition-free corporate management training programs for police administrators and officers. With support from private foundations and the National Institute for Justice, the program now extends into forty states, offering state-of-the-art management training programs that last from one day to one week and cover subjects ranging from effective supervision techniques to conflict resolution to stress management. While formal evaluation of the program has yet to be conducted, strong support has been expressed by those who have attended the programs (Bruns, 1989).

In many instances, these longer training courses are offered to senior-level personnel more as a reward for longevity rather than to personnel in positions in which they could make active use of the information provided. In addition, much of the information provided during these courses remains locked in the minds of those who attend rather than being disseminated to others in the department through in-service training sessions.

All training is, or should be, interrelated. Those with specialty skills need to update these skills on a continuing basis and can share these skills with others through in-service training. This sharing will be effective, however, only when it includes supervisory personnel who may otherwise find the concepts disseminated difficult to understand and may continue to operate using outdated information. Again, the commitment to training must come from the top, along with the recognition that training is one of the few forms of recognition available to police personnel. Merit-based selection for a specialized training course conducted at the department's expense is a rewarding experience, as is recognition of an officer's ability to train others. Without such recognition, training may be viewed in an unfavorable light.

TRAINING AND POLICE LEADERS

None of the subjects dealt with in training seminars is static. Each one is constantly changing, and what we knew to be true yesterday may turn out to be myth tomorrow (Bracey, 1990a). One way of determining the value police supervisors attach to training is to examine the extent to which they subject themselves to it. Currently, many supervisors (including chiefs) avoid training like the plague and rationalize their absences by pointing out the demands on their time in terms of meetings, planning, administrative chores, and bureaucratic requirements. In reality, the absence of police supervisors from training sessions may have more to do with other factors. Why should those at the top sacrifice their time and energy to attend training when those still striving for such positions may benefit more? Bracey (1990b) believes it is unhealthy for the functioning or morale of an organization if the people at the top cannot communicate in an informed and sophisticated manner about concepts and ideas suggested by those who work for them, as a result of their education and training. It is clearly frustrating to return from a period of training and education with an idea that seems ideal for implementation in one's own organization, only to be misunderstood or ignored by supervisors.

Last, but not least, police executives often like to operate as if they were omniscient, with no need for additional information. Related to this may be doubts about how well he will perform in the classroom. What if he appears ill-informed before classmates, including subordinates? What if his contributions to the training session are not appreciated or well received? What if his performance is exceeded by that of other, lower ranking trainees? While these concerns are real, they are worth risking in order to demonstrate that training is not a frill or simply a superficial symbol of the progressive nature of the organization, but a valued, ongoing part of that organization.

TRAINING EFFECTIVENESS

The effects of training are relatively easy to determine but infrequently are properly assessed by police agencies. Does training provide useful information? Did those attending understand the material presented? The answers to these questions lie in a simple evaluation process that is too often neglected because of the assumption that the information provided is understandable and absorbed. The only way to assess the value of training is to conduct routine evaluations. Ideally, such evaluations would include a pretest of attendees' knowledge of the material to be presented and a posttest of such knowledge. While these basic evaluation efforts may suffice for some programs, one of the major problems criminal justice training programs have encountered through the years is their lack of emphasis on evaluation with respect to the relevance and applicability of training. Many of the other professions, on the other hand, utilize sophisticated evaluation techniques to assess program effectiveness and relevancy. Similarly, most professions emphasize research that attempts to link training to job performance (Holmes, Cole, & Hicks, 1992; Bumgarner, 2001). Does training change the way employees do their job? Is the change in the direction desired by employers?

Vendors of police training are still analyzing program effectiveness by evaluating participants' attitudes only *after* instruction is completed. Research concerning CPE activities and their impact on relevancy, competency, and improved job performance suggests that evaluation efforts should concentrate on techniques such as practice audits and complex task analyses if a positive relationship between participation in CPE activities and professional competency is to be achieved (Phillips, 1987).

In his seminal research, Phillips (1987) offers insight as to why some training programs are more effective than others in producing positive changes in job performance. He analyzed eight studies that produced positive changes in performance by physicians after participation in CPE activities. There were five elements that were common to all of the studies:

1. *Specified audience:* All of the participants expressed a desire to learn something.

2. *Identified learning needs:* All participants could identify a learning need and a gap between present and optimal performance.

3. *Clear goals and objectives:* It was clear to everyone involved what was to be learned.

4. *Relevant learning methods and emphasis on participation:* Learning was participative in nature, occurred in familiar surroundings, and involved small group discussions.

5. *Systematic effort to evaluate:* In other words, assessment and evaluation procedures began the day the programs were developed, course development was based on clear definitions of learning needs, and a variety of evaluation techniques were employed.

PURPOSES OF TRAINING

A basic purpose of training is to keep police personnel up to date with respect to important changes in the profession. Police training should identify, instill, and help develop the key competencies that enable officers to do their jobs (Bumgarner, 2001, p. 34). In a larger sense, however, the purposes of training depend on the way in which the role of the police is defined. In the 1960s and 1970s, crime fighting and law enforcement were emphasized, and, to some extent, many officers still view these aspects of the police role as the most important part of police work. As a result, training courses dealing with survival techniques, patrol techniques, criminal investigation, use of force, and the law are among the most popular courses. It is typically easy to recruit officers for courses dealing with these issues.

However, in the past decade, we have come to recognize that while law enforcement and crime fighting are critical parts of the police role, they are not the most important in terms of time spent or citizen satisfaction. As we have seen (Chapter 3), police personnel spend the majority of their time negotiating settlements between spouses or lovers and between neighbors and providing other services that have little or nothing to do with law enforcement. As buffers between aggrieved parties, police personnel need to develop skills in this area. Successful intervention into the daily lives of citizens requires such skills, as well as cooperation on the part of the nonpolice citizens involved. Increasingly then, communications skills (both verbal and nonverbal) and human, community, and minority relations skills are emerging as among the most important assets of a competent, effective police officer.

But where are these skills learned? Many police training programs pay little attention to the importance of developing effective communication skills, and many police administrators assume that officers' communication skills will develop as they gain experience. Without formal training, however, officers can learn only from the examples set by others, which may or may not be appropriate (Pritchett, 1993, p. 25).

A look at basic training curriculums indicates that little emphasis is placed on these skills in the on-the-job setting. Yet communicating with others in the process of negotiating is what police officers do most often. Some police officers have excellent skills in these areas, but others have practically none. The importance of these skills is most clearly illustrated by focusing on those officers who lack them. Such officers are unlikely to get cooperation from diverse segments of the public, either because they alienate other citizens by assuming an authority figure stance as a defense for their poor communications skills, or because they cannot express clearly and convincingly what they want or need the public to do. They receive little input from the public about crime or their own performances. They routinely enforce the law in an attempt to maintain order when their more skilled colleagues could have maintained order without resorting to arrest. They become unnecessarily involved in physical encounters (Reiss, 1971; Pritchett, 1993). They create numerous and constant headaches for their superiors, or, if they are supervisors, for those who work for them.

Training in communications, human relations, minority relations, analysis of encounters, and negotiating is available, but, while more popular than a decade or two ago, such training is often not well attended unless officers are required to be present. Typically, officers who are forced to attend such training fail to see the benefits that may accrue. Such benefits are present, of course, whether a crime is being investigated (interviewing and interrogation skills), whether a police action is being questioned by the public (public relations), whether orders or directives are involved (departmental policies cannot be successfully implemented unless they are understood), or whether evaluations or promotions are involved (both require clear communication between those being evaluated or promoted and those doing the evaluating or promoting).

Such skills also are at a premium when the police are trying to educate the public, whether about a crime prevention program, new police policies, proper complaint procedures, or other issues. Such training is increasingly being recognized as a major aspect of the police role. And, not least important, communications skills are critical when the police are training their own (Pritchett, 1993; Overton & Black, 1994).

One of the major purposes of police training, then, is, or should be, to make better communicators of the public servants responsible for maintaining order. Courses dealing with both verbal and nonverbal communications should be required of all police personnel. It is also possible, however, to improve communications skills regardless of the specific content of the training. Any topic can be presented in an organized fashion, which requires feedback from the participants, and dealing with feedback can help participants learn to express themselves more clearly as well as become better listeners. Police officers who are trained to express themselves clearly and to be good listeners are likely to be better at both order maintenance and law enforcement.

WHO SHOULD DO POLICE TRAINING?

Based on the information contained in the preceding discussion, it is clear that police trainers may, and do, come from diverse backgrounds. Certainly, police officers themselves may be trainers when they have both information to share and the skills to present the information. Let us be clear that these are two separate, equally important requirements. It does little good to use an expert in any area as a trainer unless she has good communications skills. Similarly, it does little good to have an expert communicator present useless (out-of-date or irrelevant) information. Both extremes are found in the arena of police training. When an in-service or retired officer meets both requirements of a trainer, she often has a significant advantage over other trainers, provided the material presented requires an understanding of the police world. While others may have such understanding, the fact that the trainer is, or has been, a police officer often heightens her credibility among police personnel.

It is essential, however, that police training also be conducted by those outside the profession, for two very good reasons. First, many of the skills required of police officers are not frequently found among police officers. Skills needed to set up and run a computer software package, skills required to analyze interaction patterns, skills necessary to prevent infection resulting from communicable diseases are only a few examples. Second, relying only on those within the profession for training typically leads to a myopic world view, which serves to isolate members from the rest of society, and the police can ill afford further isolation. So, who should train the police? Those meeting the previously outlined requirements, regardless of the area of their expertise. Trainers may include police officers, physicians, computer experts, self-defense experts, college professors, members of minority groups, and business leaders, to name just a few. In general, the broader the spectrum of qualified trainers and the greater the exposure to different skills, the better (Marsh & Grosskopf, 1991; Bumgarner, 2001).

It has been suggested that police training must attain a positive identity within the police community and that this is difficult to accomplish because police training has few easily measurable results. The impact of training is often measured in terms of the numbers of hours or programs attended annually, but what happens when the number of hours or programs is cut? There is typically no measurable effect, because training does not often result in clearly measurable end products. Thus, training is relatively easy to cut in times of budgetary shortfalls. For training to gain and maintain a degree of importance, it must be shown that resources expended for training lead to positive results for both the police and the community they serve.

According to the Nationwide Law Enforcement Training Needs Assessment Project, areas in which such results might be attained include, among others, the following (Phillips, 1988, p. 12):

- Handling personnel stress
- Physical fitness
- Conducting interviews and interrogations
- Procedures related to evidence collection and preservation
- Emergency and pursuit driving
- Promoting a positive police image
- Testifying in court
- Report writing
- Effective supervisory procedures
- Handling domestic violence situations

Further, alternative means of delivering training need to be developed to make more training available to more officers on a cost-effective basis. Along these lines, training videos and satellite broadcasting have emerged during the past decade. These media have the potential to reach large, widely scattered groups of police personnel and, in some formats at least, still allow for interaction between trainers and trainees through the use of direct telephone communication between the two.

Yet another innovation in police training involves the use of job analysis and assessment centers. The former enables trainers to determine the nature of the skills required for performance of specified jobs, while the latter enables trainers or administrators to measure what trainees learn through the use of situational and written tests and oral presentations covering one or more areas in which training has been provided (Mullins, 1985).

Mentoring is another means of assisting police training. Experienced officers with proven skills in specific areas are assigned (or volunteer for) the task of sharing their expertise with other officers. Mentors demonstrate the skills involved, answer questions and provide instructions, and regularly assess the progress of their students (Marsh & Grosskopf, 1991, p. 65).

In the next decade, two major aspects of police training clearly require further assessment. First, further studies of the relationship between training and job performance are greatly needed. Second, more comprehensive and timely training for those wishing to fill supervisory roles must be made available. Over the past two decades, the value of traditional police training techniques—verbal harassment, harsh criticism, and physical activity as punishment—have been called into question. Techniques that build self-esteem and motivate recruits are more appropriate to applicants seeking a challenge, participation in decision making, and career development (Post, 1992).

While advances in training techniques have been made in the past decade, many questions remain to be answered, and the impact of training on the job has yet to be clarified. We believe, however, that the field of policing needs to adopt a policy of mandatory participation in CPE activities; that more of the training needs to focus on the less traditional aspects of policing, to include human relations training, communication skills, community policing strategies, ethical decision making, and the responsible exercise of discretionary authority; that executives lead by example and assume an active role in the training process; that administrators search and collaborate for innovative methods for the provision of training opportunities; and that these activities be facilitated not only by content experts, but also by experienced and knowledgeable educators.

There is no doubt that the field of policing has advanced along the continuum of professionalization during the past few decades. However, if the law enforcement community wishes to be perceived as professionals, they must demonstrate many of the same characteristics that are used to distinguish members of a profession from those of an occupation.

Regardless of the approach utilized in making such a distinction, the common denominator among all of them is a demonstrated ability to keep abreast of current trends in one's field through participation in CPE activities. It is no secret that the issues of safe practice, the technological revolution, and public accountability are some of the underlying beliefs concerning why professionals should consistently update their knowledge and skills. The history of MCE has shown us that when professional groups refuse to maintain their level of competence in a responsible and professional manner, government intervention is inevitable.

Collectively, law enforcement officers must begin to impose increased education and training standards on themselves and beat the government to the punch, so to speak. Only when the police begin to perceive participation in CPE activities as a natural extension of the preprofessional process will they achieve the desired goal of CPE—continuing professional competency.

POLICE EDUCATION

One of the most popular proposals for improving the quality of policing in the United States has focused on better educated officers. The idea that a college-educated police officer would be a better police officer spawned a federal program (LEAA) that provided millions of dollars annually in support of such education, a dramatic increase in the numbers of college programs related to policing, and an increase in the number of police officers with at least some college education (Polk & Armstrong, 2001). The debate over the importance of police education continues, federal funding for such education has diminished considerably, new federal programs are being proposed, and there are continuing concerns over the content and quality of police education.

Many of the current concerns surrounding police education result from our inability or unwillingness to decide exactly what we want the police to be and do in our society. It is extremely difficult to develop courses and curriculums for the police under these circumstances. Some believe that liberal arts courses provide the best background for police officers in a multiethnic, multicultural society; others are convinced that specialized courses in criminal justice are preferable, while still others question the value of college education for police officers. In spite of these continuing concerns, the number of programs in criminal justice and related areas increased dramatically in the 1970s.

Broderick (1987, pp. 217–218) notes, for example, that criminal justice education grew rapidly in the early 1970s, so that by 1976 there were 699 colleges and universities offering 1,245 degree programs, ranging from the associate to the doctorate: "Many of these programs, however, were of poor quality, consisting of 'war stories' and technical and vocational training." Data collected in 1985 indicated that many in academia still perceived criminal justice education as being basically technical or vocational training, often taught by faculty without proper credentials. While this may have been the case during the past couple of decades, there seems to be a glimmer of hope. The training or applied nature of many criminal justice degree programs that brought so much criticism from others in academia seems to be changing. In sharp contrast to Farrell and Koch's (1995) sentiment, that such degree programs are the "epitome of anti-intellectualism and the death of humanism" (pp. 53–54), many feel or believe that the "field has flourished intellectually and broadened its scope. Although there is little uniformity nationwide in criminal justice curricula, most contemporary programs attempt to achieve a more structured balance between the academic and applied needs of their students. Thus, it may be that a maturation process has taken root and today's programs bear little resemblance to their forerunners" (Carlan & Byxbe, 2000).

In response to the aforementioned concerns, the U.S. Department of Justice (1999) created the Office of the Police Corps and Law Enforcement Education. The goal of the program is to weave a baccalaureate education with state-of-the-art police training to produce highly qualified personnel who are able to confront the demands and intricacies of twenty-first-century policing. Highlights of the program are as follows:

- It provides scholarships to individuals who agree to earn their baccalaureate degree on a full-time basis, successfully complete Police Corps training, and serve for a minimum of four years with a state, municipal, or county law enforcement agency that participates with the program.

- It also provides funding to states that agree to participate in the program. Presently, approximately one-half of the states in the country are participating with this program.

- The Police Corps program also provides participating law enforcement agencies with monetary incentives by giving them $10,000 per year per officer hired from the program.

- Finally, those aspiring to enter the field of policing via this program can earn up to $7,500 per academic year to cover the costs of tuition, fees, books, transportation, and room and board.

Types of Police Education

Assuming that higher education for police officers is desirable, what type of education provides the best background? One survey of police departments serving cities with populations of 50,000 or more found that about half of all police executives who responded prefer to hire officers who have majored in criminal justice (Carter & Sapp, 1992). A similar number indicated no preference in college degrees or majors. Those who preferred criminal justice majors did so because of the graduates' knowledge of policing and criminal justice, while those stating no preference indicated they preferred a broader education to prepare officers to deal with a wide variety of situations, including those not dealing with law enforcement.

The same study indicated a general perception among police executives that colleges and universities do not have curriculums that meet the contemporary needs of law enforcement agencies. While the respondents found that criminal justice graduates are very knowledgeable about the criminal justice system and policing in general, they are often "narrow in ideology" and lack the broader understanding of divergent cultures and social issues confronting the police. These executives do not want colleges and universities to teach police skills; they seek graduates who can integrate the duties of a police officer with an understanding of democratic values (Sapp, Carter, & Stephens, 1989). The consensus is that liberal arts curriculums should be part and parcel of college and university criminal justice programs. Many respondents noted that a "quality" education is needed, particularly in the area of communications skills. Other areas perceived as requiring greater attention included critical thinking, decision making, research, the ability to integrate concepts, and understanding diverse cultures. Finally, the police executives indicated there is a lack of communication between colleges and universities and police agencies, with less than 25 percent indicating they were regularly consulted by these institutions and more than a fourth indicating they were never consulted about issues of common interest. The authors of the study concluded, "The results of this national study suggest that colleges and universities should be developing policies, changing and modifying curricula, and focusing on providing the educational background needed by students and society. Criminal justice educators must introspectively give detailed attention to curricula to ensure that today's curricula fit today's needs in law enforcement and other areas of the criminal justice system" (Sapp, Carter, & Stephens, 1989, p. 5).

Police Educational Requirements

In the survey conducted by Sapp, Carter, and Stephens for the Police Executive Research Forum, only about 14 percent of the responding agencies reported requiring any college at all, and less than 1 percent required a bachelor's degree. Yet almost two-thirds of these agencies had some form of educational incentive program. In part, this apparent discrepancy appears to be due to a belief among agency officials that higher education requirements could be effectively challenged in the courts or in contract negotiations. This belief is based on concerns about possible discrimination against minorities and the difficulty in demonstrating that higher education is a bona fide job requirement for police personnel (Sapp, Carter, & Stephens, 1988, p. 1; Carter & Sapp, 1992, p. 11).

As a result, it appears that while many departments do in fact give preference to recruits with college educations, few are willing to make college education a formal requirement. This conclusion is supported by the fact that the mean educational level of police officers, as determined by this survey of over 250,000 officers, is 13.6 years, compared with 12.4 years in 1967. The authors conclude that in light of the fact that some departments do require college education as a condition of initial employment and the willingness of the courts to uphold college education as a requirement in at least some cases, it is possible to establish a "defensible college education entrance requirement for employment" (and, for that matter, for promotion) in law enforcement (Sapp, Carter, & Stephens, 1988, p.23; Carter & Sapp, 1992, p. 11). This would require developing a policy outlining the rationale for the requirement by individual police agencies desiring to implement educational requirements.

Facts in support of such a rationale are available, though they may be more qualitative than quantitative. In the case of *Davis v. City of Dallas*, the United States Supreme Court allowed the Dallas Police Department's requirement of forty-five semester-hours of college coursework for entry-level officers to stand (*Davis v. City of Dallas*, 1986). Other police departments, such as in San Jose, California, and Lakewood, Colorado, have had longstanding entry-level educational requirements as well; and numerous other court decisions support educational requirements for the police (Scott,

1986). According to Stevens' (1999) work, entitled "College Educated Officers: Do They Provide Better Police Service?" it is estimated that "10 percent of all police agencies mandate college degreed candidates and 7% mandate community college degrees."

College Education and Police Performance

According to Swanson, Territo, and Taylor (1988, pp. 211–212),

> It has been argued by some that police work, especially at the local level, does not require a formal education beyond high school because such tasks as directing traffic, writing parking tickets, conducting permit inspections, and performing clerical tasks do not require higher education. In addition, it has been suggested that a highly intelligent and well-educated person would soon become bored with these mundane and repetitive tasks and either resign or remain and become either an ineffective member of the force or a malcontent.

Others have argued that the complex role of policing a multiethnic, culturally diverse society requires nothing less than a college degree as a condition of initial employment for police officers (National Advisory Commission on Criminal Justice Standards and Goals, 1973; Carter & Sapp, 1992).

In a review of the evidence on the relationship between higher education and police performance, Hayeslip (1989, p. 49) highlighted the assumed benefits of college education for police officers: greater motivation, more ability to utilize innovative techniques, clearer thinking, better understanding of the occupation/profession, and so on. Based on the studies reviewed, Hayeslip concluded that education and police performance are consistently related, though the relationship is moderate.

Sherman and Blumberg (1981) found no consistent relationship between educational level and police use of deadly force. Daniels (1982), examining the relationship between educational level and absenteeism among police personnel, found that employees without college degrees missed more than three times as many work days through unscheduled absences as those with a four-year degree.

Griffin (1980) found an inverse relationship between educational levels of patrol officers and performance ratings, but a significant relationship between educational levels and what he refers to as job achievement. Meagher (1983) examined police officer educational levels and differences in delivery of services and concluded that college graduates are more likely to explain the nature of complaints to offenders, talk with people to establish rapport, analyze and compare incidents for similarity of modus operandi, recruit confidential informants, and verify reliability and credibility of witnesses than are officers with some college or high school education. However, Meagher was unwilling to attribute these performance differences solely to educational differences.

Other studies of the relationship between higher education and police performance have found that those officers with the best performance evaluations also had significantly higher education (Baeher, Furcon, & Froemel, 1968), that college-educated police officers are less authoritarian than those without college educations (Smith, Locke, & Walker, 1968), and that those with at least some college education had fewer civilian complaints and less sick time than those without such education (Cohen & Chaiken, 1972).

A study conducted by Cox and Moore (1992) found police higher education to correlate positively with a number of variables, including more effective communication skills, better problem-solving and analytical abilities, an increase in public perception of police competence, fewer citizen complaints regarding verbal and physical abuse, and fewer disciplinary actions taken against college-educated police officers.

Worden (1990, p. 587) concluded that college education is weakly related to some police officer attitudes and unrelated to others. He found that officers' performance in police–citizen encounters, as measured by citizen evaluations, is "largely unrelated to officers' educational backgrounds."

Kappeler, Sapp, and Carter (1992) concluded that while officers with four-year degrees generated at least as many violations of departmental policy as those with two-year degrees, the former perform better that the latter in the areas of courtesy and citizen complaints.

More recent studies, which examined the relationship between higher education and police performance, seem to be positive in nature. Polk and Armstrong (2001) examined the effects of higher education on the career paths of Texas law enforcement officers. They found that higher education reduces time required for movement in rank and assignment to specialized positions and was positively correlated to promotion into supervisory and administrative posts. Implications are that higher education will enhance an officer's probability of rising to the top regardless of whether the agency requires a college degree as a precondition of employment.

In an era of community policing, many police executives expect college-educated officers to be both more open-minded and more humanitarian in nature. Carlan and Byxbe (2000) set out to link education with an increased humanistic philosophy:

> Students from three southern colleges read vignettes and sentenced a murder defendant and an automobile theft defendant to a term of imprisonment. Three hypotheses were tested. First, it was expected that police-oriented criminal justice majors would not issue more severe sentences. Second, it was anticipated that greater exposure to college from the freshman to the senior years would be accompanied by less severe sentences. Third, sentencing would be independent of social characteristics. The results provided little evidence supporting a more authoritarian and more punitive stereotype of criminal justice majors interested in pursuing police careers.

According to the American Police Foundation, a professional organization dedicated to the professionalization of law enforcement, higher education is beneficial for a number of reasons (Stevens, 1999, p. 37):

- It develops a broader base of information for decision making.
- It provides additional years and experiences for increasing maturity.

- It inculcates responsibility in the individual through course requirements and achievements.
- It permits an individual to learn more about the history of the United States and the democratic process.

Wilson (1999) attempted to measure the relationship between educational attainment of police prior to their date of hire and its effect on the frequency of citizen complaints. Examine a summary of the research:

> A ten year period of citizen complaint data from the files of 500 working police officers were retrieved and correlated with officer demographic variables of gender, age, years employed, ethnicity and level of post-secondary education. An analysis of these data produced statistics illustrating the relationship of the variables to the frequency of citizens' complaints. The main finding of this study was that certain levels of college education appear to relate favorably to the receipt of fewer citizens' complaints.

The results of Wilson's research seem to corroborate a study conducted by Johnson (1998) on citizen complaints. He, too, found that college-educated officers had a significantly lower rate of citizen complaints directed toward them.

Higher Education and the Police: A Continuing Controversy

The controversy surrounding the need for higher education for police personnel continues in spite of the fact that virtually every national commission on the police over the past half-century has recommended such education. One basic argument against college education for the police is that there is insufficient empirical evidence to indicate that such education is necessary for performing the police function. This argument is countered by recognizing the fact that there is scant evidence to indicate that college education is necessary for performing any occupation, but considerable evidence that such education may improve the performance of those in the occupation (Scott, 1986).

Some studies, however, seem to demonstrate a positive correlation between higher education and police performance. Additionally, there is a good deal of evidence that indicates that the college experience increases the ability to think critically, the amount of factual information available, self-confidence, open-mindedness, and adaptability (Feldman & Newcomb, 1969; Bowen, 1977).

While these abilities and skills may not have been deemed critical to police personnel in previous decades, they are of paramount importance to the police as order maintainers and negotiators. That is, as indicated throughout this book, the police role has changed and is changing. According to Scott (1986, p. 26),

> Police must have the ability to understand human problems in their community and they must be trained to identify and understand a variety of social, economic, and developmental ills for which they must be able to refer, recommend, or involve themselves in an effort to seek the best available solution. College education does appear to develop and enhance these abilities and skills, if the education is administered outside the narrow

parameters of a vocational training program or the classic criminal justice or law enforcement programs found in most two-year and four-year programs.

Scott concludes that entry-level requirements for police officers include a four-year degree requirement and that police officers already in the field should avail themselves of opportunities to pursue bachelor's degrees. This is the same conclusion reached by the National Advisory Commission on Higher Education for the Police some years ago.

Commitment to education, like commitment to training, should be career-long for police personnel. For officers who already have college degrees, as well as for those without such degrees, continuing education courses can be challenging, motivating, and worthwhile. Such courses also are beneficial for officers who do not wish to pursue a college degree. However, the benefits of continuing education for police officers are not limited to course content. It has been our observation over the past twenty years that a good deal of benefit accrues from having police officers and other students share the same classroom, coming to know each other as individuals, and hearing one another's perspectives on a variety of issues. This is perhaps particularly true when the class is diverse with respect to age, race and ethnicity, gender, size of hometown, and cultural background.

Departmental incentives for becoming involved in continuing education indicate to officers that their efforts are appreciated. Such incentives may include tuition reimbursement, time off to attend classes (or allowing officers to attend class while on duty in an "on-call" status), reimbursement for the cost of books, and so on. In many departments that provide these incentives, enhanced chances for promotion also exist. As is the case with training, commitment to education and continuing education must come from the top (Carter & Sapp, 1992).

The debate over the proper extent and nature of police training and education continues. An increasing body of legal evidence is accumulating and indicates that failure to train may lead to serious financial consequences for police agencies, agents, and municipalities alike. Further, there appears to be increasing legal support for higher education of police officers. Coupled with the fact that the perceived role of the police has changed dramatically in recent years, these indicators would appear to support increasingly higher standards for police training and education. The transition to police officers with higher education has not, however, been smooth or easy. Conflict and uneasiness between college-educated officers and those without such education is typical in many agencies.

This is perhaps particularly true when college-educated officers are supervised by those lacking such education. The former often consider themselves superior to the latter, based on educational background, while the latter often consider such education a waste of time and believe that street experience and common sense are far more important than a college degree. Given these conditions, developing common ground and mutual respect is not easy.

Though only a small proportion of police agencies now require college education for initial employment or promotion, informal discussions with police executives indicate that such education is of considerable importance. Similarly, the increasingly complex nature of crime and requests for police services and the laws regulating activities in these areas would appear to support the need for better educated and trained police. To reach these goals, colleges and universities, as well as police training institutes and academies, must continually revise and update curriculums while maintaining high standards. Vocational training for police officers is necessary but should not be confused with education. The two types of programs can and must coexist; and improved cooperation between proponents of each can only lead to more qualified police officers. As Carter and Sapp (1992, p. 14) note, law enforcement agencies no longer can fail to recognize the changes that are taking place in policing. These changes include an increase in the educational level of citizens and the number of police programs based on increased police–citizen interactions. These two developments require review of law enforcement educational policies. Carter and Sapp are convinced that "the question is not whether college education is necessary for police officers, but how much and how soon?"

DISCUSSION QUESTIONS

1. Why is recurrent training so important to police personnel? What are some of the possible consequences of failure to train?

2. What kinds of topics should be included in police training? Who should conduct the training?

3. How would you go about evaluating the effectiveness of a police training program? Why is evaluation so important?

4. What is the relationship between education and training? Can one replace the other? Why or why not?

5. Discuss the arguments for and against college education for police officers.

6. What are some of the weaknesses of existing college programs in criminal justice and law enforcement noted by police executives in recent surveys? How might these weaknesses be corrected?

7. Is there legal justification for requiring some college for entry-level police officers? What are the legal issues involved with this requirement?

8. Has the relationship between college education and improved police performance been thoroughly documented? What needs to be done to further examine this relationship?

REFERENCES

Baeher, E. M., Furcon, J. E., & Froemel, E. (1968). *Psychological assessment of patrolman qualifications in relation to field performance.* Washington, DC: U.S. Government Printing Office.

Baro, A., & Burlingame, D. (1999, Spring). Law enforcement and higher education: Is there an impasse? *Journal of Criminal Justice Education, 10,* 57–73.

Birzer, M. L. (1999). Police training in the 21st century. *FBI Law Enforcement Bulletin, 68,* 16–19.

Bowen, H. R. (1977). *Investment in learning: The individual and social value of higher education.* San Francisco: Jossey-Bass.

Bracey, D. H. (1990a). Future trends in police training. Paper presented at the Third Annual Sino-American Criminal Justice Institute, Taipei, Taiwan (August).

——— . (1990b). Preparing police leaders for the future. *Police Studies, 13,* 178–182.

Broderick, J. (1987). *Police in a time of change.* Prospect Heights, IL: Waveland.

Bruns, B. (1989). Operation bootstrap: Opening corporate classrooms to police managers. *NIJ Reports, 217,* 2–6.

Bumgarner, J. (2001). Evaluating law enforcement training. *Police Chief, 68,* 32–36.

Bunyard, S. R. (1991). Police higher training in England and Wales. *Crime & Justice International, 7,* 11–17.

Carlan, P., & Byxbe, F. (2000). The promise of humanistic policing: Is higher education living up to societal expectation? *American Journal of Criminal Justice, 24,* 235–245.

Carter, D., & Sapp, A. (1992, January). College education and policing: Coming of age. *FBI Law Enforcement Bulletin, 61,* 8–14.

Cervero, R. (1988). *Effective continuing education for professionals.* San Francisco: Jossey-Bass.

Cohen, B., & Chaiken, J. (1972). *Police background characteristics: Summary report.* Washington, DC: U.S. Government Printing Office.

Cox, B., and Moore, R. Jr. (1992). Toward the twenty-first century: Law enforcement training now and then. *Journal of Contemporary Criminal Justice, 8,* 235–256.

Daniels, E. (1982, September). The effect of a college degree on police absenteeism. *Police Chief, 49,* 70–71.

Davis v. City of Dallas, 777 F.2d 205 (5th Cir. 1985, certiorari denied to Supreme Court May 19, 1986).

Farrell, B., & Koch, L. (1995). Criminal justice, sociology, and academia. *American Sociologist, 26,* 52–61.

Feldman, K. A. (1969). *The impact of college on students. Vol. 1: An analysis of four decades of research.* San Francisco: Jossey-Bass.

Frye, S. (1990). Mandatory continuing education for professional re-licensure: A comparative analysis of its impact in law and medicine. *Journal of Continuing Higher Education, 38,* 16–25.

Graves, F. (1991). Trainers technique syndrome. *Police Chief, 58,* 62–63.

Griffin, G. (1980). *A study of relationships between level of college education and police patrolman's performance.* Saratoga, NY: Twenty One.

Hayeslip, D. Jr. (1989). Higher education and police performance revisited: The evidence examined through meta-analysis. *American Journal of Police, 8,* 49–59.

Holmes, G., Cole, E., & Hicks, L. (1992, November). Curriculum development: Relevancy and innovation. *Police Chief, 59,* 51–52.

Illinois Department of Professional Regulation. (1994). *Categories of regulation.* Springfield: State of Illinois.

Ilsley, P., & Young, W. (1997). Transforming criminal justice education through continuing professional education. *Crime & Justice International, 13,* 5–6.

Johnson, R. (1998, December). Citizen complaints: What the police should know. *FBI Law Enforcement Bulletin, 67,* 1–5.

Kappeler, V., Sapp, A., & Carter, D. (1992). Police officer higher education, citizen complaints and departmental rule violations. *American Journal of the Police, 11,* 37–54.

Kiley, W. (1998, October). The advanced criminal investigation course: An innovative approach to detective in-service training. *FBI Law Enforcement Bulletin, 67,* 16–18.

Lieberman, P. (1990). Facing the future. *Police, 14,* 4–71.

Maple, G. (1987). Continuing education for the health sciences. *Australian Journal of Adult Education, 27,* 22–27.

Marsh, H., & Grosskopf, E. (1991). The key factors in law enforcement training: Requirements, assessments and methods. *Police Chief, 58,* 64–66.

McCambell, M. S. (1986). Field training for police officers: State of the art. In *Research in Brief.* Washington, DC: National Institute of Justice.

Meagher, M. (1983). Perceptions of the police patrol function: Does officer education make a difference? Paper presented at Academy of Criminal Justice Sciences Meeting (March).

Mullins, W. (1985, March). Improving police officer training: The use of job analysis procedures and assessment center technology. *Journal of Police and Criminal Psychology, 1,* 2–9.

Narciso, D. (2001, July 24). New fund lets police division sell its own training programs. *Columbus Dispatch,* p. 2B.

National Advisory Commission on Criminal Justice Standards and Goals. (1973). *Report on the police.* Washington, DC: U.S. Government Printing Office.

Nowicki, E. (1990a). Police training: A sense of priority. *Police, 14,* 4.

———. (1990b). New dogs, new tricks. *Police, 14,* 31–51.

Overton, W., & Black, J. (1994). Language as a weapon. *Police Chief, 65,* 46.

Phillips, R. (1988, August). Training priorities in state and local law enforcement. *FBI Law Enforcement Bulletin, 57,* 10–16.

Phillips, L. (1987). Is mandatory continuing professional education working? *Mobius, 7,* 57–63.

Polk, O., & Armstrong, D. (2001). Higher education and law enforcement career paths: Is the road to success paved by a degree? *Journal of Criminal Justice Education, 12,* 77–99.

Post, G. (1992). Police recruits: Training tomorrow's workforce. *FBI Law Enforcement Bulletin, 61,* 19–24.

Pritchett, G. L. (1993). Interpersonal communication: Improving law enforcement's image. *FBI Law Enforcement Bulletin, 62,* 22–26.

Reiss, A. J. Jr. (1971). *The police and the public.* New Haven, CT: Yale University Press.

Rockhill, K. (1983). Mandatory continuing education for professionals: Trends and issues. *Adult Education, 33,* 106–116.

Sapp, A. (1986, November). Education and training requirements in law enforcement: A national comparison. *Police Chief, 53,* 48–62.

Sapp, A., Carter, D., & Stephens, D. (1988). Higher education as a bona fide occupational qualification (BFOQ) for police: A blueprint. *American Journal of Police, 7,* 15–59.

Sapp, A., Carter, D., & Stephens, D. (1989). Police chiefs: CJ curricula inconsistent with contemporary police needs. *ACJS Today, 7,* 1, 5.

Scaramella, G. (1997). Professionalizing the police. *Crime & Justice International, 13,* 7–8.

Schwartz, M., & Yonkers, S. (1991). Officer satisfaction with police in-service training: An exploratory evaluation. *American Journal of Police, 10,* 49–63.

Scott, W. (1986). College educational requirements for entry level and promotion: A study. *Journal of Police and Criminal Psychology, 2,* 10–28.

Sherman, L. W., & Blumberg, M. (1981). Higher education and police use of force. *Journal of Criminal Justice, 9,* 317–331.

Smith, A., Locke, B., & Walker, W. (1968). Authoritarianism in police college students and non-police college students. *Journal of Criminal Law, Criminology, and Police Science, 59,* 440–443.

Stevens, D. (1999). College educated officers: Do they provide better police service? *Law & Order, 47,* 37–41.

Swanson, C., Territo, L., & Taylor, R. (1998). *Police administration: Structures, processes, and behavior,* 4th ed. Upper Saddle River, NJ: Prentice-Hall.

United States Department of Justice. (1999). Office of the Police Corps and Law Enforcement Education, Office of Justice Programs. Available online at: http://www.ojp.usdoj.gov/opc/ee. Retrieved from the World Wide Web on August 14, 2001.

United States Department of Justice. (1997). *State and local law enforcement statistics.* Washington DC: U.S. Government Printing Office. Available online at: http://www.ojp.usdoj.gov/bjs/san-dlle.htw#education.

Wilson, H. (1999). Post-secondary education of the police officer and its effect on the frequency of citizen complaints. *Journal of California Law Enforcement, 33,* 3–10.

Worden, R. (1990). A badge and a baccalaureate: Policies, hypotheses, and further evidence. *Justice Quarterly, 7,* 580–592.

CHAPTER SIX

WOMEN AND MINORITIES IN POLICING

As indicated in Chapter 4, in recent years there have been attempts to recruit more women and minorities into policing. These attempts have come largely in response to affirmative action and equal employment opportunity requirements, rather than as a direct result of the belief that such recruits can in fact perform the police roles as well as white men. In 1990, 80.0 percent of local police personnel were white, 10.5 percent black, and 5.2 percent were Hispanic. Women comprised 8.1 percent of local police officers (Maguire, Pastore, & Flanagan, 1992). In 1999, Harris (p. 18) reported that the percentage of female officers in the United States was approximately 10 percent. In the following pages, we examine the impact of efforts to recruit women and minority group members into policing.

WOMEN IN POLICING

On September 3, 1910, in the city of Los Angeles, Mrs. Alice Stebbin Wells became the first official policewoman in the United States (Horne, 1980, p. 28). Her duties included supervising and enforcing laws pertaining to dance halls, skating rinks, theaters, and other public recreation areas. She lectured to various groups around the nation in the next few years about the place of women in police service, and her efforts resulted in the Chicago City Council passing an ordinance that provided for the hiring of police-women. By 1915, Chicago had employed thirty policewomen (Swan, 1988, p. 11). Mrs. Wells became the first president of the International Association of Policewomen in 1915. At that time, policewomen worked mainly with troubled youth and women victims and offenders. During World War I, policewomen were utilized to keep prostitutes away from military camps and to assist in the return of runaway women and girls (Bell, 1982, p. 113; House, 1993, p. 139). The "women's bureau" was a separate division; police-women did not wear uniforms, nor were they armed. They typically received less pay than their male counterparts, although their educational qualifications were consider-ably better (Horne, 1980, p. 30). Still, at the Chief's Association convention in 1922, a resolution was passed, stating that policewomen were indispensable to the modern police department (Swan, 1988, p. 11).

Very few policewomen were hired during the Great Depression, and while women were used as auxiliary police officers during World War II, this role ended with the end of the war. Not until the 1960s did opportunities for policewomen begin to improve. The President's Commission on Law Enforcement and the Administration of Justice (1967) found that policewomen could be an "invaluable asset" to modern law enforce-ment and recommended that their present role be broadened to include patrol and investigative duties as well as administrative responsibilities. The first woman assigned to full-time field patrol was hired in Indianapolis in 1968 (McDowell, 1992).

In 1972, Congress amended Title VII of the 1964 Civil Rights Act to prohibit discrimination by both private and public employers based on the sex of the applicant. At about the same time, the Police Foundation published *Women in Policing*, and the report was generally favorable toward policewomen. And, in the same time period, the Federal Bureau of Investigation and the Secret Service appointed their first female field agents. Finally, a number of cities (St. Louis, Washington, DC, New York City) placed uniformed female officers in patrol positions and conducted studies to evaluate their performance. These studies in the 1970s led to the conclusion that policewomen perform as well as policemen, although sometimes in different fashion. There was also an early study that indicated that the attitudes of policewomen and policemen are fairly similar (Koenig, 1978). Bartol, Bergen, and Volckens (1992) more recently studied thirty full-time female police officers and found that, overall, in small towns at least, they experienced stressors similar to those of their male counterparts. Other studies found that organizational commitment, job satisfaction, stress levels and job-related anxiety, and attitudes toward law and order do not differ significantly by gender (McGeorge & Wolfe, 1976; Fry & Greenfield, 1980). Felkenes and Lasley (1992) surveyed over one thousand officers and found that regardless of gender or race, levels of job satisfaction were high.

One researcher concluded that policewomen, at least in the southwestern United States, are more authoritarian and cynical than their male counterparts (Davis, 1984). Nonetheless, male officers and administrators continue to doubt the ability of female officers to perform, particularly in violent or potentially violent situations. To some extent, these doubts may be based on the development of different entry-level requirements, particularly in the area of physical ability, resulting from attempts to attract and hire female officers. To many male officers, in some cases with justification, different standards imply lower standards, and stories about being passed over for employment or promotion as a result of affirmative action requirements are rife among male officers and potential officers.

Once hired, however, Block and Anderson (1974) found that female and male officers responded to calls in a generally similar fashion and that citizen respect for the police was similar for the two groups, though male and female officers performed the jobs in somewhat different ways. According to Donna Milgram of the Institute for Women in Trades, Technology, and Science (Harris, 1999, p. 18), "Women can do this job." Kerber, Andes, and Mittler (1977) found that citizens generally judged male and female officers as equally competent, and over three-fourths of the respondents to their survey indicated that both male and female officers should be hired to improve the quality of police services. To be sure, the Kerber, Andes, and Mittler study was conducted in a university community and the results might not be representative of attitudes in other types of communities.

The authors, however, concluded that "respondents from larger cities with higher levels of education and better jobs have more liberal views on female police officers, and that, in the long run, demonstrated competence on the job is the basic criterion policewomen must satisfy to gain acceptance." Breci (1997) came to similar conclusions. Any doubt that women are as competent as men when performing police functions has largely been eliminated (Harris, 1999). In fact, women bring unique perspectives to policing—qualities that promote teamwork and effectiveness (Harris, 1999).

The number of policewomen in the United States has gradually increased so that by 1990, they accounted for about 8 percent of sworn police personnel. In that year, over 114,000 women were employed as sworn officers. The number of female police officers more than tripled between 1980 and 1990, with the increase being greatest in departments serving populations over 250,000 and in suburban departments, where women accounted for nearly 10 percent of sworn personnel. The rate of growth has been slow since 1990, with the number of women in policing increasing by only 5.3 percent by 1999 (Gold, 2000).

In spite of the fact that the Washington, DC, study conducted in the early 1970s led to the conclusion that policewomen performed capably, male patrol officers and supervisory officers continued to express predominantly negative attitudes toward their female counterparts. They continued to indicate that female officers were less capable in violent situations or as backup in such situations. More studies of policewomen soon followed. An evaluation of policewomen patrolling alone in St. Louis County (Missouri) indicated that they performed their duties as well as men, as measured by police supervisors, observers, and citizens (Sherman, 1975). The attitudes of policemen remained largely negative, though somewhat less so after the evaluation.

A study done by the California Highway Patrol in 1976 concluded that, although it cost more to recruit and train women, they performed capably (Balkin, 1988). A study done in Denver at about the same time reached similar conclusions (Bartlett & Rosenblum, 1977), as did a New York City study conducted in 1976 (Sichel et al., 1978). Numerous other studies have led to the same conclusion—women perform patrol functions acceptably (Harris, 1999). Only one study concluded that women are not as capable on patrol as men. This study, done in the Philadelphia Police Department, found that women do not project the image of power and strength that policemen project and that they do not conduct building searches as well. The report concluded that women fail to handle patrol duties as safely and efficiently as men. Critics have noted that this is true only if the major concerns of the police have to do with appearing powerful and conducting building searches (Horne, 1980).

Policewomen as Viewed by the Public, Their Supervisors, and Male Officers

Although public attitudes toward policewomen have not been extensively investigated, the information that is available indicates that these attitudes are basically positive. In fact, in the St. Louis and New York studies discussed previously, female officers were regarded more favorably than their male counterparts (Balkin, 1988). In other studies, policewomen have been rated higher than policemen by the public, when it comes to handling domestic disputes and showing appropriate concern and sensitivity. Some studies (Bell, 1982; Breci, 1997) found that while citizens generally believed policemen were preferable in violent situations, they also generally approved of policewomen. Still, public misperceptions about women who wear uniforms, patrol the streets, and command other officers continue to exist in some places (Gold, 2000).

Studies of supervisors' attitudes toward policewomen are also scarce, and those that do exist are conflicting. The Washington, DC, study, for example, indicated predominantly negative attitudes on the part of supervisors, while studies in St. Louis and New York showed supervisors to be more positive (Balkin, 1988). One chief put it in these terms: "I could see all kinds of problems . . . jealous wives, injuries. . . . It was a headache I didn't want" (Harris, 1999, p. 18).

Policemen's opinions of their female counterparts have been more well documented and, as previously indicated, have been found to be generally negative. Policemen tend to view policewomen as incompetent and unfit for police work, and working with female police officers does not appear to have a positive effect on such opinions (Balkin, 1988). A good deal of the skepticism among male officers is undoubtedly due to sex role socialization. Even though significant changes have occurred over the past decade with respect to integration of occupations by gender, some occupational groups have been slow to accept such changes. This is perhaps particularly true in occupations imbued with traditional conceptions of masculinity as a required trait, such as the construction trades, airline and fighter pilots, and, of course, the police. With changes brought on by movements for equal rights for women, by hiring better educated officers, and as a result of competent performance of women in the police role, these sex role stereotypes are gradually changing. A study by Grown and Carlson (1993), for example, found that there has been a small shift toward more favorable attitudes concerning female officers, but still about 20 percent of male officers do not want to work with female officers on patrol. Gold states, "Perhaps the problem is that some hard-liners persist in the argument that such changes [more female officers] represent a feminization of policing; that real policing was, and still is, the so-called masculine image of crime-fighting" (2000, p. 160).

Factors Affecting the Performance of Policewomen

Not surprisingly, the greatest source of work-related stress reported by female police officers is male police officers (Wexler & Logan, 1983; Fields, 2000). Bartol, Bergen, and Volckens (1992) found that policewomen experienced stress as a result of working in a male-dominated occupation, but that stress did not appear to affect their job performance, because supervisors evaluated male and female officers as performing the job equally well.

As Balkin (1988, p. 34) points out, the negative attitudes of policemen toward policewomen are most often based in personal belief, not actual experience: "No research has shown that strength is related to an individual's ability to manage success-fully a dangerous situation. . . . There are no reports in the literature of bad outcomes because a policewoman did not have enough strength or aggression."

Others have noted that agility, a cool head, and good communications skills may be more important than strength in dangerous situations (Charles, 1982; Rogers, 1987; McDowell, 1992). Some suggest that the presence of a policewoman may actually help to defuse a potentially violent situation (Sherman, 1975; Homant & Kennedy, 1985; Martin, 1993; Gold, 2000).

In spite of all these defenses of policewomen, many male police officers continue to be highly critical of them. Explanations for this persistent hostility on behalf of male officers are varied. As indicated previously, some suggest that traditional sex roles involving sex-typing of occupations are widely held by male police officers. The presence of women in what has typically been referred to as the police "fraternity" may undermine the sense of masculine identity that accompanies that subculture. Wives of male police officers sometimes object strenuously to their husbands spending eight hours a day with another woman.

Whatever the reason, policemen's attitudes toward policewomen have some very real consequences for both. First, policewomen are continually in the spotlight and must repeatedly prove themselves capable before they have a chance of being accepted as "real" police officers. Some perform most capably under this added strain, but others do not, and those who fail become legend among tradition-oriented male officers. We have heard numerous stories about policewomen who were involved in traffic accidents while on duty, policewomen who failed to qualify with their firearms the first time around, and policewomen who are never the first to arrive at a potentially violent call in their zones. These things do, of course, occur, but they also occur with a good deal of regularity among male police officers.

Second, because male officers often feel uncomfortable about dealing with potentially violent situations when their partners are women, they sometimes overprotect policewomen by instructing them to stay in the car, to stay on the radio, or to stay away from the altercation. Thus, policewomen are sometimes denied the opportunity to demonstrate their skills. Further, the same officers who required their female partners not to get involved may then criticize these partners to other male officers for failing to provide adequate backup. As Cohen (2000, p. 3) puts it, "Police work requires thinking and courage. It can be a physical job, yes, but it's first and foremost a mental exercise. As big and strong as I am, I've been tossed around like a rag doll—and any idiot with a gun and a will to do so can easily shoot me dead. We survive and get the job done by using our heads. I would sooner work with a female cop with brains and guts than any male cop who's stupid or timid, regardless of the size of his biceps."

Third, negative attitudes toward policewomen have undoubtedly played a role in promotional processes. Taking orders from a policewoman when one has no respect for women in the occupation is a bitter pill to swallow. The ability of policewomen to perform at supervisory levels thus remains to be tested, but there is little reason to believe that, given adequate preparation, they will prove less worthy than their male counterparts (Koenig, 1978; Martin, 1993).

Nonetheless, when women enter a male-dominated workplace, there is an excellent chance that they will be viewed as "tokens," at least initially. As has been noted (Kanter, 1977; Martin, 1993), this means they will be subjected to enhanced scrutiny, that differences between themselves and those who have traditionally filled the work role will be polarized, and they will be stereotyped. The stress implied by token status is over and above that experienced by others occupying the same role who are not considered tokens.

Alex (1969), in discussing the stresses experienced by black police officers, used the term *double marginality* to refer to the fact that black officers were not fully accepted by their white coworkers and were also distrusted by other blacks. The same term may be applied to women in police work who are not fully accepted as equals by their male coworkers and who often find other women (especially male officers' wives) somewhat suspect of their motives for entering police work. Based on these considerations, we might expect that policewomen would have relatively high turnover rates, and this appears to be the case at least in some departments (Fry, 1983; Harris, 1999). Martin (1993) found that such turnover is due to discrimination on behalf of male officers, lack of equal promotional opportunities, and the constant pressure to prove themselves. As might be expected, African American policewomen are even more likely to be viewed as outsiders within their own departments. There is evidence that they are often isolated from both white women and black men (Pogrebin, Dodge & Chatman, 2000).

Sexual harassment continues to be a problem for policewomen. According to McDowell (1992), the harassment that persists in many police agencies includes lewd jokes transmitted over police radios and sexists remarks in the halls. Martin (1993, p. 336) notes, "Frequent sexual jokes and gossip remind the women that they are desired sexual objects, visible outsiders, and feared competitors." Kathleen Burke, a former New York City police officers concludes, "On the surface, women seem to have all the opportunities that the men have. They are, for the most part, in every unit in the police department [New York City]. But, have all the discrimination fences been knocked down? Absolutely not, not until the last dinosaur's bones are buried" (House, 1993, p. 144). Pogrebin, Dodge, and Chatman (2000) note that patterns of sexual and racial discrimination continue to plague black policewomen. In a 1995 survey of female officers in a medium-sized department, 68 percent of the respondents indicated they had been sexually harassed while on the job (Polisar & Milgram, 1998).

Interestingly, in other studies, male officers were particularly critical of female officers who did perform well and who did not allow themselves to be treated in condescending fashion. These women were frequently stereotyped as "bitchy," "castrating," or "lesbians" by male officers (Martin, 1993; Gold, 2000).

Further, Poole and Pogrebin (1988, p. 54) found that "after just three years on the force, only a small proportion of women officers still aspire to rise in the police organization. It is likely that these officers have recognized in a relatively short period of time that few women actually get promoted; consequently policewomen lack a variety of female role models in higher ranks whom they could realistically strive to emulate." According to Gold (2000), barriers still remain when it comes to women advancing through the ranks. With very few exceptions, women are virtually absent from decision-making ranks and positions of authority. In the 1990s, there were only about 120 female chiefs of police in the United States (Polisar & Milgram, 1998). One national survey of policewomen found that 40 percent felt that their skills were being underutilized in their departments. Those with higher educational levels were more likely to report that their skills were not being utilized properly (Garrison, Grant, & McCormick, 1988).

The advantages of hiring women for police work are perhaps best summarized by Linn and Price (1985): It is illegal to discriminate on the basis of gender in hiring and promoting police officers; women are often better at collecting certain kinds of police information than are men; the presence of female officers shows commitment to serving the entire community; diverse views are needed when formulating police policies; and policewomen demonstrate that women can successfully occupy positions of authority and respect and thereby serve as role models to the community.

Linn and Price (1985, p. 75) indicate that the policeman is often resistant to change, in part, "because so little of his world is safe and predictable. His opposition to women on patrol stems in part from his not knowing *how* to treat a woman as a peer. Should he watch his language? Offer to drive? Buy her coffee? Talk about sports? Initiate friendliness? Could he share hours of tension, or even hours of boredom, and not become too involved?"

While these problems may be overcome, dealing with policemen's wives may be more difficult. Policemen's wives have protested over the assignment of women to patrol duty. The manifest concern in such demonstrations has been the safety of the male officer, but questions of fidelity appear to be not far beneath the surface.

Linn and Price (1985) conclude that the outlook for policewomen is not entirely bleak in spite of the difficulties discussed. In some communities, policewomen have been accepted by male coworkers and the public alike. Further, there is evidence that minorities and better educated officers are more likely to accept women, and their numbers are increasing. Because women account for about 51 percent of the population, and because the evidence is clear that they are capable of performing a wide variety of police functions, they should be viewed as a valuable asset in the struggle to make police departments more representative of the communities they serve and, ultimately, in the battle to reintegrate police and community. As McDowell (1992, p. 70) indicates, female police officers "are bringing a distinctly different, and valuable, set of skills to the streets and the station house that may change the way the police are perceived in the community." This is clearly one of the goals of community policing, and female officers who display negotiation and mediation skills are an important part of this movement (Fields, 2000). See Highlight 6.1, which discusses gender differences in the costs of police brutality and misconduct as a result of civil liability lawsuits.

■ ■ ■ ■ ■ ▬▬▬▬▬▬▬▬▬▬▬▬▬▬▬▬▬▬▬▬▬▬▬▬▬▬▬▬▬▬▬▬

HIGHLIGHT 6.1

GENDER DIFFERENCES IN POLICE BRUTALITY LAWSUITS: MEN COST MORE

Gender Balance in Law Enforcement Urged

With police abuse cases grabbing headlines nationwide, a new study released by the Feminist Majority Foundation and the National Center for Women & Policing documents huge gender differences in the cost of police brutality and misconduct as a result of civil liability lawsuits. The study shows male officers in the Los Angeles Police Department (LAPD) are involved in excessive force and misconduct lawsuits at rates substantially higher than their female counterparts.

"The gender gap in police brutality lawsuits is striking. The City of Los Angeles paid out $63.4 million between 1990–1999 in lawsuits involving male officers for use of excessive force, sexual assault, and domestic violence. By contrast, $2.8 million was paid out on female officers for excessive force lawsuits—and not one female officer was named as a defendant in a sexual assault or

domestic violence case," said Katherine Spillar, national coordinator of the Feminist Majority Foundation.

"Male officer payouts in cases of brutality and misconduct exceeded female officer payouts by a ratio of 23:1," continued Spillar. "Moreover, male officers disproportionately accounted for the lawsuit payouts involving killings and assault and battery." Male officer payouts for killings exceeded female officer payouts by a ratio of 43:1 and for assault and battery male officer payouts exceeded female officer payouts by a ratio of 32:1. Over the same period, male officers serving in a patrol capacity outnumbered women LAPD officers by a much lower ratio of 4:1.

"We know that women do the job of policing equally as well as men, responding to similar calls and encountering similar dangers,"

(continued)

HIGHLIGHT 6.1   Continued

said Penny Harrington, director of the National Center for Women & Policing and former chief of police of Portland, Oregon. "But more importantly for public officials in Los Angeles—and across the country—this new study shows that increasing women on the force holds the key for substantially decreasing police violence and its cost to taxpayers," continued Harrington.

"Additionally, our research revealed other types of costly male police officer violence," said Eleanor Smeal, president of the Feminist Majority Foundation. "Our study uncovered $10.4 million in payouts in lawsuits involving male officers for sexual assault, sexual molestation, and domestic violence," continued Smeal.

Noting that domestic violence calls are the single largest category of calls made to police departments, Smeal observed, "The real cost when male officers commit domestic violence and sexual assault is even greater than the $10.4 million paid out—both in financial and human terms. Failure by police to properly respond to crimes of violence against women has high consequences for women in the community."

The new study confirms earlier research both in the United States and internationally that shows women police officers rely less on physical force and more on verbal skills in handling altercations than male police officers. As a result, women police officers are less likely to become involved in problems with excessive force and are better at defusing potentially violent confrontations with citizens.

The report comes as the Los Angeles City Council is debating a series of reform measures put forward by the US Department of Justice in the wake of the unfolding LAPD Rampart Division police misconduct and brutality scandal. In response to the scandal, the Feminist Majority Foundation and the National Center for Women & Policing have called on the Department of Justice and Los Angeles city officials to incorporate gender balance hiring requirements in the negotiated consent decree.

"Hiring equal numbers of women in the LAPD would go further toward reducing police brutality and misconduct than anything else the Department could do," said Spillar. "More than nine years ago, the Christopher Commission report recommended hiring more women to reduce police brutality, and the Los Angeles City Council directed the LAPD to gender balance its academy classes," continued Spillar. "Unfortunately, the LAPD has dragged its heels, squandering an opportunity to hire significantly more women during the recent period of expansion. The consequences have now come home to roost."

Nationwide, women are severely underrepresented on police departments—averaging only 14.3% of police officers across the country. "The numbers of women in law enforcement are kept artificially low by widespread discriminatory hiring and selection practices," explained Harrington. "Not only is this unfair to women who are seeking law enforcement careers, but our study shows that depriving women jobs in policing is costly to taxpayers and results in more police brutality."

Feminist Daily Newswire; September 18, 2000.

Recruiting Female Officers

Although we discussed recruitment and selection of police officers in detail in Chapter 4, the challenges involved in successful recruitment and retention of women and minorities deserve special attention. These challenges and possible remedies are discussed here with respect to women and are addressed later in this chapter as they relate to racial and ethnic minorities.

According to the National Center for Women & Policing (2001, p. 21), "In today's economy, law enforcement agencies are facing enormous challenges recruiting qualified candidates, yet traditional strategies for recruitment frequently overlook an entire pool of qualified applicants—women." And Gold states, "That society needs more women law enforcement officers is not in question. The controversy seems to be over how long it will take to break through the barriers and achieve gender equity, and how to eliminate the barriers" (2000, p. 159).

The National Center for Women & Policing (2001, pp. 21–27) cites a number of advantages for police agencies that hire and retain women:

Enlarging the pool of competent candidates

Reducing the likelihood of the use of excessive force by officers

Assistance in implementing community-oriented policing

Improving law enforcement's response to violence against women

Reducing the incidence of sex discrimination and sexual harassment claims

Bringing about beneficial changes in policy for all officers (selection standards, etc.).

Recruitment efforts for women need to focus on positive images of female officers and should be conducted in places women frequent—women's centers, shopping malls, women's sporting events, and walk-in centers in minority neighborhoods—because traditional techniques have been largely unsuccessful in attracting large numbers of female applicants; thus a focus on "women-specific" strategies is required (Harris, 1999). Displaying posters, developing and distributing brochures, and using female officers as recruiters are among the strategies that may be employed. Reaching out to girls in high school may be required in order to encourage women to consider policing as a possible career. Designing and employing more female-friendly equipment (e.g., uniforms designed for women rather than altered male uniforms) may help retain female officers once they have been hired. Emphasis on programs designed to accommodate work–family issues and the value of insurance and retirement programs also may help recruitment efforts, which should take advantage of all available media resources (Campbell, Christman, & Feigelson, 2000).

Attracting female applicants may be less difficult than retaining them once hired. According to Kranda (1998), "The challenge lies in retaining those highly qualified women in whom the agencies have made significant investments during the recruiting process. . . . One tool that has helped some agencies to raise their retention rates for female recruits has been the establishment of a formal mentoring process." Often, this process begins even before the new recruit begins her job when a veteran officer contacts her and lets her know what to expect at the workplace. The mentor then continues to serve as an information resource and confidant.

Groups such as the National Center for Women in Policing, the National Association of Women Law Enforcement Executives, and the International Association for Women Police are available to provide guidance on recruitment and retention efforts (Gold, 2000).

BLACK POLICE OFFICERS

As noted earlier, some of the most problematic encounters involving the police occur between white police officers and minority citizens. Encounters between the police and blacks, Hispanics, Native Americans, and, increasingly, Asians indicate that a good deal of hostility remains as a result of racist attitudes, historical distrust, and past discrimination. A national survey of 1,223 adults found broad agreement that the United States has moved toward racial equality since 1963, and 71 percent of those surveyed felt equality is attainable. Yet 40 percent felt that racial equality would not occur during their lifetimes, 55 percent said that American society is racist overall, and 43 percent felt that minorities do not receive equal treatment in the criminal justice system. Interestingly, 61 percent of blacks surveyed felt discrimination occurs in the criminal justice system, compared to 40 percent of white respondents (Langer, 1988). Because the police are a reflection of society, it is not surprising that they sometimes have poor working relationships with minority group members. In fact, the National Advisory Commission on Civil Disorders found that poor minority relations were an important factor in precipitating the ghetto riots of the 1960s and recommended increased hiring of minority officers as one possible solution to the problem.

Racial tensions remain high in some parts of the United States as indicated by the now famous Howard Beach incident that occurred in 1987 and the Rodney King beating in Los Angeles in 1991. In the former case, three black men wandered into the predominantly white community of Howard Beach and were attacked by a group of white teenagers. One of the black men was hit by a car and killed while trying to flee his pursuers, and another was seriously injured. A jury eventually found three white teens guilty of manslaughter and assault charges, but the city was portrayed as an example of the racial division characterizing New York City. Protests by hundreds of blacks over various forms of racial discrimination followed (*Newsweek*, 1988).

In 1991, several white police officers were caught on videotape beating, shooting with a stun gun, and stomping Rodney King, a black motorist who had attempted to outrun the police. When the jury acquitted the officers, parts of Los Angeles erupted in violence, including the near fatal beating of a white truck driver, Reginald Denny, by blacks (Church, 1992).

In December of 1989, two black teenagers filed a federal lawsuit against two white police officers who allegedly picked the teens up in a black neighborhood, harassed them, and dropped them off in a largely white neighborhood, where they were later beaten. The suit also names the city of Chicago on grounds that there is a pattern of failure to discipline police officers who violate the civil rights of other citizens (*Journal Star*, 1989, p. 12).

The proportion of black (and other minority) officers remains relatively low, and police minority relations continue to be problematic. In fact, the number of black applicants for police positions remains extremely low in some areas, and tension between black and white officers periodically run high. This may be due to a perception among blacks that they are unwelcome or at least suspect in many police agencies (Fountain, 1991). Given these data, one may wonder why some blacks apply for police positions.

Alex (1969) noted some time ago that police work is attractive to blacks for the same reasons it is attractive to whites—reasonable salary, job security, and reasonable pension (Alex, 1969). In addition, police departments have a good deal to gain by hiring blacks in terms of the benefits of "protective coloration." Black police officers can often gather information that would be extremely difficult for white officers to gather; having black police officers on the force may make charges of racial brutality against the police less likely; and federal funding is partly dependent on equal employment opportunity and affirmative action programs. The latter benefit is self-explanatory.

It is also obvious that white police officers, whether undercover or not, will arouse suspicion in predominantly black groups. And, with respect to police brutality toward minority groups, it is apparent that when black police officers resort to the use of force in dealing with black citizens, the issue of *interracial* brutality is avoided (though the issue of police brutality remains).

The best reason for hiring and promoting qualified black applicants is the fact that a tremendous amount of talent is wasted if they are excluded from police work. Because there is no evidence that white officers perform the policing function better than black officers, it is ethically and morally appropriate to hire applicants who are black. Further, integrated police departments are more representative of the public they serve, and black officers may serve as much needed role models in the community.

Problems for Black Police Officers

Kuykendall and Burns (1980) indicate that blacks first served as police officers in Washington, DC, in 1861. Their numbers remained low until World War II, when gradual increases began. These early black officers were largely confined to black neighborhoods, and their powers of arrest did not extend to whites. In some cities, restrictions on the powers of black officers remained in place until the 1960s (Kuykendall & Burns, 1980). Leinen (1984) found that in the mid-1960s, only twenty-two law enforcement agencies employed blacks in positions above the level of patrol officers. A 1971 report of the Commission on Civil Rights affirmed the need to bring minority officers into law enforcement (Margolis, 1971). Litigation involving discrimination in hiring and promotion followed in the 1970s and 1980s, and consent decrees of the type discussed earlier in this book frequently resulted, leading to the hiring of more minority (particularly black) officers.

During the same period, the National Black Police Association and the National Organization for Black Law Enforcement Executives were established to promote minority hiring, improved community relations, and fair hiring practices (Sullivan, 1989). When these policies came under fire, the U.S. Supreme Court responded by handing down an endorsement of racial quotas in police departments that were recalcitrant in hiring and promoting minority group members. In 1987, the Court upheld promotional quotas requiring that the Alabama State Police promote one black officer for each white officer promoted until blacks held 25 percent of the top ranks in the department (Gest, 1987).

In 1992, President Bush signed into law a new civil rights act that prohibited the use of adjusting tests scores based on race, gender, religion, or national origin, except in specified cases involving, for example, physical differences between the sexes or cases in which preferential treatment is accorded to rectify past discrimination (Sauls, 1992). The effect of this new civil rights legislation is to continue a trend toward recognizing reverse discrimination, originating with *Bakke v. California* and carrying over into the late 1980s. The new legislation and an accumulating body of case law has, to some extent at least, led to a movement away from court-imposed quotas and toward new forms of ranking candidates for both entry-level and promotional positions (Gaines, Kappeler, & Vaughn, 1994, p. 73).

Black police officers confront a number of problems in addition to those confronted by their white counterparts. While many black officers are assigned to police the ghettos in hopes of alleviating racial tensions, not all black citizens prefer black officers to white. Jackson and Wallach (1973) and Alex (1969, 1976) have noted that black officers sometimes have more trouble dealing with black citizens than do white officers. As mentioned previously, Alex (1969) found that black police officers suffer from double marginality resulting from the fact that they are sometimes distrusted by their white counterparts and are often viewed as traitors by other members of the black community. Black officers may be perceived as more black than blue (i.e., police-oriented) by white officers and more blue than black by others in the black community.

As a result, black officers often report difficulties in dealing with black citizens, particularly young black males, who call on these officers to see themselves, and to act, first as racial brothers and sisters, not as police officers. Taunts and slogans indicating the role of black officers as "lackeys" for white society are commonplace in encounters between black officers and young black males. Being the target of such epithets places an additional burden on black officers to retain their composure in confrontations; and not all are able to do so. Thus, encounters between black officers and other black citizens are not always civil. In fact, there is some evidence that police brutality is largely an intraracial phenomenon, at least in high-crime areas in urban centers (Reiss, 1968).

Hacker (1992, p. 189), in discussing the fact that blacks are three times more likely to die from a police officer's bullet than are whites, notes, "As it happens, a disproportionately high number of these killings of blacks are by black policemen, which suggests that departments tend to give black officers assignments where they encounter suspects of their own race. . . . For many years, police forces hired few if any blacks; now there is a tendency to use blacks to control blacks."

Jacobs and Cohen (1978, p. 171) concluded, "Black policemen, like their white colleagues, must still arrest unwilling suspects, intervene in domestic squabbles, and keep order on ghetto streets. In the end, they represent the interests of order, property, and the status quo in an environment where large numbers of unemployed minority youth among others do not share this same commitment."

Encounters between black officers and white citizens also do not always proceed smoothly. As recently as 1988, citizens of a Chicago suburb called police to report that a black man was "impersonating" a police officer, wearing a police uniform, and driving a patrol car. This officer received, on a daily basis, "racial insults and humiliation not only from the people he has sworn to protect but also from some of his fellow officers upon whom his life may depend" (Gup, 1988, p. 25). Other black officers also report being subjected to racial slurs, distrust, and outright avoidance. Some whites are concerned about whether black officers will respond first as members of their race or as police officers when dealing with interracial situations. In some parts of the country, blacks in positions of authority are uncommon, and whites are apprehensive about being subject to such authority. In a multiracial society, these problems are perhaps inevitable to some extent, as we divide the world into "we" and "they" groups, interact with and tend to support members of the "we" group, and distrust members of the "they" groups. As long as skin color continues to be as important as, or more important than, an individual's actions, encounters between police officers and other citizens of different racial or ethnic groups are likely to remain uncomfortable, regardless of the qualifications and expertise of the officers involved.

It is important to note here that in spite of the many difficulties confronting black police officers, they report that their relationships with white officers, at least while on duty, are satisfactory. They feel confident that white officers will back them up in emergency situations, and they indicate that they would do the same for white officers. While there may be little socialization after hours, on-duty encounters are likely to be civil (Alex, 1969; Leinen, 1984). There are exceptions, of course. In some instances, black officers have formed their own associations in police departments, with agendas different from, and sometimes in sharp contrast to, those of white officers. In others, racial tension persists for other reasons (see Highlight 6.2). In 1985, for example, a federal judge awarded almost $600,000 to the Afro-American Police League of the Chicago Police Department and seven of its members after finding that discrimination had occurred in assignments, promotions, and other areas.

■ ■ ■ ■ ■

HIGHLIGHT 6.2
INTERRACIAL POLICING BREEDS RESENTMENT FROM BOTH SIDES

Last week I wrote a column saying that white cops have become so gun shy about being charged with racism, and thereby losing jobs, promotions, and careers, that many of them have stopped enforcing the law when blacks are involved. As part of the column I printed a letter from a cop in PG County saying that, yes, that is exactly what he and many of his colleagues are doing. (Incidentally, by coincidence there was a piece in National Review Online last week, from a cop in LA, who said the same thing. Cops really are backing off. It's not something I invented.)

The response I got by email was about what I expected, but worth reporting anyway. White cops said essentially, "Yep. You got it right. I'm not going to be made into a sacrificial goat enforc-ing laws for people who don't want them enforced."

I got two letters from black cops, who said that when they enforced the law in black neighborhoods, they were accused of selling out, of being Uncle Toms. Black cops don't face having their careers ruined—how do you charge a black cop with racism for giving tickets to blacks?—but they seem to get guff.

But the angriest mail came from blacks who weren't cops. The thrust was that cops single out blacks, pick on them, harass them, and refuse to enforce the law evenhandedly.

Rationally this might be debated on any number of grounds. It doesn't matter. Blacks believe, believe deeply, that they are victims of the

(continued)

HIGHLIGHT 6.2 Continued

police. For them, this isn't debatable, can barely be discussed. The sense of grievance is so nearly universal as to approach the predictability of gravitation. They are very angry about it.

Not all of these letters are angry, though. Some are almost pleading. "Why can't the police be fair? That's all we ask." I'm never sure what to think. The sense of being victimized is powerful among blacks, and doesn't always involve the police. I've seen the polls showing that a majority of blacks believe either that AIDS was invented by whites to kill blacks, or else that it may have been.

According to newspaper stories, many blacks believe that the drug epidemic was engineered by whites to destroy blacks, that whites put something in various soft drinks to make blacks impotent. I get email saying the same things, especially about drugs being targeted at blacks. To whites, these charges are nonsense. To a lot of blacks, they aren't.

My guess is that the unbridgeable chasm (which is exactly what it is) between the views of the races is in part, but only in part, the fault of the press. Any racially motivated mistreatment of blacks is national news. For example, there was the black guy dragged to death behind a truck by whites, or the black in New York who was sodomized with a broom handle by white cops. Both happened. Both were racial.

But racially motivated atrocities committed by blacks are not played up. They occur: Blacks aren't saints any more than whites. The recent Wichita massacre of whites by blacks is an example. It was all over the Internet, but not much in the press, and not too many blacks spend a lot of time on the Net.

If I were black, and saw unending news stories about brutality by white cops, and never saw anything about misbehavior by black cops, or blacks at all, I would not unreasonably conclude that blacks were being singled out.

The practical point, it seems to me, is that the resentment of cops among blacks is both potent and, in the foreseeable future, irremediable. It's too deep-seated, too vigorously reinforced by the press, too much a part of the worldview of blacks.

SO WHAT TO DO?

As I've said before, a lot of tension might be eliminated by having neighborhoods predominately of one race policed by cops of that race. Same departments, same training, same pay, same equipment, but different beats. Blacks didn't burn Los Angeles because cops were acquitted of beating Rodney King, but because white cops beat him, and were acquitted. The potential for explosion is still there, in many cities, and interracial encounters with cops are the likely spark.

Which is better—to keep pushing interracial policing that doesn't work very well, because we think it ought to work, or go to same-race policing that people seem to want, but think they shouldn't want?

I'd like to know what people, certainly including blacks, think about the idea.

Promotions of black officers appear to be problematic in many departments. There is a general consensus that officers of all minority groups are greatly underrepresented at levels above the patrol level (Williams, 1988; Sullivan, 1989, p. 342). In part, this may be due to their relatively recent entry into police in many locales, but it is also in part due to institutional discrimination (e.g., biased testing procedures, job assignments, and educational requirements) and to the fact that federal agencies wishing to satisfy affirmative action requirements often recruit minorities from the ranks of municipal departments. The increasing number of black politicians occupying positions as mayors and chiefs of police may, over time, alleviate the promotional dilemma.

HISPANIC POLICE OFFICERS

Demographics in the United States are changing rapidly. As this occurs, police agencies in some communities are burdened with high rates of crime in many ethnic communities. According to the National Crime Prevention Council (1995, p. 5), "As was true with newcomers in earlier periods of immigration, many recent immigrants and refugees have tended to remain in physical and cultural isolation, leaving them vulnerable to crime victimization both from members of their own ethnic group and the indigenous community. When they have had occasion to interact with police, the results have often been alienating and laced with misunderstanding." Police agencies characterized by ethnic diversity serve the public better, especially under the community and problem-solving approaches, by providing sworn officers who can deliver effective services within their own ethnic communities and well as to the community as a whole. Hiring minority officers (as we have seen in the preceding section) helps the police to break down barriers that might hinder an effective partnership (NCPC, 1995, p. 11).

The Hispanic population in the United States, for example, has increased dramatically in the past decade. The Hispanic population was estimated at almost thirty million in 1997, up by more than eight 8 million over 1990 numbers, making Hispanics one of the fastest growing minorities in the United States. About 25 percent of Hispanic families are living below the poverty line (Schaefer, 2000, p. 300). All of these facts taken together indicate that police contacts with Hispanics are already frequent and are likely to increase dramatically as this minority group increases in size. These contacts are likely to be somewhat problematic because of language differences as well as the fact that, in addition to whatever immediate reason the police have for initiating contact with Hispanics, they may also be dealing with illegal immigrants, who can be deported if detected and reported to the Immigration and Naturalization Service. Further, some authorities indicate that Hispanics tend to view the police in a less favorable light than do whites and about as favorably as do blacks (Carter, 1983; Bartollas & Hahn, 1999, p. 323).

Hispanics in the United States are not a homogeneous group, but consist of those whose origins are in Mexico, Cuba, Puerto Rico, and other Central and South American countries. Further, some of these groups are concentrated in specific areas (Cubans in southern Florida, Mexican Americans in the Southwest), although most metropolitan areas include sizable numbers of Hispanics. In these areas, if the police are to be representative of the communities they serve, Hispanic officers must be recruited.

The rationale for recruiting Hispanic officers is much the same as for recruiting women and blacks, with the additional consideration of being bilingual and, ideally perhaps, bicultural. It should be noted here that if being bilingual is an important job-related qualification, this should be specified when advertising the vacancies, because there are many individuals with Hispanic (and Chinese, Korean, and Japanese) surnames who do not speak Spanish (or Chinese, Korean, and Japanese). Because many Hispanics are not fluent in English, police officers serving in heavily Hispanic areas need to speak at least basic Spanish in order to render assistance as well as to engage in order maintenance and law enforcement functions. Further, a basic understanding of Hispanic culture is likely to make the officer who polices in Hispanic neighborhoods more comfortable with his surroundings and more understanding of the lifestyle encountered.

There is little information about Hispanic police officers, in part because their numbers have been very small until recently. In a study of fifty of the largest police departments in the United States, Walker (1989) found that 42 percent of those responding reported significant increases in the number of Hispanic officers employed between the years 1983 and 1988, about 11 percent reported reductions, and 17 percent reported no change. A study by Carter (1986) concluded that Hispanic police officers in an Hispanic American community perceive that they are discriminated against by the police organization, even though the department in question consisted of 70 percent minority group members.

A study by Winters (1991) of Hispanic police officers in the Chicago area discovered that fewer dollars for policing and a high dropout rate among Hispanic high school students accounted for many of the hiring problems that existed. Carter and Sapp (1991) noted that college education is still disproportionately inaccessible to blacks and Hispanics, raising the possibility that a college-degree requirement for entry-level officers may be discriminatory.

The language barrier, physical size requirements, the general belief that Hispanics were not highly sought after by police departments, and the belief that other occupations or professions were to be more highly prized by Hispanics probably account for the relatively small number of Hispanic officers in the past. With changing physical requirements, greater emphasis on unbiased, job-related tests, and affirmative action programs, opportunities for Hispanics in policing have increased.

What we know suggests that Hispanics seek police positions for the same reasons as officers from all other racial and ethnic groups and share basically the same problems, including the double marginality and discrimination in promotions and assignments discussed previously with respect to black police officers. In 1988, for example, a U.S. District Court judge found that hundreds of Latino agents had been victims of discrimination by the FBI. The judge found that Hispanics were often given unpleasant assignments that were rarely meted out to their white counterparts. Kennedy (1998, p. A2) noted, "A frequent complaint supported by the preponderance of the evidence is that an Hispanic agent with five years of Bureau tenure who has ridden the 'Taco Circuit' may not have the experience of an Anglo on duty for two years." The obvious result of such discrimination can be seen in terms of promotions, which often depend on a variety of different police experiences as well as other factors.

By 1997, several states had made progress in employing Hispanic police officers in departments with at least one hundred sworn officers. Forty-two percent of New Mexico's state police officers were Hispanic, while some 20 percent of sworn employees with the Texas Department of Public Safety were Hispanic. About 15 percent of sworn employees in the Arizona Department of Public Safety and the California Highway

Patrol were Hispanic. As you can see, these departments are concentrated in the Southwest, and no agency outside of that geographic area reported that more than 10 percent of its sworn personnel were Hispanic (Bureau of Justice Statistics, 1999, p. 263). Reasons for failure to recruit more Hispanics continue to include a history of negative stereotypes of the police in Hispanic communities, lack of interest in law enforcement careers among young Hispanics, misdirected recruitment efforts, and lack of role models (Shusta et al., 1995).

In 1998, over two hundred African American and Hispanic officers were awarded $10,000 each by a U.S. District Court judge, who ruled against the City of Chicago in a case involving discriminatory promotional practices (Bartollas & Hahn, 1999, p. 324). "[P]olice departments across the nation have not treated minorities who wanted to become police officers well. . . . Hispanic/Latino American officers have been largely ignored in examinations of policing in the United States. Consequently, without the benefit of empirical studies, it is difficult to draw many conclusions about these officers as a separate group" (Bartollas & Hahn, 1999, p. 330). The same may be said of Asian American officers.

ASIAN AMERICAN POLICE OFFICERS

As the Asian American population continues to increase, as crime rates in Asian American communities increase, and as Asian Americans become more organized in pursuit of equality, the need for Asian American police officers becomes apparent. While there is little information about Asian American police officers, one study of Chinese American officers has been completed (Lin, 1987). In this study, all 120 Chinese American police officers in New York City were sent questionnaires soliciting information about their attitudes and self-conceptions.

Seventy of the questionnaires were returned, and the results indicate that Chinese American police officers share many of the same problems as other minority officers. For example, over three-fourths of the officers responding indicated that they have good working relationships with other Chinese American officers as well as with officers of all other ethnic groups. However, only 3 percent preferred Chinese American partners, while 41 percent indicated a clear preference for partners who are not Chinese American. Only 7 percent preferred Chinese American supervisors, while 46 percent indicated a preference for supervisors who are not Chinese American. Over two-thirds felt the department should hire more Chinese American police officers, but only 10 percent indicated they would seek the advice of other Chinese American officers with respect to their work. While over 60 percent felt that Chinese Americans would prefer to make complaints to Chinese American officers, only 20 percent expressed a preference for policing in heavily Chinese American neighborhoods. Less than half felt that choosing policing as a career had improved their social status, though 86 percent viewed policing as a worthwhile career, and more than half would encourage friends or relatives to pursue a career in policing. Unlike members of some other minorities in policing, 86 percent agreed that there are promotional opportunities for them in policing, 78 percent felt they were fairly evaluated, and 68 percent agreed that their duties had been fairly assigned.

Lin concludes that Chinese American officers are well integrated into policing in New York City and that they tend to distance themselves from other Chinese Americans in some ways, much as some officers who represent other minority groups tend to distance themselves from their racial or ethnic groups. It appears, as seems to be the case with black officers as well, that Chinese American officers prefer to be viewed first and foremost as police officers, at least while on duty.

Other Asian minorities also require the attention of the police. Refugees from Vietnam, Cambodia, and Laos have formed enclaves in many urban areas, establishing subcultural pockets as their numbers increase. Numerous officers have reported difficulties communicating with, and understanding the culture of, such refugees. Korean and Japanese neighborhoods also exist in cities around the United States, and residents of these areas, too, may present difficulties in terms of providing (or requesting) police services. Further, Asian and Oriental neighborhoods are not the crime-free areas they were once thought to be. There is clear evidence of Chinese involvement in organized numbers operations and racketeering, of Vietnamese involvement in drug rings, of Korean involvement in illegal massage parlors, and so on (O'Connor, 1985).

The Houston Police Department continues to try to recruit police officers that reflect the varying Asian cultures and languages of the community. The department has established the Asian-American Office of the Year Award to recognize the contributions made by officers of Asian decent (*Crime Control Digest*, 1999).

RECRUITING AND RETAINING MINORITY POLICE OFFICERS

The recruitment and promotion of qualified minority group members is essential for several reasons. When police agencies do not represent the communities they serve in terms of race and ethnicity, and perhaps to some extent gender as well, suspicion and distrust arise among members of both the police organization and the minority groups in question. Research has shown that interaction that occurs among those equally well qualified for the positions they occupy tends to reduce such suspicion and distrust. Further, understanding and communicating with members of different racial and ethnic groups that are characterized by different cultural or subcultural values, attitudes, and beliefs are essential for any public servant in a multicultural, multiethnic society. In addition, minority group members who become police officers may serve as living proof that it is possible to "get up and get out" for minority youngsters who need such role models. Finally, equal treatment, regardless of race, ethnicity, religion, or gender, is the foundation for a truly democratic society.

However, there may be a downside to minority recruitment. In some cases, minority group members are recruited or promoted for reasons other than ability and competency. When this occurs, members of the dominant group are adversely affected, and a backlash may be expected. Minority group members, whether qualified or not, are in the spotlight in many police organizations. Their behavior is critically scrutinized at every turn, and this is especially true if the standards according to which they were hired are different from those applied to dominant group members. This may make the minority group members feel as if they are on trial or have been singled out for close observation and criticism, increasing the stress under which they operate, which, in turn, may make it more difficult for them to perform well.

In some cases, as a result of the desire to correct past wrongs as quickly as possible, some personnel are hired and promoted who should not have been. When the City of Miami responded to demands from minority communities that more minorities be hired by consenting to hire 80 percent minorities, minority citizens were pleased, but police administrators and many white police officers were outraged. In what some perceive as a direct result of hiring and promoting large numbers of minority group members in a relatively short (seven-year) period, some twenty-five Miami police officers have been arrested for crimes ranging from burglary to murder, the morale of the police is extremely low, and there is considerable talk about a need for change in city and department administration (Dorschner, 1987). Lott (2000), in a cross-sectional study of U.S. cities between 1987 and 1993, found that lowering hiring standards in order to recruit more racial and ethnic minority officers reduced the overall quality of officers hired and led to increased crime rates.

The solution to this dilemma is obvious but difficult to achieve. In simple terms, race, ethnicity, and gender should not be considerations when hiring or promoting police personnel. There is no evidence to support the belief that any of these factors determines success, or lack of success, in policing. Eliminating these factors in the hiring and promotional process means developing tests that are not inherently biased in terms of such factors, and herein lies the difficulty. Such tests are likely to be considerably different from those traditionally employed and are likely to be perceived as inferior to those taken by officers who were hired in the past. Of course, *different* does not necessarily imply *inferior*, either in testing or with respect to race, ethnicity, and gender, and we must find ways to make this point clearly and with certainty.

As is the case with recruitment efforts aimed at women, minority recruitment efforts must overcome a number of obstacles. First, of course, members of minorities must be reached, and many conventional efforts fail to do so. Use of minority publications, recruitment efforts directed at colleges and universities, and recruitment efforts aimed at recognizing and supporting high school students who have an interest in law enforcement have all shown positive results. Enlisting the aid of national organizations such as the NAACP, local church leaders, and civic and local leaders who are members of minority groups also may prove beneficial. Addressing the issues confronting minorities entering policing and moving to new communities with the help of the resources mentioned is crucial. Questions concerning establishment of a "comfort level" at work and in the community should be addressed. If the new officer is the first black, Asian, or Hispanic officer hired by the agency, he is bound to have concerns about acceptance, both in the agency and in the larger community. These questions may extend to family members and their acceptance within the new community. Civic and religious leaders may help to answer some of these questions.

Recruitment teams that include women and/or minorities also may help in minority recruitment, as may recruitment efforts of current employees. Some departments have instituted incentive pay for successful recruitment (McKeever & Kranda,

2000). Other departments have found that developing citizen police academies to familiarize the public with police activities is a beneficial strategy. Community speaking engagements by officers reflecting diversity and interest in minority recruitment, development of linkages with the military, and formation of partnerships with the media also are worthwhile minority recruitment activities (McKeever & Kranda, 2000).

Until the suggested reforms in hiring and promoting become widespread, we must work hard when dealing with biases of those already employed in police work. Occupational discrimination continues to occur on a regular basis in various squad rooms, locker rooms, and patrol cars. While most police officers are smart enough to understand that racial slurs to other citizens are likely to lead to disciplinary action sooner or later, many continue to use such terms among themselves and in regard to minority officers. Indeed, to be more accepted into the fraternity, some minority group members use derogatory terms to describe members of their own racial or ethnic groups, allowing white officers to rationalize their own behavior by pointing to this fact. In spite of their lack of widespread popularity, human relations and community relations courses need to be offered on a regular basis, if for no other reason than to combat occupational discrimination that too often becomes institutionalized.

To sum up the current situation with respect to minority police officers, we offer the following observations. Minority officers (women excepted) have largely achieved representation commensurate with their population share and now have the same legal rights and responsibilities as other police officers. However, it is clear that minority officers still face discrimination in duty assignments and promotion. While numerous law enforcement agencies have made attempts to eliminate discrimination in hiring and promoting minority officers, this has proven to be a difficult and complex task. Minority recruits sometimes lack the skills necessary to gain access to higher education, and many do not compete well using traditional measures such as written tests. As a result of these factors, court decisions, and civil rights legislation, police entry-level and promotional requirements have sometimes been changed. Such changes have caused some to argue that police agencies are lowering their standards and recruiting unqualified minorities.

These fears that hiring minorities for police work will result in a more negative image of the police, based on lower standards and performance, remain real for many white, male police officers. It is our belief that such changes will lead to better, more representative police departments and that changing standards so that they are equitable to members of both sexes and all racial and ethnic groups need not be equated with lowering standards and poor performance.

DISCUSSION QUESTIONS

1. Why and how have women and minority group members been excluded from police work over the years?

2. Summarize the research relating to the performance of policewomen on patrol. Are you convinced that policewomen are as capable as policemen? Why or why not?

3. What are the basic advantages police departments gain when hiring members of racial or ethnic minorities?

4. Do affirmative action programs sometimes result in reverse discrimination? What pressures do affirmative action programs place on minority group members who are hired?

5. What stresses do minority officers experience in addition to those experienced by white police officers?

6. What steps can be taken to address occupational discrimination? To improve understanding among police officers of different racial or ethnic groups?

REFERENCES

Alex, N. (1969). *Black in blue.* New York: Appleton-Century-Crofts.
———. (1976). *New York cops talk back.* New York: Wiley.
Balkin, J. (1988). Why policemen don't like policewomen. *Journal of Police Science and Administration, 16,* 29–37.
Bartlett, H. W., & Rosenblum, A. (1977). *Policewomen effectiveness.* Denver, CO: Denver Civil Service Commission.
Bartol, C. R., Bergen, G. T., & Volckens, J. S. (1992). Women in small-town policing: Job performance and stress. *Criminal Justice and Behavior, 19,* 240–260.
Bartollas, C., & Hahn, L. S. (1999). *Policing in America.* Boston: Allyn & Bacon.
Bell, D. J. (1982). Policewomen—Myths and reality. *Journal of Police Science and Administration, 10,* 112–120.
Block, P., & Anderson, D. (1974). *Policewomen on patrol: Final report.* Washington, DC: Urban Institute.
Breci, M. G. (1997). Female officers on patrol: Public perceptions in the 1990s. *Journal of Crime & Justice, 20,* 153–166.
Bureau of Justice Statistics. (1999). *Law enforcement management and administrative statistics, 1997: Data for individual state and local agencies with more than 100 officers.* Washington, DC: U.S. Government Printing Office.
Campbell, D. J., Christman, B. D., & Feigelson, M. E. (2000). Improving the recruitment of women in policing: An investigation of women's attitudes and job preferences. *Police Chief, 67,* 18–28.
Carter, D. L. (1983). Hispanic interaction with the criminal justice system in Texas: Experiences, attitudes, and perceptions. *Journal of Criminal Justice, 11,* 211–227.
———. (1986). Hispanic police officers' perception of discrimination. *Police Studies, 19,* 204–210.
Carter, D. L., & Sapp, A. D. (1991). *Police education and minority recruitment: The impact of a college requirement.* Washington, DC: Police Executive Research Forum.
Charles, M. T. (1982). Women in policing—The physical aspect. *Journal of Police Science and Administration, 10,* 194–205.
Church, G. L. (1992, May 1). The fire this time. *Newsweek,* pp. 19–25.
Cohen, B. (2000). Are female cops a safety risk?: One cop's answer. *Women Police, 34,* 3.
Crime Control Digest. (1999, May 21). Asian-American officers recognized, p. 11.
Davis, J. A. (1984). Perspectives of policewomen in Texas and Oklahoma. *Journal of Police Science and Administration, 12,* 395–403.
Dorschner, J. (1987). The dark side of the force. In Dunham, R. G., & Alpert, G. P. (eds.), *Critical issues in policing: Contemporary readings.* Prospect Heights, IL: Waveland.
Felkenes, G. T., & Lasley, J. R. (1992). Implications of hiring women police officers: Police administrators' concerns may not be justified. *Policing and Society, 3,* 41–50.
Fields, G. (2000, March 30). Study: Police forces lack female officers. *USA Today,* p. 4A.
Fountain, J. W. (1991, October 20). Minority cops making gains in suburbs. *Chicago Tribune,* sec. 2, pp. 1–2.
Fry, L. (1983). A preliminary examination of the factors related to turnover of women in law enforcement. *Journal of Police Science and Administration, 11,* 149–155.
Fry, L., & Greenfield, S. (1980). An examination of attitudinal differences between policewomen and policemen. *Journal of Applied Psychology, 65,* 123–126.

Gaines, L. K., Kappeler, V. E., & Vaughn, J. B. (1994). *Policing in America.* Cincinnati, OH: Anderson.

Garrison, C. G., Grant, N., & McCormick, K. (1988, September). Utilization of police women. *Police Chief, 55,* 32–72.

Gest, T. (1987, March 9). A one-white, one-black quota for promotions. *U.S. News and World Reports,* p. 8.

Gold, M. E. (2000). The progress of women in policing. *Law & Order, 48,* 159–161.

Grown, M. C., & Carlson, R. D. (1993). Do male policemen accept women on patrol yet? Androgyny, public complaints, and dad. *Journal of Police and Criminal Psychology, 9,* 10–14.

Gup, T. (1988, October 17). Racism in the raw in suburban Chicago. *Time,* pp. 25–26.

Hacker. A. (1992). *Two nations: Black and white, separate, hostile, and unequal.* New York: Ballantine.

Harris, W. (1999). Recruiting women: Are we doing enough? *Police, 23,* 18–23.

Homant, R. J., & Kennedy, D. B. (1985). Police perceptions of spouse abuse—A comparison of male and female officers. *Journal of Criminal Justice, 13,* 29–47.

Horne, P. (1980). *Women in law enforcement.* Springfield, IL: Charles Thomas.

House, C. H. (1993). The changing role of women in law enforcement. *Police Chief, 60,* 139–144.

Jackson, C., & Wallach, I. (1973). Perceptions of the police in a black community. In Snibbe, J. R., & Snibbe, H. M. (eds.), *The urban police in transition* (pp. 382–403). Springfield, IL: Charles C. Thomas.

Jacobs, J. B., & Cohen, J. (1978). The impact of racial integration on the police. *Journal of Police Science and Administration, 6,* 179–183.

Johnson, W. (1992, May 17). Breaking ground wasn't always easy. *Journal Star,* p. B5.

Journal Star. (1989, December 15). Police officers named in bias suit, p. 12.

Kanter, R. (1977). *Men and women of the corporation.* New York: Basic Books.

Kennedy, J. M. (1988, October 1). Latino FBI agents bias victims: Judge. *Journal Star,* p. A2.

Kerber, K. W., Andes, S. M., & Mittler, M. B. (1977). Citizen attitudes regarding the competence of female officers. *Journal of Police Science and Administration, 5,* 337–347.

Koenig, E. J. (1978). An overview of attitudes toward women in law enforcement. *Public Administration Review, 38,* 267–275.

Kranda, A. H. (1998). Women in policing: The importance of mentoring. *Police Chief, 65,* 54–56.

Kuykendall, J., & Burns, D. (1980). The black police officer: An historical perspective. *Journal of Contemporary Criminal Justice, 1,* 103–113.

Langer, G. (1988, August 8). Americans say racism persists. *Journal Star,* p. 2.

Leinen, S. (1984). *Black police, white society.* New York: University Press.

Lin, T. (1987). *Chinese-American police officers in New York City.* Unpublished Master's Thesis. Macomb, IL: Western Illinois University.

Linn, E., & Price, B. R. (1985). The evolving role of women in American policing. In Blumberg, A. S., & Niederhoffer, E. (eds.), *The ambivalent force: Perspectives on the police,* 3rd ed. (pp. 69–80). New York: Holt, Rinehart and Winston.

Lott, J. R. Jr. (2000). Does a helping hand put others at risk? Affirmative action, police departments, and crime. *Economic Inquiry, 38,* 239–277.

Maguire, K., Pastore, A. L., & Flanagan, T. J. (1992). *Bureau of justice statistics sourcebook of criminal justice statistics—1992.* Washington, DC: U.S. Government Printing Office.

Margolis, R. (1971). *Who will wear the badge? A study of minority recruitment efforts in protective services.* United States Commission on Civil Rights. Washington, DC: U.S. Government Printing Office.

Martin, S. E. (1993). Female officers on the move? A status report on women in policing. In Dunham, R. G., & Alpert, G. P. (eds.), *Critical issues in policing: Contemporary issues* (pp. 312–329). Prospect Heights, IL: Waveland.

McDowell, J. (1992, February 17). Are women better cops? *Time,* pp. 70–72.

McGeorge, J., & Wolfe, J. A. (1976). Comparison of attitudes between men and women police officers—A preliminary analysis. *Criminal Justice Review, 1,* 21–33.

McKeever, J., & Kranda, A. (2000, Summer). Recruitment and retention of qualified police personnel: A best practices guide. *Big Ideas for Smaller Departments, 1,* 3–14.

National Center for Women & Policing. (2001). *Recruiting & retaining women: A self-assessment guide for law enforcement.* Los Angeles: National Center for Women & Policing.

National Crime Prevention Council. (1995). *Lengthening the stride: Employing peace officers from newly arrived ethnic groups.* Washington, DC: U.S. Government Printing Office.

Newsweek. (1988, January 4). A mixed verdict on Howard Beach, p. 24.

O'Connor, C. (1985, December 30). Crime: An equal-opportunity employer. *Newsweek,* p. 22.

Pogrebin, M., Dodge, M., & Chatman, H. (2000). Reflections of African-American women on their careers in urban policing. Their experiences of racial and sexual discrimination. *International Journal of the Sociology of Law, 28,* 311–326.

Polisar, J., & Milgram, D. (1998). Strategies that work. *Police Chief, 65,* 42–52.

Poole, E. D., & Pogrebin, M. R. (1988). Factors affecting the decision to remain in policing: A study of women officers. *Journal of Police Science and Administration, 16,* 49–55.

President's Commission on Law Enforcement and the Administration of Justice. (1967). *Task force report: The administration of justice.* Washington, DC: U.S. Government Printing Office.

Reiss, A. J. (1968, July-August). Police brutality—Answers to key questions. *Transaction,* 10–19.

Rogers, C. J. (1987). Women in criminal justice: Similar and unique obstacles to their acceptance in law enforcement and corrections, cited in Balkin, 1988.

Sauls, J. G. (1992, September). The Civil Rights Act of 1991: New challenges for employers. *FBI Law Enforcement Bulletin, 61,* 25–32.

Schaefer, R. T. (2000). *Racial and ethnic groups,* 8th ed. Upper Saddle River, NJ: Prentice-Hall.

Sherman, L. J. (1975). Evaluation of policewomen on patrol in a suburban police department. *Journal of Police Science and Administration, 3,* 434–438.

Shusta, R. M., Levine, D. R., Harris, P. R., & Wong, H. Z. (1995). *Multicultural law enforcement: Strategies for peacekeeping in a diverse society.* Englewood Cliffs, NJ: Prentice-Hall.

Sichel, J. L., Friedman, L. N., Quint, J. C., & Smith, M. E. (1978). *Women on patrol—A pilot study of police performance in New York City.* New York: Vera Institute of Justice.

Sullivan, P. S. (1989). Minority officers: Current issues. In Dunham, R., & Alpert, G. (eds.), *Critical issues in policing: Contemporary readings.* Prospect Heights, IL: Waveland.

Swan, R. D. (1988). The history of American women police. *Women Police, 22,* 10–13.

Walker, S. (1989). *Employment of Black and Hispanic police officers, 1983–1988.* Omaha, NE: Center for Applied Urban Research.

Wexler, J. G., & Logan, D. D. (1983). Sources of stress among women police officers. *Journal of Police Science and Administration, 11,* 46–53.

Williams, L. (1988, February 14). Police officers tell of strains of living as a "Black in Blue." *New York Times,* pp. 1, 26.

Winters, C. A. (1991). Hispanics and policing in Chicago and Cook County, Illinois. *Police Journal, 64,* 71–76.

CHAPTER SEVEN

THE POLICE SUBCULTURE AND THE PERSONAL COSTS OF POLICE WORK

In Chapter 2, we focused on organizational and administrative aspects of policing, on the formal structure and the impact of police leaders. While these formal considerations are crucial to an understanding of the police role, there are two other contributing factors that must be considered in our attempt to understand policing as an occupation:

the police subculture and the pressures and stresses of police work. Police administrators and the law specify the broad parameters within which officers operate, but the police subculture tells them how to go about their tasks, how hard to work, what kinds of relationships to have with their fellow officers and other categories of people with whom they interact, and how they should feel about police administrators, judges, the law, and the requirements and restrictions they impose.

Combined, the effects of formal pressures and the pressures generated by the police subculture often lead police officers to experience a great deal of stress in their occupational, social, and family lives, resulting in cynicism, burnout, and retirement, as well as a host of physical and emotional ailments. Further, many officers, at least initially, fail to recognize the extent to which the police subculture and their chosen occupation affect the way in which they view and act towards others.

According to Hernandez (1989, p. 85), "Unlike most other occupations . . . (the police) view of reality may be rejected by the very people they are trying to serve. . . . The result for the police is that they must function while juggling the two worlds of fact and fiction, each of which carries its own risks. They can't escape the reality because they deal with it every day, nor can they act without a constant awareness of the differing ways in which their client populations perceive both the world and the public."

Inciardi (1990, p. 227) indicates that police officers develop resources to deal with isolation from the community resulting from the job and the police socialization process. These police subcultural attributes include "protective, supportive, and shared attitudes, values, understandings and views of the world," which result in a "blue fraternity," or closed police society. Furthermore this process of socialization or the creation of a blue fraternity begins at the police academy, but as with most forms of occupational socialization, it is an ongoing process throughout the police officer's career. At the academy, the new officers learn language, cultural norms, and associated factors that create the sociobehavioral infrastructure of policing (Carter & Radelet, 1999, pp. 168–170). These factors interact and are reinforced by other officers, eventually leading to the development of attitudes, behaviors, beliefs, and perceptions that reflect the dominant beliefs of almost all police officers. Ultimately, police officers cope with their organizational environment by taking a "lay low" or "cover your ass" attitude and adopting a crime-fighter or law enforcement orientation (Paoline, Myers, & Worden, 2000, p. 578). They quickly discover that when they are recognized, it is usually for a mistake or a violation, rather than for an achievement or effective policing, and they learn that hard work entails the risk of exposure and sanction. Some believe that the professionalization of the police (i.e., removing politics from policing, scientific advances and anti-police misconduct strategies) has been the catalyst for this isolation and strengthening of the "us versus them" attitude associated with the police culture (Sparrow, Moore, & Kennedy, 1990; Paoline, Myers, & Worden, 2000, p. 579).

THE POLICE SUBCULTURE

According to Westley (1970), the police subculture is a crucial concept in the explanation of police behavior and attitudes. The subculture, in his view, characterizes the public as hostile, not to be trusted, and potentially violent; this outlook requires secrecy, mutual support, and unity on the part of the police. Manning (1977) suggests that the inherent uncertainty of police work, combined with the need for information control, leads to police teamwork, which in turn generates collective ties and mutual dependency.

More recently, Manning (1989, p. 362), reviewing twenty-five years of research on police cultures, concludes that researchers "grant the occupational culture a signifi-cant place in determining officer behavior." Further, he states (p. 363) that as a result of the uncertain nature of police work, "The police officer is *dependent* on other officers for assistance, advice, training, working knowledge, protection in case of threats from internal or external sources, and insulation against the public and periodic danger."

The presence of an organizational culture in policing is not unique. Almost all organizations have a form of culture associated with the values, beliefs, and norms that are unique to the occupation and even to the individual organization. Generally, three levels of culture affect police behavior: the culture of the profession, the culture of an individual department, and the culture of the city (U.S. General Accounting Office, 1998, p. 17). Furthermore, Adcox (2000, p. 20) indicated that police officers are influenced by formal organizational structures and expressed organizational values, but also informal values, beliefs, norms, rituals, and expectations of other police officers that are passed along through the organizational culture. According to Crank (1998, p. 6), "Carried in the minds of street cops who work together, culture enables a wide variety of police activities to link together in ways that are, though not systematic, sensible enough to give meanings to different kinds of situations in which cops find themselves."

Champoux (2000, pp. 56–68) indicated that there are different but related forms of organization culture: artifacts, values, and basic assumptions. The artifacts are the most visible parts of the organizational culture and include sounds, architecture, smells, behavior, attire, language, products, and ceremonies. For example, police recruits quickly learn police jargon, how to address superiors, how to communicate on the radio, where to file reports, and a host of other behavior unique to policing. Swidler (1986, pp. 273–286) reported the existence of a "cultural tool-kit" carried by police: "ways of using a commanding voice in routine encounters, abrading a citizen's personal space, a sense of authority and righteousness regarding one's beat, all are aspects of the tool-kit that officers carry into their daily work routines."

Another form of police artifact is the patrol officer's uniform, which is a symbol of law and order and allows all members of society to readily identify a police officer. Some departments have researched the use of blazers or a more casual form of dress to encourage police–community interactions and avoid the paramilitary style of uniform. However, today, almost all police departments have uniformed patrol divisions patrol-ling in squad cars with the phrase "to serve and protect" in a decal on the squad car doors.

The second form of organizational culture involves the values embedded in the organization. Champoux (2000, pp. 56–68) indicated that the in-use values are the most important because they guide the behavior of the organization. Often, in policing, as in many occupations, conflicts exist between values. More (1998, pp. 44–47) cited the examples of a fellow police officer engaging in corruption and not being reported, or an officer drinking on duty and the incident being forgotten. He concluded in these incidents that the value of loyalty to a fellow officer overrode the professional conduct values of the department. Alpert and Dunham (1997, p. 113) indicated that peer influence or loyalty is at the core of the police subculture and is one of the most profound pressures operating in police organizations.

The third and final form of organizational culture is the basic assumptions of the organization. According to Champoux (2000, pp. 56–68), veteran employees of an organization are not consciously aware of the basic assumptions that guide the organization's behaviors. These assumptions develop over the history of the organization and include many aspects of human behavior, human relationships in the organization, and relationships with the organization's external environment. Nelson and Quick (2002, pp. 453–455) indicated that organizational "assumptions are the deeply held beliefs that guide behaviors and tell members of the organization how to perceive and think about things." Gaines, Kappeler, and Vaughn (1999, pp. 307–309) described the presence of a police *ethos* (fundamental spirit of a culture). They identified three concepts of the utmost importance in policing: bravery, autonomy, and the ethos of secrecy.

Crank (1998, p. 226) concluded that secrecy is "a cultural product, formed by an environmental context that holds in high regard issues of democratic process and police lawfulness, and that seeks to punish its cops for errors they make. Secrecy is a set of working tenets that loosely couple the police to accountability, that allow them to do their work and cover their ass so that they can continue to do the work they have to do without interfering oversight." Evidence of secrecy is clearly articulated in postulates who say, "Watch out for your partner first and then the rest of the guys working," "Don't give up another cop," "Don't get involved in anything in another cop's sector," "If you get caught off base, don't implicate anybody else" (Reuss-Ianni, 1983, pp. 14–16).

Many police officers view themselves as teammates linked together by portable and car radios, part of a team that is no stronger than its weakest member. As members of the team, they feel a good deal of pressure to live up to the expectations of other team members and support the practice of secrecy. Among the attitudes and values identified as characteristics of a police culture are adhering to a code of silence, with grave consequences for violating it, and maintaining loyalty to other officers above all else. Cynicism or disillusionment about the job, the criminal justice system, and public support for those who performed properly are characteristics of the subculture, as is on-the-job indoctrination as to what is acceptable behavior (U.S. General Accounting Office, 1998, p. 170).

Thus, police officers tend to socialize with other officers (not unlike members of other occupational groups) and come to realize (unlike members of many other occupational groups) that their identities as police officers sometimes make them socially unacceptable, even when off-duty. That is, in some circles at least, there is a kind of stigma attached to those who are perceived as being "too close" to police officers; and police officers themselves are sometimes suspicious of the motives of non-police who become too friendly. Others see the police as pursuing their own interests (e.g., improving their salaries) in cases in which money collected through traffic citations is returned to the police department. And, in some instances, the families of the officers get to know one another, and a kind of mutual protection society develops, furthering the alienation and isolation from the public (Barker, Hunter, & Rush, 1994).

The police subculture, or blue fraternity, or brotherhood, consists of the informal rules and regulations, tactics, and folklore passed on from one generation of police officers to another. It is both a result and a cause of police isolation from the larger society and of police solidarity. Its influence begins early in the new officer's career when he is told by more experienced officers that the "training given in police academies is irrelevant to 'real' police work" (Bayley & Bittner, 1989, p. 87).

What is relevant, recruits are told, is the experience of senior officers who know the ropes or know how to get around things. Recruits are often told by officers with considerable experience to forget what they learned in the academy and in college and start learning real police work. Among the first lessons learned are that police officers share secrets among themselves; that these secrets, especially when they deal with activities that are questionable in terms of ethics, legality, and departmental policy, are not to be divulged to others; that administrators cannot often be trusted; and that the police are at war with criminals and, sometimes, with other citizens in general. This emphasis on the police occupational subculture as unique results in many officers regarding themselves as members of a "blue minority" (Cox & Fitzgerald, 1996; Skolnick & Fyfe, 1993). According to Kunen (1986, pp. 127–128), "The general feeling among police officers is that the public is not to be trusted . . . that people are very finicky about supporting the police. People will say that they think police officers do a hard job, and they respect them. But if you're giving somebody a ticket, then suddenly you become the bad guy, and they think you're doing a lousy job and you're stupid."

Thus, officers tend to divide the world into "us" and "them," the former consisting of other police officers, the latter encompassing most everybody else. To be sure, members of other occupational groups also develop their own subcultures and world-views, but often not to the same extent as the police (Skolnick, 1966). Skolnick notes, "Set apart from the conventional world, the policeman experiences an exceptionally strong tendency to find his social identity within his occupational milieu" (p. 52). Postulates indicative of the we–they view include the following (Reuss-Ianni, 1983, pp. 14–16):

1. Don't tell anybody else more than they have to know; it could be bad for you, and it could be bad for them.
2. Don't trust a new guy until you have checked him out.
3. Don't give them (police administrators) too much activity.
4. Keep out of the way of any boss from outside your precinct.
5. Know your bosses.
6. Don't do the bosses' work for them.
7. Don't trust bosses to look out for your interests.
8. Don't talk too much or too little.
9. Protect your ass.

Skolnick (1966) goes on to indicate that factors inherent in police work contribute to this tendency. Among these factors are danger, authority, and the need to appear efficient.

Danger, Authority, and Efficiency

Although police work is not the most dangerous occupation, danger is always a possibility. Who knows when the traffic stop at midday will lead to an armed attack on the police officer involved? Who can predict which angry spouse involved in a domestic dispute will batter a police officer (or, for that matter, whether both spouses will)? Who knows when a sniper firing from a rooftop will direct his shots at the windshield of a patrol car? Under what circumstances will a mentally disordered person turn on an officer attempting to assist? Will drivers approaching an intersection heed the flashing lights and siren of an officer's car? Will minority group members organize, take to the streets, and single out police officers as targets? Does the fleeing youthful burglar have a firearm under his shirt? Danger is always a possibility in policing and is highly unpredictable except in certain types of situations. The potential to become the victim of a violent encounter, the need for backup from other officers, and the legitimate use of violence to accomplish the police mandate all contribute to a subculture that stresses bravery, which is ultimately related to the perceived and actual dangers of policing (Gaines, Kappeler, & Vaughn, 1999, p. 307). See Highlight 7.1 for a discussion concerning the affects of stress on police officers.

In fact, because of the unpredictable nature of danger in policing, police officers are trained to be suspicious of most, if not all, other citizens they encounter. They are encouraged to treat other citizens encountered as "symbolic assailants," to approach

■ ■ ■ ■ ■ ▬▬▬▬▬▬▬▬▬▬▬▬▬▬▬▬▬▬▬▬▬▬▬▬▬▬▬▬▬▬▬▬▬

HIGHLIGHT 7.1

POLICE STRESS AFFECTS OFFICERS AT WORK, TUCSON AUTHOR SAYS

Allen R. Kates has never worked as a cop. He's not related or married, to one.

But Kates, a Tucson author, feels he knows police officers better than most. He spent six years and nearly $100,000 of his own money researching, writing and self-publishing a book to help cops understand how to avoid, or recover from, stress-related illness.

"I think it's real important," Glenn Brasch, a recently retired Tucson police officer, said of Kates' book.

"A police officer may deal with something in one day that an average person may not deal with in a lifetime," Brasch said.

"Unless a person has a good (emotional) support system, they may be in trouble."

Kates' book is *CopShock: Surviving Posttraumatic Stress Disorder.* Posttraumatic stress disorder, once called "combat fatigue," is caused by

exposure to extreme violence. Victims may experience nightmares, flashbacks, unexplained anger, emotional numbness, addictions or suicidal thoughts.

Law-enforcement officers, repeatedly exposed to low-grade violence and horrific brutality, are at high risk for developing the condition. One study estimated that up to one-third of U.S. police officers experience the disorder or some of its symptoms. That estimate is borne out in statistics associated with the profession: high rates of suicide, addiction and divorce.

"We as a general public should care a great deal" about post-traumatic stress among police, Kates said. "If cops are not healthy emotionally and psychologically, it is going to affect how they treat us."

CopShock is used as a training manual at the San Francisco Police Academy and to train volun-

(continued)

HIGHLIGHT 7.1 Continued

teer police peer counselors at the Patrolman's Benevolent Association, a union representing uniformed New York City police officers.

"When cops read this book, the first thing they say is, 'Jesus, I'm normal,' " Kates said. "The second thing they say to me is, 'Now I know I'm not crazy.' "

Police have difficulty seeking help because of the twisted perception that comes from working in a profession where lies, isolation, fear, mistrust and assaults on the badge are commonplace, according to Kates.

"Cops start to think these situations they're in, the stabbings, the shootings, are normal," Kates said. "By reading my book, they come to understand that the situations they're in are abnormal, but their feelings are normal."

CopShock tells the stories of law-enforcement officers whose lives were nearly destroyed by the disorder, and how they brought themselves back from the brink.

The book introduces readers to people like Terry Nunn, a Toronto constable tortured by his decision not to shoot two armed assailants for fear of injuring schoolchildren nearby.

Nunn was praised in the Canadian press for his composure but shunned by fellow constables who felt he could no longer be trusted in high-pressure situations.

He began experiencing classic symptoms of post-traumatic stress disorder: flashbacks, nightmares that woke him daily at 3 A.M, and an eating disorder that had him living on booze, cigarettes and chocolate.

He eventually found help in a post-shooting support group.

"Cops themselves have started to believe this myth (that trauma can't affect them)," Kates said. "They look at themselves as this superhuman group that cannot show emotion or even ask for help."

Although 53 percent of municipal police departments offer in-house mental-health units, many officers don't use them. For that reason, cops must learn to recognize post-traumatic stress disorder symptoms and discover other ways to stay healthy.

"We often think of police officers as doing a job, but policing is a calling just like the ministry is a calling," Kates said. "They go out there to genuinely help people and contribute to society and in doing so come up against some of the worst and best of what society offers."

Bryn Bailer, *Arizona Daily Star*, (2001, July 23). p. B4.

them in certain ways, to notify headquarters of their whereabouts when making a stop, to wait for a "cover," or backup car, to arrive before proceeding in potentially dangerous cases, and so on (Skolnick, 1966; Barker, Hunter, & Rush, 1994). Examples of symbolic assailants include two men walking in a quiet residential neighborhood at 3 A.M. and a group of teenagers walking into a dense wooded area in a public park. La Grange (1998, p. 162) indicated that "symbolic situations" that signal trouble to police also exist. Examples of symbolic situations include store lights left on or off at odd hours, a clean car with dirty license plates, or a moving van at a house without a For Sale sign.

Van Maanen (1978) identified three types of people with whom police must interact: "suspicious persons," "assholes," and "know-nothings." *Suspicious persons* include those persons who are most likely about to commit or might have already committed an offense. The *assholes* include those individuals who disrespect the police and do not accept the police definition of the situation. These individuals often are the recipient of "street justice" or "a physical attack designed to rectify what police take as a personal insult." The *know-nothings* are the typical citizens who interact with the police when they request service.

Academy instructors teach police officers to assess others with whom they are involved in terms of their ability to physically "handle" those others if it becomes necessary and to be aware that, in most instances, their encounters with other citizens will be perceived as creating "trouble" for those citizens. We teach them that they work in an "alien" environment in which everyone knows who they are, while they lack such information about most of the people with whom they interact (Rubinstein, 1973).

Additionally, of course, we tell police officers that as representatives of government, they have specific authority to intervene in a wide array of situations. We equip them with a baton, a side arm, handcuffs, a portable radio, a shotgun for their vehicle, mace, partners, backup officers, and a uniform to be sure that their image as authority figures is complete and unmistakable. And we tell them that when dealing with a dispute in progress, their definition of the situation must prevail, that they must take charge of the situation. Police are taught that, as a part of their role, they must give orders, exercise control over law enforcement and order maintenance situations, place restraints on certain freedoms, enforce unpopular laws and ones they do not agree with, conduct searches, make arrests, and perform a number other duties (Alpert & Dunham, 1997, p. 109).

What we don't routinely tell them, but what they learn very quickly on the streets, is that other citizens, not infrequently, resent their intervention. And other citizens, when treated suspiciously by the police, may react with hostility, resentment, contempt, and occasionally, physical violence. Nor do we teach them routinely that certain segments of the population hate them or hold them in contempt simply because they wear the badge and uniform. When members of these groups challenge the authority of the police, the police, based on their training, sometimes resort to threats of force or the use of force to impose their authority, which often escalates the level of danger in the encounters. On those relatively rare occasions in which the challenge to authority is prolonged or vicious, danger may become the foremost concern of all parties involved, and the capacity to use force, including deadly force in appropriate circumstances, becomes paramount (Bittner, 1970). Under the circumstances, the need for police solidarity and the feelings of isolation and alienation from other citizens become apparent. Alpert and Dunham (1997, pp. 112–113) suggest that police unity bolsters officer self-esteem and confidence that enables the police to tolerate the isolation from society and the hostility and public disapproval.

At the same time, Skolnick (1966) has argued, we expect the police to be efficient, and the police themselves are concerned with at least giving the appearance of efficiency, if not the substance, because performance evaluations and promotions often depend on at least the former. Concerns with efficiency and the resulting pressures they produce have increased dramatically with the computerization of the police world and other technological advances. Simultaneously, taxpayers have begun to demand greater accountability for the costs involved in policing and more well-educated (and therefore more costly) police personnel. The resulting "do more with less" philosophy has led many police executives to emphasize even more the importance of efficient performance. According to Carey (1994, p. 24), "Citizens expect professional police behavior, respectful treatment, maintenance of human dignity, responsiveness, and a high value on human life. In addition, these increasingly sophisticated taxpayers also insist that the police achieve maximum effectiveness and efficiency in the use of their tax dollars."

However, the police subculture has established standards of acceptable performance for officers and resists raising these standards. Officers whose performance exceeds these standards are often considered "rate-busters" and threats to those adhering to traditional expectations. For example, fueling the patrol car, in some departments, is an operation for which the officer is expected by the subculture to allot twenty to thirty minutes. Because the operation may actually take less than five minutes, administrators concerned about accountability, totaling the amount of time lost in this operation for, say, ten cars, recognize they are losing two to three hours of patrol time if they fail to take action to modify the fueling procedure. At the same time, however, officers concerned about accountability who wish to patrol an additional fifteen to twenty minutes and fuel the car in less time make those officers adhering to the twenty- to thirty-minute standard look bad, and are under considerable pressure to conform to the established standard. Similar expectations and conflicts exist with respect to the number of drunk drivers who can be processed in a shift, the number of felonies that may be processed, the number of subpoenas that may be served, or the number of prisoners who may be transported. Officers must make choices as to whose expectations are to be met and sometimes operate in a no-win situation, in which meeting one set of expectations automatically violates the other, leaving the officer under some stress no matter how she operates.

Sparrow, Moore, and Kennedy (1990, p. 51) argue that the police subculture creates a set of truths, according to which officers are expected to live. Note that there is some basis in fact for each of these subcultural truths, and that each makes integrating the police and the citizens they serve more difficult.

1. The police are the only real crime fighters.
2. No one understands the nature of police work but fellow officers.
3. Loyalty to colleagues counts more than anything else.
4. It is impossible to win the war on crime without bending the rules.
5. Other citizens are unsupportive and make unreasonable demands.
6. Patrol work is only for those who are not smart enough to get out of it.

As discussed in previous chapters, society has witnessed major changes in the concept of police in the past decades. Kappeler (1999, p. 481) indicated that American society no longer reflects the values, attitudes, or social organization that distinguished the first half of the twentieth century. Accordingly, through these changes and others in policing, the police culture has experienced a change. For example, Paoline, Myers, and Worden (2000, p. 581) believes that the adoption of and experimentation with community policing may have altered both the occupational and organizational environments of policing, and within these environments, the stresses and strains experienced by police officers. They cite the greater attention to officers' efforts to reduce disorder, solve problems, and build rapport with the public that could result in a modification of the "us versus them" outlook. Furthermore, as police agencies include proportionately more women, more members of racial and ethnic minorities, and more college-educated personnel, the police culture may experience more fragmentation and greater heterogeneity (Paoline, Myers, & Worden, 2000, p. 583).

THE POLICE PERSONALITY: MYTH OR REALITY?

Some have suggested that the impact of police work and the police subculture itself lead to the development of a distinctive police personality. Burbeck and Furnham (1985), in reviewing the literature on police attitudes, found that police officers, in comparison with the general population, place more emphasis on family security and sense of accomplishment and less on social equality. Further, experienced officers appear to deemphasize affective values.

Over the years, the literature on the police has characterized them as more authoritarian and prejudiced than other occupational groups. Authoritarian personalities tend to be conservative, rigid, punitive, and inflexible, and to emphasize authority and rules (Adorno et al., 1950). As Burbeck and Furnham (1985) have noted, studies do not support the contention that individuals possessing these traits seek out police work; thus, the presence of the traits may be the result of occupational and subcultural pressures. In addition, it may be argued that the military background of large numbers of police personnel, particularly in the time period between the Civil War and the middle of the twentieth century, may have been a factor in authoritarianism (and may still be, because some of these personnel are now chief executive officers in police agencies) (Hernandez, 1989). However, because of the changes in the police role, departments are seeking officers with the personalities and characteristics that are consistent with quality-of-life issues and problem-solving expertise (Carter & Radelet, 1999, p. 183).

Prejudice (in this case, unfavorable attitudes toward a group or individual not based on experience or fact) appears to be more common among those with authoritarian traits. Prejudiced individuals tend to develop and adhere to stereotypes based on race, ethnicity, occupational group, and other factors. Police actions based on such stereotypes are discriminatory and clearly inappropriate in a democratic society. There is little doubt that many police officers have negative stereotypes of particular groups in the public, or that the police subculture creates, sustains, and supports such stereotypes (Van Maanen, 1978; Cray, 1972; Chevigny, 1969; Kirkham, 1977; Cox & Fitzgerald, 1996; Rudovsky, 1992). Because these stereotypes and prejudices are attitudes and cannot be directly observed, they are difficult, if not impossible, to eliminate among police officers as well as among the general public. Discriminatory actions, however, are observable, and steps to prevent such actions can and must be taken. The extent to which prejudices and stereotypes translate into discriminatory action remains an empirical question, though there is no doubt that it does sometimes happen.

Cynicism is another feature of the police officer's working personality that is addressed by students of the police. As defined by Niederhoffer (1967, p. 96), cynicism involves a loss of faith in people, of enthusiasm for police work, and of pride and integrity. Niederhoffer and others (Regoli & Poole, 1978) found that cynicism peaked

The occupational culture sometimes calls for aggressiveness on the part of police officers.

in the seventh to tenth year of police service, and the latter noted that the level of cynicism varies with the organizational style of the department and the type of department (urban or rural). However, the classic 1967 study did find that cynicism set in shortly after graduation from the police academy. According to Graves (1996, p. 17), this is related to the reality of the streets, particularly in large cities that have high crime rates and more anonymity, which shocks the new officers, causing them to lose faith in others and only trust other police officers. In another study, cynicism was found to vary inversely with rank and preferred assignment (day shift) and in a curvilinear fashion with the police officer's length of service (Dorsey & Giacopassi, 1987, p. 1–16). Dorsey and Giacopassi also concluded that race and gender influenced the development of cynicism, and that white female officers were the most cynical and male black officers were the least.

Neiderhoffer (1967, p. 95) defined four stages that lead to police cynicism:

1. Stage One—Pseudo Cynicism: New recruits are idealistic, their desire is to "help people."

2. Stage Two—Romantic Cynicism: Involves the first five years of police work; these officers are the most vulnerable to cynicism.
3. Stage Three—Aggressive Cynicism: Failures and frustrations, resentment, and hostility are obvious and prevalent at the tenth-year mark.
4. Stage Four—Resigned Cynicism: Detachment, passiveness, an acceptance of the flaws of the system.

Within different police subcultures, cynicism is thought to involve different issues, including the public, the police administration, the courts, training and education, dedication to duty, and police solidarity (Regoli, 1976; Bouza, 1990). Alpert and Dunham (1997, p. 112) conclude, "[T]here is some evidence for the existence of a police working personality. Most of the evidence points to the influence of socialization and experiences after becoming a police officer as the main source of the unique traits." Broderick (1987, pp. 22–115) believes there are four working personalities of police: enforcers, idealists, realists, and optimists. Enforcers emphasize the law enforcement function, while idealists focus on individual rights. Realists place little emphasis on social order and individual rights. Optimists view policing as the opportunity to help people (Broderick, 1987, pp. 22–115; Peak, 1997, pp. 92–94). Each of these working personalities will include a different level of cynicism. For example, the Enforcer is a crime fighter rather than problem solver and becomes easily frustrated with the criminal justice system, the public, and others.

In contrast, Terry (1989) reviewed numerous studies that found essentially no differences between police officers and those in other occupations with respect to either authoritarianism or prejudice, and studies that have found police officers to be intelligent, emotionally stable, and service oriented. Carpenter and Raza (1987, p. 16) report that police applicants differ from the general population in several positive ways: "[T]hey are more psychologically healthy than the normative population, as they are generally less depressed and anxious, and more assertive and interested in making and maintaining social contacts." Terry (1989, p. 550) concedes that while some of the research on police personalities does appear to distinguish certain traits, no one has been able to "disentangle the effects of a person's socioeconomic background from the demands that police work and its subculture places upon individual officers."

Lundman (1980, p. 74), summarizing police socialization practices at the end of the 1970s, noted that in contrast to the largely white high-school-educated men of the recent past, more of today's police recruits are college educated and members of minority groups. He found that quasi-military training is giving way to other, less rigid alternatives: "Some academies feature technical training with primary emphasis given to the maintenance of order under the rule of law. A few academies offer non-stress training, featuring a condensed liberal arts curriculum. Some departments select 'coaches' for new officers in terms of their police skills and adherence to a 'softer' approach to policing. A possible effect of these slow and uneven changes is diversity in the working personalities of patrol officers." Changes during the past decade have followed the patterns discussed by Lundman and others (Post, 1992), and the number of departments and academies featuring such changes has clearly increased. As a result of these and other changes, it is difficult to say that there is currently a distinct police personality. The research does not support the existence of a single dominant personality type among police officers. Yarmey (1990, p. 42) states, "There is no evidence for such a thing as a typical police personality showing a cluster of traits that is constant across time and space."

STRESSES AND STRAINS OF POLICE WORK

Previously we discussed the formal police organization and the police subculture, both of which contribute to the stress levels experienced by police. The effects of formal pressure from police organizations and pressures generated by the police subculture often lead police to experience a great deal of stress in their occupational, social, and family lives, resulting in cynicism, burnout, and retirement on the job, as well as a host of physical and emotional ailments. Furthermore, recent research concluded that police officers increasingly view stress as a normal part of their job, but they also see themselves as being under significantly more pressure than their colleagues were ten to twenty years ago (National Institute of Justice, 2000, p. 19).

THE PERSONAL COSTS OF POLICE WORK

In spite of the fact that there does not appear to be a cluster of personality traits that distinguish police officers from other occupational groups, there is no doubt that the nature of police work and the subculture in which it occurs creates difficulties for officers, their families, and friends (see Highlight 7.2). The need to perform under stress is a concern in many professions; policing is probably not as stressful as some other occupations. However, according to Adams (2001, p. 420), stress is one of the most common of all occupational hazards for police and can be extremely debilitating, leading to early stress-related illness.

According to Nelson and Quick (2002, p. 190), *stress* is one of the most creatively ambiguous words in the English language. For most people, stress has a negative perception, something to be avoided. However, stress is a great asset in managing legitimate emergencies and achieving peak performance. According to Champoux (2000, p. 302), a person experiences stress when an event in their environment presents a constraint, an opportunity, or an excessive physical or psychological demand.

Nelson and Quick (2002, pp. 193–197) used four approaches to define stress. These approaches, which emphasize demands or sources of stress in organizations, include task demands, role demands, interpersonal demands, and physical demands.

Task Demands

Task demands or the lack of task demands can impose high stress levels on police. Quantitative input overload is a result of too many demands for the time allotted, while

■ ■ ■ ■ ■

HIGHLIGHT 7.2
SYSTEM TO GAUGE POLICE STRESS:
INDICATORS OF TROUBLE TO POP UP ON COMPUTER

Pressures on the 102 recruits of the newest Cleveland Police Academy won't stop with graduation, so the department wants to ensure they handle them the right way.

Cadets who successfully complete the 4½-month course will be tracked by a new computer system designed to allow supervisors to gauge how officers are dealing with the stress of the job. The $45,000 Risk Analysis Management System will keep a record of eight indicators that an officer could be headed for trouble.

The indicators include excessive use of sick time, on-duty preventable auto accidents, use-of-force incidents and citizen complaints—excluding those complaints determined to be unfounded.

The system will alert a staffer when an officer has a certain number of flags from the tracked indicators. The staffer will prepare a report for the officer's commander. The commander and the officer's direct supervisor will decide if intervention is necessary.

The system will be a part of the proposed Employee Intervention Program, which Police Chief Martin L. Flask said he will have running within a week. It will be an expansion of the department's Employee Assistance Unit, which provides counseling referrals for officers.

"Any progressive law enforcement agency has something like this in place," he said. "This is a stressful job we have. Besides the stressors of the job, we have all the stressors of a father, a husband, a wife or a mother. I've seen too many officers have their careers go up in flames and even in some cases take their own lives."

The growing number of arrests of Cleveland officers for serious crimes and the suicides of two officers prompted Flask to jump-start the longstanding request for a tracking system.

Roy Rich, president of the Fraternal Order of Police, supports the idea. He sent Flask a list of recommended changes to the first draft of the proposal, most of which were implemented. Rich heads the union that represents ranking officers.

Flask said he would welcome suggestions from Bob Beck, president of the Cleveland Police Patrolmen's Association. He said he asked Beck several months ago for his support with the program.

Beck said he will sit down to talk with Flask about the program this week. He said he wants to ensure that the program protects the officers' confidentiality and anonymity.

"Our Employee Assistance Unit does a good job, so I'm not sure of the need" for the new program, Beck said. "Anybody who knows anything about rehabilitation knows the importance of safeguarding information."

The program will be voluntary and outside the discipline process. Data from records already kept by the department will be fed into the system.

The Risk Analysis Management System was developed by the Police Foundation, a Washington-based private, nonprofit group, to help police departments track their officers. Twelve departments in the United States and one in Canada use the software.

Officers in several of the cities that use the program said it has been an effective management tool.

"It has spotted some people headed for trouble," said Newark, N.J., Detective Lillian Carpenter. The department has about 1,400 officers. "It's a good system. I haven't seen any better."

qualitative input overload is the result of complexity and limited time (Whisenand, 2001, p. 206). These two types of input overload are known as *hyperstress*. Quantitative overload occurs when police officers experience stacking of calls or more calls are being received than can be answered. Emergency calls are prioritized by 911 systems, but minor theft cases, criminal damage to property cases, trespassing violations, and other non-emergency calls are answered in the order in which they are received. In other words, an officer on a busy shift might respond to twenty-five calls for service, with little time for patrol or personal breaks. Obviously, with this number of calls, the quality of the police interaction with the public can suffer. However, investigators assigned a large number of a cases more readily experience quality overload. Each case must follow case management criteria and may include interviews, interrogations, evidence collection, search warrants, and numerous reports. The number of cases assigned by supervisors and the pressure generated by prosecutors to complete an investigation have an effect on the quality of investigation and the extent of overload experienced by individual officers.

Whisenand (2001, p. 206) found that low levels of mental and physical activity cause hypostress, which is the result of quantitative and qualitative input underloads. Police officers who work a third shift with no calls experience high levels of boredom when the only activity is random patrol and personal breaks.

Role Demands

Role demands develop two types of role stress in the work environment: role conflict and role ambiguity (Nelson & Quick, 2002, p. 196). *Role conflict* is a result of the inconsistent or incompatible expectations communicated to the person. A role conflict can occur when society's expectations of police behavior conflict with certain police principles, beliefs, and behaviors. For example, for many decades, society has condemned the use and sale of illegal drugs. However, the police are limited in their ability to successfully reduce drug abuse. According to Caldero (1997), police have to become a link in the distribution of drugs, including introducing new users to dealers and buying and selling drugs. Society would not readily condone nor comprehend the involvement of police officers in these activities. Crank (1998, p. 246) concluded that "cops must avoid the harsh glare of the external observation which would reveal that they are in violation of the law and that they are doing exactly what the public wants them to do, generate arrests for drugs the only way they can—fabricating evidence, dropsy, lying on the witness stand, entrapment, in a word, by being more criminally sophisticated than the criminals." Thus, the perceptions of society and the actual behaviors of police performing undercover drug enforcement can generate high levels of stress, especially for police who must become a part of the drug culture, appear in court as a professional police officer, and still maintain relationships with spouses, children, and other family members.

Role ambiguity is the confusion a person experiences related to the expectations of others (Nelson & Quick, 2002, p. 196). For example, according to Manning (1977, p. 100), the police are seen by the public as "alertly ready to respond to citizen demands, as crime-fighters, as an efficient, bureaucratic, highly organized force that keeps society from falling into chaos." However, as we have seen in other chapters, this is an exaggeration of actual police work. Manning concluded that "most police work resembles any other kind of work: it is boring, tiresome, sometimes dirty, sometimes technically demanding, but it is rarely dangerous. And to add to the role confusion, the public has demanded an even higher of level of the crime fighting activities which are grossly exaggerated in books, movies, electronic games and television shows. In one study it was determined that officers who experienced role ambiguity had low self-confidence, higher job-related tension, and lower job satisfaction (More, 1998, p. 251).

Interpersonal Demands

Abrasive personalities, sexual harassment, and the leadership style in the organization are interpersonal demands for people at work (Nelson & Quick, 2002, p. 196). Even with general support by the public, police typically encounter individuals with abrasive personalities. According to Alpert and Dunham (1997, p. 105), many citizens feel the police are just a little above the evil they fight or believe that the police are against them and misuse their right to use force to uphold the law. However, the police often perceive a more extreme negative evaluation by citizens, leading to increased levels of occupational stress. Peak (1997, p. 347) concluded that police are never completely "off-duty" and are accosted at home and while attending social functions by people who want to complain about police actions. This diminished private life can become stressful, compelling police to withdraw from public interactions, enhancing the "us versus them" attitude.

Sexual harassment has contributed to high stress levels and the resignation of female police officers. Even with the increased visibility of laws relating to sexual harassment, increased prevention training, and more litigation, sexual harassment still occurs. Unfortunately, the police environment may be more conducive than others to sexual harassment because of the nature of the work, investigating sex crimes and pornography (Bennett & Hess, 2001, p. 364). Dealing with sex crimes and pornography on a recurring basis makes discussion of these topics commonplace and the boundaries of propriety are sometimes erased. Furthermore, they concluded there is some evidence to suggest that sexual harassment is significantly higher in male-dominated occupations. Sexual harassment behaviors, including unwelcome sexual advances and verbal and physical assaults, contribute to the adjustment problems of female police officers on the job.

Leadership styles are another interpersonal demand that can create stress in the work environment. Management styles play an important role in work-environment stress levels. Various management styles, such as allowing little or no participation in organizational decision making, providing ineffective consultation, and imposing restrictions on employee behaviors, are characteristics that can be potentially stressful for employees (Greene, 1997, p. 70). This is especially true in police organizations that are characteristically authoritarian but attract college-educated personnel. Roberg, Crank, and Kuykendall (2000, p. 414) concluded that college-educated police would be less willing to work in, and be less satisfied with, authoritarian departments and managerial practices.

Physical Demands

Extreme environments, strenuous activities, and hazardous substances create physical demands for people in the work place (Nelson & Quick, 2002, p. 197). While once believed to be a very high stress occupation, more recent research suggests that policing may not be as stressful as originally believed (Roberg, Crank, & Kuykendall, 2000, p. 466). This change may be in part due to different hiring processes, stress-reduction training classes, and individual characteristics of the officers. However, police, on a regular basis, are exposed to situations rarely experienced by other members of society. Death, extreme physical abuse, and fear of the unknown have significant affects on the physical and mental health of police. Stevens (1999, pp. 1–5) found that the top five stress producers for police officers are child abuse, killing an innocent person, conflict with regulations, domestic violence, and killing or hurting a fellow police officer. For example, a police officer responding to a trouble call finds that the father has shot his two young children, his wife, and then himself. The public will read only a short abstract about this tragedy in the newspaper, but the image of the young child gripping her doll just before being shot in the head with a shotgun by her father will remain with the officer forever.

FORMS OF POLICE STRESS

Bartol (1983) says that stress occurs when a stimulus leads to a response that does not lead to greater perceived or actual control over the stimulus. He lists the following as major causes of stress among police officers: inefficiency in the courts, court decisions, poor equipment, shift work, working conditions, eating habits, pay, boredom and inactivity, role conflict, and alienation from the public. To this list we might add excessive paperwork, red tape, lack of participation in decision making, and competition for promotion among others. One study found new and more severe sources of stress for police: increased scrutiny and criticism from the media and the public and anxiety and loss of morale as a result of layoffs and reduced salary raises (National Institute of Justice, 1997, p. 3). The National Institute of Justice concluded that even positive changes, such as the movement to community policing, has caused increased levels of stress for many officers.

Peak (1997, pp. 343–351) divided stressors experienced by police into four major categories: stressors originating within the organization, stressors external to the organization, stressors connected with the performance of police duties, and stressors particular to the individual officer.

1. Stressors originating within the organization: Poor supervision, absence of career development opportunities, inadequate reward system, offensive policies, and paperwork

2. Stressors external to the organization: Absence of career development (not able to transfer to another department), jurisdictional isolation, seemingly ineffective corrections system, courts, distorted press accounts, unfavorable minority and majority views, derogatory remarks, and adverse government actions

3. Stressors connected with the performance of police duties: Role conflict, adverse work schedules, fear and danger, sense of uselessness, and absence of closure

4. Stressors particular to the individual officer: Feeling overcome by fear and danger, pressures to conform

Finn and Tomz (1997, pp. 1–39) found that the cumulative effects of stressors unique to police can lead to impaired performance and reduced productivity, public relations problems, and labor–management friction. The number of civil law suits may well increase, along with tardiness, absenteeism, and turnover. Finally, there may be an added expense of hiring and training as personnel experiencing high levels of stress leave the organization (Finn & Tomz, 1997, pp. 1–39).

Stratton (1978) classified police stressors into four groups: external, internal, occupational, and individual. He also identified some of the specific stressors occurring in police work as a result of these four categories: situations that require the officer to be in an alert state (autonomic nervous system response) whether or not action is taken, situations in which the officer is responsible for the lives of others, rotating shift assignments, and the accompanying biological and social changes required to adapt to shift work. To these stressors others have added low self-esteem and constant exposure to the darker side of life. In a later study, Pranzo and Pranzo (1999, pp. 1–209) examined police occupational stress and classified the following as sources of police stress: "the need to live with extremes; oppressive work schedules; work in high-crime neighborhoods; fear of injury or death; the operation, administration, and policies of a police agency regarding discipline and promotion; the possibility of internal investigation and lawsuits; and changed expectations with the integration of women into police work."

Carter and Radelet (1999, p. 292) devised a typology of seven police stressors that selectively interact with a police officer's job activities, decision making, and organizational life:

1. Life-threatening stressors (ever-present potential of injury or death)
2. Social isolation stressors (cynicism, isolation, and alienation from the community, prejudice and discrimination)
3. Organizational stressors (administrative philosophy, changing policies and procedures, morale, job satisfaction, misdirected performance measures)
4. Functional stressors (role conflict, use of discretion, and legal mandates)
5. Personal stressors (police officer's off-duty life, including family, illness, problems with children, marital stresses, financial constraints)
6. Physiological stressors (fatigue, medical conditions, and shift-work effects)
7. Psychological stressors (possibly activated by all of the above and the exposure to repulsive situations)

The National Institute of Justice (NIJ) (2000, p. 19) concluded that today's police are experiencing new levels of stress based on a perceived increased public scrutiny and adverse publicity and a perceived decline in police camaraderie. Fear of contracting air- and blood-borne diseases (TB, HIV, hepatitis), the focus on cultural diversity and political correctness, and the transition to community policing have also increased stress levels, according to the Institute. Furthermore, these newly perceived stressors have serious emotional and physical effects on police. The NIJ concluded that the consequences of stress reported by police include cynicism, suspicion, and emotional detachment from everyday life. In addition, stress leads to reduced efficiency, increased absenteeism, and early retirement, as well as excessive aggressiveness, alcoholism, and other substance abuse. Marital and family problems (extramarital affairs, divorce, domestic violence) and posttraumatic stress disorders are yet other products of stress. Other symptoms include heart attacks, ulcers, weight gain, and suicide (National Institute of Justice, 2000, p. 20).

STAGES OF STRESS

All occupations involve stress, but stress need not always be harmful. In fact, moderate stress appears to be positively related to productivity. Elimination of all stress is neither possible nor desirable. However, the effects of prolonged high levels of stress are clearly dysfunctional, producing both debilitating psychological and physical symptoms. In part, the damage caused by stress occurs because of the *general adaptation syndrome* identified by Selye (1974). In the first stage of this syndrome, the body prepares to fight stress by releasing hormones that lead to an increase in respiration and heartbeat. In the second stage, the body attempts to resist the stressor and repair any damage that has occurred. If the stress continues long enough and cannot be successfully met through flight or fight, the third stage, exhaustion, occurs. Repeated exposures to stressors that cannot be eliminated or modified by the organism eventually lead to stage three.

Often, a police officer's career is divided into significant phases, according to the development of stress at various periods of his career. Flynn states, "These stages include the initial phase, which involves academy training; the middle phase, which deals with years of working various assignments and promotions; and the final stage, which examines the time immediately preceding retirement and the subsequent return to civilian life" (1997, p. 1). Police officers experience such stressors repeatedly in the performance of their duties as well as during off-duty time (as when they are required to carry an off-duty weapon).

Violanti and Marshall (1983, p. 3) concluded that four transitory stages exist in a police officer's career.

1. *Alarm Stage (0–5 years).* Stress increases as the officers adjust to new experiences, including death, an authoritarian style of management, and the dangers of policing. The officer quickly learns that the academy training, education classes, and television do not truly reflect the street environment.

2. *Disenchantment Stage (6–13 years).* Stress levels continue to increase in this stage as the officer realizes that crimes do not have easy resolutions and that many of the problems they encounter do not have a resolution.

3. Personalization Stage (14–19 years). During this stage, there is a substantial decrease in the stress levels experienced by police officers. In all sizes of department, the officer has become somewhat comfortable with the job and has seen almost every type of call.

4. *Introspection Stage (20 years and over).* Stress continues to decrease during this stage. Police officers are concerned about retirement and personal issues and are very secure in their job. If the officers experience frustration, they can retire at any time. (Violanti and Marshall, 1983)

From this study, it is apparent that stress reduction training be provided early in a police officer's career. The National Institute of Justice (2000, p. 22) reported that doing so during the initial training period is a possibility because police recruits are a "captive audience" and because the information may remain with them throughout their entire police career. However, others believe that recruit training is not the most effective time or approach because most academy attendees are not experienced enough to recognize the stresses of the job. They believe the optimal time to reach a new police officer is after she has worked the street for six to eight months.

The transitory stages discussed earlier exist in small, medium, and large departments. Thus, the size of a police agency does not affect police stress. However, the environment in which the officers work, or the officers' perceptions of working conditions (e.g., danger, impersonality, public adversity) do affect the perceived levels of stress (Brooks & Piquero, 1998, pp. 1–18). Brooks and Piquero concluded that officers working in large police departments experienced high levels of stress related to administrative procedures, the criminal justice system, and personal demands, but less stress from exposure to suffering than do officers in small police agencies. When only patrol officers were considered in this study, police from larger departments experienced more administrative, personal challenge, and criminal justice stress; more stress relating to the public; more stress from demands placed on them; and more stress from worries about danger.

BURNOUT

The inability to find a way to relieve stress may lead to burnout, characterized by emotional exhaustion and cynicism. Champoux (2000, p. 308) defined *burnout* as a chronic state of emotional exhaustion stemming from an unrelenting series of on-the-job pressures with few moments of positive experience. Repeated exposure to high levels of stress results in emotional exhaustion. Depersonalization of relationships follows emotional exhaustion as a coping response. Police suffering from these stages view victims and complainants as case numbers, and with little empathy or individual attention. The final stage of burnout involves reduced personal accomplishment, in which the officer loses interest in the job, performance declines, and motivation is lacking.

More (1998, pp. 248–249) states that the onset of burnout occurs through five stages:

1. *Honeymoon, enthusiasm phase.* New police officers are excited, ready to help people, and want to save the world from crime. If coping mechanisms are not in place, these officers move to the next stage.

2. *Stagnation stage.* Police in this stage expend less energy, new challenges have disappeared, and police work becomes boring and routine. Veniga and Spradley (1981, pp. 7–10) state that the following symptoms begin to appear: job dissatisfaction, inefficiency, fatigue, sleep disturbance, and escape activities. Vila et al. (2000, pp. 1–122) report that police who work excess hours display fatigue six times higher than that found among shift workers in industrial and mining occupations.

3. *Frustration stage.* Police exhibit anger and resentment, and begin to withdraw from the job.

4. *Apathy stage.* Officers become obsessed with the frustrations of the work environment.

5. *Hitting the wall/intervention.* Burnout becomes entwined with alcoholism, drug abuse, heart disease, and mental illness. (More, 1998, pp. 248–249; Veniga & Spradley, 1981, pp. 1–68)

As noted, officers experiencing such stress sometimes turn to alcohol or other drugs, physical aggression, and even suicide in attempting to alleviate it. In fact, of course, these perceived solutions simply make the problem worse and increase the stress level of the officer. In addition, stress symptoms experienced by police officers may influence other members of the family. For example, Ryan (1997, pp. 1–4) reported no significant differences in levels of depression, posttraumatic stress disorder, communication, and attitudes toward police issues and stress symptoms between police officers and their spouses. The literature on the police is replete with data on high rates of divorce (though there is conflicting research here), alcoholism, and suicide (Terry, 1989; Wagner & Brzeczek, 1983; Hill & Clawson, 1988; Josephson & Reiser, 1990; Swanson, Gaines, & Gore, 1991).

Perhaps an example of the incidents occurring in the first few hours of a police officer's tour of duty will help clarify the stressors to which officers are routinely subjected. Shortly after reporting "in service," the officer receives a call that another officer requires immediate assistance. The officer responding to the call for help turns on red lights and siren and drives as rapidly as possibly to reach his colleague. On the way he is preparing for the possibility of a physical struggle or armed resistance, and the physical changes described are taking place. The officer is tense and excited, but also frightened. The fear experienced may have to do with anticipation about what will happen when he arrives at the scene, but it also has to do with what other drivers, noting the red lights and siren—or failing to note them—will do. Will they yield at intersections? Will they pull off to the right? Will they pull to the left? Will they stop in the middle of the street? Will they slow down or speed up? What will the chief say if he is involved in an accident?

Arriving at the scene, the officer finds the situation under control, a suspect in custody, and his colleague uninjured. As the officer gets back into the patrol car, another call comes from the dispatcher. This call involves an accident with serious injuries. The officer proceeds to the scene (with the same set of concerns about arriving safely). As the first emergency officer to arrive, he finds that several people have been seriously injured and an infant killed. After the accident has been "handled," the officer gets into his vehicle and is told to come to the station to meet with the chief. His concerns on the way are somewhat different but perhaps equally stressful. For the next several hours and, in some cities, for the next several days, weeks, and years, these scenarios are repeated. The ups and downs of police work take their toll, and the officer experiences repeated stress, tension, and perhaps burnout.

The literature on police stress is extensive and suggests that the interaction of personality and situational factors determines the amount and type of stress experienced by the individual. Fell, Richard, and Wallace (1980) examined police death certificates and concluded that they indicated a high rate of premature death due to stress-related factors. They also noted that the suicide rate among police officers was the third highest among 130 occupations. Wagner and Brzeczek (1983) found that Chicago police officers were five times more likely than other citizens of the city to commit suicide, but the authors' sample size was quite small (221 suicides). Josephson and Reiser (1990), however, found the rate of suicide among Los Angeles police officers to be about the same as that of the general population. Stack and Kelley (1999, pp. 1–14) found similar results after analyzing data on police suicides from sixteen states. They controlled for the socioeconomic variables, concluded that being a police officer is not associated with the odds of death by suicide, and challenged the assumption that police have a higher suicide rate than others in the work force.

Gaines, Kappeler, and Vaughn (1999, pp. 321–322) claim that comparing suicide rates of the general public and police may be deceptive because there are drastic differences between the two groups. These differences include male domination in policing, all are over 21 years of age, all have access to firearms, and most police officers work in urban areas. Further, they concluded that besides the stress of police work, other factors contribute to police suicides. Among these are abuse of alcohol and drugs, involvement in deviance and corruption, depression, and working in a male-dominated organization. Family and economic problems, alienation, and cynicism associated with the police culture; role conflict; and physical and mental health problems are other contributing problems (Gaines, Kappeler, & Vaughn, 1999, p. 322).

Cottle and Ford (2000, pp. 1–9) also examined the stress associated with policing by administering the Minnesota Multiphasic Personality Inventory (MMPI) to police officers. They found that compared to pre-employment MMPI scores, current MMPI scores for the police increased significantly on scales related to hypochondriasis, depression, hysteria, psychopathic deviance, paranoia, psychasthenia, schizophrenia, and social introversion. The authors concluded that police may have a greater tendency to develop and/or express potentially maladaptive characteristics due to the pressures associated with policing, which requires them to control dangerous and emotional situations while remaining emotionally controlled.

Storms, Penn, and Tenzell (1990) examined police officers' self-perceptions and compared them with police officers' perceptions of the "ideal" police officer. They found that the ideal officer was perceived as good, decisive, active, strong, fast, right (versus wrong), responsive, masculine, flexible, and considerate. Police officers perceived themselves to possess most of these same characteristics but to a lesser degree than the ideal officer. The authors concluded that while officers perceive themselves as falling a little short of the ideal, they basically have a positive self-image.

Spielberger et al. (1981) indicate that organizational and administrative factors are as important in determining levels of police stress as are physical danger and emotional stress resulting from the police role. Stratton, Parker, and Snibbe (1984) studied posttraumatic shooting situations and documented psychological reactions ranging from sleep disturbances to anger. Violanti, Marshall, and Howe (1985) found that stress was an important factor in alcohol use among police officers. Burke and Deszca (1986) noted that older officers, with higher rank and more years service, drank and smoked more and exercised less than their younger, less experienced, and lower ranking colleagues. Pendergrass (1999) indicates that estimates of alcohol abuse among police officers suggest that abuse is about twice as high as that of the general population. Violanti, Vena, and Marshall (1986) found that police officers have significantly higher rates of death from cancer and suicide than does the general population. Shift work is a source of stress among police officers who cannot maintain regular sleep patterns during days off, who cannot be present at holiday gatherings, and whose family life may suffer as a result (Bartollas & Hahn, 1999, p. 199). Haar and Morash (1999, pp. 1–34) identified several additional strategies police officers use to cope with occupational stress:

1. Change of job assignment
2. Escapist tactics
3. Expression of feelings
4. Co-worker camaraderie
5. Racial bonds
6. Support from superiors, co-workers and family
7. Co-worker positive reactions to oneself

STRESS AND POLICE FAMILIES

Yet other studies have focused on the effects of police work on the police family. Maynard and Maynard (1982) found that police wives viewed inherent job demands, shift rotation, changing schedules, and promotional practices as sources of strain on police families. Kureczka (1996) found that long-term serious consequences for family members may result from police shootings and police use of excessive force. Hageman (1989) notes that while the family is often viewed as a stress reducer in other occupations, in policing, the spouse often becomes identified as one of the stressors. Hageman also points out that while police divorce rates appear to be no higher than those in the general population, officers' perceptions of the impact of the job on their marriages often differed significantly from those of their spouses, indicating a potential for misunderstanding and distrust.

Family-related stress has the potential to adversely affect the job performance of employees. Police officers not experiencing job stress can be adversely affected by problems in the home environment. Borum and Philpot (1993, pp. 122–135) reported several sources of stress commonly cited by police officers' spouses: shift work and overtime, inability to express feelings, the fear that a spouse will be injured or killed, and officers' excessively high expectations of their children. Other sources of stress included avoidance, teasing, and harassment by other children because of the officer's job, the presence of a gun in the house, and the officer's twenty-four-hour role as a law enforcer. There is also the perception the officer prefers to spend time with co-workers rather than the family, that there is either too much or too little discussion of policing, and the family member's perception that the officer is overprotective (Borum & Philpot, 1993, pp. 122–135; National Institute of Justice, 2000, p. 20).

In 1985, Blumberg and Niederhoffer (p. 371), in discussing the police family, state,

> The police profession is a jealous mistress, intruding in intimate family relationships, disrupting the rhythms of married life. The danger of police work arouses fears for the safety of loved ones. The revolving schedule of a patrol officer's "around-the-clock" tours of duty complicates family logistics. . . . Although wives adapt to the pressures of the occupation on family life, they, nevertheless, gripe about the injustices and inconsistencies. They resent the "secret society" nature of police work that obstructs free-flowing communication between spouses. Paradoxically, although they are treated as aliens in the police world, their family lifestyle is scrutinized by a curious public.

This may also be true of husbands of female officers.

The literature on the police contains discussions of the impact of policing on not only the primary marital relationship, but also the relationships between police parents and their children. The cycle of initial enthusiasm over the job leading to daily or nightly discussions of the workday between spouses, the hardening of the police spouse emotionally, and the alienation of the spouses have been described vividly by other writers as well (Doerner, 1985; Wambaugh, 1975).

PROMOTIONAL STRESS IN POLICE ORGANIZATIONS

The announcement that promotional opportunities exist within a police department typically generates a good deal of stress among officers. This response should not be unexpected when one considers the hierarchical, paramilitary organizational structure of most police agencies. The organizational chart looks like a pyramid, with very little room at the top, indicating that promotional opportunities occur only periodically and that one may have only a limited number of chances to be promoted during a twenty-year career. For those desiring to move up the rank ladder, every opportunity must be grabbed and pursued energetically. Yet only a few individuals, sometimes only one individual, will be selected for advancement. How are these few to be selected?

In most departments, advancing through the ranks depends on success in passing a written examination and an oral examination, and having attained and maintained high performance standards in the current rank. However, in many, if not most, police agencies, the belief prevails that these are not the only considerations. Also in the mix is that officers who are well connected at the upper levels of the department, or in political circles, have the edge, and this belief is coupled with the almost equally strong one that subjective elements play a major role in determining who gets promoted.

To some extent, current promotional procedures contribute to these concerns. For example, once the written test, performance evaluations, and oral examinations have been conducted and scored, the chief executive officer is often allowed to pick any of the top three candidates for the position. This raises questions as to the importance of the overall score attained on the three components of the testing procedure in determining promotability. If the tests are valid, reliable, and job related, why isn't the top scorer automatically given the position? Is the testing process followed because it is objective or merely to give the appearance of objectivity? Suppose you attain the highest score but are passed over for the position? Suppose you take but fail the written examination? Suppose you take the written examination whenever it is given, score well on it and the other portions of the promotional process, but are never promoted? What if promotions are determined by race or gender regardless of test scores, or worse, what if test scores are altered so that only certain individuals are eligible for promotion? These and a host of other concerns relating to the promotional process make it a stressful event in many police departments (Schaefer, 1983).

POLICE SHOOTINGS AND CRITICAL INCIDENTS AS A SOURCE OF STRESS

According to Wright (1986, p. 1), "Each year, some 30,000 Americans die through the suicidal, homicidal, or accidental abuse of guns; many hundreds of thousands more are injured; many hundreds of thousands more are victimized by gun crime." The National Institute of Justice survey discussed by Wright, based on 1,800 convicted and incarcerated adult male felons indicated that 50 percent were "gun criminals" and another 11 percent were armed with other potentially deadly weapons. In 1993, a new gun death occurred every 14.8 minutes, and there were at least 220 million guns in America (Davis, 1994).

Although it is extremely difficult to predict future dangerous behavior, police officers must attempt to do so on a regular basis. Their failure to do so accurately may cost them their lives. Since 1976, an average of seventy-nine police officers have been murdered each year in the line of duty, but the annual number is dropping (Brown & Langan, 2001, p. 19). The factors that likely influenced this decrease include the use of body armor or bullet-proof vests, better communications, increased training, and better police practices. Firearms were used in 92 percent of the murders of police in the line of duty between 1976 and 1998. During this period, 12 percent of the murdered officers were killed with their own firearms. The Bureau of Justice Statistics Report found that 1,820 law enforcement officers were murdered between 1976 and 1998. The majority of police officers murdered were killed while responding to disturbance calls or arrest situations. A substantial number of police officers were murdered while enforcing traffic laws and investigating suspicious persons or circumstances, or they were killed in an ambush.

Clearly, being shot, or shooting someone else, is a possibility for police officers, though the probability is low. Sherman and Cohn (1986) found that in Jacksonville, Florida, a city with a high rate of police killings, an officer could expect to work 149 years before killing a citizen. Similar figures for officers working in Milwaukee and Honolulu were 1,299 years and 7,692 years, respectively (Burns & Crawford, 2002, p. 37). In addition, police officers are more likely to be killed in the United States than are officers in most other countries (Burns & Crawford, 2002, p. 40). In any case, the stress of actually being involved in a shooting, whether as shooter or victim, is very real. Vaughn (1991, pp. 143–148) indicates that 70 percent of the police officers who use deadly force exit law enforcement within five years after the incident. The impact of such an incident is far reaching, affecting the officer, the officer's family, the organization, other officers, and the public. Kureczka (1996, pp. 1–9) reported that this form of police stress leads to faulty decision making, disciplinary problems, excessive sick leave, tardiness, on-the-job accidents, citizen complaints, and high officer turnover.

Most research involving police stress has involved police shootings. More recently, however, the research has expanded to include stress induced by critical incidents. As Kureczka (1996, p. 10) notes, "A critical incident is any event that has a stressful impact sufficient to overwhelm the usually effective coping skills of an individual." Examples of critical incidents (Kureczka, 1996) include line-of-duty death or serious injury of a coworker, a police suicide, an officer-involved shooting in a combat situation, a life-threatening assault on an officer, a death or serious injury caused by an officer, an incident involving multiple deaths, a traumatic death of a child, a barricaded suspect or hostage situation, a highly profiled media event, or any other incident that appears critical or questionable. Kureczka concluded that the most important element of combating critical incident stress is preincident stress education.

ATTEMPTS TO COMBAT POLICE STRESS

Recognition of the fact that police work can exact a high toll in personal costs has led to numerous attempts to identify and deal with such stress. Many of the factors identified as related to police stress have been discussed previously. This section examines the attempts to lessen the impact of these factors, keeping in mind our earlier statement that stress cannot be entirely eliminated and, unless it is prolonged and severe, serves some useful functions.

Farmer (1990, pp. 210–215) summarized various managerial attempts at dealing with police stress. These attempts are made to help police officers better manage the stresses they encounter.

1. Programs and activities designed to increase officer participation in decision making and to improve the quality of work-life through enhanced communication or participation
2. Development of training programs in stress awareness
3. Establishment of specific police stress programs such as psychological services, health and/or nutrition programs, and exercise programs
4. Development of peer counseling programs
5. Development of operational policies that are directed at reducing stress (shift assignments, scheduling, etc.)
6. Developing managerial skills that are people-oriented
7. Improved understanding of the nature of stress and coping alternatives through stress training
8. Use of relaxation and other stress-reducing techniques
9. Use of spouse, family orientation, and involvement programs
10. Development of support groups
11. Implementation of total wellness (physical and emotional) programs

The Los Angeles County Sheriff's Department is an example of an agency that has developed an organizational consultant program designed to provide police supervisors with the tools needed to recognize and remedy police officer stress (Higginbotham, 2000, pp. 1–3). The program takes a proactive approach to stress and trains supervisors in prevention and early intervention. The Sheriff's Department's program teaches police supervisors how to deal with difficult people, how to manage police stress, and strategies for counseling police officers. Another example for dealing with stress is the Spousal Academy. The Collier County, Florida, Sheriff's Office offers training to spouses and other domestic partners of deputies and recruits who are enrolled in the regular training academy (National Institute of Justice, 2000, p. 21). The program includes an introduction to law enforcement work and discussions concerning the effect policing will have on family lives. In addition, spouses discuss the structure of the department, stress management, and conflict resolution techniques.

The movement toward community policing also may be important in the reduction of stress among police officers. If a good deal of the stress officers experience results from constant contact with the criminal elements in the community, and from constantly working in an environment in which the police are regarded as causing trouble for other citizens, then increasing contact with law-abiding citizens under positive circumstances should help alleviate stress. To some extent, this gain may be offset by the additional problem-solving responsibilities placed on community policing officers, but if the administration accepts risks and occasional failures as part of the growing process in community-oriented policing (COP), this stress, too, can be reduced.

DEALING WITH STRESS IN POLICE ORGANIZATIONS

By now, it is clear that policing can be a stressful occupation. Whether it is more stressful than other occupations is debatable, but the point is that efforts should and can be made to reduce stress in the interests of the officer, the department, the officer's family, and the public served. Police officers often either fail to recognize the signs of stress or fail to seek help when they do recognize the symptoms. This may be due, in part, to the influence of the police subculture, which holds that "real" police officers can handle their own problems and do not need the help of "shrinks," employee assistance programs, clergy, or other "outsiders" (Bouza, 1990).

To the extent that stress results from discrepancies between the official expectations of police administrators and the unofficial expectations of the police subculture, these discrepancies need to be confronted. Because both official and subculture expectations will continue to play roles in policing, efforts must be made to reduce existing differences between the two. To the extent that stress is created and sustained by administrative policies that frustrate and befuddle officers, revisions need to be made.

As an example, we might look once again at police promotional practices. Promotions are recognized as being stressful, but unnecessary stress can be reduced. Promotional opportunities should induce healthy stress associated with preparation and enthusiasm for the testing process. However, the longer the process takes, the greater the stress involved. One way to reduce promotional stress is make the process as rapid as possible. Frankly, many departments do the opposite. The written examination is given, and there is a time lag until the results are known. When the results are known, oral interviews are scheduled, often at the convenience of board members, over several days or even weeks. Then the performance evaluations are completed, the scores are tabulated, and an eligibility list is posted. Sometime thereafter, the actual promotion is made. Although some time is required for each of these steps, the waiting period for those participating in the promotional procedure, for those waiting for a new subordinate to be appointed and for those waiting for a new supervisor to be appointed, should be reduced as much as possible. Recognition and handling of problems that increase stress levels enables us to be proactive rather than reactive in dealing with the problems.

DISCUSSION QUESTIONS

1. What is the police subculture, and in what ways does it conflict with the official mandates of police work?

2. What are the forms of organizational culture? Give an example of each form.

3. Why is it so difficult for police officers to avoid getting caught up in the subculture? Give specific examples.

4. Is subculture affiliation unique to the police? If not, should we be concerned about participation in and support of a subculture? If so, why?

5. Is policing a stressful occupation? Why and in what ways?

6. What are some of the major sources of police stress? How might some of these stresses be alleviated? Can they be eliminated?

7. What are the relationships among police stress, alcoholism, suicide, and family disruption?

8. How are police stress and the police subculture interrelated?

9. Discuss the ways in which community policing may help to reduce police stress. Can community policing also increase stress levels among officers? If so, how?

REFERENCES

Adams, T. F. (2001). *Police field operations*, 5th ed. Upper Saddle River, NJ: Prentice-Hall.

Adcox, K. (2000). Doing bad things for good reasons. *Police Chief, 67*, 16–27.

Adorno, T. W. et al. (1950). *The authoritarian personality.* New York: Harper and Brothers.

Alpert, G. P., & Dunham, R. G. (1997). *Policing urban America*, 3rd ed. Prospect Heights, IL: Waveland.

Barker, T., Hunter, R. D., & Rush, J. P. (1994). *Police systems & practices: An introduction.* Englewood Cliffs, NJ: Prentice-Hall.

Bartol, C. R. (1983). *Psychology and American law.* Belmont, CA: Wadsworth.

Bartollas, C., & Hahn, L. D. (1999). *Policing in America.* Boston: Allyn and Bacon.

Bayley, D. H., & Bittner, E. (1989). Learning the skills of policing. *Law and Contemporary Problems, 47*, 35–59.

Bennett, W. W., & Hess, K. M. (2001). *Management and supervision in law enforcement*, 3rd ed. Belmont, CA: Wadsworth/Thomson Learning.

Bittner, E. (1970). *The functions of the police in modern society.* Chevy Chase, MD: National Institute of Mental Health.

Blumberg, A. S., & Niederhoffer, E. (1985). The police family. In Blumberg, A. S., & Neiderhoffer, E. (eds.), *The ambivalent force: Perspectives on the police*, 3rd ed. (pp. 371–372). New York: Holt, Rinehart and Winston.

Borum, R., & Philpot, C. (1993). Therapy with law enforcement couples: Clinical management of the high-risk lifestyle. *American Journal of Family Therapy, 21*, 122–135.

Bouza, A. V. (1990). *The police mystique: An insider's look at cops, crime, and the criminal justice system.* New York: Plenum.

Broderick, J. J. (1987). *Police in a time of change*, 2nd ed. Prospect Heights, IL: Waveland.

Brooks, L. W., & Piquero, L. (1998). Police stress: Does department size matter? *Policing, 21*, 600–617.

Brown, J. M., & Langan, P. A. (2001). Policing and homicide, 1976–1998: Justifiable homicide by police, police officers murdered by felons. Washington, DC: Bureau of Justice Statistics Clearinghouse.

Burbeck, E., & Furnham, A. (1985). Police officer selection: A critical review of the literature. *Journal of Police Science and Administration, 13*, 58–69.

Burke, R., & Deszca, E. (1986). Correlates of psychological burnout phases among police officers. *Human Relations, 39*, 487–502.

Burns, R. G., & Crawford, C. E. (2002). *Policing and violence.* Upper Saddle River, NJ: Prentice-Hall.

Caldero, M. (1997, March). Value consistency within the police: The lack of a gap. Paper presented at the Annual Meeting of the Academy of Criminal Justice Sciences, Louisville, KY.

Carey, L. R. (1994). Community policing for the suburban department. *Police Chief, 61*, 24–26.

Carpenter, B., & Raza, S. (1987). Personality characteristics of police applicants: Comparisons across subgroups and other populations. *Journal of Police Science and Administration, 15*, 10–17.

Carter, D. L., & Radelet, L. A. (1999). *The police and the community*, 6th ed. Upper Saddle River, NJ: Prentice-Hall.

Champoux, J. E. (2000). *Organizational behavior.* Cincinnati, OH: South-Western.

Chevigny, P. (1969). *Police power: Police abuses in New York City.* New York: Vintage Books.

Cottle, H. D., & Ford, G. G. (2000). Effects of tenure police officer personality functioning. *Journal of Police and Criminal Psychology, 15,* 1–9.

Cox, S. M., & Fitzgerald, J. D. (1996). *Police in community relations: Critical issues,* 3rd ed. Dubuque, IA: Wm. C. Brown.

Crank, J. P. (1998). *Understanding police culture.* Cincinnati, OH: Anderson.

Cray, E. (1972). *The enemy in the streets: Police malpractice in America.* Garden City, NY: Anchor Books.

Davis, R. (1994, January 3). Attitude change proves lethal for police. *USA Today,* p. 3A.

Doerner, W. G. (1985). I'm not the man I used to be: Reflections on the transition from prof to cop. In Blumberg, S., & Niederhoffer, E. (eds.), *The ambivalent force: Perspectives on the police* (pp. 394–399). New York: Holt, Rinehart and Winston.

Dorsey, R. R., & Giacopassi, D. J. (1987). Demographics and work-related correlates of police officer cynicism. In Kennedy, D. B., & Homant, R. J. (eds.), *Police and law enforcement* (pp. 173–188). New York: Ames Press.

Farmer, R. E. (1990). Clinical and managerial implications of stress research on the police. *Journal of Police Science and Administration, 17,* 205–218.

Fell, R., Richard, W., & Wallace, W. (1980). Psychological job stress and the police officer. *Journal of Police Science and Administration, 8,* 139–144.

Finn, P., & Tomz, J. E. (1997). Developing a law enforcement stress program for officers and their families. National Institute of Justice, Document NCJ 63175. Rockville, MD: National Criminal Justice Reference Service.

Flynn, R. S. (1997). Stress reduction techniques for police officers. Western American Doctoral Dissertation, National Criminal Justice Reference Service NCJ 171561. Available online at ncjrs.ord.

Gaines, L. K., Kappeler, V. E., & Vaughn, J. B. (1999). *Policing in America,* 3rd ed. Cincinnati, OH: Anderson.

Graves, W. (1996). Police cynicism: Causes and cures. *FBI Law Enforcement Bulletin, 65,* 16–20.

Greene, L. W. (1997). Uplifting resilient police families. *Police Chief, 64,* 70–72.

Hageman, M. J. (1989). Family life. In Bailey, W. G. (ed.), *The encyclopedia of police science* (pp. 187–190). New York: Garland.

Haarr, R. N., & Morash, M. (1999). Gender, race, and strategies of coping with occupational stress in policing. *Justice Quarterly, 16,* 303–336.

Hernandez, J. Jr. (1989). *The Custer syndrome.* Salem, WI: Sheffield.

Higginbotham, C. E. (2000). Organizational consultant program takes aim at officers' stress. *Police Chief, 67,* 104–106.

Hill, K. Q., & Clawson, M. (1988). The health hazards of "street level" bureaucracy: Mortality among the police. *Journal of Police Science and Administration, 16,* 243–248.

Inciardi, J. A. (1990). *Criminal justice,* 3rd ed. San Diego: Harcourt Brace Jovanovich.

Josephson, R. L., & Reiser, M. (1990). Officer suicide in the Los Angeles Police Department: A twelve-year follow-up. *Journal of Police Science and Administration, 17,* 227–229.

Kappeler, V. E. (1999). *The police and society,* 2nd ed. Prospect Heights, IL: Waveland.

Kirkham, G. (1977). *Signal zero.* New York: Ballantine.

Kunen, J. S. (1986). Praised, admired, feared and mistrusted, cops are seen not in true colors, but only blue. *People Weekly, 26,* 127–131.

Kureczka, A. W. (1996, Feb/Mar). Critical incident stress in law enforcement. *FBI Law Enforcement Bulletin, 65,* 10–16.

LaGrange, R. L.(1998). *Policing American society,* 2nd ed. Chicago: Nelson-Hall.

Lundman, R. J. (1980). *Police and policing: An introduction.* New York: Holt, Rinehart and Winston.

Manning, P. K. (1977). *Police work.* Cambridge, MA: MIT Press.

———. (1989). Occupational culture. In Bailey, W. G. (ed.), *The encyclopedia of police science* (pp. 360–364). New York: Garland.

Maynard, P., & Maynard, N. (1982). Stress in police families—Some policy implications. *Journal of Police Science and Administration, 10,* 302–314.

More, H. W. (1998). *Special topics in policing*, 2nd ed. Cincinnati, OH: Anderson.

National Institute of Justice. (2000). On-the-job stress in policing. *National Institute of Justice Journal*, 19(24 (NCJ 180079).

Neiderhoffer, A. (1967). *Behind the shield: The police in urban society*. Garden City, NY: Doubleday.

Nelson, D. E., & Quick, J. C. (2002). *Understanding organizational behavior*. Cincinnati, OH: South-Western.

Paoline, E. A., Myers, S., & Worden, R. (2000). Police culture, individualism, and community policing: Evidence from two police departments. *Justice Quarterly, 17*, 575–605.

Peak, K. J. (1997). *Policing America*, 2nd ed. Upper Saddle River, NJ: Prentice-Hall.

Pendergrass, J. M. (1999). Alcohol abuse in policing: Prevention strategies. *FBI Law Enforcement Bulletin, 68*, 16–18.

Post, G. M. (1992). Police recruits: Training tomorrow's workforce. *FBI Law Enforcement Bulletin, 61*, 19–24.

Pranzo, P. J., & Pranzo, R. (1999). *Stress management for law enforcement behind the shield: Combating trauma*. Longwood, FL: Gould.

Regoli, R. M. (1976). An empirical assessment of Niederhoffer's police cynicism scale. *Journal of Criminal Justice 4*, 231–241.

Regoli, R. M., & Poole, E. D. (1978). Specifying police cynicism. *Journal of Police Science and Administration, 6*, 98–104.

Reuss-Ianni, E. (1983). *Two cultures of policing*. New Brunswick, NJ: Transaction Books.

Roberg, R., Crank, J., & Kuykendall, J. (2000). *Police and society*. Los Angeles, CA: Roxbury.

Rubinstein, J. (1973). *City police*. New York: Farrar, Straus and Giroux.

Rudovsky, D. (1992). Police abuse: Can the violence be contained? *Harvard Civil Rights–Civil Liberties Law Review, 27*, 465–501.

Ryan, A. H. (1997). Afterburn: The victimization of police families. *Police Chief, 64*, 63–68.

Schaefer, R. B. (1983). The stress of police promotion. *FBI Law Enforcement Bulletin, 52*, 3–6.

Selye, H. (1974). *Stress without distress*. Philadelphia: Lippincott.

Sherman, L. W., & Cohn, E. C. (1986). *Citizens killed by big city police*. Washington, DC: Crime Control Institute.

Skolnick, J. (1966). *Justice without trial*. New York: John Wiley & Sons.

Skolnick, J. H., & Fyfe, J. J. (1993). *Above the law: Police and the excessive use of force*. New York: Free Press.

Sparrow, M. K., Moore, M. H., & Kennedy, D. M. (1990). *Beyond 911: A new era for policing*. New York: Basic Books.

Spielberger, C., Westberry, L., Grier, K., & Greenfield, G. (1981). *Police stress survey—Sources of stress in law enforcement*. Tampa: University of South Florida Human Resources Institute.

Stack, S., & Kelley, T. (1999). Police suicide. In Kennedy, D. J., & McNamara, R. P. (eds.), *Police and policing: Contemporary issues*, 2nd ed. Westport, CT: Praeger.

Stevens, D. J. (1999). Police officer stress. *Law and Order, 47*, 77–81.

Storms, L. H., Penn, N. F., & Tenzell, J. H. (1990). Policemen's perception of real and ideal policemen. *Journal of Police Science and Administration, 17*, 40–43.

Stratton, J. G. (1978, May). Police stress: Considerations and suggestions. *Police Chief, 45*, 73–76.

Stratton, J. G., Parker, D., & Snibbe, J. (1984). Post-traumatic stress-study of police officers involved in shootings. *Psychological Reports, 55*, 127–131.

Swanson, C., Gaines, L., & Gore, B. (1991, August). Abuse of anabolic steroids. *Law Enforcement Bulletin, 60*, 19–23.

Swidler, A. (1986). Culture in symbols and strategies. *American Sociological Review, 51*, 273–286.

Terry, W. C. (1989). Police stress: The empirical evidence. *Police Science and Administration, 9*, 61–75.

United States General Accounting Office. (1998). Law enforcement information on drug-related police corruption. Washington, DC: U.S. Government Printing Office.

Van Maanen, J. (1978). The asshole. In VanMaanen, J., & Manning, P. K. (eds.), *Policing: A view from the street* (pp. 221–238). Santa Monica, CA: Goodyear.

Vaughn, J. (1991). Critical incidents in policing. In Reese,, J., Horn, J., & Dunning, C. (eds.), *Critical incidents in policing* (pp. 143–148). Washington, DC: U.S. Government Printing Office.

Veniga, R. L., & Spradley, J. (1981). *How to cope with job burnout.* Englewood Cliffs, NJ: Prentice-Hall.

Vila, B. J., Kenney, D. J., Morrison, G. B., & Reuland, M. (2000). *Evaluating the effects of fatigue on police patrol officers: Final report.* Washington, DC: Police Executive Research Forum.

Violanti, J. M., & Marshall, J. R. (1983). The police stress process. *Journal of Police Science and Administration, 11,* 389–394.

Violanti, J., Marshall, J., & Howe, B. (1985). Stress, coping, and alcohol use—The police connection. *Journal of Police Science and Administration, 13,* 106–110.

Violanti, J., Vena, J., & Marshall, J. (1986). Disease risk and mortality among police officers—New evidence and contributing factors. *Journal of Police Science and Administration, 14,* 17–23.

Wagner, M., & Brzeczek, R. J. (1983, August). Alcoholism and suicide: A fatal connection. *FBI Law Enforcement Bulletin, 52,* 8–15.

Wambaugh, J. (1975). *The choirboys.* New York: Dell.

Westley, W. (1970). *Violence and the police.* Cambridge, MA: MIT Press.

Whisenand, P. M. (2001). *Supervising police personnel,* 4th ed. Upper Saddle River, NJ: Prentice-Hall.

Wright, J. D. (1986, November). The armed criminal in America. In *Research in Brief,* National Institute of Justice. Washington, DC: U.S. Government Printing Office.

Yarmey, A. D. (1990). *Understanding police and police work: Psychosocial issues.* New York: New York University Press.

CHAPTER EIGHT

POLICING IN A MULTICULTURAL SETTING

It should be apparent from discussions in Chapters 2 and 3 that the police, whatever their perceived role, cannot be effective or efficient without public support. Without such support, they will be uninformed of most crimes, are likely to receive inadequate resources, will not be able to collect information needed to solve cases and apprehend offenders, and will be unsuccessful in recruiting quality employees. There is little doubt that, in democratic societies at least, community relations are the cornerstone of good policing. Burden (1992, p. 19) notes, ". . . the police are—or should be—the protectors of a citizen's civil liberties and civil rights, as well as his life and property. They are, for example, the first line of defense for the First Amendment rights to assemble peaceably and speak freely. Few unpopular ideas would ever get a public hearing unless the police were on hand to ensure the speaker's safety and maintain order." If the police are to serve the community effectively and in a manner acceptable to citizens, there must be a reasonable working relationship between the two.

Developing such working relationships in a rapidly changing, multicultural society is difficult. Indications from the U.S. Bureau of Census are that the rapidly growing Asian population is now 10.9 million (4% of the population), the Hispanic population is now 31.7 million (11.7% of the population), and the African American population is now 35.1 million (13% of the population) (U.S. Cenus Bureau, 2000). Most authorities agree that within fifty to sixty years, people of color will be a numerical majority in the United States (Takaki, 1993). Pomerville (1993, p. 30), for example, notes, "In the next few decades, the population will shift from a dominant Anglo-American society to a dominant multi-cultural majority of African-Americans, Asian-Americans, and Hispanic-Americans." According to Barlow and Barlow (2000, p. 7), "Groups whose numbers in the census polls indicate they might be described as racial/ethnic minorities already exist as majorities in most major U.S. cities."

The elderly constitute an increasing proportion of our population. Gays and lesbians, the homeless, religious minorities, neo-Nazi skinheads, and refugees from Balkan countries, Central and South America, and island countries continue to seek asylum. Immigrants come to this country bringing different languages, religious observances, dress, and lifestyles, and different views of the police. Some, having come from countries where the police are integrated with the military and police actions are not regulated by strong constitutional and human rights guarantees, have very negative images of the police (Scott, 1993, p. 26; Barak, Flavin, & Leighton, 2001, pp. 257–259).

There are basically two ways of attempting to develop good working relationships between the police and other citizens. The first, community policing, is discussed in detail in Chapter 9. The second consists of police–community relations efforts. The two are not, of course, mutually exclusive, but neither are they identical, as Highlight 8.1 indicates.

THE NATURE OF POLICE–COMMUNITY RELATIONS

As O'Brien (1978, p. 304) once indicated, "The central position of the police in the community critically affects all sections of society. The multiple duties of the police at all times and in all areas of the community dictate that they must influence the daily life of each citizen. . . . Unfortunately, in recent times there has been a rupture of mutual trust between the police and some segments of the community."

Actually, of course, as we have seen, the "rupture of mutual trust" noted by O'Brien is not a recent occurrence but has deep historical roots in American policing. Conflict between the police and other citizens is rooted in the basic structure of American society and the values on which it rests. The extent to which this is so can be seen in numerous discussions of police–community relations that are described, presumably unintentionally, in terms of police encounters with citizens. The language employed here makes it

■ ■ ■ ■ ■

HIGHLIGHT 8.1
NEW CHIEF TO LOOK FOR TROUBLE SPOTS

Mack Vines vows his department will pursue community policing with a mission, concentrating on drug corners and high-crime areas.

In 1974, Mack Vines inherited a St. Petersburg Police Department in disarray. Crime was up. The department's relationship with the black community was poor. During six years in charge, he promoted minorities and got residents more involved in the department, though he still dealt with his share of racial tensions in the city.

After he retired, he took a jog along Coffee Pot Boulevard and thought, "I'm going to return to this city some day."

He did more than that. On Friday, he returned to the very job he left 21 years ago.

A lot has changed between Vines' first and second tours of duty as police chief, including civil disturbances in 1996. Now that the chief's job is his again, what does Vines plan?

He does not have any specific changes in mind yet, but in an interview with the *St. Petersburg Times*, Vines, 63, touched on:

- Keeping community policing.
- Saturating drug areas with officers.
- Doing more with the existing staff.

"My management style is that I am not a micromanager," Vines said. "I am a detail person. I like information, but I like to place tasks with people. I want them to perform and be productive, creative and innovative. Just make a decision and do it. We don't want them to be afraid of anything."

Vines, who worked half of his 41-year law enforcement career in St. Petersburg, said much of what police do is problem-solving.

"We must police through empathy," he said.

Community policing—solving quality of life problems such as drug dealing, vagrants and loud music—is here to stay, Vines vowed.

"I have always felt that the community and the police together can solve many problems and contributing factors to discord in the community," Vines said. "During the 1970s, as a lieutenant, I was sent to numerous cities throughout the nation to study efforts being made to more involve citizens in the fight against crime and disorder. Later, the department submitted a federal grant request, which was funded, and team policing, the forerunner of community policing, started in the south side of town."

He said there should be no difference in the way officers treat residents, particularly minorities. "The officer's initial approach, not necessarily the citizen's, will dictate how successful the encounter is," Vines said. "If the approach is abrupt, more than likely the reception will be the same."

Vines said to fight drugs, he will increase officer presence in known drug-dealing areas through "directed patrols."

"We're going to have to address these people who think they can run havoc over these citizens," Vines said.

He will find trouble spots by having his staff analyze crime statistics and then assign officers there. As an example, he talked of officers in the Childs Park neighborhood to move dealers off street corners.

"If they move, we move," Vines said. "It's proactive, effective patrolling." The Police Department must follow the dealer until the activity ends or the suspect is arrested, he said.

Officers also should do field interrogation reports, street interviews in which they ask people their names, dates of birth and other information. Officers pass the information to detectives to compare with descriptions of possible suspects to solve crimes. Vines sees it as an important crime-fighting tool, though the practice has come in for some criticism in the past in St. Petersburg, after records showed that between January 1996 and August 1997 black residents were three times more likely to be stopped than white residents.

In addition to fighting crime, Vines will have to sort out a department with some staffing troubles.

Many officers have said discipline isn't fairly applied, and the police union is negotiating a new contract and is concerned about raises for officers.

Whether problems with morale are real or perceived, Vines said, he intends to talk with the rank and file about their concerns.

Meanwhile, earlier this year, a computer analysis suggested that nearly half an officer's day is devoted to free time or activities the department doesn't know about.

The findings suggest the number of patrol officers the city has is adequate. But the department needs to make significant improvements in allocating, scheduling and deploying officers. So far, no changes have been made. To Vines, hiring more police officers is not the answer.

"You've got to deploy people based on need," he said. "More is not always better. It's much more feasible to manage smarter."

Vines said positions in the department that do not require a gun and badge should be farmed out to civilians at lower pay.

"I'll be reviewing and reviewing and reviewing issues," Vines said.

He won the job after Mayor Rick Baker decided to stick with his gut feelings.

"Whether it was calm or crisis, who would I feel had the experience, background, knowledge and temperament?" Baker asked himself. The answer kept coming back "Vines."

Vines will begin shadowing Chief Goliath Davis III on Sept. 24. He officially takes over Oct. 5 and will earn $111,400 annually. He also will draw an annual city police pension of $47,750.

Said Vines, "I have a real burning desire to get back at the helm of the department and see if there's any way all of us together can improve on what we're doing internally and externally."

Leanora Minai, *St. Petersburg Times*, (2001, September 9, p. 1B). Copyright St. Petersburg Times.

appear that the police are not, themselves, citizens and points to a dichotomy that has emerged in our society between the police and other citizens.

In many respects the police have come to be viewed as adversaries not only by those involved in criminal activities, but also by basically law abiding citizens who occasionally violate speed limits or drive when they have had one too many drinks or protest what they consider to be legitimate grievances without going through proper channels to obtain a permit. In fact, of course, police officers are first and foremost citizens, historically, traditionally, and legally. Yet the language we use to describe things often indicates the way in which we view them, and, to some extent, some of us tend to view the police as somehow distinct from "citizens." While the use of such terminology may not widen the gap between the police and other citizens, it does little to close the gap. Police encounters with other citizens are, at base, encounters between fellow citizens.

Another point needs to be made here. When we are talking about police–community relations, we tend to think in terms of police encounters with the public. In fact, we are not dealing with one large homogeneous group called a public, but with many diverse publics. These publics are divided by factors such as geography, race, sex, age, social class, respect for law and order, and degree of law-abiding behavior (Cox & Wade, 1998, p. 13). These different publics have unique interests and concerns that separate them from one another in many ways. The police, as public servants, are to serve all these various publics, and they themselves organize in various ways to meet what they perceive to be the needs of the publics they serve. Because the expectations of members of these different publics are often dissimilar, providing effective service is often difficult, leading to many of the problems in policing. According to Hennessy (1993, p. 48),

> Our communities are changing quickly—often too quickly for law enforcement to keep up. Failing to understand many of these changes, and still trying to conduct business as usual, we find that the tools and rules that worked before don't work now. For many seasoned officers, their main concern is to make it through each shift and go home in one piece. This only serves to reinforce a force-oriented culture that brings officers closer to each other and further from the community they serve.

In addition, members of the various publics are often apathetic about most issues involving the police but have very specific expectations when they, or other members of their group, require police services.

The necessity of attempting to satisfy these different, sometimes conflicting, expectations should alert us to the fact that good police–community relations are not easy to achieve. In a large, industrialized, multiethnic society, one based on values that include democratic decision making, individual freedom, and tolerance for diversity, the need for social order and the demand for freedom will inevitably lead to conflict on some occasions (Cox & Fitzgerald, 1996).

To some extent, then, conflict between the police and other citizens is inevitable and perhaps even healthy within limits. The problem cannot be ignored when the conflict becomes extensive or certain groups experience differential treatment by the police. Solutions to conflicts of this type are not found easily and are not the sole responsibility of the police. Yet we cannot easily force other citizens into classes on human or public relations, even though we recognize that successful programs in either of these areas require reciprocity. Therefore, the burden of trying to improve police–community relations often rests with the police.

Police–community relations comprise both human and public relations. The concept of human relations refers to everything we do to, for, and with other people. Included under this concept are such things as showing respect for one another, being sensitive to the problems of others, tolerating divergent points of view, and showing respect for human dignity. Public relations, from the police perspective, include all of the activities in which they engage while attempting to develop and/or maintain a favorable public image (Cox & Fitzgerald, 1996). Let's examine each of these concepts as they relate to police encounters with other citizens.

Human Relations in Policing

With respect to police–community relations, human relations in the millions of day-to-day encounters that take place are the foundation for community relations, good or bad. It is important to recognize that these encounters between individuals do not occur in a vacuum. When we enter into encounters with others, we often know, or think we know, a good deal about them, even though we have never met them before. Thus, for example, we have preconceived notions about members of different racial or ethnic groups and about police officers. These preconceived notions, or stereotypes, are based on prior encounters, word of mouth/rumor/gossip, and/or information provided by the media. These notions may be accurate or inaccurate. Whichever is the case, we act in terms of these perceptions, at least until the encounter in which we are involved gives us additional and/or different information on which to base our beliefs and actions.

Consider an encounter between a uniformed police officer and another citizen. The officer is easily identifiable because of the uniform, badge, nightstick, handcuffs, and gun, and all of these help identify her role in the encounter. The role that is, in part, defined by the tools of the trade includes the fact that the officer has authority and may use force under certain circumstances to gain compliance with her wishes. This should indicate, and for the most part appears to indicate, to other parties to the encounter that the officer's definition of the situation will be the prevailing one—that is, that the officer is in control or will gain control.

For this definition of the situation to prevail, certain obligations must be fulfilled by the other party or parties to the encounter. These include deferring to the officer's authority, treating the officer with some degree of respect, and complying with her directions. To do otherwise is to risk offending the officer, who may then resort to more drastic actions in light of what may be viewed as a challenge to her authority. Some officers are extremely sensitive to such challenges and to the perceived loss of face that accompanies them. Such officers may feel compelled to respond quickly and forcefully to maintain their control. Obviously, such a response may lead to suspicion and hostility on behalf of the other party to the encounter, and the encounter may become nasty in short order.

This is especially true when the two parties to the encounter bring negative impressions of each other into the encounter, as sometimes occurs when the police and racial or ethnic minority group members interact. Such negative impressions also often exist when the police are called into a domestic violence situation in which they regard the offender with suspicion and the offender believes that police intervention into his home into an essentially private matter is improper.

The extent to which encounters between the police and other citizens become problematic depends on a number of factors. These include the impressions brought to the encounter, the setting in which the encounter occurs (private or public, familiar or unfamiliar), the number and types of participants involved, the degree of control exercised by the participants, and what actually happens during the encounter. For example, the mere sight of a police officer puts some people on guard. They drive more slowly and more carefully; if they are involved in illegal activities, they may try to appear innocent, and they may treat other persons more civilly. For their part, police officers are trained to be suspicious of others, especially when past experience or present knowledge leads them to believe an offense may be involved. Thus the danger and difficulty of police encounters ranges from very great, as in an encounter with a known felon in the process of committing a felony in an isolated location, with the officer and the felon being the only participants involved, to very little, as in the case of locating a missing child lost in a shopping mall where other participants are attempting to assist.

It is possible to exaggerate the difficulties involved in police encounters with other citizens. Most such encounters are civil, characterized by some degree of mutual concern, understanding, and respect (Reiss, 1968). Still, there is no denying that encounters between the police and some citizens are more likely to be problematic than others. As we have seen, police–minority encounters in our society have been particularly problematic over the past quarter of a century, and it is to these encounters that we now turn our attention.

Police–Minority Encounters

One of the most controversial areas of police–community relations in our society involves the police and racial/ethnic minority group members, particularly police interactions with blacks and Hispanics, though members of other racial and ethnic minorities are sometimes involved as well (see Highlight 8.2). Our country has a long history of conflict between the police and minorities. In the 1960s there were five years of riots involving blacks and the police, and in the 1990s a number of incidents, beginning with the highly publicized Rodney King beating by Los Angeles police officers, again illustrated the poor relationships that exist between the police and blacks in many parts of this country (*Crime Control Digest*, 1999, p. 6). Similar problems exist in many communities with respect to Hispanics and Native Americans (Walker, Spohn, & DeLone, 1995).

■ ■ ■ ■ ■ ▬▬▬▬▬▬▬▬▬▬▬▬▬▬▬▬▬▬▬▬▬▬▬▬▬▬▬▬

HIGHLIGHT 8.2

LAPD OFFICERS, PROJECT RESIDENTS EXPLORE WAYS TO EASE TENSIONS

After a week and a half of clashes in and around South Los Angeles housing projects that have left seven police officers injured, residents and police got together at a meeting Thursday and agreed on some steps to ease tensions.

Although the meeting at the Jordan Downs gymnasium was heated at times, police, residents and politicians agreed to increased foot patrols, to hold monthly meetings and to try to bring back federal funding for a once-popular community policing program.

Tensions have resulted in violence five times recently at the Jordan Downs, Nickerson Gardens and Imperial Court housing projects, usually as police tried to make a stop or an arrest, said Los Angeles Police Capt. Patrick M. Gannon. Crowds have quickly formed each time, with the suspects sometimes becoming the objects of a kind of tug-of-war, he said.

The latest incident occurred Wednesday after a drive-by shooting that left two people in critical condition. Firefighters and then police were pelted with objects, but no one was hurt.

However, on Tuesday night, two police officers were kicked, beaten and bitten by about a dozen people after they tried to arrest a parolee at Nickerson Gardens, Gannon said.

Sunday night, a foot chase at Imperial Court took an even more dangerous turn when an 11-year-old girl became "so incensed she picked up a broomstick to strike officers. Her grandmother took it away and [the girl] picked up a butcher knife," Gannon said.

"If not for the actions of the grandmother, a tragedy could have occurred," he said.

Last Friday, three police officers at Jordan Downs were injured by a crowd after they made a traffic stop of a bicyclist, Lt. Rick Angelos said. The officers, who suffered cuts and scratches, returned to work Tuesday.

"If there's a guy running through the development carrying a gun or carrying drugs, that's a legitimate chase. But there's a belief that every time we do that, it's wrong," Gannon told about 100 people assembled at the Jordan Downs Recreation Center.

The meeting was attended by Chief Bernard C. Parks, Congresswoman Juanita Millender-McDonald, Councilwoman Janice Hahn and other local leaders.

Parks urged residents not to get caught up in perceived past slights and to think instead about solving problems.

"To provide good service, there needs to be a level of trust on both sides," Parks said. "We cannot be successful without your help."

Some residents complained that police officers should treat them with more respect.

Dorothy Toliver, 65, a longtime Jordan Downs resident, said that years ago, police officers "walked the beat."

"Now, when they come around, they come like you just done stole the world," she said.

"They need to try to get to know people in the community."

Resident Richard Alford, 30, said too many officers "have no people skills. They act like we're all suspects, and we're not."

Other residents expressed a common fear that affects their relationship with police: retaliation by suspects if they report crimes. The Southeast Division consistently has the highest murder rate in the city, police say.

Gannon said that as of Wednesday night, his division had increased the number of police officers on foot patrol at the three housing developments. That will continue from now on, he said.

Millender-McDonald said she would take a petition signed by residents to Washington to ask the federal government for funding to bring back the Community Oriented Policing on the Streets—or COPS—program.

Becerra, Hector. (2001, August 17 Section 2; p. 3) *Los Angeles Times.*

A minority group is comprised of individuals who are accorded unequal treatment from dominant group members in the form of discrimination; who are relatively easy to identify because of their physical and/or cultural characteristics, which differ from those of the dominant group. Using this definition of discrimination, the police themselves might well be considered members of a minority because they are often victims of discrimination, are generally easy to identify, and have, as we have seen, some distinctive cultural characteristics (masculinity, authority, use of force, cynicism, etc.). One basic difference between police officers and members of racial/ethnic minorities is that the former are voluntary members while the latter are not. Traditional beliefs in our society hold that members of some racial/ethnic minorities are inferior to whites in some ways, even though scientific research indicates there is no basis for such beliefs. Because many police officers come from traditional backgrounds, it is not surprising to find that many agree that minority group members are inferior, especially when they police in areas with high crime rates that are inhabited principally by members of a minority who often view the police as intruders or members of an army of occupation (Baldwin, 1962; Hacker, 1992).

It is important to point out the difference between prejudice (a feeling about a person or persons based on faulty generalizations) and discrimination (which involves behavior that, in its negative form, excludes all members of a certain group from some rights, opportunities, or privileges [Schaefer, 2000]). We all have prejudices that may or may not result in discrimination. The existence of prejudice among police officers has been documented (Bayley & Mendelsohn, 1969; Reiss, 1970), and though we might hope that these proclivities have changed in recent years with changes in civil rights legislation and hiring practices of police agencies, there is little we can do in a direct fashion to alter peoples' feelings, and precious little research has been done in this area in the past decade or so (Bayley & Mendelsohn, 1969; Schaefer, 2000; Walker, Spohn & Delone, 1995).

When these feelings carry over into behavior (discrimination), however, serious problems result for both the police and minority group members. Thus when police officers harass or abuse individuals because they are members of a minority, or treat individuals as if they are above the law because they belong to another minority, community relations suffer. Harassment and abuse result in loss of face and human dignity as well as occasional physical injuries, and they cannot be tolerated on the part of police officers. There is little doubt that members of many minorities—racial and ethnic as well as behavioral (alcoholics, homosexuals, prostitutes, drug addicts, etc.)— believe that such harassment and abuse are commonly directed to members of their groups. According to Walker, Spohn, and DeLone (1995, p. 102), "Verbal abuse by police officers is one of the most common complaints expressed by citizens. In 1990, about 40 percent of the complaints received by the New York City Civilian Complaint Review Board involved discourtesy or ethnic slurs. . . . Racial or ethnic slurs . . . not only demean citizens but also deny them equal treatment on the basis of their race or ethnicity." As a consequence, as well as for historical reasons, individuals belonging to minority groups resent and are sometimes openly hostile toward the police. They often respond by harassing and verbally abusing the police. These actions escalate the danger and hostility involved and ensures poor community relations. It is essential, then, to realize that prejudice and discrimination are not limited to the police and, therefore, that the police alone cannot ensure good community relations.

It is equally important to recognize that many police officers who might not otherwise be involved in discriminatory practices fall victim to occupational discrimination. That is, even though an individual officer may not believe in acting in a discriminatory fashion, his colleagues may exhibit such behavior. To be perceived as a part of the subculture described earlier, this officer may emulate the behavior of his peers, thus harassing or abusing minority group members, not because he believes it is right, but because he wishes to be perceived as a member of the "in-group."

Similarly, minority group members may not believe that harassing the police is appropriate behavior, but in the presence of other members of their group, may do so. Some blacks in the United States, for example, have several centuries of historical reasons for disliking the police, whom they see as representatives of the establishment that, they believe, made and keeps them second-class citizens. As Sykes (1978, p. 395) pointed out, "In a democratic social order, the police are expected to be fair in their enforcement of the law and accountable to those who are policed. They are not to be an alien force imposed on a community, an autonomous body ruling by coercion, or agents of a tyrannical state, but servants of society maintaining a commonly accepted body of law in evenhanded fashion."

However, as we have pointed out elsewhere (Cox & Fitzgerald, 1996), the police in our society have often been an alien force when dealing with blacks and other minority group members. The police traditionally enforced the laws that made blacks second-class citizens. And, in contemporary society, the police expend a disproportionate amount of their resources in minority neighborhoods. Here again, conflicting points of view and the difficulty of finding solutions to police–minority relations problems are obvious. As Weaver (1992, p. 2) states, "Simply mixing culturally different people together does not resolve misunderstandings. Quite the contrary. Differences usually become more apparent and hostilities can actually increase during encounters between culturally diverse individuals."

While minority group members regard the numbers of police in their neighborhoods as excessive and a form of harassment, the police are correct in arguing that minority neighborhoods typically have high crime rates and therefore require police presence. Although it may be argued that police presence contributes to high crime rates (the more police, the more crimes they discover), it is equally true that the number of victims and offenders found in such neighborhoods makes it difficult for the police to respond in any other fashion (Walker, Spohn, & DeLone, 1995). This fact, however, does not justify the use of discriminatory tactics in minority neighborhoods.

What are some of the forms of police discrimination in minority neighborhoods? As noted, the basic form of discrimination is psychological harassment based on the use of racial slurs and other attempts to embarrass or humiliate members of the minority group in question. Failure to use proper forms of address (e.g., use of first name rather than Mr. or Ms. and last name) has been and remains a major complaint of minority group members (National Advisory Commission, 1968; Cox, 1984; Hacker, 1992; Walker, Spohn, & DeLone, 1995). Failure to respond rapidly to calls in ghetto or barrio areas also has been an issue. Unreasonable use of stop-and-question and stop-and-frisk tactics alarm minority group members. And, of course, the relatively infrequent but totally unacceptable use of excessive force on the part of the police in dealing with members of minorities (or, for that matter, the dominant group) is of major concern (Reiss, 1970; Chavis & Williams, 1993; Walker, Spohn, & DeLone, 1995). Such incidents become legend in minority neighborhoods and further the negative image of the police already present as a result of historical differences between the parties.

According to Walker, Spohn, and DeLone (1995, pp. 85, 89), "Minorities are arrested, stopped and questioned and shot and killed by the police out of all proportion to their representation in the population. . . . The police play a far more visible role in minority group neighborhoods compared with white neighborhoods. . . . An African-American or Hispanic American is much more likely than a white American to see or have personal contact with a police officer." Police use arrests as a strategy for resolving a variety of problems (many of which are noncriminal in nature) in the ghettos. In some instances, the probability of a black man being arrested during his lifetime approaches 90 percent (Barlow & Barlow, 2000, p. 94).

The patrol car in the ghetto or barrio may be perceived by blacks and Latinos as police harassment, while the police may believe they are acting in the best interests of these minority groups by providing as many personnel as possible in those areas where citizens are most likely to commit and be victims of crime. Alternatively, the young black or Latino males who use the slang and dress of their subcultures may be perceived by the police as challenging their authority. Such negative stereotypes are often inaccurate, and their persistence makes sharing a definition of the situation or mutual understanding difficult, if not impossible.

We should note here that human relations problems involving the police and minority group members are definitely not a thing of the past. Kane (2001, p. 3) states, "One national study found that more than half of all black men report they have been victims of racial profiling by law enforcement. Overall, nearly four in 10 blacks believe they have been unfairly stopped by the police simply because they are black—52% of black men and 25% of black women" (see Highlight 8.3). Further, a 1999 survey revealed that only 31 percent of black respondents and only 33 percent of other non-whites rated the honesty and ethical standards of police officers as "very high" or "high" compared to 52 percent of white respondents. Additionally, only 30 percent of black respondents (compared to 67% of white respondents and 48% of Hispanic respondents) felt their local police treated people fairly. And, 43 percent of black respondents and 28 percent of Hispanic respondents reported fearing that the police would stop and arrest them, even though they were innocent (compared with 16 percent of white respondents) (Maguire, Pastore, & Flanagan, 1999, pp. 109–111).

Police–minority problems are likely to increase in number for all of the reasons we have presented unless steps are taken now to prevent this from occurring. Unless dramatic changes in the socioeconomic status of many minority group members occur, the number of encounters between them and the police will continue to increase, making resolution of some of the problematic aspects of such encounters even more important.

Police Public Relations

Police–community relations are comprised of two components. The first of these, human relations, we have just discussed. The second component, public relations, consists of those efforts on behalf of the police to develop and present a favorable image. While it is true that community relations programs are doomed to failure if the day-to-day human relations practices of participants are poor, publicizing the positive practices and programs of police departments can certainly affect the impression of the police in the minds of other citizens. The uniform of the officer, the symbol on the squad car, and the response of the dispatcher or receptionist at police headquarters all create an impression of the police, and they are all parts of police public relations efforts.

Police pamphlets, public-speaking engagements, department-sponsored programs, news conferences, widely advertised training in cultural diversity, and many other activities also fall within the public relations domain. Public relations involve two interdependent components. The first of these, *policy*, consists of decisions, statements, and plans made by management in an attempt to influence public opinion. The second component, *practice*, is the process of putting the policies into action (Nolte, 1979). In most police agencies, policies are formulated by the chief in consultation with her staff and those for whom the chief works (city manager, mayor, councilpersons), while putting the policies into operation is typically a task of rank-and-file officers. In Chapter 4, we

HIGHLIGHT 8.3

IN 2001 AMERICA, WHITES CAN'T BELIEVE BLACKS TREATED UNFAIRLY

Maybe you heard about how blacks pay more for car loans from Nissan.

A recent study showed black customers in 33 states consistently paid more interest on their loans than white customers, regardless of credit histories.

Or, perhaps you heard about the study on asthmatic African-Americans whose health care falls consistently short of standards compared to that received by whites.

Here in Milwaukee, no doubt you've heard that minorities seeking home loans are denied at a greater rate than whites—more than 3-to-1—for the 11th straight year, making our hometown the largest such gap in the nation.

These are the hard numbers behind the racial divide, the accumulated data that strongly suggest there are still plenty of reasons for African-Americans to continue to make demands on society to become more equal and fair.

We haven't even addressed racial profiling yet; another national study found that more than half of all black men report they have been victims of racial profiling by law enforcement.

Overall, nearly four in 10 blacks believe they have been unfairly stopped by police simply because they are black—52% of black men and 25% of black women.

You could cite numbers and statistics ad infinitum, but clearly, some people will never accept the reality; despite hard-earned gains, many blacks still don't get equal treatment in this society.

Keith Reeves of Swarthmore College, a political scientist who worked on *The Washington Post*-Kaiser Foundation-Harvard University study, provides a possible explanation:

"The results (of the survey) suggest there is the overwhelming sense among most whites that this is 2001—we could not possibly be saddled with segregation and discrimination and, therefore, things can't possibly be as bad as black Americans say they are." I can testify to that.

Because I write a column that addresses racial attitudes in Milwaukee—one of the nation's most segregated cities—many white readers regularly complain to me about the "whining" attitude of blacks here and elsewhere over perceived discrimination.

What's clear from listening to their constant complaints is they simply don't believe the hype.

Their attitude: This is America, 40 years after the modern civil rights movement. There is no more racial discrimination, no more institutional racism, no more barriers preventing black people from achieving everything they want from society, as long as they're willing to work at it.

You can't change their minds by throwing hard facts at them, because they simply don't want to hear it.

Whether the subject is home mortgage loans, health care treatment or opportunities for education, whenever blacks are found to have received less than equal treatment, excuses start flying.

Usually, the consensus is that blacks themselves are to blame for the way society treats them.

While noting there have been many significant improvements in black life—including the growth of the black middle class and an increase in the numbers of blacks attending college and entering the work force—the Post-Kaiser-Harvard study found most whites hold misconceptions about the black-and-white reality of where things stand today.

How did they find that out? Mainly by asking people what they believe and contrasting it with the truth.

For example, six in every 10 whites believed blacks had equal or better access to health care, according to the study. Yet, according to the census, blacks are far more likely to be without health insurance than whites.

About half of all whites—49%—believed blacks and whites have similar levels of education.

(continued)

HIGHLIGHT 8.3 Continued

The truth: One in six blacks—17%—has completed college, compared with 28% of whites.

Eighty-eight percent of whites are high school graduates, compared with 79% of blacks 25 years old or older.

Half of all whites believe the average black is about as well off as the average white in terms of employment, according to the survey. But where approximately one-third of all whites hold professional or managerial jobs, only one-fifth of blacks have a comparable job status.

Black people are about twice as likely as whites—23% vs. 12%—to hold lower-paying, less-prestigious jobs, according to the Post-Kaiser-Harvard study.

Blacks are also twice as likely as whites to be unemployed.

The study found rampant misperceptions by whites of the true status of blacks in America, something that no doubt accounts for widespread resistance to things like affirmative action, slavery reparations and even modest diversity initiatives.

For far too many whites, there's a belief that black people don't know what they're talking about when they complain about unequal treatment in society.

Actually, it's the other way around.

Posing questions about income levels, health care, education and job status, the study found most whites—seven in 10—had at least one or more misconceptions about the true status of blacks.

It's a clear indication of the denial that runs rampant whenever racial issues are addressed, evident in the angry callers and e-mailers who fill my mailbox whenever I write about a subject that examines race.

About the only time white readers truly want to discuss race is when it concerns crime. They are more than willing to point to a spurt of murders in Metcalfe Park as evidence why blacks—even law-abiding blacks—don't deserve acceptance into mainstream society.

Which is the very definition of racist thought.

One of the most provocative studies I've ever run across was one in which white college students were presented with a intriguing premise.

Suppose you were changed into a black person tomorrow? How much money would you require to make that transformation?

The students, who were given information about racial disparities in jobs, income levels and education, each came up with a monetary figure. For some, it was $250,000. For others, it was far greater, topping $2 million.

The motivation behind that kind of thinking was best articulated during a concert by black comedian Chris Rock (a personal favorite), who talked about how beneficial it was to be white in America.

His conclusion: "There's not a single white person in here who would change places with me, and I'm RICH!"

It's a challenge I will present to the next reader who calls to say most black complaints are groundless because, today, the color of your skin just doesn't matter.

"If that's true, would you change places with a black person tomorrow?"

I'm not expecting many takers (Kane, 2001).

discussed the importance to police personnel of good communications, and there is perhaps no better example than in the area of public relations. Policies formulated but not acted on, or formulated but not explained or understood, can hardly be expected to result in sound practice.

Similarly, policies developed without communication with those who will eventually be responsible for putting them into action are often of little value. Policy and practice go together. Both must be present, and some coordination between the two is necessary if either is to be valuable. It is here that many police administrators fail at implementing good community relations programs. Some administrators recognize the importance of policy making and appoint special community relations officers or teams to create such policy. Some recognize the importance of human relations and emphasize to every officer the importance of encounters with other citizens. Far fewer recognize that policy making and practice are intimately intertwined, so that policymakers and those who implement the policies must be in constant communication to allow for feedback and evaluation on a routine basis.

Such feedback and evaluation should focus on measuring and evaluating public opinion concerning the police, on developing and implementing policies to maintain favorable public opinion or to change it so that it becomes more positive, and then on reevaluating policies, practices, and opinions (Nolte, 1979, p. 20). Public relations is a process that is repeated over and over as conditions and opinions change. And, we should emphasize once again, police public relations programs will lead to a favorable image only if they accurately reflect practices that are acceptable to the public. No amount of image building will convince citizens that they have a professional police department if the daily encounters between police and these other citizens are conducted in an unprofessional fashion. The current widespread concern with biased enforcement in the form of racial profiling serves as an excellent illustration of this point.

Biased Enforcement/Racial Profiling

According to Hoover (2001, p. 1), "The practice of discriminatory law enforcement has been a long-standing issue in American law enforcement. Concern about the practice predates the civil rights movement and has been the topic of legislation, litigation, and professionalization of law enforcement for decades." Currently, however, the controversy over racial profiling as one form of biased enforcement engaged in by some police officers has reached the boiling point. Legislation requiring recording of detailed information on race or ethnicity of persons involved in encounters with the police, by the police, and/or requiring sensitivity training for police officers on a recurring basis has been passed or introduced in a number of states.

Racial profiling by police officers occurs when officers base their actions solely on the perceived race/ethnicity of the citizens they observe. This type of racial profiling occurs in practice when officers stop citizens solely because of their skin color or other identifiable racial or ethnic characteristics. In other words, there is no legitimate probable cause for the stop. Most observers, including most police officers, would agree that this practice is unacceptable. As Jurkanin (2001, p. i) notes, "Police are sworn to uphold the 'rule of law' in the protection of individual rights, while dutifully enforcing traffic and criminal laws for the protection of the public at large. . . . It is essential that law enforcement administrators take every necessary action to ensure zero tolerance regarding enforcement actions that are discriminatory against any segment of the population."

Yet there are a certain number of police officers that engage in such practices. The fact is, we do not know how many such officers exist. For a variety of reasons, we suspect that the proportion of officers involved in such practices is small, but all officers should be taught that taking official action based solely on race is unacceptable and is grounds for disciplinary action. Harassment of individuals short of taking unofficial action also is unacceptable.

We all have the right to go into any neighborhood we choose at any time of day or night without police interference. Yet the experience of police officers often tells them that our presence in certain areas at certain times may indicate involvement in illegitimate behavior. They believe that the citizens of their communities, as well as their police supervisors, would want them to take action under such circumstances (Hoover, 2001; Cox & Hazlett, 2001).

Similarly, police officers frequently respond to calls from the public concerning "suspicious persons." In some cases, these calls are based on observations of suspicious behavior, but in others the only thing suspicious about the person is his race. Having learned from the media that young black males are overrepresented in crime statistics, whites observing young black males in predominantly white neighborhoods may well regard them as suspicious persons. They call the police and then watch to see what happens. How, police officers say, are we supposed to respond? Not to respond may be perceived as dereliction of duty by both superiors and the public. And common sense suggests to the officer that "something" be done. Taking no action goes against all the training the officer has received.

Should the officer involved in situations of this type choose to stop and question the so-called suspicious person, allegations of racial profiling/discrimination may be expected. This is especially true when the stop or questioning become harassing in nature. Telling people to "move along" or "go back to your own neighborhood" or threatening to take (unjustified) official action is very likely to result in the belief that racial factors are playing a major role. When such communication characterizes inter-action with persons of one racial or ethnic group but not those of another, the allegations should be considered factual.

As mentioned, in the rush to determine whether racial profiling exists in various communities or states, legislation mandating that officers record race/ethnicity has been introduced. The concern with confronting racial profiling where it exists is easy to understand and appropriate. Yet the legislation may have numerous unintended consequences.

First, such legislation may cause officers (including all those who do not participate in racial profiling) to focus on exactly the characteristics we wish them to ignore as a basis for making stops or arrests. Such reporting clearly causes officers to focus on racial/ethnic characteristics precisely because they have to record them.

Second, the legislation may lead to a good deal of intentional misreporting. This may happen as a result of officers fearing that they have stopped or arrested too many minority group members in a given period of time and deciding not to accurately report the race or ethnicity of those they stop or arrest, or deciding not to even report stops that do not lead to official action. In effect, officers may develop their own quota systems. At best, this will lead to false reporting, and at worst, it may motivate officers not to make stops or arrests that they would normally make because they fear being reprimanded for stopping too many persons of a particular race or ethnicity.

Racial profiling, as one form of biased enforcement, "inevitably leads to questions as to whether biased enforcement exists at the departmental level as a result of policy decisions" (Cox & Hazlett, 2001, p. 97). Police allocation of resources based on crime rates may lead to higher arrest rates for minorities who are disproportionately located in high-crime areas (Taylor & Whitney, 1999). If the police withdraw their resources from such areas, cries of biased enforcement in terms of lack of police services are likely to be heard (Cox & Hazlett, 2001, p. 98). In fact, some have argued that race is totally irrelevant to the police in most high-crime neighborhoods because nearly all of the residents are minorities (MacDonald, 2001).

Solving such dilemmas is difficult precisely because discrimination in law enforcement can occur in a variety of contexts, ranging from traffic stops to field interrogations to provision of shabby services (Hoover, 2001, p. 2). Developing partnerships between neighborhood groups and the police may be a partial solution (Hartnett & Skogan, 1999). A comprehensive plan involving policy reform, officer training, and voluntary data collection also may help in this regard (Carrick, 2000). Ultimately, however, the issue of racism must be dealt with by the larger society if biased enforcement and racial profiling are to be alleviated.

Citizen Complaints

An important part of the process of evaluating police–community relations consists of soliciting, evaluating, and acting on citizen complaints. Good community relations require that citizens feel free to discuss with appropriate authorities their complaints about police officers or police behavior. Systematic efforts to determine what those served by the police think of the services they receive should be an integral part of police management. Such efforts may be conducted by department personnel, by university personnel, or by private consultants, and should attempt to establish a baseline of public opinion and then compare these opinions with those collected on a regular basis over time. A part of this process should include the development and publicizing of policies related to citizen complaints. Citizens should know who to contact and what to expect when they make such contact. Further, those complaining should be kept advised of the efforts made to investigate their complaint and the final disposition of the complaint.

Many citizens who feel they have been abused or harassed by the police do not know how to make a complaint, or they fear retaliation from the officer involved or her colleagues if they do complain. Public relations messages indicating the desire of police administrators to know about such complaints, coupled with prompt, fair action when such complaints are received, can only help to improve community relations. While we can do a great deal to help improve the citizen complaint process (see Highlight 8.4), we should be aware that most citizens who have complaints about the police will

■ ■ ■ ■ ■

HIGHLIGHT 8.4
POLICE REFORM COMPLAINT SYSTEM

The city will let police internal affairs investigate complaints against officers, instead of immediate supervisors, in a move officials say will lead to fairer, more independent reviews.

The city says the move has nothing to do with a lawsuit filed against it by the Justice Department in 1999 that alleges police violated people's civil rights. "This is something we've been talking about," Mike Brown, spokesman for Mayor Michael Coleman, said Thursday after neighborhood leaders and the media were briefed on the reforms. "This is the right thing to do." Under the plan that went into effect Monday, complaints will be turned over to the department's internal affairs bureau for investigation. Previously, an officer's supervisor conducted the review, a system that allowed a supervisor to immediately dismiss a complaint by classifying it as "inquiry."

Now, internal affairs sergeants will investigate each complaint and inform the deputy chief in charge of the officer whether the complaint is valid. The deputy chief will determine whether any discipline is appropriate.

Reforms have been suggested since 1996 by various police and Safety Department officials. Chief James Jackson approved the idea last year, and the city added $1.2 million to the 2001 budget to add 15 sergeants and two lieutenants to the bureau.

Cmdr. Kimberly Jacobs acknowledged that the changes were prompted by perceptions, mainly in the black community, that complaints were not being fairly and objectively investigated.

The changes and publicity about them are expected to lead to more complaints, city officials said.

Under the old system, there were about 600 complaints a year and often 200 to 300 other complaints classified as inquiries.

The number of complaints could rise to about 1,000, Jacobs said.

"What this does is it ensures accountability, independence and a thorough review of every complaint," she said.

Complaints about police are handled differently throughout the state.

In Cincinnati, the scene of three days of rioting in April after a white officer shot an unarmed black man, citizens who have filed minor complaints against officers have face-to-face meetings with the officer and a supervisor.

There also is a Citizens Review Police Panel to review complaints, but the panel has complained about a lack of support from the city. Police officials say they should be able to handle minor complaints on their own.

In Toledo, an 11-member citizens board reviews complaints against officers. The board, formed in 1991, includes representatives from the city's minority community.

Cleveland removed the citizen complaint process from the Police Department in January, when Chief Martin Flask transferred the function to the Office of Professional Standards.

Although investigators are plainclothes police sergeants, the office is in turn evaluated by a five-member Civilian Review Board.

Flask criticized the department's dissolved Complaint Investigations Unit as "time consuming and cumbersome."

Reprinted with permission of The Associated Press.

probably never voice these complaints directly to the police (Homant, 1989; Walker, Spohn, & DeLone, 1996, pp. 106–107; Walker, 2001, pp. 20–21, 53–80). Similarly, we should note that some citizens who strongly support the police file complaints in the hope of helping the police improve, rather than with negative intent.

Police–Media Relations

Surette (1992, p. 81) acknowledges, "People live today in two worlds: a real world and a media world. The first is limited by direct experience; the second is bounded only by decisions of editors and producers." According to Palmiotto (2000, p. 169),

> The mass media reinforce the same stereotypes and display unrealistic attitudes about outgroups that are found in school materials. The depiction of minorities in the media is most often a caricature. . . . In analyses of the depiction of minorities in print media in one midwestern city, it was found that Native Americans and Asian Americans were virtually invisible in the local paper, whereas Hispanic Americans were somewhat more visible and African Americans were highly visible. However, the areas in which African Americans had a major presence were crime, sports, and entertainment; their visibility in business and government was low.

As indicated in Chapter 3, any police agency concerned about good community relations will want to develop a good working relationship with the media. Information presented on television, on the radio, or in the newspapers is a major source of influence on public opinion. Police administrators today typically prefer to develop open, honest relationships with representatives of the media, although this has not always been the case. In the past, police administrators often had a policy requiring officers to tell media representatives only what they had to, thus engendering mutual suspicion and distrust.

Because many citizens never have direct contact with the police, their view of the police is based on media presentations. These include, but are not limited to, documentaries, news broadcasts, interviews with police personnel and those they serve, and police-produced or -assisted informational programs. These presentations also include those television shows and movies that deal with police activities, many of which are highly misleading in their portrayal of violence and gun battles and crime fighting as the major activities of the police. In such presentations, the police often appear to be violent, sadistic, corrupt, and/or stupid, and their work appears to consist of going from one violent situation to another. To be sure, most viewers realize that there is no direct correspondence between what appears on the screen and what happens in reality, yet it is sometimes difficult to separate fact from fiction and to correct inaccurate impressions.

By creating a positive public image, the police can benefit in many ways. Cooperation and support on the part of the public can be encouraged in a number of ways. Police ride-along programs allow other citizens to observe the daily activities of the police. Open-house days allow members of the public to view the internal workings of the police department from communications through investigations to incarceration. Walk-in centers provide the opportunity for neighborhood residents to discuss whatever is on their minds with citizen-oriented police officers. School resource officer programs, drug resistance programs, and police athletic programs provide opportunities for youth to get to know police officers as individuals, and vice versa. Providing Public Information Officers (PIOs) who are available to meet with media representatives on a regular basis to provide accurate, timely information is still another beneficial strategy (Surette, 2001). These and other public relations efforts on behalf of the police can improve community relations when accompanied by positive human relations efforts.

Other Police–Community Relations Efforts

There are other things police administrators can do to improve the relationship between their departments and the communities they serve. We have discussed the recruitment and hiring of minority officers at length in Chapter 6. Clearly, the police department that represents the community it serves in terms of race and ethnicity has an initial advantage in community relations. This is perhaps particularly true when segments of the community served fail to comprehend English well or not at all. It is difficult for Hispanics, for example, to believe that a police department with no Spanish-speaking officers is concerned about their well-being. If it is true that mutual trust and understanding are important components of police–community relations, the language barriers must be broken wherever possible. Training that familiarizes police officers with the cultural characteristics of the populations they serve, and courses that help those from different cultural and linguistic backgrounds understand the justice system in the United States (discussed later), are also both possible and important.

Programs aimed at specific minorities other than those based on race or ethnicity also are important. Police efforts to prevent crime against senior citizens, to organize neighborhood watch groups, and to help youth resist drugs or gang influence are widespread. School liaison programs in which police officers are assigned to the schools for the academic year and in which the officers participating serve as counselors and sometimes confidants to youth are more and more common.

Police departments also are becoming more involved with training in community relations. An example of the progress being made in this sector is the program developed in Clearwater, Florida. Prior to the commencement of training, both police officers and black city residents were surveyed to learn their impressions of one another. The results of this survey were used as the foundation for the training that followed, which involved exchanges between members of the black community and police officers concerning the issues brought forth by both groups. The training was conducted as a preventive measure, not as a response to a crisis, and it seems to have been perceived positively by all parties (Teagarden, 1988; see also Field, 1990).

In Arvada, Colorado, the police department initiated a senior liaison officer (SLO) program in which officers worked proactively with senior citizens to identify concerns and needs. The goals of the program were to meet these needs and reduce fear of crime among senior citizens (Palmiotto, 2000, pp. 299–300).

The Orange County (California) Sheriff's Office developed another method for improving police community relations. The basic tool employed is the Community Feedback Questionnaire designed to gather information about police behavior as perceived by victims and informants. The questionnaires, along with cover letters from the sheriff, are sent to about 10 percent of those who call the sheriff's department as victims or with information. This simple survey instrument provides a chance to evaluate police performance, and it also indicates that the department is interested enough in those served to care about what they think. The information collected is then passed on to the officers involved, providing direct feedback not only to those officers, but also to the supervisory staff. The program represents a "valuable and inexpensive means of assessing community perceptions of department performance" (LaDucer, 1988, p. 224).

To address crime problems in an apartment complex occupied by Hispanic and Vietnamese immigrants, the Garden Grove (California) police department opened a storefront office. Research showed that the storefront office had a positive effect on both groups. Hispanics reported less fear of crime after the storefront opened and also reported improved perceptions of the police. Vietnamese residents also reported less fear of crime, and their already very positive attitudes toward the police remained positive (Torres & Vogel, 2001).

PUBLIC OPINION AND THE POLICE

Based on the material presented thus far in this book, it is clear that how the public perceives their police is a critical determinant of police–citizen interaction. Over the years, numerous attempts have been made to assess public opinion concerning the police, and the results have been consistently favorable to the police, although opinions appear to vary by age, race (as we saw earlier in this chapter), residence, and other factors, and notwithstanding the fact that suggestions for improvement are frequently made by respondents. Inquiries concerning public attitudes toward the police have been made as a part of the National Crime Survey (NCS) since 1972; the results have been consistently positive, indicating that over three-fourths of those surveyed rate police performance as either good or fair. In earlier studies conducted by the Harris group, about two-thirds of those surveyed responded favorably to items concerning police performance (Ennis, 1967; Garofalo, 1977).

Although respondents rate the police favorably, whites are more likely to view the police favorably than are non-whites (Sampson & Bartusch, 1999; Carter & Brown, 1999). Some research indicates that these differences may be more related to socioeconomic status than to race, and in at least one study, racial differences in attitudes disappeared when neighborhood context was taken into account (Sampson & Bartusch, 1999).

Overall public support for the police has remained consistently high over the past three decades, and the level of support is consistently higher than is commonly believed by the police. We should be aware, however, that attitudes are difficult to measure, and the correlation between attitudes and behavior is certainly not one to one. An example of current attitudes toward the police can be seen in Table 8.1, which deals with attitudes toward honesty and ethicality of police officers over a twenty-year period. As you can see, the attitudes expressed are consistent and relatively positive.

The police cannot, however, rest on their laurels, because in spite of the positive findings, there are indications in most studies that room for improvement exists. Let us

TABLE 8.1 Respondent's Ratings of the Honesty and Ethical Standards of Police Officers between 1977 and 1997

Honesty/Ethicality	1977	1981	1985	1990	1995	1997
Very High	8%	8%	10%	9%	8%	10%
High	29%	36%	27%	40%	33%	39%
Average	50%	41%	41%	41%	44%	40%
Low	9%	9%	7%	7%	11%	8%
Very Low	3%	4%	3%	2%	3%	2%

Source: Adapted from G. Gallup Jr. (1999). *The Gallup Report,* as it appears in *Sourcebook of Criminal Justice Statistics—1998* (p. 109). Washington, DC: U.S. Department of Justice.

turn our attention to the roles of the police and the public, respectively, in making such improvement.

THE POLICE AND PUBLIC IN COMMUNITY RELATIONS

The Police Role in Police–Community Relations

In spite of the fact that the police sometimes feel separate from and in conflict with other citizens, they are nevertheless members of the community in which they serve. Both groups are controlled by the same government, both pay taxes to support the police and other public service agencies, the children of both groups attend the same schools, and both share in the fate of the community. By and large, the police are recruited from, hired by, and sworn to serve this same community. Further, the functions of the police are essential to the community, but no more essential than the services provided by others. Good police–community relations depend on emphasizing this common community membership.

To indicate their willingness to participate as partners in the community, the police need to recognize and reflect the racial and ethnic composition of that community. Active efforts to recruit qualified minorities into policing are essential in this regard, as are promotions based strictly on merit. An all-white police department in an ethnically diverse community provides "proof" that the police are different in a very obvious way and raises suspicions that the police also may be different in many other, less obvious ways. A multiethnic police department will not be problem-free, but it has a definite advantage in developing good community relations. Some progress is being in this area if Gabor (2001, p. 15) is correct when he concluded, "For the most part, police departments across the country are becoming a reflection of the cultural makeup of the community they serve. In fact, while it may still be the exception rather than the rule, in some California police departments, minority officers are the majority, while white officers in some departments are in the minority."

Innovative, regular training in human and public relations skills is an important requirement for police officers, as is training in cultural diversity. Cultural diversity or awareness programs are designed to familiarize police officers with people and customs different from those to which they are accustomed. Assigning a police officer to police a ghetto or barrio without such an introduction virtually guarantees community relations problems. Programs designed to anticipate the types of crises that might arise in the community alert officers to the possibility that they may occur, while providing them with some structure and preparation.

Cultural Diversity/Awareness Training

Training in cultural diversity has become increasing popular over the years. Such training typically focuses on improving communications skills, recognizing signs of prejudice and bias, understanding the perspectives of people of different backgrounds, and appreciating the benefits of diversity (Scott, 1993; Hennessy, 1993; Bickham & Rossett, 1993; Cox & Fitzgerald, 1996; Barlow & Barlow, 2000). Before being assigned to a beat, officers should receive orientation on the various groups residing in the area. Further, as police agencies become more culturally diverse, internal problems may develop, so training should address derogatory language, racial and ethnic slurs, and ethnic jokes in the context of the police organization (Scott, 1993; Barlow & Barlow, 2000).

Bickham and Rossett (1993, p. 43) believe the outcomes of cultural diversity training should include learing about cultures and groups present in the service area; development of a positive, caring attitude toward cultural differences; and development of action plans that serve diverse communities. Hennessy, Hendricks, and Hendericks (2001) indicate that all cultural awareness training sessions should include active participation and establishment of a meaningful context.

According to Himelfarb (1991, p. 53), the Royal Canadian Mounted Police identified six principles necessary for culturally sensitive policing:

1. Respect for and sensitivity to diverse communities served
2. A broad-based multicultural strategy
3. Multicultural training
4. Training on a continuing basis (not just one or two courses)
5. A philosophy of policing that addresses multicultural issues and establishes operations to deal with these issues
6. Multicultural training and strategies developed in consultation with the ethnocultural communities served by the police

Training programs such as these require that police administrators recognize that community relations require effort on behalf of every individual officer and the police management team. The former determine the nature of human relations in daily encounters, and the latter, in consultation with these officers and the various publics in the jurisdiction, determine and evaluate the policies to be implemented and their effectiveness in practice. As we have seen, community policing efforts are intended to deal with these very issues by empowering patrol officers and personalizing police efforts.

Police Responsiveness and Accountability

Two key terms for the police in community relations are *responsiveness* and *accountability* (Cox & Fitzgerald, 1996, pp. 210 6218). A department that is responsive provides appropriate services as promptly and competently as possible and refers cases not within their jurisdiction in the same fashion. This requires that police administrators recognize and convey to the public the fact that it may be impossible and/or inappropriate for the police to respond to all citizen requests for service. Priorities may have to be established and differential response strategies developed in order to best allocate available resources. These tasks should be accomplished in partnership with the community, and the policies and strategies resulting from this effort should be communicated clearly to residents, thus, to the extent possible, preventing potentially negative reactions. The department must make it clear that requests for service on behalf of citizens are taken seriously and will be dealt with accordingly.

Accountability is the second key to police efforts to establish and maintain positive community relations. Police officers are employees of the community they serve. Like other employees, they are accountable to their employers for their actions. Accountability may be accomplished in a variety of ways, ranging from periodic reports to the public on police activities, to annual reports, to developing and utilizing an internal affairs unit, to cooperation in developing a civilian review to hear complaints concerning the police (Walker, 2001).

The two extremes of police concern with community relations, by imagining what police departments at each end of the continuum might look like, are illustrated in Figure 8.1. While few departments match the ideal types shown in Figure 8.1, all can be evaluated in terms of where they stand along the continuum of concern with community relations. Specifically, the following concerns should be taken into account.

POLICE ADMINISTRATION

1. Recognize, attempt to assess, and meet the needs of diverse publics.
2. Emphasize training and indoctrination in community relations skills.
3. Develop policies based on assessment and evaluations of officers' and other citizens' opinions.
4. Communicate policies effectively to publics and officers.
5. Provide for supervision of policy implementation.
6. Reevaluate periodically.
7. Form teams with members of diverse publics to assist in policy development.

POLICE OFFICERS

1. Communicate concerns to the public and the administrators.
2. Implement policies.
3. Evaluate policies in practice.
4. Provide feedback to administrators.
5. Treat all citizens with respect and preserve human dignity.

Officer/Department Characteristics	Reactions to Encounters with Diverse Populations	Possible Consequences
Type 1 Traditional, authoritarian structure	Uncertainty, anxiety, high fear/ stress, suspicion, hostility, stereotypes, secret brutality	Ineffectiveness psychological and/or physical
Homogeneous in terms of race, gender, lack of representativeness Minimal educational requirements Minimal prior contact with diverse publics Little emphasis on community relations in terms of training, assessment of public attitudes, evaluation of programs Strong subcultural "us–them" feelings Strict law enforcement orientation Forced participation in affirmative action and equal employment opportunity programs Unenlightened management Secret complaint investigations		
Type 2 Participatory structure	Less uncertainty Less anxiety Less fear Less suspicion Less stress Less hostility Fewer stereotypes	Less psychological and physical brutality Better relations with diverse publics and more public cooperation, more professional conduct
Heterogeneous with respect to race, gender More representative of the publics served Higher educational/training requirements More contact with diverse publics Emphasis on assessment and evaluation of public attitudes Less subcultural closeness Strong service orientation Open complaint investigations More enlightened management		

FIGURE 8.1   Polarized Police Department Concern with Community Relations

The Role of the Community in Police–Community Relations

We have noted the fact that the police are predominantly reactive rather than proactive. That is, the community in which they operate determines, in most instances, when the police act, about what they act, and on whom they act (Reiss, 1970; Walker, 2001). Thus, the community plays, and must accept, an important role in police–community relations. If the community does not do its part in building positive community relations, police-initiated programs cannot succeed (Cox & Fitzgerald, 1996).

To demonstrate good faith in police–community relations, community residents and civic action can develop programs to support police efforts and recognize police performance. Neighborhood Watch programs and "officer of the month" programs are two examples of community efforts to demonstrate support for the police. Community resident willingness to serve as reserve or auxiliary officers also demonstrates support, as do joint programs to divert youth from drugs and delinquency. Providing the police with information concerning matters important to the community and being willing to serve as witnesses are yet other ways in which community residents can show appreciation for their police. While the police may be required to take the lead in developing community relations efforts, the public is an important part of the team necessary for such efforts to produce the desired results, making the task of the police easier and the community a better place in which to live. It is important that members of all communities have continual, open dialogue with police officials in order to deal with specific issues. According to Walker (2001, p. 44), "Citizen oversight of the police was an established fact of life in American law enforcement by the end of the century. It existed in many large cities and was steadily spreading to smaller communities. The spread of oversight marked a momentous change since the tumultuous 1960s. Most important, citizen involvement in the complaint process was increasingly recognized as an important means for achieving police accountability."

DISCUSSION QUESTIONS

1. Trace the historical origins of some of the current problems in police–community relations.

2. What characteristics of a multiethnic, industrial, democratic society make police community relations problematic?

3. Why are affirmative action and equal employment opportunity programs important to police–community relations?

4. What is the general perception of the police as reflected in public opinion surveys? What are some of the important factors in determining these perceptions?

5. List and discuss four specific steps the police can take to help improve community relations. List and discuss the same thing from the public perspective.

6. How are human relations and public relations different? How are they related to community relations?

7. What is the impact of biased law enforcement on police–minority relations? Are the police unique in the criminal justice network when it comes to bias?

REFERENCES

Associated Press. (2001, July 12). Police reform complaint system.

Baldwin, J. (1962). *Nobody knows my name*. New York: Dell.

Barak, G., Flavin, J. M., & Leighton, P. S. (2001). *Class, race, gender and crime*. Los Angeles: Roxbury.

Barlow, D. E., & Barlow, M. H. (2000), *Police in a multicultural society: An American story*. Prospect Heights, IL: Waveland.

Bayley, D. H., & Mendelsohn, H. (1969). *Minorities and the police*. New York: Free Press.

Bickham, T., & Rossett, A. (1993). Diversity training: Are we doing the right thing? *Police Chief, 60*, 43–47.

Burden, O. P. (1992, June). Peacekeeping and the "thin blue line." *Police Chief, 59*, 19–28.

Carrick, G. (2000). Professional police traffic stops: Strategies to address racial profiling. *FBI Law Enforcement Bulletin, 69*, 8–10.

Carter, T. B., & Brown, D. (1999). Evaluations of police performance in an African American sample. *Journal of Criminal Justice, 27*, 457–465.

Chavis, B. F., & Williams, J. D. (1993). Beyond the Rodney King story: NAACP report on police conduct and community relations. *NAACP News, 93*, 42.

Cox, S. M. (1984). Race/ethnic relations and the police: Current and future issues. *American Journal of the Police, 3*, 169–183.

Cox, S. M., & Fitzgerald, J. D. (1996). *Police in community relations: Critical issues*, 3rd ed. New York: McGraw-Hill.

Cox, S. M., & Hazlett, M. H. (2001, July). Biased enforcement, racial profililng, and data collection: Addressing the issues. *Illinois Law Enforcement Executive Forum*, 91–99.

Cox, S. M., & Wade, J. E. (1998). *The criminal justice network: An introduction*, 3rd ed. New York: McGraw-Hill.

Crime Control Digest. (1999, January 15). Killing sparks racial tensions, p. 6.

Ennis, P. H. (1967). *Criminal victimization in the United States: A report of a national survey*. Washington, DC: U.S. Government Printing Office.

Field, M. W. (1990, October). Evaluating police services through citizen surveys. *Police Chief, 57*, 69–72.

Gabor, T. (2001). Racial profiling: A complex issue made simple. *Journal of Cailifornia Law Enforcement, 35*, 15–17.

Garofalo, J. (1977). The police and public opinion: An analysis of victimization and attitude data from 13 American cities. Washington, DC: U.S. Government Printing Office.

Hacker, A. (1992). *Two nations: Black and white, separate, hostile, unequal*. New York: Ballantine Books.

Hartnett, S. M., & Skogan, W. G. (1999). Community policing: Chicago's experience. *National Institute of Justice Journal, 239*, 3–11.

Henness, S. M., Hendricks, C., & Hendricks, J. (2001). Cultural awareness and communication training: What works and what doesn't. *Police Chief, 68*, 15–19.

Hennessy, S. M. (1993, August). Achieving cultural competence. *Police Chief, 60*, 46–54.

Himelfarb, F. (1991, November). A training strategy for policing in a multicultural society. *Police Chief, 58*, 53–55.

Homant, R. J. (1989). Citizen attitudes and complaints. In Bailey, W. G. (ed.), *The encyclopedia of police science* (pp. 54–63). New York: Garland Press.

Hoover, L. T. (2001, July). Police response to racial profiling: You can't win. *Illinois Law Enforcement Executive Forum*, 1–13.

Jurkanin, T. J. (2001, July). Editorial. *Illinois Law Enforcement Executive Forum*, i.

Kane, E. (2001, July 15). In 2001 America, whites can't believe blacks treated unfairly. *Milwaukee Journal Sentinel*, p. B3.

LaDucer, D. W. (1988, July). The community feedback program. *Police Chief, 55,* 24.

MacDonald, H. (2001). The myth of racial profiling. *City Journal, 11,* 14–27.

Maguire, K., Pastore, A. L., & Flanagan, T. J. (1999). *Sourcebook of criminal justice statistics—1998.* The Hindelang Criminal Justice Research Center, U.S. Department of Justice. Washington, DC: U.S. Government Printing Office.

National Advisory Commission on Civil Disorders (Kerner Commission). (1968). *Report.* Washington, DC: U.S. Government Printing Office.

Nolte, L. W. (1979). *Fundamentals of public relations: Professional guidelines, concepts, and integrations.* New York: Pergamon.

O'Brien, J. T. (1978). Public attitudes toward the police. *Journal of Police Science and Administration, 6,* 303–310.

Palmiotto, M. J. (2000). *Community policing: A policing strategy for the 21st century.* Gaithersburg, MD: Aspen.

Pomerville, P. A. (1993). Popular myths about cultural awareness training. *Police Chief, 60,* 30–42.

Reiss, A. J. (1968, July/August). Police brutality—Answers to key questions. *Trans-action, 5,* 15–16.

———. (1970). *The police and the public.* New Haven, CT: Yale University Press.

Sampson, R. J., & Bartusch, D. J. (1999). Attitudes toward crime, police, and the law: Individual & neighborhood differences. *Alternatives to Incarceration, 5,* S14–S15.

Schaefer, R. T. (2000). *Racial and ethnic groups,* 8th ed. Upper Saddle River, NJ: Prentice-Hall.

Scott, E. L. (1993). Cultural awareness training. *Police Chief, 60,* 26–28.

Surette, R. (1992). *Media, crime & justice: Images and realities.* Pacific Grove, CA: Brooks/Cole.

———. (2001). Public information officers: The civilianization of a criminal justice profession. *Journal of Criminal Justice, 29,* 107–117.

Sykes, G. (1978). *Criminology.* New York: Harcourt Brace Jovanovich.

Takaki, R. (1993). *A different mirror: A history of multicultural America.* Boston: Little, Brown.

Taylor J., & Whitney, G. (1999). Crime and racial profiling by U.S. police: Is there an empirical basis? *Journal of Social, Political, & Economic Studies, 24,* 485–510.

Teagarden, R. B. (1988, November). Effective community relations training. *Police Chief, 55,* 42–44.

Torres, S., & Vogel, R. E. (2001). Pre- and post-test differences between Vietnamese and Latino residents involved in a community policing experiment: Reducing fear of crime and improving attitudes towards the police. *Policing, 24,* 40–55.

U.S. Census Bureau. (2000, September). *Current population reports.* Washington, DC: U.S. Government Printing Office.

Walker, S. (2001). *Police accountability: The role of citizen oversight.* Belmont, CA: Wadsworth.

Walker, S., Spohn, C., & DeLone, M. (1995). *The color of justice: Race, ethnicity, and crime in America.* Belmont, CA: Wadsworth.

Weaver, G. (1992). Law enforcement in a culturally diverse society. *FBI Law Enforcement Bulletin, 61,* 1–9.

CHAPTER NINE

ETHICAL PRACTICE AND THE USE OF DISCRETION IN POLICING

"Have we really reached the point that it requires the use of anonymous informants to uncover police wrong doing? Do we have to develop a 'witness protection program' to shield officers from other officers? Are we at such a low point that the techniques primarily used against organized crime will now be used against police themselves?"

—Sykes, 1999

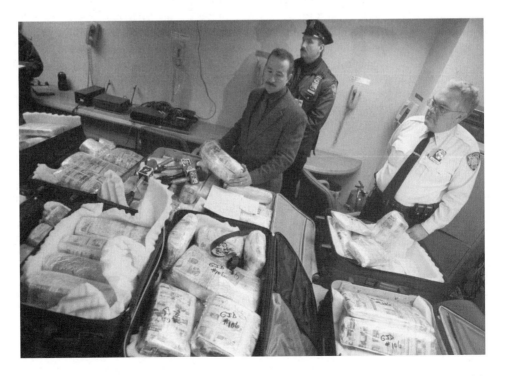

INTRODUCTION

The preceding epigraph refers to an administrative policy that the New York City Police Department (NYPD) and other agencies have adopted to encourage and protect honest officers who come forward to expose the malfeasance of their coworkers from the psychological and physical brutality often directed at them by their colleagues and superior officers. While the need for such a policy seems to indicate a sad state of affairs, it may be necessary in light of the scandals that continue to plague many law enforcement agencies.

Such scandals, resulting from unethical and often illegal police behavior, may be the result of a number of factors:

1. The infamous code of silence or conspiracy of silence, an inherent trait of the larger police subculture that frequently results in the reluctance of police officers to report the misdeeds of their coworkers
2. Inadequate and lax supervision
3. Poor recruitment, selection, and hiring practices
4. Organizational and individual retaliatory action by members against officers who dare expose corruption, as well as other archaic or inappropriate administrative policies
5. Insufficient training and continuing professional education activities that emphasize the importance of professional practice.

All of these factors at analyzed in detail throughout this textbook.

Due to the multiple roles the police are expected to perform, along with the myriad external and internal influences that tend to shape police policy and public expectations, the exercise of a wide range of discretionary authority is required if the police mission is to be achieved. Fulfilling this mission in a competent and responsible fashion, however, also requires a sustained organizational and individual commitment to the underlying tenets of ethics and professionalism, both of which are largely dependent on the judicious use of discretion. The critical issues of ethics and discretion in policing are the foci of this chapter, in which we

1. discuss the importance of ethics in policing, providing a framework for the professionalization of the field;
2. characterize the rationale, exercise of, and factors influencing police discretion;
3. identify the unintended consequences of discretionary authority; and
4. offer recommendations to mitigate the magnitude, frequency, and duration of the various dilemmas posed by unethical police practices and the abuse of discretionary authority enjoyed by law enforcement officials.

THE IMPORTANCE OF ETHICS IN POLICING

From an early age, most parents teach their children to tell the truth, not to steal, or not to cheat. And yet, by the time they take college classes, the vast majority of criminal justice students indicate that they would not turn in a classmate who lied, cheated, or stole (Cox, 2002). A significant proportion indicate at this stage that, upon becoming police officers, they would not turn in a fellow police officer who lied, cheated, or stole (Scaramella, 2001). Where did they get the message that it is acceptable to let others do these things without taking action? How did doing the right thing become the wrong thing to do?

Some 30 years ago, the Knapp Commission discovered that the majority of New York City police officers did not aggressively seek out opportunities to engage in unethical conduct (Knapp Commission, 1972). These officers, referred to by the Commission as "grass-eaters," chose not to get involved in such conduct, but refused to turn in fellow officers who did, thus, in effect, condoning unethical acts. Are we creating generations of grass-eaters outside as well as inside policing? Do we teach youth in general, and police recruits specifically, to condone unethical conduct?

In many cases, the answer appears to be yes. Although we teach our children not to lie, steal or cheat, many of us also teach them not to get involved when others lie, steal, or cheat. "It's not your business, stay out of it!" "Don't get involved!" "You just worry about yourself, not about other people." These and other similar pieces of advice may indeed lead youth to become grass-eaters who simply turn away from lying, cheating, and stealing. They learn very early that "ratting" on another individual is unacceptable behavior in many settings, perhaps as bad as being directly involved in unethical conduct. Of course, the police subculture often builds on exactly this consideration. Loyalty to the group (other officers) is held out as a virtue, even when it means engaging in unethical conduct (covering, making excuses, telling "white lies") to protect unethical individuals (involved, for example, in perjury or theft from victims and/or crime scenes). Yet police officers are required by the Code of Conduct, as well as by federal law (Civil Rights Act, Title 42 United States Code section 1983), not to condone such behavior.

Perhaps equally important are the lessons we have learned about "whistleblowers." Far too often, those who do the right thing by telling the truth and exposing corruption and brutality are the victims of vicious attacks from within their ranks. The lessons of Serpico have been learned well. Expose unethical conduct and you risk your life. Do the right thing and you become pariah. Confronting unethical conduct under these circumstances requires bravery above and beyond the call of duty and many would simply prefer to keep their distance.

Recent research has shown that many police agency policies allow or encourage officers to accept precisely those gratuities, favors, subscriptions, and gifts that the Code of Conduct prohibits (Dorn, 2001). Other policies prohibit accepting such favors, but are ignored in practice, sending the message that it is acceptable to violate policy in at least some instances. Where do such violations stop? We found no policies that allow or encourage perjury, theft, or brutality, so all such acts are clearly recognized as violations of policies as well as the Code of Conduct and the law.

In some cases, policy issues are reflective of administrators who are not committed to ethical conduct. According to Trautman (2002, p. 118), "After researching thousands of incidents of serious misconduct, the single most damaging category of misconduct in law enforcement is administrators intentionally ignoring obvious ethical problems. There is nothing as negative as a chief, sheriff, director or superintendent knowing his department has ethical problems and intentionally looking the other way, trying to make it to retirement." Some administrators role model unethical conduct on a regular basis, allowing officers to rationalize that their misconduct is no worse than the administrator's. Putting all the blame for unethical conduct on administrators, however, may encourage individual officers who engage in such conduct to attempt to escape responsibility for their actions.

It must be stated clearly at this point that we firmly believe that the vast majority of police officers in the United States perform their duties honestly, ethically, and professionally. It is a very small minority of officers who tarnish the field by engaging in inappropriate behavior. Unfortunately, these select few do a tremendous amount of damage to the reputation of policing and place the field in the uncomfortable position of having to constantly convince the public that acts of police malfeasance are not widespread.

Before proceeding to an analysis of ethics and its related principles, a working definition of the term is needed. While there are many different bases for the study of ethics, for our purposes, *ethics* may best be described as "the study of right and wrong, duty, responsibility, and personal character . . . [we] should regard all of these concepts . . . as having an implicit modifier—'moral'—attached to them. Ethics is concerned with moral duty, what is morally right and wrong. . . ." (Close & Myer, 1995, p. 3).

The maintenance of ethical standards within the field of policing is important for several reasons, all of which are obvious and none of which can be taken lightly. First, and foremost, the police are public servants, agents of the government sworn to uphold the laws of the land. As such, they must be role models for all of society, on and off the job. When police officers violate the public trust by engaging in unethical behavior, illegal or otherwise, the trust and confidence between themselves and the public they serve is shaken. Furthermore, and perhaps even more devastating, when the bond between the public and police is severed, the ideals of the entire criminal justice system may be called into question.

Ethics in policing are important because true ethical practice encapsulates a host of intimately related characteristics that are the essence of professionalism, an end state that most law enforcement practitioners seek to achieve so that they can deal with the multitude of social problems they encounter effectively. Professional police officers are those who

1. possess excellent personal character;
2. understand the concepts of justice, temperance, and truthfulness;
3. respect laws, policies, and credos consistent with democratic ideals;
4. remain accountable to both their organizations and their respective communities;
5. possess a commitment to higher education and continuous learning throughout their careers; and
6. remain intolerant of misconduct within their ranks (Delattre, 1996).

Ethical police conduct is imperative for policing twenty-first-century society. No longer can we argue that policing has so many gray areas that providing clear ethical guidelines is impossible. As Myron (1992) has noted, there are a number of behaviors sometimes engaged in by the police that are absolutely unethical. Among these are theft, brutal violations of human rights, planting evidence, and lying in court or to supervisors. There is no offender so important that the police should violate the Constitution or statutory law to arrest him or her (Myron, 1992, pp. 26–27).

To encourage ethical conduct, police agencies must recruit, select, hire, and promote individuals of excellent character, and they must demonstrate a sustained commitment to professionalism. In addition, they should emphasize ethics in recruitment, selection, and hiring practices, and increase educational standards for entry-level positions. Criminal justice curriculums in higher education institutions should be designed to incorporate and emphasize the study of ethics. In an attempt to ascertain whether four-year public institutions, which offer baccalaureate degrees programs in criminal justice, do in fact incorporate a course or courses in the study of ethics as a part of their core curriculum, Scaramella (2001) examined six public universities in the state of Illinois. Unfortunately, none of the six mandated a class in the study of ethics as a component of its core curriculum at the time of the study.

Using a survey instrument, Scaramella also attempted to assess the ethical attitudes of students who were enrolled in criminal justice classes. This instrument included scenarios that described common police encounters along with a corresponding scale of potential responses from which students could select. The responses ranged from ethical on one end of the scale to criminal behavior on the other end. The individual scenarios included a wide range of misconduct: on-duty consumption of alcohol, acceptance of gratuities, use of excessive force, verbal abuse, acceptance of kickbacks, perjury, theft, and nonfeasance. The results of the research were not only interesting, but also proved useful in discussions of ethical decision making with students of criminal justice. Examine the following highlights of the research results:

- Overall, the unethical responses generated by the table data ranged from 6 percent to 93 percent, with a mean of 45 percent.
- A willingness on behalf of the respondents to ignore illegal and unethical acts committed by police officers (nonfeasance) accounted for the vast majority of responses in this regard, with unethical responses ranging from 34 percent to 82 percent.
- Regarding the gender variable, women tended to provide higher indicators of ethical responses compared to those of male respondents, with the exception of questions concerning perjury. In the perjury scenario (courtroom testimony), men provided clearly higher ethically appropriate responses.
- Older respondents (21 to 30 years of age) consistently answered more ethically than did their younger counterparts.
- Another significant and interesting difference came with the variable that introduced academic status (freshman to senior). Those respondents who had attained more educational credits responded more ethically.
- Some of the more surprising data, and perhaps an important signal to both law enforcement executives and academicians, resulted from the relationship between those who had prior work experience in the criminal justice field compared with

those without any previous experience. Those with experience tended to answer *less ethically* than did those without such experience.

- Equally alarming data emerged when the variable of "academic major/minor" was introduced. *Non–criminal justice majors and minors* were much more willing to report acts of misconduct by their coworkers.

Regardless of how they are interpreted, the data describe an alarming situation. Unethical and criminal conduct committed by police officers is intimately related to the police subculture. As Cox (1996) and others point out, the influence of the police subculture begins early in a police officer's career. Most disturbing about Scaramella's research is that the vast majority of those respondents have yet to begin their careers in the field of criminal justice and have already reported tendencies associated with behavior that is consistent with the unethical characteristics of the police subculture. Moreover, the fact that those respondents who have never worked in the field, and who were non–criminal justice majors and minors, reported being more likely to take official action against a coworker for various acts of misconduct, may well indicate that the perceptions of potential law enforcement officers are shaped even before occupational contact with the subculture. Perhaps future research should address how and why some undergraduate criminal justice students, who were less likely to report that they would take official action against a coworker, develop these unethical attitudes prior to joining the workforce.

Criminal justice educators may help address this issue by incorporating the study of ethics into their core curriculums. Once students are required to engage in the study of ethics, researchers will be able to determine whether exposure to ethics can mitigate unethical and unprofessional attitudes and behavior. It is hoped that such exposure may afford future criminal justice graduates the strong ethical foundation needed to effectively confront the many ethical dilemmas they will experience in the field.

Although past and current research attributes the vast majority of corrupt practices in policing to a small minority of officers, the widespread media attention that envelops acts of official misconduct seems to belie that fact with important implications for public perceptions and confidence. Most recently, the police have been under attack by the media for alleged biased enforcement practices, or what journalists and other public watchdog groups are calling "racial profiling." Racial profiling is a component of biased enforcement involving the practice of disproportionately targeting minority group members for various law enforcement initiatives (i.e., selective traffic enforcement, narcotics interdiction efforts, etc.). These allegations, true or not, have brought about increased judicial, legislative, and public concern, so much so that the proposed remedies that address these allegations have become the primary concern of police executives throughout the country. Needless to say, any form of discriminatory or biased police practice is unethical, serves only to erode the public trust and confidence in the police, and is indicative of the fact that ethical conduct should be emphasized more that it has been.

Finally, other contemporary research focusing on issues pertaining to police/public integrity indicates a need for increased emphasis on the study of ethics and its related principles, both at the recruit and in-service level (U.S. General Accounting Office, 1998; U.S. Department of Justice, 2001). More specifically, the DOJ report recommends that basic and in-service training curriculums be expanded to include and stress the importance of subjects such as ethical decision making; responsible use of discretionary authority; racial, ethnic, and cultural diversity; and the development of effective interpersonal communication skills.

PROFESSIONALISM AND THE POLICE

As ethics is one of cornerstones of professionalism, various professions have adopted codes of ethics on which practice should be based. Accordingly, the International Association of Chiefs of Police (IACP), the most recognized professional association representing the field of policing, adopted the original "Law Enforcement Code of Ethics" in 1957. It has since been revised and was renamed the "Police Code of Conduct" in 1989 (*Police Chief*, 1992, p. 14).

A special code of ethics or conduct is required for the police because of two special ethical problems confronting police officers. First, the police are entitled to use coercive force. Second, they are entitled to lie to and otherwise deceive others in the course of their duties (e.g., while conducting undercover operations or interrogating suspects). Further, special standards of conduct appear to be necessary in policing because police officers, over the years, have engaged in activities that have offended the moral sensibilities of a good number of people. Finally, the need for special ethical standards arises whenever certain types of conduct are not subject to control by other means, usually when practitioners exercise considerable discretion and those affected must trust them to be ethical. As noted throughout this book, this is clearly the case with the police.

A code of ethics is, however, only one of several components of a profession. An early attempt at defining a profession and offering a framework to distinguish a profession from a vocation was provided by Flexner (1915). According to Flexner, there are objective criteria that can be used to identify a profession:

- Full-time commitment to their work
- A degreed workforce
- Realization by members that their practice is constantly changing and evolving
- Involvement of intellectual operations in the practice
- Responsibility for problem solving
- Material being derived from science
- Possession of an educationally communicable technique
- Common set of objectives
- Creation of a strong "class consciousness"
- Production of literature to the field or advancement through research
- Altruistic in nature

Another popular attempt at characterizing professional status was offered by Larson (1978). In contrast to Flexner, Larson defines what a profession is not by identifying a list of objective criteria that characterize professional behavior, but by examining the relationship between a profession and society. Also referred to as the socioeconomic approach, Larson and other proponents of this viewpoint believe that there is neither an absolute profession nor a set of criteria associated with one. They simply believe that occupations are either regarded by society as professions or they are not. A profession is merely a title or symbol that is valued by society, the value being high social status and/or economic reward. Consequently, achieving professional status depends on society's belief that the group's credentials are necessary to provide a service that would otherwise be unattainable.

More specifically, Larson believes the key elements of the professional process to be the standardization of a relatively abstract body of knowledge and the creation of a monopoly on the services that professions supply (market control). This rather complex task is achieved by the following:

- The group's ability to produce a distinctive commodity or services that are intangible in nature
- Standardizing the knowledge that the group draws on in their practice, beginning at the point of "production of producers," thus creating an atmosphere of "cognitive commonality among members"
- Standardizing the minds of consumers by having the authority to define persons as clients, determine their needs, and prescribe a remedy
- Attaining cognitive exclusiveness or having the appearance of cognitive superiority
- Gaining the protection of public authorities (licensing bodies that serve to insulate the group from public criticism)

According to Larson (pp. 26–27), "It is the monopolization of knowledge, not the knowledge itself, that makes professionals different. . . . Professions are in conflict with other groups in society for power, status, and economic reward. . . . Professionalism is seen as an ideology for controlling an occupation, rather than as an end-state . . . for the betterment of society."

Another framework for making this distinction was offered by Houle (1980). His research focused on the professionalization process. Also referred to as the process approach, this framework views all "occupations as existing on a continuum of professionalization" (Cervero, 1988, p. 7). The question is not whether a particular occupation is a profession, but how professionalized an occupation is. This approach allows us to view some occupations as following a sequence of steps toward professional status. Houle (1980) identified several characteristics or qualities that occupations should strive toward in their journey along the continuum of professionalization:

- Having a central mission
- Mastery of theoretical knowledge

- Self-enhancement
- Capacity to problem-solve using theory
- Use of practical knowledge
- Formal training
- Provisions for credentialing
- Creation of a subculture
- Legal reinforcement
- Public acceptance
- Ethical practice
- Establishment and enforcement of penalties
- Maintenance of a close relationship with related groups
- Well-defined provider–client relationships

The point that needs to be emphasized with regard to the characteristics set forth by Houle is they are not absolute, nor is there a cluster of criteria that an occupation must completely conform to if they are to be viewed as a profession. This approach views it as wrong to deny occupations at least a degree of professionalization simply for not exhibiting the aforementioned characteristics simultaneously.

If policing is examined using the process approach, most would agree that the field has attained at least a degree of professionalization, particularly in the past ten to fifteen years, and especially with respect to the higher education requirement espoused by Houle. Many law enforcement agencies across the country have raised their minimum education and basic recruit training requirements for entry-level positions. Although these accomplishments are important in the eyes of many police administrators and criminal justice scholars, malfeasance of duty consistently emerges as the major obstacle to further professionalization. Ricciardi and Rabin (2000), for example, note in their ten-year analysis of corruption within the ranks of the Los Angeles Police Department, one of the major culprits is lack of training relevant to ethics and racial/cultural diversity issues.

In addition, Arnold's (1997) in-depth analysis of police ethics training in Illinois found a similar state of affairs. Examine the following key findings of his research:

- Less than 1 percent of police academy training focuses on ethical and moral decision making.
- As a topic of continuing professional education or in-service training, ethics and moral decision making are seldom offered.
- There is very little consistency in training programs with respect to instructor qualifications, instructional philosophy and methodology, and course content.
- Training in ethics at the in-service level is sporadic at best and normally has little support from police executives.
- Data also demonstrate that there is little to no agreement among police executives, regional training directors, and police academy training directors concerning what constitutes police ethics.

Thus, the evidence seems to warrant significant changes in the areas of training curriculums, organizational/executive-level commitment, instructional philosophies, and instructor qualifications, topics that are discussed in more detail in Chapter 5.

Ethical practice is a requisite for professional status, and if the field of policing is to progress further along the path to professionalization, all parties concerned must commit themselves to achieving this end. Whether the police are able to attain this end, though, in large part depends on the responsible and accountable exercise of discretionary authority.

POLICE DISCRETION: RATIONALE AND INFLUENCES

Police discretion involves the use of individual judgment by officers in making decisions as to which of several behavioral responses are appropriate in specific situations. According to Sykes, Fox, and Clark (1985, p. 172), police "discretion exists whenever an officer is free to choose from two or more task-relevant, alternative interpretations of the events reported, inferred, or observed in a police-civilian encounter."

Discretion is a normal, desirable, and unavoidable part of policing that exists at all levels with a police agency. Administrative discretion involves decisions to selectively enforce laws and establish role priorities. Supervisory discretion involves decisions by supervisors to allocate resources in specific ways at specific times in response to specific requests for services.

Such discretionary behavior is required because the code of criminal law, to say nothing of departmental policies, is expressed in terms that often make difficult a clear interpretation of the writer's intentions. In addition, police resources are limited; the police cannot be everywhere at once. Further, policing, like many other occupations, consists of a number of specializations, and not all departments have the specialized personnel to investigate all types of crime or provide all types of services. Finally, the police are well aware that all other components of the criminal justice network also have limited resources (court time, jail cells, etc.).

While police officers are not, in the strictest sense of the words, judges or jurors, they must and do perform the functions of both on certain occasions. That is, they must decide what the facts are in any given encounter, what the law has to say with respect to the encounter, and how best to bring the encounter to a successful conclusion. They also consider matters in extenuation and mitigation because each individual wants to provide her own account of the circumstances leading up to the encounter.

The extent to which police officers are encouraged to exercise discretion varies from department to department, from shift to shift, and among divisions within the same department, but the exercise of discretion is routine in all police agencies (Reiss, 1992, p. 74). This is true because, as mentioned, the police simply cannot enforce all the laws all of the time or perform all of the services demanded at the same time. Thus, both law enforcement and policing are selective processes in which some laws are enforced and some services are provided most of the time, while others are not. The determination of which, and when, services are provided rests to some extent with police administrators, the general public, prosecutors, judges, and other politicians, but police officers do not typically operate under immediate, direct supervision. Therefore, they are relatively free to determine their own actions at any given time. Their decisions are typically influenced by the following factors (Cox, 1996, pp. 46–47):

1. The law
2. Departmental policy
3. Political expectations
4. The situation/setting
5. The occupational culture in which they operate

The Unintended Consequences of Discretionary Authority

Clearly, the exercise of discretion is necessary for effective policing. Problems arise, though, when the public perceives discretion as being applied in a discriminatory or biased fashion. For many years now, minority group members, particularly African Americans, and many criminal justice scholars have been pointing to the disproportionate number of minority group members who enter the criminal justice system, from the point of arrest through the point of incarceration. While some empirical studies do lend support to such concerns, others do not. What is clear, though, is that concerns of this nature consistently appear in the press, the most recent and notable of these being what the press has labeled racial profiling or "Driving While Black," defined simply as the targeting of minority group members by police for traffic and/or other law enforcement practices.

Law enforcement practices that turned the spotlight on racial profiling and that evoked a huge public outcry in this regard occurred in the states of New Jersey and

Traffic stops should be made without regard for race, ethnicity, or gender.

Maryland in 1998, when members of the New Jersey and Maryland State Police were formally accused of stopping black motorists on their states' respective highways for no reason other than race (Barovick, 1998). Empirical evidence resulting from data collection efforts regarding traffic stops, detention/investigation, and arrests of black drivers on those states' highways paints an alarming picture. In New Jersey, researchers wanted to ascertain whether state troopers stopped, ticketed, and/or arrested black motorists at rates significantly higher than other racial and ethnic groups. To determine this, the researchers measured the rate at which blacks were being stopped, ticketed, and/or arrested on the relevant part of the highway, and . . . the percentage of blacks on that same stretch of road (Harris, 1999).

The results of the data collection efforts in New Jersey were direct and disturbing. Of the approximate 42,000 cars involved in the study, the following was determined:

- There was little or no difference concerning the frequency and type of traffic violations committed by black and white motorists.
- Approximately 73 percent of the motorists stopped and arrested were black, but only about 13 percent of the vehicles involved in stops had a black driver or passenger.
- Blacks drove or occupied only about 13 percent of the vehicles in question, but accounted for 35 percent of the total number of traffic stops.

Results from a similar study in Maryland yielded remarkably similar results. In this case, six thousand vehicles were included in the data collection, and as in the New Jersey study, the purpose was to discover whether Maryland state troopers were stopping, issuing citations, searching, and/or arresting predominately minority-group motorists. The following quotation summarizes the Maryland results in clear fashion (Harris, 1999, pp. 265–326):

> . . . blacks and whites drove no differently; the percentage of blacks and whites violating the traffic code were virtually undistinguishable. More importantly . . . analysis found that although 17.5% of the population violating the traffic code on the road . . . studied was black, more than 72% of those stopped and searched were black. In more than 80% of the cases, the person stopped and searched was a member of some racial minority.

Since the coverage of these incidents, dozens, perhaps hundreds, of law enforcement agencies have come under scrutiny for similar biased-enforcement practices, opening the floodgates, so to speak, for civil and criminal civil rights litigation and prompting legislatures from all levels of government to sponsor and adopt laws designed to eradicate this form of malfeasance by police. So numerous were the complaints from the minority citizenry, the American Civil Liberties Union (ACLU) posted an online complaint form/questionnaire on the World Wide Web in their effort to compile statistical data to bolster their plea to various units of government for support in eliminating these law enforcement practices.

A point that needs to be emphasized is that public perceptions of biased enforcement are not limited to the minority communities in this country. The Gallup organization conducted numerous national polls addressing these issues when these alleged law enforcement issues began receiving increased media attention. What follows is a synopsis of the public opinion polls resulting from Gallup's efforts:

- When racial profiling is operationalized as "police officers stop motorists of certain racial or ethnic groups because the officers believe that these groups are more likely than others to commit certain types of crimes" (Newport, 1999), 59 percent of the adults surveyed, regardless of race and/or ethnicity, believe this practice to be widespread. In addition, 81 percent of the respondents disapprove of this practice.
- When broken down by race, more than four out of ten African Americans believe they have been stopped by the police just because of their race. Moreover, of those who claim to have been stopped because of their race, six out of ten say they have been stopped three or more times. It should also be noted that the responses varied significantly by age and gender within the African American community: ". . . it is black men, and especially young black men, aged 18 [to] 34, who are most likely to report having been stopped because of their race" (Newport, 1999).
- When respondents were asked to give their opinions of both their local and state police, among whites there is barely a difference, with 85 percent giving favorable opinions of their local police and 87 percent giving favorable opinions of their state police. Newport (1999) states that blacks have a less favorable opinion of both, with 58 percent having a favorable opinion of their local police, and 64 percent of state troopers. Once again, age was a significant factor. More than 50 percent of young black men, aged 18 to 34, had unfavorable opinions of both groups of police. Unfavorable opinions of the police from the respondents in the 35 to 49 age group dropped to 36 percent.
- When respondents were asked if they felt they were treated unfairly during interactions with their local and state police, race, age, and gender seemed to account for the most pronounced differences. For whites, the number of those who reported being treated unfairly was small: 7 percent for local police and 4 percent for state police. Black respondents reported quite differently: 27 percent for local police and 17 percent for state police. When age was factored in, 53 percent of young black men, aged 18 to 34, reported being treated unfairly by their local police, and 29 percent reported being treated unfairly by their state police (Newport, 1999).

Dellatre (1996) strongly advises police executives to never be reluctant to justify their policies, procedures, and actions to the public or any other source of inquiry. As alluded to earlier in this section, reluctance to conform to public demand arouses suspicion of wrongdoing and acts as a barrier to the trust and confidence of the public in the police that are absolutely essential if the police are to operate effectively. The following quotation says it all:

> When authority, power, and discretion are granted to public officials . . . rational people presume that they will not use more than they need for their legitimate purposes, because rational people would never grant more authority or discretion to abridge liberty or use force than they believed necessary. The presumption is not of guilt but of official respect

for restraint. Citizens expect public officials to justify their use of authority or power when questions arise. (Dellatre, 1996, p. 63)

Whether the practice of racial profiling is as widespread as the media portrays is not the central issue; rather, police administrators must realize that this emotionally charged subject must be dealt with competently, responsibly, and swiftly.

Controlling Discretion and Encouraging Ethical Behavior

According to Manning (1978, pp. 11–12), the police occupational subculture emphasizes the following assumptions:

1. People are not to be trusted and are potentially dangerous.
2. Personal experience is a better action guide than abstract rules.
3. Officers must make the public respect them.
4. Everyone hates a cop.
5. The legal system is untrustworthy; police officers make the best decisions about innocence or guilt.
6. People must be controlled or they will break laws.
7. Police officers must appear respectable and be effective.
8. Police officers can most accurately identify crime and criminals.
9. The basic jobs of the police are to prevent crime and enforce laws.
10. More severe punishment will deter crime.

The consequences of these assumptions, if carried over to the realm of police discretion, might (and in fact quite often do) lead to the following behaviors on behalf of police officers:

1. Ignoring abstract rules and principles (including laws)
2. Resorting to the threat or use of force to make the public show respect for police officers
3. Displaying paranoid behavior
4. Using street justice
5. Preferring efficiency over effectiveness
6. Regarding non-enforcement tasks as less than real police work
7. Adding charges when making arrests in order to try to ensure that some punishment or more severe punishment will result

The police subculture, important though it is, is not the only determinant of police discretion, nor are street level officers the only police personnel who exercise such discretion. Among other important considerations in the exercise of discretion are the law, the seriousness of the offense in question, departmental policy, personal characteristics of those involved in a given encounter, the safety of the officer involved, and the visibility of the decision (Sykes, Fox, & Clark, 1985; Reiss, 1992; Gaines, Kappeler, & Vaughn, 1994, pp. 195–202).

Further, the education, training, and length of service of the officer and the wishes of the complainant have been shown to affect decisions rendered by police officers (Brooks, 1993). A department involved in community policing may provide more education and training in the exercise of discretion, and more encouragement to use discretion than would a more traditional department. Still, the department's policy will have differential impact on officers with different lengths of service and different levels of education who may be assigned to vastly different neighborhoods.

Failure to recognize and communicate the importance of discretion at all levels in policing may lead to a pretense of full enforcement and equal treatment in similar conditions, when the reality is selective enforcement and unequal treatment. Thus, a necessary first step in dealing with discretion is to recognize its existence and importance. Once we admit that discretion exists in police work, we can talk about its proper and improper uses. We can stop attempting to deceive the public, and we can provide training with respect to the appropriate uses of discretion.

For example, we agree that a driver who is exceeding the speed limit by three or four miles per hour should not be subject to arrest. We might thus establish a "tolerance limit" of five miles per hour, instruct officers that those driving over the speed limit, but within the tolerance, need not be arrested. While this does not guarantee absolute control over officers' behavior (they could, for example, still cite a driver for driving two or three miles per hour over the speed limit), it does let them know that it is permissible to ignore or warn those who are marginally speeding (Langworthy & Travis, 1994, pp. 294–295).

Similarly, we might agree that an officer who decides to render service or enforce the law based solely on the gender, race, or physical appearance of the other citizen involved is exercising discretion inappropriately (based on personal characteristics). Supervisors could then discourage such behavior and explain why decisions based solely on personal characteristics of subjects are unacceptable. In effect, we would be enhancing the value of police discretion by providing the officer with appropriate education and training.

Because the police are a public service agency, honesty and accountability to the public are particularly important. Admitting that selective enforcement does occur and that not all police officers respond in the same way to similar situations (already "open secrets") are steps in the right direction. Although a comprehensive set of guidelines for the exercise of police discretion may not be possible, improvement of current guidelines is clearly possible. Such clarification will not only assist the community in understanding police actions, but also might remove some of the confusion among police officers themselves as to how much and what types of discretion are available to and expected of them. Simply telling an officer to exercise his discretion, in the traditional police world, is likely to have little effect, because there are other indicators that innovation is seldom rewarded and mistakes seldom go unpunished.

Unfortunately, a typical response to controlling police discretion is often the use of negative sanctions to prevent or correct discretionary behavior. A number of side effects are likely to accompany the punitive approach: temporary rather than permanent change, inappropriate emotional behavior, inflexibility, possible changes in desirable behavior, and fear or distrust of those administering the negative sanctions.

Further, the stigma accompanying punishment may have negative effects on self-esteem and status as well, which may lead to anger and hostility in those punished. A better approach to controlling discretion is the use of incentives to promote voluntary compliance with policies concerning discretion. Such incentives include officer participation in policy formulation, establishment of specialized units to deal with specific tasks, positive disciplinary practices (aimed at correcting the aberrant behavior without humiliating the officer involved), and more and better training with respect to the exercise of discretion and the social and historical context, which requires the police to be accountable to several audiences (public, administration, colleagues) for their behavior. Similarly, training and education dealing with police ethics may provide the foundation for making appropriate discretionary decisions in a variety of different situations (Brooks, 1993; Gaines, Kappeler, & Vaughn, 1994, pp. 221–230).

There are a number of other steps police administrators can take in mitigating instances of unethical and illegal practices and improving organizational and individual decision making.

Commitment to the Importance of Ethical Decision Making

Leaders set the tone for the entire organization; therefore, without a strong commitment stressing the importance of ethical decision making by the chief executive officer and her entire command staff, instances of unethical and perhaps illegal practices are sure to follow. As stated by O'Malley (1997, p. 22) in his work, *Managing for Ethics: A Mandate for Administrators,*

> The importance of upper-level management in determining a department's ethics and overall quality cannot be overstated. A common thread in most widespread police corruption cases is an absence of oversight from above. A recent examination of multi-officer corruption cases uncovered an unwillingness by police executives to acknowledge corruption and found, in some cases, a "willful blindness" to unethical behavior.

Police administrators also can mandate the study of ethical decision making in their in-service training and bring pressure to bear on state training directors to stress this activity at the recruit level as well. In addition, those responsible for directing training practices should revisit their curriculum designs and ensure that the training is delivered or facilitated by experienced educators and trainers who understand and emphasize the importance of ethical considerations and discretionary activities. All policies governing individual and collective police behavior should be consistent with the ideals of justice and morality.

Improved Hiring Practices

Presently, most state, county, and municipal law enforcement agencies utilize the services of merit boards and/or boards of police and fire commissioners, comprised chiefly of civilians from the community at large, to oversee their hiring and promotional practices. Normally mandated either by state statute or county/local ordinance, this practice guarantees that the communities these agencies serve have at least some input with respect to their law enforcement personnel. While this process may be good in theory, practically speaking, these boards and commissions may not be effective in selecting and hiring the best candidates for policing. Members of these boards and commissions are often political appointees and in many cases have little or no experience in the field of policing or in the area of human resource development. Perhaps it is time to change the composition of board members so that those in the community who have expertise in one or both of these areas are included. It may be that policing can benefit from the experiences of the private business sector, whose hiring and promotional practices are quite different and, by most accounts, more effective. For example, private-sector practices differ in the following ways:

- Place less emphasis on outdated and at times prejudicial physical agility and power tests
- Increase reliance on in-depth oral interviews conducted by experienced and knowledgeable professionals within the field
- Increase minimum education requirements for those seeking admission and/or promotion. Perhaps it is time for the minimum requirement of a baccalaureate degree to be implemented, at least for those desiring promotion within police ranks
- Utilize appropriate and complex task analyses for the position sought
- Use appropriate testing procedures to evaluate effective written and oral communication skills—from our perspective, the single most important set of skills to bring to the job
- Conduct extremely thorough background investigations

These recommendations should significantly increase the probability that those selected will fulfill the requirements of the agency in question and the field of policing. This, in turn, should increase the level of professional policing and mitigate or decrease the incidence of malfeasance (see Highlight 9.1).

Elimination of Quotas

Most administrators, when asked whether officer performance is, in large part, based on ticket and arrest activity, would answer that there are no quotas in their respective agencies. Rather, they would most likely point to "performance standards," which tend to identify acceptable ticket and arrest activity of department members, using measures of central tendency, such as means and medians. Regardless of what they are called, either *quotas* or *performance standards*, officers' performance evaluations are based almost entirely on the number of tickets and arrests that are made. What must be emphasized is that, in many cases, this may cause some officers to engage in biased enforcement practices in order to meet agency expectations. We can recall an instance when a police officer told us that whenever the end of the month nears, more stops of vehicles driven by male Hispanics occur because of the assumption that they are poor and often operate

■ ■ ■ ■ ■

HIGHLIGHT 9.1
STATE'S LAW OFFICERS GATHER TO DISCUSS ETHICS

Their profession tarnished by recent scandals, hundreds of high-ranking law enforcement officers from around the state convened in Long Beach on Tuesday for the region's first police ethics symposium.

The two-day conference at the Queen Mary ocean liner is delving into such sensitive issues as corruption, abuses of power, civil rights violations, and changing police culture to improve the way officers do their jobs.

Task force members say they want to strengthen integrity and avoid repeating such controversies as the Branch Davidian deaths in Waco, Texas, the recent case of an FBI agent arrested as a Russian spy and the Rampart scandal now engulfing the Los Angeles Police Department.

"There has been a loss of law enforcement credibility," said James V. DeSarno Jr., assistant director of the FBI office in Los Angeles. "Not even the FBI has been saved from criticism. We need to regain our position of trust. This is the beginning of the discussion."

The conference, which attracted about 300 participants, stems from a regional task force on law enforcement ethics established six months ago by federal, state and local police agencies.

They include the FBI, the state attorney general's office, the U.S. attorney's office, the Los Angeles County Sheriff's Department, the Los Angeles Police Department, the Los Angeles County district attorney's office, and a variety of professional associations.

"We have played a game in our profession over the last 20 years. We talk about free coffee and meals, but not about fudging police reports and how we treat people," said Pasadena Police Chief Bernard K. Melekian, who heads the Los Angeles County Chiefs of Police, an association of law enforcement leaders.

Also appearing at Tuesday's symposium were Los Angeles Police Chief Bernard C. Parks, Alejandro N. Mayorkas, the U.S. attorney in Los Angeles, and Los Angeles County Sheriff Lee Baca, who have been facing questions about the integrity of some of their recent actions. They briefly attended a news conference, but stepped away before the question-and-answer period.

A recent report by the inspector general for the Los Angeles Police Commission concluded that Parks made misleading statements about the Rampart scandal to the news media and to the inspector general's office during its investigation. The report, obtained by The Times this week, was written in December.

Later in the day, Parks strongly contested the conclusions of Inspector General Jeffrey Eglash.

Baca and Mayorkas have been linked to the furor over one of former president Bill Clinton's last-minute pardons and clemency cases. In conversations with White House aides, they talked about Carlos Vignali, a convicted cocaine trafficker whose 15-year sentence was commuted by Clinton on his last day in office. The Vignali case involved 800 pounds of cocaine.

Mayorkas has repeatedly declined to discuss the matter.

In a statement last week, Baca said he returned telephone calls to White House officials, but denied that he supported or requested clemency for Vignali during the discussions. The sheriff maintains that he only vouched for the truthfulness of Vignali's father, Horacio, who was seeking clemency for his son.

Parks, Mayorkas and Baca told the audience during opening remarks Tuesday that they strongly supported the ethics conference and the effort to restore an unwavering respect for the law within the profession.

"A locker room mentality pervades what happens on the street and that is different from a department's core values," Baca said. "These are critical times in shaping the future of law enforcement. The biggest challenge is to lift our people up and get the best out of them."

Baca said the Sheriff's Department recently created an independent review panel of six civil rights attorneys to oversee and evaluate charges of wrongdoing by deputies. Disciplinary cases used to be handled almost exclusively by the department's Internal Affairs Division.

Other departments, including the LAPD and Long Beach police, have set up police commissions or civilian review boards.

"The civil rights community is not our enemy. That is a wrong way of thinking," Baca said. "We should join in and embrace every aspect of civil rights in American life."

Officials hosting the conference said they hope the event will provide police managers with new ideas and raise the level of discussion about ethics within the region's law enforcement agencies.

New York City police official Charles V. Campisi, who oversees one of the largest internal affairs units in the world, said in an interview that ethics conferences have been valuable in New York state, where at least seven have been held since 1994.

Although the ranks of the New York Police Department grew by 40% in the last six years, Campisi said, the number of corruption cases against officers has declined 41%. He attributed the drop partly to ethics conferences.

"Everyone learns from each other at these things," said Campisi, a conference panelist. "You come away with practical solutions. You can see measurable results."

Weikel, Dan. (2001, March 7). *Los Angeles Times.*

ill-equipped vehicles. Multiple citations can then be issued, thus allowing the department ticket quota or standard to be met.

Zero-tolerance arrest policies also are notorious for increasing the probability of biased enforcement practices. These policies are normally reserved for "high crime" areas, usually found in geographic areas of low socioeconomic status and high minority populations. When narcotics, gang crime, and vice enforcement are conducted in this fashion, allegations of unethical and otherwise inappropriate police behavior are sure to follow. These policies are not consistent with the goals and objectives of community-oriented policing strategies either, and for this reason, as well as the ones cited previously, arrest quotas and zero-tolerance policing initiatives should be changed.

Intolerance of Malfeasance

Rather than focus on zero-tolerance arrest policies, police administrators might adopt zero-tolerance policies concerning malfeasance by department members. As stated earlier in this chapter, the vast majority of our nation's police officers perform their duties ethically, professionally, and competently. The small minority of officers who do engage in unethical and criminal activities damage the reputation of the entire field of policing. The sad truth of the matter is that most honest, hard-working officers know who these miscreants are. Unfortunately, for many of the reasons cited in Chapter 10, "Police Misconduct," there is a great reluctance on the part of many of these honest officers to report the wrongdoings of their coworkers.

Moreover, these unprofessional officers are known not only by rank-and-file personnel, but also by command staff. To make matters worse, these "bad apples" are usually identified as such very early in their careers, normally during their field training or probationary period of employment. Unfortunately, many of these officers are not terminated at that time. Administrators point to the high cost of training and the amount of money they have invested in these relatively new officers, so rather than fire those individuals, they keep them, hoping that they will improve as time goes by. More often than not, though, these officers end up costing their agencies a lot more during the course of time, not only in terms of dollars, but even more in terms of community relations and public perception. For these reasons, chief executive law enforcement officers are encouraged to revisit their policies on disciplinary actions regarding malfeasance by their personnel from time to time.

In-Car Video Cameras

In recent years, many police departments have adopted policies that allow placement of video cameras, capable of recording sight and sound, inside their marked squad cars. Purported reasons for use of this technology include those that focus on officer safety. Recently, however, installation of these devices comes as the result of allegations concerning racial profiling. These video cameras, which activate from the beginning to the end of an officer's shift, can be shut on and off only by supervisory personnel. All tapes are collected and maintained for review, if the need arises. Because the videotape is always rolling during a shift, many officers claim that this makes them better officers, more professional and more than ever willing to abide by department policy.

In 2000, the Cook County Sheriff's Police Department (CCSPD) (Cook is the county in which the city of Chicago is located) placed video cameras in a number of their squad cars as a test program to evaluate the usefulness of this relatively new phenomenon. The responses from both line and staff personnel were overwhelmingly positive (Keoun, 2000, p. 2C2):

> Advocates of the cameras, which in recent years have been adopted by police departments across the nation, say they provide officers with additional evidence to convict traffic offenders, especially in drunken-driving cases. But the cameras are also touted as a way of protecting officers against false complaints of brutality and racial profiling. Motorists benefit from the camera because officers are less likely to misbehave during traffic stops if they know they are being taped.

As one CCSPD officer put it, "With the video camera, it makes you a better officer because you know you're being videotaped. . . . I would never want to work without a camera. If I had to, I'd feel it was a disadvantage" (Keoun, 2000).

Based on numerous similar accounts, police agencies throughout the country have adopted these cameras for the benefit of both the public and their officers. The advantages in terms of improved community relations and increased professionalism far outweigh any conceivable disadvantages.

Responsible and Proactive Data Collection Efforts

As previously stated, legislative acts and judicial orders are forcing many law enforcement agencies to collect data regarding the race or ethnicity of all motorists and passengers who are stopped by police on our nation's roadways. As noted earlier, the methodologies established for collecting these data do not always paint an accurate picture due to a number of factors. The lack of accurate baseline demographics from which to compare agency statistics is a significant limitation. This has formed a genuine conundrum for many police executives, for now, no matter what they do, allegations of racial profiling are sure to surface.

This is not the case, however, for the Bloomingdale, Illinois, Police Department, which has not come under scrutiny for biased enforcement practices. In 1991, long before the term *racial profiling* was coined, the Bloomingdale Police Department (BPD) decided to examine and monitor the racial makeup of all motorists ticketed that year by first establishing a minority roadway population on their city's major thoroughfares, collecting the racial composition of all motorists ticketed, and comparing the statistics for abnormalities. Examine the highlights from their analyses:

- Of the thousands of traffic tickets issued during that time period (1991–1992), black drivers accounted for 9 percent of the tickets issued, the town having a 6.5 percent minority population.
- There were three officers who were writing 40 percent or more of their tickets to black motorists, a clear indicator that those individuals were targeting certain drivers. The officers in question were then counseled, sent to sensitivity training, and afterward closely monitored by supervisory personnel. Those corrective actions seemed to take care of the problems.
- The BPD attributed these biased enforcement practices to their former use of ticket quotas. That policy of performance evaluation was quickly abandoned by the agency (Higgins, 2000).

The significance of the last highlight cannot be overemphasized. Ticket quotas have a way of encouraging biased enforcement practices. As stated by a BPD commander,

> The problem officers let the work go to the end of the month, and they've got to catch up. Who catches the brunt of the enforcement effort? It's the people who can't afford the good car—people who are on the lower socioeconomic rung. . . . They're easier targets . . . (Higgins, 2000, p. 205).

The members of the BPD who initiated this study are to be commended for their professionalism and proactive policing style. Among a host of allegations of racial profiling recently directed at agencies in close proximity to their borders, the BPD received none. More important than that, they were not caught off guard and had sound, empirical data to negate allegations of biased enforcement practices. According to David Harris, a law professor and noted expert in the area of racial profiling, "This early foray into monitoring the racial breakdown of ticketed drivers is impressive. . . . My hat is off to them. . . . It's very unusual. For 1991, it's stunningly unusual" (Higgins, 2000, p. 2D5). Police executives from across the country may be well advised to voluntarily follow the lead of the BPD.

Good Police–Media Relations

As indicated in Chapter 3, in our present age of technology, the media, both print and broadcast, have the ability to transmit news stories throughout the world in a matter of seconds—an awesome power indeed. Unfortunately, in the name of sensationalism and profit, that power is subject to abuse. The allegations of racial profiling perhaps exemplify the essence of sensationalism and unprofessional behavior on the part of many in the media. As discussed throughout this chapter, statistical data are easily manipulated and do not always portray events or phenomena accurately.

Unfortunately, the history of police–media relations in this country is poor at best. For a variety of reasons, many police officials, line and staff personnel alike, tend to shun media representatives whenever possible, withholding information on newsworthy events, even when disclosure of information could not possibly harm anyone or compromise a criminal investigation. When clashes like this occur, the information garnered for the news story is usually provided by unreliable sources and often leads to inaccurate depictions of the incidents in question.

Aside from large, urban police departments, such as those of New York, Chicago, and Los Angeles, very few agencies dedicate personnel on a full-time basis to maintaining good media relations with the local press. Agencies that are successful in this regard can almost, without exception, be guaranteed fair and impartial reporting by their local media representatives. Imagine two local police departments, A and B, that have recently come under public scrutiny regarding allegations of racial profiling. Department A enjoys a long-standing, professional relationship with the local press. Department B, on the other hand, has no relationship to speak of with the local press and ignores media representatives whenever possible. Which department do you suppose will receive fair and impartial reporting? Department A would more than likely have the ability to take the initiative and invite and assist members of the local press in its search for the truth. Provided the department in question has nothing to hide, reporters could be invited to examine official data, as well as ride along with the officers to observe enforcement practices firsthand. At the very least, Department A will be assured an accurate portrayal of the facts.

The power of the press cannot be ignored, and command personnel throughout the nation are urged to develop policies that foster a positive relationship with their local media. The benefits of such policies will come back tenfold. Simply stated, the police need the press more than the press needs the police.

To perform their role competently and effectively, the police must maintain a high degree of discretionary authority. This level of power and authority, though, must be exercised ethically and responsibly if the public trust is to be reestablished and maintained. Without this level of public confidence, the journey toward increased professionalism in the field of policing will come to an end.

The implications of discretionary authority are both clear and considerable. Police agencies throughout the nation need to revisit practices with respect to hiring and strive to hire men and women of excellent character. Police executives must both lead by example and be intolerant of acts of malfeasance by their personnel. Policies that emphasize the importance of an ethical foundation for the exercise of discretion are critical in this regard (see Highlight 9.2, for example).

HIGHLIGHT 9.2
MODEL AGENCY POLICY REGARDING RACIAL PROFILING

I. PURPOSE The purpose of this written directive/policy is to establish procedures for officers in the conduct of their relations with traffic violators for the uniform enforcement of traffic laws.

II. POLICY It is the policy of the [ ] Agency to conduct traffic stops and interactive patrols for the purpose of deterring motor vehicle violations, and to provide law enforcement visibility to assist in deterring more serious crimes. Officers should strive to make each contact educational and leave the violator with the impression that the officer has performed a necessary task in a professional and friendly manner. Officers shall not stop, detain, search or arrest any traffic violator based solely on the person's race, national origin, citizenship, religion, ethnicity, age, gender, color, creed, sexual orientation or disability.

III. PROCEDURES
Field Officer Responsibilities

1. An officer may stop a motor vehicle upon a reasonable suspicion that the driver or an occupant committed a motor vehicle violation or other offense. Such stops shall conform to [agency] policy and procedures.

2. This directive does not preclude an officer from stopping a vehicle to offer assistance (e.g., to inform a driver of an item left on the roof, or of a substance leaking from the car). Such actions should be reported as an "assist motorist" call.

3. Officers are prohibited from stopping, detaining, searching or arresting anyone because of the person's race, national origin, citizenship, religion, ethnicity, age, gender, color, creed, sexual orientation or disability unless they are seeking an individual with one or more of those identified attributes (e.g., Officers may consider a person's apparent age when investigating a

possible violation when age is an element of such).

4. Each officer will complete a [Traffic Stop Form] after stopping the driver of a vehicle. The following information is required when completing the form:
   a. The age, gender and race or minority group of the individual stopped;
   b. The traffic violation or violations alleged to have been committed that led to the stop;
   c. Whether a search was conducted as a result of the stop;
   d. If a search was conducted, whether the individual consented to the search, the probable cause for the search, whether the person was searched, whether the person's property was searched, and the duration of the search;
   e. Whether any contraband was discovered in the course of the search and the type of any contraband discovered;
   f. Whether any warning or citation was issued as a result of the stop;
   g. If a warning or citation was issued, the violation charged or warning provided;
   h. Whether an arrest was made as a result of either the stop or the search;
   i. If an arrest was made, the crime charged; and
   j. The location of the stop.

5. The [Traffic Stop Form] requirement only applies to officer observed statutory/ordinance motor vehicle violations.

6. Officers shall treat every person with courtesy and respect. An officer shall provide his/her name, serial/badge number and reason for the vehicle stop, per department policy.

7. Whenever a person complains that an officer has engaged in practices prohibited by this directive, the officer will notify their supervisor, per department policy.

(continued)

HIGHLIGHT 9.2 Continued

Supervisor Responsibilities

1. Supervisors shall ensure that officers follow the policies and procedures outlined in this directive.
2. If a supervisor is available he/she shall respond to the stop location when advised that a person is making a complaint alleging profiling or other improper conduct.
3. After discussion with the person, the supervisor shall provide the complainant with a [Citizen Complaint Form] if the matter is not resolved. The citizen shall be provided guidance in completing and filing of the complaint, per department policy.

Review/Reporting Requirements

1. The department will periodically review the statistical information collected from the [Traffic Stop Form] to determine compliance with RSMO 590.650.
2. If the review reveals a pattern, an investigation will be conducted to determine whether any officers of this agency routinely stop members of minority groups for violations of vehicle laws as a pretext for investigating other violations of criminal law.
3. Officers found to have engaged in race-based traffic stops shall receive appropriate counseling and training within ninety days of the review.
4. Annually the department will forward statistical information, as required by statute, to the Missouri Attorney Generals Office. (RSMO 590.650)

Training

1. Employees of this department who are empowered to make traffic stops of motor vehicles shall receive training regarding this directive.
2. Annual sensitivity training shall be provided to employees who may conduct stops of motor vehicles regarding the prohibition against racial profiling.

COMPLIANCE Violations of this policy, or portions thereof, may result in disciplinary action.

OFFICERS ASSIGNED TO OTHER AGENCIES Officers of this department assigned to or assisting other law enforcement agencies will be guided by this policy.

APPLICATION This order constitutes department policy, and is not intended to enlarge the employee's civil or criminal liability in any way. It shall not be construed as the creation of a higher legal standard or safety or care in an evidentiary sense with respect to third party claims insofar as the employee's legal duty as imposed by law.

DISCLAIMER: This draft policy is provided by Meadowbrook Insurance Group only as a guide to the drafting of a policy by the local agency. Every effort has been made to ensure that this draft policy incorporates the most current information and judgment on this issue. However, no draft policy can meet all of the needs of any given agency because each agency operates in unique environments regulated by federal and state laws and court decisions, regulations, local ordinances and other legal constraints. Therefore, this draft should not be adopted by any agency without it being reviewed by local counsel for current compliance with federal, state and local laws, regulations, and judicial decisions.

Policy History: Adopted September 15, 2000 Amended Procedural Instructions Effective Date: LEAF Subject: Race Based Traffic Stops Reference: CALEA Standard 61.1.8; 590.650 and 590.653 RSMO.

DISCUSSION QUESTIONS

1. What is police discretion? How extensive is its use?

2. Why is the police subculture important in understanding discretion?

3. What are some possible negative consequences of the exercise of discretion? What are some positive consequences?

4. What factors besides the police subculture affect the exercise of police discretion?

5. Can we eliminate the exercise of police discretion? How might we gain better control over it?

6. Discuss racial profiling as an example of poor discretionary decision making.

7. Discretion is exercised by police administrators and supervisors as well as by line officers. Discuss some of the discretionary prerogatives of police managers.

8. Discuss the evolution of the police code of ethics/conduct. Why are ethics especially important for the police?

9. How effective are police academies at teaching ethics? Where and how do most officers learn police ethics?

10. List and discuss some steps that might be taken to encourage police officers to become more ethical in exercising discretion.

REFERENCES

Arnold, T. (1997). A case study analysis of police ethics training in Illinois. Doctoral dissertation, Northern Illinois University, 170 p. *Dissertation Abstracts International*, Vol. 58-12, Sec. A, p. 4522.

Barovick, H. (1998, June 15). DWB: driving while black. *Time.com*, 151 (23). Available online at: http://www.pathfinder.com/time/magazine/1998/dom/980615/nation_driving_while.html.

Brooks, L. W. (1993). Police discretionary behavior: A study of style. In Dunham, R. G., & Alpert, G. P. (eds.), *Critical issues in policing: Contemporary readings*, 2nd ed. (pp. 140–164). Prospect Heights, IL: Waveland.

Cervero, R. (1988). *Effective continuing education for professionals.* San Francisco: Jossey Bass.

Close, D., & Meier, N. (eds.). (1995). *Morality in criminal justice.* Belmont, CA: Wadsworth.

Cox, S. M. (2002, May 20). Personal interview with Cox. Macomb, IL.

———— . (1996). *Police: Practices, perspectives, problems.* Boston: Allyn & Bacon.

Dellatre, E. (1996). *Character and cops*, 3rd ed. Washington, DC: AEI Press.

Dorn, D. (2001). *Police officer gratuity policies: An exploratory story.* Unpublished Master's Thesis, Macomb, IL: Western Illinois University.

Flexner, A. (1915). Is social work a profession? *School and Society, 1*, 901–911.

Gaines, L. K., Kappeler, V. E., & Vaughn, J. B. (1994). *Policing in America.* Cincinnati, OH: Anderson.

Harris, D. (1999). The stories, the statistics, and the law: Why "driving while black" matters. *Minnesota Law Review, 84*, 265–326. Available online at: http://www.udayton.edu/race/03justice/dwb01.htm.

Higgins, M. (2000, May 26). 1992 ticket-writing lesson helped Bloomingdale cops. *Chicago Tribune* (Internet Edition).

Hoover, L. (2000, July). Why the resistance to collecting race data on police traffic stops? *Police Labor Monthly*, 1–6.

Houle, C. (1980). *Continuing learning in the professions.* San Francisco: Jossey Bass.

Keoun, B. (2000, May 22). Video cameras in squad cars gain popularity among police. *Chicago Tribune* (Internet Edition).

Knapp Commission. (1972). *Report on police corruption.* New York: George Braziller.

Langworthy, R. H., & Travis, L. F. (1994). *Policing in America: A balance of forces.* New York: Macmillan.

Larson, M. (1978). *The rise of professionalism: A sociological analysis.* Berkeley, CA: University of California Press.

Manning, P. (1978). The police: Mandate, strategies, and appearances. In Manning, P., & Van Maanen, J. (eds.), *Policing: A view from the street* (pp. 7–13). Santa Monica, CA: Goodyear.

Myron, P. (1992). Crooks or cops: We can't be both. *Police Chief, 59*, 23–29.

Newport, F. (1999, December 9). Racial profiling is seen as widespread, particularly among young black men. *Gallup News Service.*

O'Malley, T. (1997, April). Managing for ethics: A mandate for administrators. *FBI Law Enforcement Bulletin* (Internet Edition).

Reiss, A. J. (1992). Police organization in the twentieth century. In Tonry, M., & Morris, N. (eds.), *Modern policing* (pp. 51–98). Chicago: University of Chicago Press.

Ricciardi, N., & Rabin, J. (2000, March 13). Report echos Christopher Panel's findings. *Los Angeles Times*, p. A5.

Scaramella, G. (2001, February). Attitudes of undergraduate criminal justice majors toward ethical issues in criminal justice. *Illinois Law Enforcement Executive Forum, 1*, 9–25.

Sykes, G. (1999). NYPD blues. *Ethics Corner, 6*, Southwestern Law Enforcement Institute, Center for Law Enforcement Ethics: http://web2airmail.net/slf/clee.html.

Sykes, R., Fox, J., & Clark, J. (1985). A socio-legal theory of police discretion. In Blumberg, A., & Niederhoffer, E. (eds.), *The ambivalent force: Perspectives on the police* (pp. 171–183). New York: Holt, Rinehart, and Winston.

Trautman, N. (2002). Administrator misconduct. *Law and Order, 50*, 118–126.

U.S. Department of Justice. (2001). *Principles for promoting police integrity: Examples of promising police practices and policies.* Washington, DC: U.S. Government Printing Office.

U.S. General Accounting Office. (1998). *Drug-related police corruption.* Washington, DC: U.S. Government Printing Office.

CHAPTER TEN

POLICE MISCONDUCT

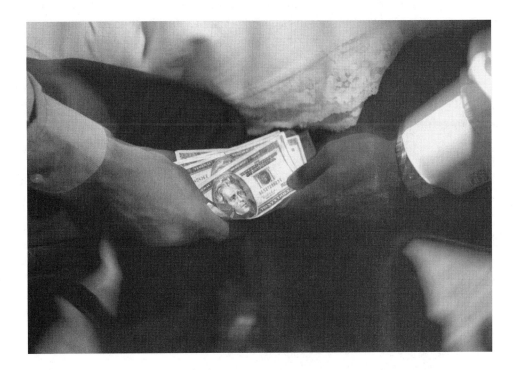

Police misconduct is a complicated topic with a long and convoluted history in the United States. Misconduct may be broadly divided into two categories—corruption and physical/emotional abuse—and may be either organizational or individual in nature. Each of these categories includes numerous subcategories, the categories often overlap, and both are violations of the ethical standards of police officers. As pointed out in earlier chapters, in a general sense, *ethics* refers to the moral obligations of humans to act in ways that are good and proper. Applied specifically to police officers, ethical conduct is especially important because of the authority granted officers and because of the difficulty of overseeing the daily behavior of police officers on the street.

The "police possess at least two capacities whose use raises special ethical problems. Police are entitled to use coercive force and to lie and deceive people in the course of their work. Moreover, as sociologist Egon Bittner reminds us, while 'few of us are constantly mindful of the saying, He that is without sin among you, let him cast the first stone, only the police are explicitly required to forget it.'" (Klockars, 1989, p. 427).

Additionally, of course, police performance has traditionally been subject to a good deal of moral controversy, partly because they deal with moral issues on a regular basis and partly because their behavior has sometimes offended the moral sensitivities of others. Finally, the police engage in discretionary behavior regularly, and other citizens must place a good deal of trust in their conduct with little in the way of assurances that their conduct is subject to adequate control (Klockars, 1989). Many ethical violations by the police fall under the general heading of conduct unbecoming a police officer and are investigated by other police officers. In light of the potential for police misconduct resulting from the periodic need to coerce and/or deceive the public, there is clearly a need for more attention to police ethics than is commonly paid.

In our present era of community policing, law enforcement executives, government officials, community groups, and academicians all advocate policing strategies that include partnerships with the public in the control and suppression of crime, thus providing for an overall improvement in the quality of life. Such strategies, as sound as they are, require an atmosphere of trust and confidence between the citizenry and those who have been sworn to serve and protect them—the police. Unfortunately, various acts of misconduct by a significant number of these public officials consistently occur, serving to create an aura of suspicion, mistrust, and uncertainty between the police and the public they serve. When allegations of corruption arise and are confirmed, effective policing strategies are severely inhibited.

This critical issue in the field of policing is the focus of this chapter, and we provide a brief historical analysis of police conduct; identify various forms, causes, and consequences of police corruption; and offer recommendations for an improved response to this serious problem.

POLICE CORRUPTION

One need only briefly examine daily media accounts to realize the breadth of corrupt and unethical law enforcement practices. Consider the following:

- The Los Angeles Police Department (LAPD) is currently in the midst of what many officials are calling LAPD's worst scandal, referred to as the Rampart Division Scandal. It involves a variety of misdeeds by numerous officers, including false arrests, the planting of evidence, and unjustified shootings (Glover & Lait, 2000).
- The Chicago Police Department (CPD) has come under public and legal scrutiny regarding three recent scandals. One involved the forced resignation of the superintendent of police for violating department rules and regulations prohibiting members from associating with convicted felons (Jackson, 2000). Another incident involved the indictments of veteran Gang Crimes Unit officers on

charges ranging from narcotics trafficking and extortion to unjustified shootings, robbery, and case fixing (Slater, 2000). The latest allegation of police corruption involves the indictment of veteran officers for "shaking down" and stealing money from Polish immigrants (Main, Sadovi, & Sweeney, 2000). See Highlight 10.1.

- In New York, several officers from both New York City and Buffalo police departments are facing suspensions and indictments for official misconduct, possession of stolen property, and associations with known organized crime figures (Claffey & Weir, 2000).
- In Michigan, the former Detroit police commissioner has been indicted for protecting an organized crime gambling enterprise (Hawk, 2000).

■ ■ ■ ■ ■

HIGHLIGHT 10.1
FOUR CITY COPS CHARGED WITH SHAKEDOWNS

Four veteran Chicago police officers suspected of shaking down Polish immigrants outside taverns were charged with felonies Tuesday after three of them were videotaped stealing cash from an undercover FBI agent, officials said.

One day in April, the agent was robbed by one of the officers and then was shaken down a half hour later by two other officers on the same block, sources said.

Officers Steven G. Miller, 55; James P. Petruzzi, 47; Michael W. Simpson, 52; and William J. Tortoriello, 50, were arrested Tuesday morning at their Northwest Side homes—without the usual courtesy of advance notice. "The superintendent wanted to treat them like any other thieves," a top police source said.

Assigned to the Jefferson Park District on the Northwest Side, the officers targeted dozens of Polish immigrants on Belmont and Milwaukee avenues, ordering them to "empty their pockets" after approaching them on sidewalks or stopping their cars, police sources said.

Miller stopped an undercover agent posing as a Polish immigrant in the 5100 block of West Belmont on April 9, authorities said. Miller allegedly took the agent's wallet, removed some money and then returned it, sources said.

A half hour later, Simpson and Tortoriello approached the same agent in the same block, authorities said. Simpson stayed in the car while Tortoriello patted down the agent, took his wallet, removed money and gave it back, sources said.

Tortoriello had shaken down the same agent on March 12, also in the 5100 block of West Belmont, authorities said. "We adamantly deny the charges; the burden will be on the state to prove them," Simpson's lawyer, Tamara Cummings, said.

The department had tried to fire Simpson in 1985, but he was found not guilty of administrative charges, said a police source, who did not provide details. Cummings said she was unaware of any past disciplinary actions against Simpson.

Petruzzi was the only officer not accused of stealing from anyone. On Feb. 5, he and Simpson, his partner, allegedly filed a bogus accident report unrelated to the shakedowns.

Simpson and Petruzzi were riding in a squad car when it was struck by another vehicle in the 3000 block of North Newcastle in the Grand-Central District, authorities said. But the two claimed the car was parked in the Jefferson Park District when it was struck, sources said.

"My understanding is that this was an ongoing investigation. If this is the extent of their charges, it really bodes well for my client," Petruzzi's lawyer, Rick Beuke, said. "People know him as a hard-working, aggressive police officer. He's considered a valuable asset wherever he's worked."

(continued)

HIGHLIGHT 10.1 Continued

Police moved Tuesday to suspend the officers without pay. Five other officers remain under investigation after being placed on desk duty. The department plans to try to fire them on administrative charges. A top police official said he expects more criminal charges in the case. Tuesday's charges were the result of a nearly two-year investigation by the police Internal Affairs Division and the FBI.

The nine officers are suspected of stopping Polish immigrants, threatening them with deportation and going through their wallets. Undercover agents posed as immigrants and videotaped several of the officers. Some of the officers used the loot to support their gambling habits, sources said.

The officers arrested Tuesday were not given any warning by the department so they could surrender with their lawyers, customary in criminal cases against officers, a police source said. Miller was picked up at his home at 6:30 a.m., his lawyer, Marc Martin, said. "He was supposed to go in for outpatient surgery for a herniated disk," Martin said.

Miller was charged with theft and official misconduct; Petruzzi with disorderly conduct and official misconduct; Simpson with theft, two counts of official misconduct and one count of filing false police reports; and Tortoriello with two counts of theft and two counts of official misconduct, police said.

They were released Tuesday after posting bail. Judge Neil Linehan set bond for Miller and Petruzzi at $25,000, and for Tortoriello and Simpson at $35,000.

The shakedown investigation came to light in August after the head of the Fraternal Order of Police publicly raised questions about surveillance equipment that officers had found in two police vehicles. When the FOP asked whether the department was randomly snooping on officers, the department responded that the devices were being used in a targeted probe against specific officers.

At a news conference, First Deputy Supt. John Thomas said the union disclosure "did not have any impact at all" on the probe. Asked why the officers were not charged with robbery, which carries a stiffer penalty than theft, he insisted the charges were proper. Thomas also said it "would take a quantum leap of faith" to conclude that the shakedowns were part of an organized conspiracy.

Word of the officers' charges was greeted enthusiastically by several Jefferson Park officers and a sergeant. "Good," the sergeant said. "We're all being brushed with the same paint. It's giving us all a black eye.... We have a lot of good officers. Now we're all embarrassed to be from 16 (the Jefferson Park district)."

Edward Moskal, president of the Polish National Alliance, said he was satisfied with the police department's reaction to the alleged shakedowns. Police have distributed 65,000 fliers explaining to Polish immigrants what to expect during traffic stops. Police Supt. Terry Hillard's office also worked with the Polish National Alliance to air public service announcements on proper police procedures.

"The superintendent is doing exactly what he promised," Moskal said. "(But) it is a sad commentary for the police to do this to our community. We've been getting calls that some of the Asians have been getting harassed, too."

John Milkowski, co-owner of Bristol tavern at 3084 N. Milwaukee and a Polish immigrant in 1968, said he hopes the officers "get what they deserve." "I hope it sends a message to the police not to pick on the Polish immigrants and contractors unless they break the law like everybody else," he said.

In August of 2001, Tortoriello and Miller entered guilty pleas to single counts of official misconduct. They were sentenced to thirty months probation, fined $1,000 each, and forfeited their police pensions. Cases against Petruzzi and Simpson are pending (Sadovi, 2001).

Even more alarming than the aforementioned allegations and acts of misconduct is the fact that media coverage exposing the majority of those instances occurred during a period of approximately six weeks—an amazingly short period of time considering the frequency of occurrence and the nature of the malfeasance involved. In addition, while those accounts pertain to allegations of criminal conduct, criminal offenses perpetrated by police officers represent only a small percentage of the activities routinely classified as police misconduct. Before examining the various forms of police misconduct, a few words regarding the history of police corruption are in order.

THE BACKGROUND OF POLICE CORRUPTION

The history of the American municipal police is replete with example and discussions concerning corruption. Reform movements have been initiated periodically to reduce or eliminate corruption but have largely failed to achieve their goals (see Highlight 10.1). The reform movement of the middle 1800s attempted to remove blatant, undesirable political influence from policing. The civil service reforms of the late 1800s sought the same goal and, though there were some successes, were bitterly opposed and circumvented by those wishing to retain undue influence over the police (Richardson, 1974; Johnson, 1981; Trojanowicz, 1992). According to Bracey (1989, p. 175),

> In 1894 the Lexow Commission, an investigative group appointed at the instigation of a coalition of concerned citizens and good government groups, closed its hearings into police corruption and ineffectiveness in New York City. It reported that corruption was systematic and pervasive, a condition that it attributed in large part to malfeasance, misfeasance and nonfeasance in the higher ranks. The next fifteen years found similar investigations and similar findings in almost every major American city.

Reforms in the early and middle 1900s emphasized the importance of professionalism as a means of reducing corruption of all types, and reform-oriented chiefs were appointed in many cities across the nation. Yet the problem of corruption resurfaced, sometimes in departments previously marred, other times in departments previously untouched by scandal. Lacayo (1993, p. 43) reported, "For cops as for anyone else, money works like an acid on integrity. Bribes from bootleggers made the 1920s a golden era for crooked police. Gambling syndicates in the 1950s were protected by a payoff system more elaborate than the Internal Revenue Service." In 1971, Frank Serpico brought to light police corruption in New York City, and the Knapp Commission investigation that followed uncovered widespread corruption among officers of all ranks. According to Lacayo, "In the 1980s Philadelphia saw more than 30 officers convicted of taking part in a scheme to extort money from [drug] dealers" (1993, p. 43). A major corruption scandal "hit Miami in the mid-1980s, when about 10% of the city's police were either jailed, fired, or disciplined in connection with a scheme in which officers robbed and sometimes killed cocaine smugglers on the Miami River, then resold the drugs."(Lacayo, 1993, p. 44). As Cooksey (1991, p. 7) states, "The Los Angeles County Sheriff's Department discharges approximately 20 officers a year, primarily as the result of misconduct." And, in 1993, twenty-two years after Serpico's disclosures in the same department, Michael Dowd and fifteen to twenty other New York City police officers led "a parade of dirty cops who dealt drugs and beat innocent people [which] has shocked the city during seven days of corruption hearings" (Frankel, 1993b, p. 3A).

Some departments were, of course, built on foundations of corruption, with politicians requiring payments for positions while others gave police positions away in return for political favors. Allegations of corruption still occur on a regular basis in many large departments, as noted. Our observations in recent years indicate that corruption of authority remains widespread in small- and medium-size (under 500 sworn personnel) departments as well. Several of the other forms of corruption also have been noted in these smaller departments.

Corruption occurs when a police officer acts in a manner that places his personal gain ahead of duty, resulting in the violation of police procedures, criminal law, or both (Lynch, 1989). According to Barker and Carter (1986, pp. 3–4), "Corrupt acts contain three elements: (1) they are forbidden by some law, rule, regulation, or ethical standard; (2) they involve the misuse of the officer's position; and (3) they involve some actual or expected material reward or gain."

Police corruption is best viewed not as the aberrant behavior of individual officers, but as group behavior guided by contradictory sets of norms. It involves a number of specific patterns that can be analyzed in terms of several dimensions, including the acts and actors involved, the norms violated, the extent of peer group support, the degree of organization, and the police department's reaction. It is difficult to estimate the proportion of police officers directly involved in police corruption, but it is probably small. Still, the actual number of police officers involved nationwide is quite large, and these officers attract a good deal of negative attention when their acts of corruption are made public (see Highlight 10.2). And, while most police officers are not directly involved in corrupt activities, large numbers do condone such activities by their failure to speak out or take action against them. These are the officers, referred to as "grass eaters" by the Knapp Commission, who passively accept the presence of corruption as a part of the police world (Knapp Commission, 1973). "Meateaters" are those officers, typically far fewer in number, who actively seek out the opportunity for corrupt activities. Recognition that those officers who actively seek out corrupt activities are relatively few has led many police administrators to espouse the "rotten apple" theory, which holds that while there are a few corrupt officers in policing, most officers are unaffected by corruption.

In fact, it is virtually impossible for a single corrupt officer to survive (other than in a one-person department). In other words, most forms of corruption require some degree of organizational support, at least in the sense that others within the organization turn their heads and refuse to confront the corrupt officer. This failure to take action against corrupt officers, even on the part of other officers who clearly dislike such activities, may be due in part to the police "code" or subculture.

Some time ago, Stoddard (1968) discussed the informal code of silence that exists among police officers with respect to a variety of types of deviant behavior. He and others (Bouza, 1990; Frankel, 1993a) have indicated that such deviance is an "open secret" within the fraternity, but its existence is denied to those outside the group.

■ ■ ■ ■ ■

HIGHLIGHT 10.2
COP'S BRAGGING WAS HIS DOWNFALL

Editor's note: The following article and excerpts from FBI tapes give readers a sense of Joseph Miedzianowski's world. The language, though edited, might be offensive to some readers.

In the end, the crooked cop was convicted by his own words. Former Chicago police officer Joseph Miedzianowski was found guilty this week of drug conspiracy and racketeering after a 12-week federal court trial. He was dubbed the "most corrupt" cop ever prosecuted by the U.S. attorney's office in Chicago.

While the drug-selling officer took the stand in his own defense, the jurors heard even more of him on tape—more than 250 secretly taped conversations in all. One juror said those tapes were key to the conviction in the case, prosecuted by Brian Netols, Victoria Peters and John Lausch.

FBI agents secretly wiretapped two home phone lines at the officer's home from mid-September to mid-December 1998. Miedzianowski is heard arranging drug deals, advising gang-bangers on how to beat criminal charges, bragging about his brutality, griping about his mistress, and talking about the importance of loyalty. His attorneys said the conversations were taken out of context.

In one conversation, Miedzianowski corrects one drug dealer when he states there is no honor among thieves.

"Ah, there is some, there is some, but you got (to have) the right thieves. You know what I mean?" Miedzianowski says. He tells the former girlfriend of another drug dealer why they have to work together and not turn on each other. "I promise you because I told you once, if it happens to you, it happens to me," he says.

What follows are lengthier excerpts from government transcripts of the conversations played to the jury at trial. In one conversation on Nov. 17, the officer tells Francisco "Frankie" Figueroa, who cooked cocaine into crack for the drug ring, that there's no honor left in the world and why they need to stick together.

Miedzianowski: It's just a, it's a ——up world, Frank. There ain't no honor out there.

Figueroa: Yeah.

Miedzianowski: There ain't no honorable —— out there. They're all the, I'm telling you they're all out to stick your ass up, everyone of 'em, in one way or another. They're gonna stick ya up for your money, they're gonna stick ya up for your product, they're gonna stick ya up for your bitch, they're gonna stick ya up for your car. They ain't got no roots, those guys got no roots. . . .

In an Oct. 19 call, he tells drug dealer Juan "Casper" Martir his philosophy on dealing and arresting people.

Miedzianowski: I don't go out there and —— pull those dumb ass shots where I pull some guy over and start slappin' him in the face or, or make him look stupid in front of his friends. No, I approach everybody like a man. You —— over a friend of mine, or you —— over me then I will come for your ass. I will —— your —— life up. I will —— your dog, your cat, your mom, your dad, I don't give a ——. I won't stop, but I mean that's 'cause you —— up, not me.

Martir: Right.

Miedzianowski: I don't go out lookin' to —— nobody and all the people you've known I —— , I don't —— nobody unless they—— with a friend of mine or with me. That's it, that's the end of it.

Miedzianowski is captured on tape bragging to gang members and drug dealers that he often helps them out. Prosecutors said he fixed dozens of cases and even helped harbor a killer

(continued)

HIGHLIGHT 10.2   Continued

from the Latin Lovers named Nelson Padilla. The former cop even shot a photograph of Padilla with his arm around Miedzianowski's little boy at the former officer's home.

In a lighter conversation Nov. 6, drug dealer Jesus "Flip" Cuevas calls Miedzianowski from his cell phone to ask for advice after Cuevas has been pulled over in his car by a Chicago police officer.

> **Cuevas:** Man, I just got pulled over by blue boys, man.
>
> **Miedzianowski:** Right now?
>
> **Cuevas:** Yeah. Do you think you can talk to them? I just ran a stop sign, I think.
>
> **Miedzianowski:** Yeah, just tell 'em you're coming to meet me.

The officer, still on the phone, later shares Cuevas' predicament with his wife.

> **Miedzianowski:** Honey?
>
> **Nancy Miedzianowski:** Yeah?
>
> **Miedzianowski:** Flip gets pulled over by the police. He's got me waiting on the ph . . .
>
> **Wife:** Oh, great.
>
> **Miedzianowski:** Got pulled, he got no license, you know? And I can hear the voice in the background . . . well, sir . . . a female police officer. What do you think the chance of him getting out of this ticket are . . . He has no ID. She hadn't searched him. But all she keeps, I can hear her yelling for, do you have an insurance card, do you have an insurance card? This guy could have a kilo of dope and a gun in a lap.

Miedzianowski also was accused of being a brutal cop, and one recorded talk that he had with another officer stood out during the trial. In a Dec. 5 conversation, Miedzianowski brags about beating a black man with a sledgehammer for showing disrespect to the police.

Miedzianowski is talking to his friend Billy Jarding, a Cook County corrections officer now on desk duty. Miedzianowski says he had to hit the man because two other officers did nothing when the man disrespected them while the police were executing a search warrant.

> **Miedzianowski:** Do you know why I had to hit him? Because him and his partner were doing nothing. This ―― was talking down to 'em like they were a couple pieces of ―― .
>
> **Jarding:** Mmm.
>
> **Miedzianowski:** Billy, we're doing a search warrant on a guy's house, OK?
>
> **Jarding:** Mmm hmm.
>
> **Miedzianowski:** So, what you do is, we pull up in the alley, ya know, we're pulling the cars over. Now, when you do a search warrant, the element of surprise is very important.
>
> **Jarding:** Absolute.
>
> **Miedzianowski:** We pull over, emptying the trucks, this ―― pulls up behind them and starts laying on the horn, like a ―― . And it, well, ya know, we get out, and guy says, "Whadda you doin'?" I gotta get in my place! I said, we're the police. I don't give a ――! I, I, and that's the part I heard. Now, they go up to the car, the ―― gets outta the car. He's about six-five.
>
> **Jarding:** Mmm hmm.
>
> **Miedzianowski:** About three hundred pounds. The biggest ―― ―― I ever seen.
>
> **Jarding:** Mmm hmm.
>
> **Miedzianowski:** (The victim says,) That's my space. You move your ――! Like that. So, I go to him and I go . . . what the ――'s your problem? He goes, what the ――'s my problem? ――! Before he could say . . . I hit him right in the forehead with that ―― sledge.

Jarding: (Laughs)

Miedzianowski: Billy, Billy, he started, did ya ever see the cartoons where a guy is standing in one spot and he's kinda weaving in a circle?

Jarding: Mmm hmm.

Miedzianowski: He was doing that and then when I got him coming like weaving past, toward me again, I hit him a second time. And his head, literally there's a bubble from the first hit.

Jarding: Hmm.

Miedzianowski: That bubble blew up and there was blood everywhere.

Jarding: Hmm.

Miedzianowski: This guy fell down.

Jarding: We, we not only executed the warrant, did the recovery, put the prisoners . . . (got) the dope in the car. He (the victim) was still laying there in the alley.

Miedzianowski: And we drove away. Paul's going, I think you killed him! —— him! That was the first words outta my mouth. —— him! He's lucky he ain't going to jail.

Later in the same conversation, Miedzianowski brags how he throws the man out of the station house when he comes to complain about an officer beating him up.

Miedzianowski: This —— . . . comes . . . first of all I thought it was a Hindu, some Hindu come in 'cause he had a big, big like thing on top of his head. Well, it was the bandage. He went to the hospital. He comes to the desk, complaining how some white policeman hit him. I saw him. I go, what? Do you want some more? And he went running out of the station and I never seen him again.

In an earlier conversation with Jarding, Miedzianowski describes how he could get away with such brutality—by making up credible police reports.

Miedzianowski: Man, Bill, I've thrown guys out third-floor windows, I —— beat 'em with hammers, I've run over them with cars. None of these —— got the balls to do that anymore. It's ridiculous.

Jarding: It's 'cause they'd all get jammed.

Miedzianowski: And why don't I?

Jarding: Don't know, it's the magical touch.

Miedzianowski: 'Cause I'm papa.

Jarding: Mmm.

Miedzianowski: 'Cause I always remember one thing.

Jarding: Hmm?

Miedzianowski: What you put down on paper today will come to haunt you tomorrow.

Jarding: That part is true.

Miedzianowski: So I always put down the right stuff.

(Miedzianowski's attorneys, Thomas Breen and Randy Rueckert, said none of the brutality ever happened. It was just empty bragging by the former officer, they said.)

Miedzianowski and his partner, John Galligan, who faces trial later this year, are caught bragging on a different topic—that they endured all the official complaints against them over the years.

Miedzianowski: I mean, how many guys, John, from my recruit class, got fired? . . . For stealin'.

Galligan: Yeah.

Miedzianowski: For doin' something wrong on the job. For off-duty drinkin' beefs. . . . The amount of beefs we've had and never a sustained beef ever?

Galligan: Yeah.

Miedzianowski: Ever, John. Ever!

Galligan: Thank God.

(continued)

HIGHLIGHT 10.2   Continued

Even Miedzianowski's realization that the feds were onto him and tapping his phone line was captured on tape. He accidentally got a phone order for a wiretap with his name on it.

Miedzianowski didn't order it.

He was the target of the tap.

Miedzianowski: Now, this a request by me?

AT&T employee: Well, not necessarily. It's um, it has your name on the order. Later, the employee says: I wanted to make sure that we . . . had given you everything you had needed.

Miedzianowski assures her she has.

But that insight did Miedzianowski little good.

When he is sentenced in August, prosecutors will seek a life term for him.

According to the Associated Press (2002), as of April 12, 2002, Miedzianowski is still awaiting sentencing.

Reprinted with special permission from the Chicago Sun-Times, Inc., 2001.

Frankel (1993a, p.1A) reports that, for Bernie Cawley, a New York police officer, it was "nothing to lie to grand juries, to steal drugs, weapons, and money, and to protect other cops doing the same thing." His fellow officer, Michael Dowd, testified, "Cops don't want to turn in other cops. Cops don't want to be a rat" (Frankel, 1993a, p. 3A).

In some departments, officers who are "straight" are regarded as stupid or as failing to take advantage of the benefits of corrupt activities that have come to be defined as inherent in the job. When an officer does decide to take action against corrupt colleagues, the fraternity may react violently and is very likely to ostracize the officer who has violated the code or broken faith with those in the subculture.

Police corruption has been recognized as a problem in this country for at least one hundred years, and various reform movements and departmental programs to reduce or eliminate corruption have been attempted, as we shall see shortly. Given these initiatives, why does police corruption remain problematic? The answer seems to lie, at least in part, in the relationship between the police and the larger society. It has been said that police are a reflection of the society or community they serve, and this is nowhere more true than with respect to police corruption. Simply put, police corruption could be stopped overnight if we wanted to eliminate it. If other citizens stopped offering bribes, free services, and other gratuities, and started reporting all police attempts to benefit in unauthorized fashion from their positions, it would be very difficult for corrupt police officers to survive unscathed.

To some extent, it appears that we want our police to be corrupt or at least corruptible. It gives us something to talk and write about, it provides us with a sense that the police are not morally superior to others, and it perhaps gives some of us a feeling of power over those who are recognized as having a good deal of power. Do we want our police to be totally honest and trustworthy? Or would we prefer to believe that they would overlook at least minor violations as a result of the favors we have provided them? Are we satisfied regarding the police as morally superior because they routinely turn down opportunities to earn thousands of dollars by accepting payoffs from drug dealers, gunrunners, pimps, and those involved with other illegal activities? If the police do in fact adhere to high ethical standards, and if they are, after all, basically citizens like ourselves, and if we would be tempted by opportunities to earn large sums of money by simply failing to enforce the law, are we less ethical, less moral? Or are we, too, convinced that corruption is inherent in the police role and that there is little we could do about it even if we wanted to?

Two publicized commissions were formed to investigate police corruption and offer recommendations for change, the first of which was the Christopher Commission. Created by former Los Angeles Mayor Tom Bradley in 1991 in response to several high-profile media accounts of various acts of misconduct by LAPD members, the Commission specifically addressed structure and operation, recruitment and training practices, internal disciplinary procedures, and citizen review and oversight issues (Human Rights Watch, 1998). Headed by attorney and former U.S. Secretary of State, Warren Christopher, the final report, entitled "The Christopher Commission Report," painted a disturbing, but all too familiar picture of the LAPD for both the public and the police. Key findings of the report included the following:

- A small, but significant number of police officers systematically engaged in acts involving excessive force.
- Police administrators clearly knew who these "problem officers" were but took little or no preventive measures to address the problem.
- The Commission recommended that a new policy be adopted to hold both individual officers and command staff personnel strictly accountable for future acts of malfeasance (Human Rights Watch, 1998; Christopher Commission Report, 1991).

Whether the LAPD adopted any of these recommendations stemming from the Christopher Commission Report is subject to debate. Many remain skeptical that any fundamental changes occurred within the LAPD, and their skepticism seems to be justified in light of the LAPD's most recent and notorious scandal of all time—what has come to be known as the Rampart Division Scandal, highlighted briefly earlier in this chapter.

For many of the same reasons cited by Los Angeles public officials and enraged citizen groups, Mayor Rudolph Giuliani of New York City formed a special commission to investigate allegations of corruption within the ranks of the NYPD. Officially formed in 1994 and commonly referred to as the Mollen Commission, headed by retired New York State Supreme Court Justice Milton Mollen, the charge of the Commission was to investigate allegations of misconduct, analyze the effectiveness of anticorruption mechanisms within the department, and offer recommendations for improvement. Key findings and recommendations included the following:

- Much of the corruption was closely tied to the illegal drug market and the use of excessive force.

- Many of the corrupt acts were perpetrated by police officers acting in concert with on another, sometimes with as many as fifteen officers conspiring with one another.
- Corruption occurred primarily in crime-ridden precincts, populated predominantly by minority group members.
- The leadership structure of the Department demonstrated no sense of commitment to rooting out corrupt practices.
- There existed a strong police subculture that frowned on honest officers reporting the wrongdoings of corrupt coworkers.
- The internal mechanisms responsible for uncovering and investigating misconduct were ineffective and, in many instances, focused on the whistle-blowers rather than the perpetrators.
- There existed a department-wide belief that the identification of corruption would cause the Department administrators to retaliate for bringing discredit on the LAPD.
- A recommendation was made to create a permanent, external panel to monitor internal anticorruption measures and conduct investigations (Treaster, 1994; Tran, 1994).

The mayor and police administrators have yet to adopt the recommendations of the Mollen Commission and strongly object to oversight outside the control of the NYPD. This reluctance may be, in part, responsible for the continued allegations of misconduct plaguing the NYPD.

Clearly, a brief comparison of the major findings and recommendations of both the Christopher and Mollen commissions reveals many more similarities than differences: the inability of these two agencies to police themselves, reluctance to proactively and seriously confront this issue and/or encourage independent oversight, subcultures that discourage honest police officers from reporting coworker misconduct, and leadership structures that do not actively promote and support anticorruption measures.

While the aforementioned reports focused on two of our nation's largest police departments, the critical issues that formed the core of both investigations seem to ring true, albeit in differing magnitude, for all size departments and in all regions of the country. These issues are discussed in more detail in the Recommendations for Improvement section of this chapter. For now, an examination of the different types of police misconduct is in order.

TYPES OF MISCONDUCT

Because of their vast legal and discretionary power and authority, and the multiple roles that they perform and assume in a democratic society, police officers consistently find themselves in the midst of a wide range of ethical dilemmas. The structural and functional opportunities for all forms of misconduct are unfortunately omnipresent in the everyday world of policing. While few would argue that the vast majority of the men

Unethical conduct can lead to serious consequences for police officers.

and women who serve their communities do so in an exemplary fashion, it is equally true that the minority of officers who bring discredit on their departments by compromising the Law Enforcement Code of Conduct causes severe damage to their respective agencies in the areas of public trust, department morale, and overall community relations.

Rosoff, Pontell, and Tillman (1998), in their work on police corruption and in their analyses and interpretation of earlier research by Barker and Roebuck (1974), set forth a typology that encompasses a variety of misconduct ranging from violations of departmental rules and regulations to statutory violations of state and federal law. A brief examination of each category follows.

Corruption of Authority

The corruption of authority is the most widespread form of police misconduct and includes "a wide variety of unauthorized material inducements, anything from discounted underwear to free commercial sex" (Rosoff, Pontell, & Tillman, 1998, p. 298). While this acceptance of gratuities on the part of the police often violates department policy, it does not violate criminal law statutes when the gratuities are offered voluntarily. In many cases, they are viewed as coming with the job and are overlooked by police departments unless they become a matter of public concern. In other words, the acceptance of gratuities is often condoned if not approved.

The difficulty with accepting gratuities is that the officer never knows when the corruptor may expect or request special services or favors in return. This may, of course, never happen, but if it does, it places the officer who has accepted the gratuities in a difficult position, although she may certainly refuse to grant such requests. In addition, it becomes difficult to draw a line between such gratuities and other types of corrupt activities in terms of monetary value and violation of ethical standards.

Such actions also may have an effect on the police image. For example, two police officers were recently witnessed during lunch hour at a fast food chain. One officer was in uniform, the other in plain clothes. In front of a large number of lunch-hour customers, the person taking the orders told the uniform officer he would receive a 50 percent discount on the price of his meal. This started some murmuring in the crowd. The second officer then informed the cashier that he, too, was a police officer, and entitled to a 50 percent discount, and he showed his badge to prove it. The cashier apologized, saying she hadn't recognized him as a police officer and assured him that he would receive his discount. Needless to say, the muttering in the crowd became rather negative, with other patrons indicating that they now understood why so many police officers ate at the establishment in question.

DeLeon-Granados and Wells (1998) explored an ecological model called the "gratuity exchange principle," which predicts that the mere act of retrieving a gratuity is likely to offset police patrol practices. Their research found that gratuities increased police coverage, in that establishments that offered free or discounted menu items received greater police coverage compared with similar types of establishments that did not offer gratuities to police officers. DeLeon-Granados and Wells (1998) indicated the need for further discussions of the social costs of police receiving gratuities.

Kickbacks

Kickbacks constitute a second type of police corruption and refer to the practice of obtaining goods, services, or money for business referrals by police officers (Rosoff, Pontell, & Tillman, 1998). The other individuals involved in these quid pro quo schemes include lawyers, doctors, towing contractors, auto body shop operators, and others who reward police officers who refer customers to them. In 1988, several Chicago police officers were involved in a kickback scheme with local morticians. A number of officers were convicted on various charges stemming from allegations that they received money from referring grieving parties to select funeral home directors (Gorman, 1988).

While many of the forms of misconduct in this category are not illegal per se, the preceding examples should serve as a warning to police officials concerning how easy it is to cross the line between violations of department rules and regulations and illegal activities. The difficulties inherent in such activities are obvious, but in some police departments, they too are condoned unless a public issue arises as a result.

Shakedowns

The third type of misconduct involves shakedowns and occurs when officers take money or other valuables and personal services from offenders they have caught during the commission of a crime (Rosoff, Pontell, & Tillman, 1998). Drug dealers, prostitutes, and motorists seem to be favorite targets, though incidents like these occur when any arrestee is willing to buy his or her way out of an arrest.

Bribes

This type of malfeasance can assume many different forms. Sometimes referred to as "the fix," it involves police officers taking no enforcement action when they are normally required to do so, usually in exchange for monetary remuneration (Rosoff, Pontell, & Tillman, 1998). Common examples include officers who, in exchange for money, will not write a motorist a ticket or officers who deliberately misdirect an investigation or perjure their court testimony to ensure a favorable outcome for the defendant (Hyatt, 2001, p. 79).

Opportunistic Theft

This form of misconduct pertains to police officers who steal money or other valuables when, for example, they are guarding a crime scene, as in the case of a burglary, or steal other such goods from unconscious, inebriated, or dead people (Rosoff, Pontell, & Tillman, 1998). Similar activity also may occur when money and other property are stolen from arrestees either prior to or during the booking process.

Protection of Illegal Activities

Protection of illegal activities is one of the most egregious forms of misconduct and involves police officers taking money or other valuables in exchange for their protection of criminal activities (Rosoff, Pontell, & Tillman, 1998). The most common forms of criminal activity protected by police are narcotics trafficking, gambling, prostitution, the fencing and/or sale of stolen property, and chop shop/auto theft operations. Unfortunately, allegations of this type of behavior occur all too frequently. To protect the illegal behaviors, a good deal of organization is often required. It does little good for one officer to look the other way when gambling occurs if his replacement for days off and vacations or officers on other shifts, fail to protect the parties involved.

Even more disturbing than this review of unethical and criminal conduct by police officers are the results of research conducted by Barker and Wells (1982) and Annarino (1996), cited in Hyatt's (2001) work on police misconduct. They surveyed police chiefs in the southeast region of the United States in an effort to ascertain whether their respective agencies had official regulations explicitly covering the range of misconduct cited previously and their opinions regarding the type of disciplinary action these activities would warrant. The following is a brief summary of the results:

- Kickbacks: More than 50 percent of the chiefs indicated that they would reprimand or suspend officers involved in kickbacks.
- Opportunistic thefts: Approximately 60 percent of the departments had regulations pertaining to this category of malfeasance. However, only 35 percent of the chiefs indicated a willingness to pursue criminal charges.
- Shakedowns: Approximately 60 percent of the respondent departments had regulations pertaining to this activity, and only 37 percent of the police chief respondents considered the initiation of criminal charges.

■ Bribes: Even more disturbing was that only 39 percent of departments had regulations governing this form of conduct, and less than 30 percent of the chiefs believed this activity to be serious enough to recommend criminal prosecution (Barker & Wells, 1982; Annarino, 1996; Hyatt, 2001, pp. 79–80).

The reluctance by chief executive officers to take appropriate disciplinary action against officers engaged in unethical behavior serves only to strengthen the force the police subculture exerts on so many officers. Moreover, these types of attitudes by chiefs send a very disturbing, but clear message to subordinates—that more often than not, at least with respect to this research population, the penalty for malfeasance will not be commensurate with the seriousness of the offense. In any event, this view of corruption by chiefs of police is an issue that begs more attention, both through research and professional development activities.

Although one type of corruption does not necessarily lead to another, where one finds more serious types of corruption, one is also likely to find most of the less serious types. Consider, for example, a department that condones internal payoffs. If a supervisor attained her position by paying someone for it, it becomes difficult to deal with less serious forms of corruption among those supervised, who may have knowledge of the way in which the promotion was obtained. In the long run, such a department is likely to be characterized by all other forms of corruption. In addition, services to the public are likely to be less efficient and effective than they might otherwise be, because promotions are not usually based on merit, and less competent or incompetent people may become supervisors.

As Richardson (1974) stated,

> Discipline may be especially weak since any action might lead to unpleasant publicity. If a large portion of a police department is implicated in such corrupt relations, no one can enforce the law against the police themselves. Officers outside the network of payoffs have to turn their backs on what goes on around them and deny publicly that any such activity exists. . . . Moreover, what is the effect on a young patrolman who learns that his colleagues and commanders are often more interested in profiting from the law than enforcing it? (p. 154)

Frankel (1993b, p. 3A) reported the same logic. "Daniel Sullivan, former head of the [NYC] department's Internal Affairs division, testified that the message from the top brass to his investigators was simple: 'We shouldn't be so aggressive because the department doesn't want bad press. . . . Honest officers testified that their efforts to report and investigate corruption ran into resistance and retaliation."

CAUSES AND CONSEQUENCES OF POLICE MISCONDUCT

While not specifically included in the original typology developed by Barker and Roebuck (1974), Rosoff, Pontell, and Tillman (1998), and others, there are additional categories of malfeasance we believe need to be identified, along with associated causes and consequences.

Nonfeasance

As mentioned earlier in this chapter, nonfeasance in the context of policing refers to the reluctance of most police officers to report wrongdoings committed by their coworkers. Why is this so? Can the situation be changed as we enter the twenty-first century? The former question has intrigued researchers and practitioners alike since the early days of policing, and although it has been the subject of intense scrutiny for as long, the answer is clear. The latter question is addressed in the Recommendations for Improvement section of this chapter.

The code of silence among police officers results in collective feelings and attitudes, as misdirected as they may be, of cynicism, isolation from the community in which the police live and work, and a sense of blind loyalty to their colleagues. Cox (1996) describes the police culture as consisting of the informal rules and regulations, tactics, and folklore passed on from one generation of police officers to the next. The code of silence is both a result and a cause of police isolation from the larger society and of police solidarity.

A 2000 study conducted by the National Institute of Justice (NIJ) illustrates the power and influence of the effects of this "conspiracy of silence" on police corruption. This national survey was designed to assess American police officers' views on several key issues pertaining to the abuse of police authority. When respondents were asked if officers should report coworker misconduct, "responses on this subject suggest[ed] the possibility of a large gap between attitudes and behavior. That is, even though officers [did] not believe in protecting wrongdoers, they often [did] not turn them in" (NIJ, 2000). Note some of the highlights of this study.

- While approximately 80 percent of the respondents claim to not accept the code of silence as essential component of policing, nearly 25 percent agreed that reporting misconduct is not worth the trouble it can cause.
- Nearly 68 percent of the police officers surveyed believed that the officers who report acts of internal misconduct are likely to be given the "cold shoulder" by their coworkers.
- Approximately 52 percent of the respondents agreed that it is not unusual for officers to "turn a blind eye" to coworker malfeasance.
- A majority (61 percent) of respondents indicated that officers do not often report even serious misconduct perpetuated by their coworkers.

The results of this study and other related research clearly articulate the challenges the code of silence presents for police administrators. First and foremost, the cycle of corruption is allowed to perpetuate because honest police officers, due to fear of retaliation from coworkers and supervisors, often hesitate to report the illegal and unethical acts of coworkers. Until this aspect of the police subculture can be significantly diminished, and honest police officers develop the courage to do the right thing, police corruption will continue to flourish. The effects of this continued pattern of corruption will then spread and exert even more strain on the already tenuous relationship that exists between many police departments and their respective communities.

Evidence in support of this belief can be found by examining a poll cited in 1997 NIJ report entitled "Police Integrity: Public Service with Honor." This poll focused on the assessment of public confidence regarding the ability of members of various professions and occupations to do the right thing. Respondents were asked to rank the level of confidence regarding twelve professions or occupations, with a rank of 1 being the most confidence and 12 being the least confidence. Examine the results:

1980	**1995**
1. Pharmacist	1. Firefighter
2. Clergy	2. Pharmacist
3. Firefighter	3. Teacher
4. Teacher	4. Dentist
5. Police officer	5. Clergy
6. Doctor	6. Stock broker
7. Dentist	7. Doctor
8. Accountant	8. Accountant
9. Stock broker	9. Funeral director
10. Lawyer	10. Police officer
11. Funeral director	11. Lawyer
12. Politician	12. Politician

Apparently, public confidence in the police had been shaken during the fifteen-year period between polls, with police officers dropping five positions, ahead only of lawyers and politicians. Even more disturbing is that when race was analyzed, there was a significant difference between Caucasian and African-American respondents. Among blacks, police officers were ranked in the ninth position in 1980 and in the eleventh position in 1995 (NIJ, 1997).

Although this decline in public perception of confidence in the police may not be based in fact, the message is clear—those involved in corruption should not be protected. If the law enforcement community desires to progress along a continuum of professionalization, this silent obstacle needs to be removed permanently.

Drug-Related Corruption

Another form of police misconduct involves drug-related corruption. A 1998 study by the U.S. General Accounting (GAO), entitled "Drug-Related Police Corruption," provided insight into the systematic, narcotics-related corruption in the field of policing. The study analyzed federal drug-related investigations and prosecutions of police officers from several state and municipal police departments. Through its examination and analyses of government and academic reports and interviews with numerous federal law enforcement sources specializing in the investigation of public integrity matters, the GAO generated interesting new data to be considered in the study of police corruption. The following is a summary of the major conclusions of the GAO report:

- Drug-related police corruption differs from other forms of police misconduct.
- Officers involved in this corrupt practice "were more likely to be actively involved in the commission of a variety of crimes, including stealing drugs and/or money from drug dealers, selling drugs and lying under oath about illegal searches." (p. 3)
- Power and vigilante justice were found to be additional motives for drug-related corruption.
- A recurring pattern of this form of corruption was that the misconduct involved small groups of officers who consistently conspired and helped one another commit a variety of crimes.
- The culture surrounding drug-related corruption was characterized by the all too familiar code of silence, blind loyalty to group members, and cynicism about the criminal justice system.
- Younger officers, as well as those lacking experience and at least some form of higher education, were found to be more susceptible to these corrupt practices.
- A variety of critical management and administrative issues were also associated with this form of corruption, such as lax and/or incompetent supervision; no real commitment from department brass to promote integrity; weak or ineffective investigative methodologies used to combat corruption; inadequate training, both basic and in-service, particularly in the area of ethical decision making; police brutality; and informal pressures stemming from officers' personal friendships and affiliations with neighborhood figures. (GAO, 1998, pp. 3–5)

Noble Cause Corruption

As the phrase implies, this form of misconduct typically pertains to various situations in which officers circumvent the law in order to serve what they perceive to be the greater good. Perhaps Delattre (1996, p. 191) describes this behavior best by proposing the following dilemma to both officers and administrators: "If you have a perpetrator in custody, and he has information that could save the life of an innocent victim, is it right to use extreme methods to get the information?"

Although questions such as that posed by Delattre always generate enthusiastic debate on both sides of the issue, the answer is actually quite clear—police officers are sworn to uphold the law and should never, under any circumstances, willfully violate the rights of anyone in their custody. Those who disagree point to the life-and-death nature of Delattre's scenario. The question that begs an answer, however, is how often do "Dirty Harry" cases like this occur in the daily lives of police officers? Most would argue that they occur rarely, if ever, during an officer's career. The debate underlying noble cause corruption then must focus around more commonplace activities encountered by our nation's police officers. Imagine plainclothes officers approaching an individual on the street to conduct a field interview. The person in question then abruptly turns a corner, and while temporarily out of view of the officers, drops a quantity of illegal narcotics to the ground. The police then find the contraband and arrest the subject (Delattre, 1996, p. 20). What should the officers do? If they tell the truth, the case will most likely be dismissed in court. If they elect to fabricate their report and possibly perjure themselves in court, they have removed a dope dealer from the street. Herein lies the problem with adhering to the noble cause corruption philosophy—two wrongs never make a right, and if left unchecked, the collective behavior of officers may eventually even assume a vigilante-like mentality.

Incidents like Delattre's occur all too often, and officers and administrators who approve of this manifestation of the police subculture, even though their approval may be tacit, run the risk of systemic corruption taking hold in their respective agencies. According to Harrison (1999, p. 5), no matter how routine or exigent the circumstances may be,

> When officers use unlawful means to gain a desired end, they damage the system they represent. Beyond the damage to the justice system, however, officers who engage in illegal behavior denigrate not only the uniform of the guardian but also the individual within. The eventual result to society is a loss of confidence in those charged with the protection of others, leading to a fraying of the tapestry of the culture that binds communities together.

PHYSICAL AND EMOTIONAL ABUSE

Police misconduct is not limited to corrupt activities, but includes perjury, emotional abuse/harassment, and physical abuse, and even murder. To some extent, perjury and other forms of unauthorized deception serve as links between corruption and other forms of misconduct. What is the difference, for example, between a police officer perjuring himself in order to fix a ticket in return for payment from the defendant and one who perjures herself in order to cover up the fact that she used physical force unnecessarily against a defendant? How does one draw the line between lying to informants and drug dealers and deceiving one's superiors? Once perjury and deception gain a foothold, they tend to spread to other officers and to other types of situations until, in some cases, the entire justice system becomes a sham.

This is the case, for instance, when police officers perjure themselves in criminal cases in which the defendant is also perjuring himself, the respective attorneys know that perjury is occurring, and the judge knows that none of the parties is being completely honest. The outcomes of such cases seems to ride on who told the most believable lie, or the last lie. The overall impact is to increase the amount of suspicion and distrust of the justice system among all parties, and this is certainly not the desired end product if we wish citizens to participate in and believe in the system.

Chevigny (1969), Cray (1972), Manning (1974), Skolnick (1966), and Roberg and Kuykendall (1993), among others, have addressed the issue of police lying and all agree that the behavior, in some cases, becomes accepted as an inherent part of the job in much the same way as does corruption. This appears to be true particularly in cases in which police misconduct has occurred and the officers involved are trying to cover up the misconduct. Police officers who stop other citizens without probable cause and/or harass them, and police officers who use force unnecessarily, must attempt to justify their actions or face relatively severe sanctions.

Perhaps some examples will help illustrate the kind of behavior in question here. Activists protested police brutality in a trial involving white officers charged with the death of a black man while he was in custody. The county coroner said the man died of suffocation due to either a choke-hold or the weight of police officers falling on him as he was taken into custody for questioning about drug trafficking (Cornwell, 2001).

A 23-year veteran Chicago police officer faces possible fifty-seven-month prison sentence after admitting he helped his partner run a Miami-to-Chicago drug ring. As a part of a plea agreement, the officer admitted handing crack to an informant in the parking lot of a city police station. He also admitted that he fabricated a search warrant and gave false testimony to cover another police officer's theft of 2.2 pounds of cocaine from a drug suspect (Associated Press, 2001).

The preceding examples are not intended as an indictment of the police. They are meant to illustrate the extent, nature, and seriousness of the behavior included under the umbrella of police misconduct.

Emotional Abuse/Psychological Harassment by Police Officers

As indicated previously, police officers, like those in other occupational groups, sometimes employ stereotypes and divide the world into "us" and "them," or insiders versus outsiders. Those who are perceived as outsiders are often labeled, and occasionally these labels are used openly to refer to the members of groups so designated. The use of ethnophaulisms or racial slurs is but one example of the kind of harassment under consideration. Other special categories and labels are created for those belonging to particular types of "deviants," for example, drug dealers, homosexuals, prostitutes, and protestors. The creation of special categories and the ensuing labels are not unique to the police, but as public servants who represent the authority of the government, the police are in a unique position when it comes to using the labels created.

First, the police are supposed to represent all other citizens, regardless of race, creed, nationality, gender, political beliefs, or sexual orientation. When they use dehumanizing terms or harass others, the impression may be that because they represent government, they are expressing the attitudes of those who govern, though in fact they may simply be expressing personal dislikes, contempt, or hostility. Second, because of the fact that they represent governmental authority, they are in turn very likely to be subject to harassment, name calling, and challenges. When those being policed use dehumanizing terms, and deliberate attempts to harass or provoke the police occur, the possibility that the police will reciprocate in kind is heightened. Third, the occupational subculture legitimizes the use of labels behind squadroom doors or among police officers, keeping these labels alive and meaningful. Fourth, few of those other citizens harassed or verbally abused are likely to report the abuse, which tends to reinforce the abusive behavior. Fifth, as an alternative to arrest, many of those harassed probably view the harassment as the lesser of two evils (homeless people, for instance, who are "escorted" to the city limits by police officers with a warning not to return).

Members of minority groups (both racial and behavioral), particularly in high-crime areas, report that psychological/emotional abuse is a routine part of their encounters with the police. And, in fact, the best available evidence supports this contention. Although his study is now dated, Reiss (1968, pp. 59–60) provides information concerning the incidence of police psychological mistreatment of other citizens:

> What citizens object to and call "police brutality" is really the judgment that they have not been treated with the full rights and dignity owing [sic] citizens in a democratic society. Any practice that degrades their status, that restricts their freedom, that annoys or harasses them, or that use physical force is frequently seen as unnecessary and unwarranted. More often than not, they are probably right. . . . Members of minority groups and those seen as nonconformists, for whatever reasons, are the most likely targets of status degradation.

Hacker (1992, p. 189), for example, notes that "most black Americans can recall encounters [with the police] where they were treated with discourtesy, hostility, or worse. . . . And it would appear that at least a few police officers still move in circles where no censure attaches to using the word 'nigger.'"

It is clear, then, that what constitutes police brutality is, at least in part, a matter of definition, and that police definitions and those of other citizens may not always agree. What some segments of the public see as police harassment or brutality, the police are likely to view as aggressive policing, necessary for their survival on the streets as well as for maintaining some degree of order and crime control. Is a police officer in a high-crime area, where many residents are known to carry deadly weapons, harassing a citizen when she approaches cautiously, pats the citizen down for weapons, appears suspicious, and has another officer back her up?

The answer depends, in part, on whether one is the police officer or the person being stopped, questioned, and searched, because while the latter knows whether he is a dangerous or criminal person, the officer typically does not. Obviously, the way in which such encounters are carried out is important. Reiss notes that it is not always what the officer says, but how she says it that is degrading, and that whites, as well as racial/ethnic minority group members, are also victims of psychological harassment. The conclusions drawn by Reiss are supported by the findings of the National Advisory Commission on Civil Disorders (1968), which concluded that foremost among the complaints of minority group members about the police were the use of improper forms of address (use of terms such as *boy, nigger,* and a first name when a surname is appropriate) and stopping and questioning people for no apparent reason other than their race or ethnicity.

All of these findings and incidents, and others as well, imply that harassment and psychological brutality, if not actual physical brutality, continue to occur in police encounters with at least certain other citizens.

EXCESSIVE USE OF FORCE

Nothing seems to grip the attention of the public more than the accounts of police officers overextending their legal authority by using excessive force to either effect an arrest of or to coerce information from individuals with who they interact during the course of their duties. Celebrated cases such as the Rodney King incident in Los Angeles and the Abner Louima case in New York City are indelibly etched into the minds of many Americans, but are the abusive tactics in question commonplace in policing? Has police brutality reached epidemic proportions? To answer these questions and ascertain whether abuses similar in nature occur frequently and by a significant number of police officers requires a systematic examination of data pertaining to the overall use of force by police.

One relevant study examined citizen complaints filed against police officers in Florida, Illinois, Missouri, Pennsylvania, and Washington. Approximately 50 percent of all the complaints focused on the verbal conduct and overall demeanor of the officers. An additional quarter of the total complaints involved a wide variety of nonviolent, illegal conduct committed by officers on and off duty. The remaining quarter of complaints dealt with excessive force issues, once again by officers on and off duty (Johnson, 1998, p. 3).

Actual complaints arising from on-duty arrest situations were responsible for less than one-quarter of the complaints filed against police officers. While these numbers are significant, the author did not indicate whether these complaints were sustained or whether the officers exonerated of wrongdoing. Either way, the data "reveals that excessive force by police officers while effecting an arrest represents a problem to address, but it does not appear as widespread as the media portrays" (Johnson, 1998, p. 3).

A much more representative investigation of issues involving use of force by police was conducted by the NIJ in a 1999 study entitled "Use of Force by Police: Overview of National and Local Data." According to this and other NIJ reports, only a small percentage of police–public interactions involve the use of force, with an even smaller percentage resulting in incidents of conduct, that would be classified as excessive. Data used in their analyses were gathered from a variety of sources, including police reports, citizen complaints, victimization surveys, and ethnographic methodologies. A summary of the highlights of their research follows:

- With respect to custody arrests of adults, of the 7,512 cases studied, police used physical force less than 20 percent of the time. In those instances, nonviolent or weaponless tactics such as "grabbing" were used in the majority of cases.
- Approximate 2 percent of the cases involved the use of weapons by police, and chemical agents such as pepper spray were used in the majority of those cases.
- Use of force by police typically occurs when a suspect is resisting arrest.
- When physical injuries do occur as a result of arrest, they are usually minor (i.e., bruises or abrasions).
- Instances of the use of force do not seem to be associated with officers' demographic characteristics, such as age, gender, and ethnicity. (This finding seems to be at odds with an earlier study in which officers who received the bulk of citizen complaints, albeit not all were for excessive force, tended to be male, white, under 30 years of age, had less than five years of experience, and had little or nor formal education (Johnson, 1998).
- Use of force by police occurs more often when dealing with individuals who are under the influence of alcohol or drugs and with emotionally disturbed persons.

■ A small number of police officers tend to be involved with an unusually high percentage of use-of-force incidents.

No matter how one interprets the data, the evidence seems to suggest that cases that involve severe beatings with fists, feet, and batons are not at all typical of the use of force by police. When these cases do occur, however, data also demonstrate, as they do with many other forms of police misconduct, that excessive use of force is committed by a disproportionately small number of officers (NIJ, 1999).

The 1999 NIJ report also identified areas in need of further research, areas that may further assist in helping us understand the sources of and the answers to issues pertaining to excessive use of force by police. These areas include administrative policies, hiring practices, disciplinary procedures, use of technology, and the various influences of situational characteristics on the use of force.

Reiss (1971, p. 2) observed, "At law, the police in modern democracies such as the United States possess a virtual monopoly on the *legitimate* use of force over citizens." Bittner (1970) described the capacity to use force as the core of the police role. And Rubinstein (1973) discussed the police officer's body as his most important tool and the process by which he evaluates other citizens in terms of his physical ability to "handle" these other citizens if an encounter should turn nasty. That the police have the capacity to use force is indicated by the baton, mace, and side arm they carry into every encounter, as well as by their sheer numbers in certain types of encounters. It should not be surprising, therefore, that the issue of misuse of force by the police should arise occasionally. This is perhaps especially true when we recognize that we live in a society characterized by violence. Spouse abuse, child abuse, and drug-related street violence are common occurrences in our society; and the police are routinely involved in dealing with all three.

Physical brutality by the police involves the use of unnecessary and/or excessive force by the police. Others (Chevigny, 1969; Cray, 1972) conclude that the police sometimes provoke other citizens to resist in order to create the need to use force, and then use force and cover their deeds by adding charges of resisting arrest or obstruction of justice to the original charge in an attempt to ensure that the alleged offender is found guilty of some violation. Chevigny refers to such proceedings as a pattern involving the use of force, arrest, and "cover charges."

What is clear is that the perception that such incidents occur is widespread in minority communities in cities of all sizes across the country. This perception becomes the reality for those involved, whether the perception is grounded in reality or not. The perception creates hostility and resentment on behalf of some citizens who view themselves as particularly likely to be victims of harassment and brutality, and on behalf of the police who view themselves as particularly likely to be harassed, challenged, and criticized by certain segments of the population. In spite of these misgivings on both sides, the vast majority of police encounters with other citizens occurs without physical brutality on the part of either party.

Occasionally, however, suspicion, fear, resentment, and hostility escalate, resulting in physically violent encounters. In addition, of course, the police must be concerned about the possibility of violence that has nothing to do with harassment or social status but is based on felonious behavior. The possibility of physical violence always exists when the officer responds to calls involving domestic disputes, bar fights, robberies in progress, burglaries in progress, bomb threats, street protests, gunrunning, and drug trafficking, to mention just a few. In a small proportion of these cases, the result will be the use of deadly force by one or more of the parties involved.

Management and Administrative Issues

We can think of no phrase or cliché more relevant than the following when directed toward command staff personnel in the context of police corruption—"the buck stops here." Since the early days of policing, and following a review of major law enforcement scandals and the reports of the various commissions that investigated the misconduct in question, one common denominator surfaced—the leadership structures of the agencies in question demonstrated no real sense of commitment to investigating and ferreting out corruption from within. As Delattre (1996) and others point out, with respect to police corruption, the problem does not lie with the few "rotten apples" that many police chiefs espouse as the problem; rather, it is the result of "rotten" leadership structures and administrative policies that seem to avoid rather than promote strict accountability for all department members who engage in misconduct. Moreover, these structures and policies do not support sound investigative methodologies that are necessary to proactively investigate malfeasance (pp. 87–88).

Even more alarming are the results of the Mollen Commission report, which pointed to the existence of a department-wide belief that the identification of corruption would cause department administrators to retaliate for bringing adverse public attention to the agency. These retaliatory actions, in part, would many times then be directed toward the whistle blowers. Unfortunately, the history regarding the treatment of officers who came forward with the intent of exposing corruption is replete with instances of unpleasant and, in many cases, threatening actions bestowed on them by their superiors and coworkers.

In response to data such as these, many chiefs emphasize the harm done to community relations when corruption becomes public. Thus, many mistakenly believe that covering up, ignoring, and/or simply having wrongdoers resign, rather than face the disciplinary ramifications commensurate with their misdeeds, is for the greater good.

According to Bracey (1989, p. 176),

> Management accountability is perhaps the most important, effective and most difficult proactive tool for preventing and detecting police corruption. This is not a program or a device, but rather a thorough rethinking of the meaning of supervision and management responsibility. The driving assumption underlying accountability is that commanders are responsible for all police activity that takes place on their command. At its simplest, a policy of accountability means that commanders may not plead ignorance and surprise when corruption is discovered in their areas.

Bracey goes on to indicate that while the accountability approach clearly can work, it can be carried to extremes by supervisors so concerned with protecting themselves from liability that they trivialize the process.

Trojanowicz (1992, p. 2) notes that supervisors can have an impact on corrupt activities, but they "must go the extra distance to ensure that the officers under their command treat people with respect and that they have not crossed the line. . . . [T]he good news is that departments which have embraced Community Policing have taken an important step in fostering a climate where average citizens may well feel encouraged to share any such concerns or suspicions."

No matter how one analyzes the situation, any administrative action short of holding all members of the organization strictly accountable for their misdeeds is improper and serves only to perpetuate the problem, as well as send a disturbing message down the organizational ladder—a message that tacitly approves of corrupt practices. Perhaps chief executive officers can learn from the actions of Chicago Police Superintendent Terry Hillard. After concluding a two-year joint Internal Affairs Division–FBI investigation into the allegations that some police officers were shaking down Polish immigrants, Superintendent Hillard had the officers involved arrested at their residences, without affording them the usual custom of advance notice. Stated by one official in the Hillard administration, "[T]he superintendent wanted to treat them like any other thieves" (Main, Sadovi & Sweeney, 2000, p. 1).

Other administrative issues that may unwittingly lead to corrupt practices are related to the various get-tough-on-crime, no-nonsense, zero-tolerance policing strategies initiated by many law enforcement executives. While their intentions may be noble, do the results of such endeavors outweigh the possible negative consequences associated with them?

Such strategies are normally reserved for locales often ridden with crime, generally the lower socioeconomic areas of our nation's cities. Officers who are assigned to police these areas usually work in specialized units such as gang crimes, narcotics, and vice control, and many times are forced to work under quota-type pressure if they wish to remain assigned to those units. Consequently, the pressure to make arrests will lead to increased citizen encounters, substantially raising the possibility of an increased number of citizen complaints concerning activities that range from illegal searches and seizures to excessive force and discriminatory or biased enforcement practices. When poor or inadequate supervisory practices and the "conspiracy of silence" are added to the mix, the result can prove to be disastrous for agencies in terms of public relations and department morale.

In addition to the negative consequences associated with zero-tolerance policies, the underlying tenets of these techniques are, in many cases, diametrically opposed to the principle of community policing. The "us versus them" mentality that tends to accompany get-tough-on-crime crusades serves more to alienate the public than to reduce crime and solve other social problems through collaboration and partnership with members of the community. Moreover, it must be emphasized at this point that the majority of society that views the police most suspiciously reside in the geographic areas most likely to be targeted by these traditional, zero-tolerance policing initiatives.

Other techniques used by management to detect corruption include the use of field associates, "turning" officers who have been found to be corrupt, and rotation of assignments. Field associates are those officers specially trained and sometimes recruited to obtain information on corrupt activities while performing normal police functions. This information is relayed to management without other officers knowing who the informants are, creating an atmosphere of suspicion among officers when the existence of the program is known. "Turning" involves offering leniency or immunity to corrupt officers who agree to provide information on other corrupt officers. Rotation of personnel across shifts and geographic assignments is a technique used to disrupt possible corruption by making it difficult for officers and the other citizens they police to establish permanent ties. While this may have a positive impact on corruption, it disrupts the flow of information between officers and the citizens they police, may negatively impact on community relations, and makes community-oriented policing impossible (Bracey, 1989).

Another strategy, which may be employed to reduce corruption, is recruitment. Recruiting police personnel of high moral character and providing training in ethics early in their careers appear to be steps in the right direction (Lynch, 1989; Cooksey, 1991). If the department and subculture also foster an anticorruption attitude, promote on the basis of merit, and pay relatively well, the allure of corruption may be somewhat reduced. Internal affairs units and external review boards have also been used to help curb corruption by identifying and charging those involved.

It is difficult to assess the extent to which anticorruption programs have been successful. To some extent, police corruption may be related to economic conditions, but the relationship appears to be curvilinear. That is, when police and other wages are low, the temptation to accept dirty money may be great. Alternatively, as Lynch (1989, pp. 166–167) indicates, "[W]hen the wages of sin are incredibly lucrative, as they are in so many instances today, the appeal of corruption is proportionately more alluring. . . . Let me suggest to you that given the potential for misuse of police power, the wonder is that police officers, who witness crime, inhumanity and degradation every day, do not lose their sense of integrity and do not violate their oath of office more frequently."

In the long run, the only way to significantly reduce police corruption is to prosecute, to the fullest extent of the law, those involved, sending a clear message to the corrupt, uncorrupt, and corruptors that such action will be taken and that the consequences may be severe. While such actions in and of themselves may have limited impact on corrupt police officers, when widely publicized they may alert the community to the fact that reform in the police department is required. Although such reform is seldom sweeping enough to keep the problem from reemerging, it is possible to make it so. And, at a minimum, it disrupts the corrupt activities already in progress and alerts those involved to the fact that their activities are not secret and may result in official action.

RECOMMENDATIONS FOR IMPROVEMENT

The complexities of our society are a challenge for today's police administrators. Effective police operations, however, become even more difficult when acts of misconduct continue to surface. As the public, legislative bodies, and judicial decisions increase the level of accountability placed on the police, law enforcement administrators must respond accordingly and begin by rooting out corrupt practices to the best of their abilities. This is no easy task, but there are many sound recommendations that, if followed, should significantly mitigate instances of corruption.

A 2001 report issued by the U.S. Department of Justice (DOJ), entitled "Principles for Promoting Police Integrity: Examples of Promising Police Practices and Policies," offers sound recommendations for curbing police misconduct and the continued professionalization of the field. The following is a summary of the various recommendations from the DOJ report.

- *Accepting Complaints:* Many police department have policies that require those wishing to file a complaint against a police officer to do so in person, oftentimes requiring them to submit a formal written statement. It is recommended that citizens be allowed to file a complaint using any medium of communication (e.g., telephone, mail, facsimile, or e-mail). Not to allow these options is tantamount to discouraging reports of wrongdoing.
- *Reports of Misconduct:* This portion of the DOJ report deals with the nonfeasance issue identified earlier in the chapter. Police departments must begin to adopt formal policies that hold officers responsible for not reporting the wrongdoings of their coworkers. In addition, it is recommended that the disciplinary action reserved for acts of nonfeasance be commensurate with the serious nature of this code of silence.
  - Departments should also have mechanisms in place that encourage and allow officers to come forward and report acts of misconduct, anonymously if necessary. Currently, the NYPD and other agencies seem to be moving in that direction, and "this policy change attempts to insure protection of officers who come forward and report other officers' misconduct and corruption" (Sykes, 1999). Many critics of such policies warn about potential constitutional abuses and liken this practice to the treatment of confidential informants and protected witnesses. We agree that, in a perfect world, police departments should not have to employ such tactics. At this point in time, however, this policy of anonymity appears to be a good starting point. Perhaps, in the years to come, there will be no need for anonymity.
  - Formal policies addressing retaliation against officers reporting misconduct should be implemented and rigorously enforced. If officers are afraid to report misconduct, the problem of corruption will continue to grow.
  - Police departments are also advised to request notification from prosecutors and judges when they have reason to believe that an officer may have engaged in inappropriate behavior during the course of a criminal investigation or court proceeding. Incidents involving perjury and bringing false charges against a defendant to justify malfeasance must not be tolerated.
- *Investigative Methodologies:* It is recommended that investigations that focus on allegations of serious misconduct, such as constitutional deprivations or other illegal acts, be conducted by a special unit or body charged only with these responsibilities. It must be emphasized that individuals working in these specialized units be competent and experienced investigators, with access to state-of-the-art investigative aids. Most important, investigators in these units need the support and encouragement of the entire command structure of their agencies.
- *Resolution of Misconduct Investigations:* When the evidence warrants, and officers are found to be culpable for misconduct, they should be held strictly accountable

and punished accordingly. On deciding disciplinary action, police chiefs are urged not only to look at the seriousness of the misconduct, but to consider the officer's history of similar misdeeds.

- After resolution, the complainant should be notified, in writing, of the disposition of the case, the reasons for the decision, and the disciplinary action taken.
- *Accountability and Effective Management:* According to the DOJ (2001, p. 10), "Studies of law enforcement agencies yielded empirical data that a small number of police officers are responsible for a disproportionate amount of problematic police behavior." In light of this information, police departments are advised to maintain a computer database that would identify potentially problematic behavior patterns of officers. Information entered into the database should include, but not be limited to, incidents involving the use of force; number of citizen complaints, as well as commendations and honorable mentions; criminal and civil actions initiated against officers; disciplinary record; and training history.
  - Rather than use the statistical data for punitive purposes, it is recommended that supervisors treat this information as an early warning that inappropriate behavior patterns may be beginning to develop. Armed with this information, nondisciplinary remedial actions can be taken before serious problems develop.
- *Supervision:* Supervisors must lead by example and must at all times be alert for signs of misconduct. Nothing hurts morale more than when supervisors either ignore the misdeed of their subordinates or engage in inappropriate behavior themselves. If supervisory personnel are held accountable for the actions of individuals within the span of their direct control, acts of misconduct should diminish substantially.
- *Public Information, Feedback, and Civilian Input:* It is recommended that police administrators actively seek feedback from the public regarding performance of the agency. A relatively convenient and inexpensive way to elicit this information is by the random distribution of what is commonly referred to as community satisfaction surveys. The key is to act accordingly on the feedback provided by the public.
  - It is also suggested that regular meetings be held to disseminate all relevant information to members of the community. These meetings also give residents an opportunity to voice their concerns regarding police operations.
  - With respect to the goals of community-oriented policing, it is recommended that police departments utilize some form of citizen oversight when investigating allegations of misconduct. For example, Walker (2001) concluded that citizen oversight agencies have resulted in the development of more open and accessible complaint procedures, compared to the traditional procedures used by many police departments. He concluded that many police agencies have failed to investigate complaints in a thorough and fair fashion and have failed to use hostility from citizen complaints as a learning tool. Thus, in many agencies, citizen oversight agencies have improved police accountability and resulted in positive changes in the police organization. However, many citizen oversight agencies have not been successful. Walker (2001) found that these agencies were unable to establish independence from the police agency, suffered from leadership problems, and, in many cases, faced unrelenting police. While

the effectiveness of citizen oversight remains subject to debate, the inclusion of community members in this process goes a long way toward the removal of barriers that for decades have prevented the police and the communities they serve from coming together.

- *Training:* Basic and in-service training curriculums must be expanded to include and stress the importance of such subjects as ethical decision making; responsible use of discretionary authority; racial, ethnic, and cultural diversity; and effective interpersonal communication.
  - It is also recommended that individuals who serve as academy instructors and facilitators of continuing professional education be well versed not only in the topics they are assigned to cover, but also in the basic principles of learning.

CONCLUDING REMARKS

The issue of misconduct is a problem that has plagued the field of policing since its early days. Even though the range of activities that are categorized as malfeasance occur infrequently and are committed by a relatively small number of officers, the harm caused by these actions often takes years to repair. The costs in terms of community relations, department morale, and reputation are too devastating to bear any longer. The message is clear—it is no longer acceptable for police departments to operate with impunity or without accountability.

As we enter the twenty-first century, police executives should strive to continuously advance the field of policing along the continuum of professionalization. If they adopt the recommendations set forth by the Department of Justice, acts of malfeasance should diminish significantly. To do otherwise is tantamount to nonfeasance, thus making leaders part of the problem rather than the solution. One theme that consistently emerges from the literature is that police misconduct tends to flourish, absent real commitment from the top rungs of the organizational ladder to put an end to corrupt policing practices.

DISCUSSION QUESTIONS

1. What are some of the more important ethical issues in policing? Should police recruits be taught ethics?

2. What constitutes police corruption? Can you cite examples of police corruption from your own experiences?

3. Why is corruption of authority (accepting gratuities such as free coffee, food, etc.) critical in understanding police corruption in general?

4. Does society desire or demand police who are incorruptible? Why or why not?

5. What are the relationships between internal corruption in police agencies and other forms of corruption?

6. How are police corruption, police perjury, and police use of force interrelated?

7. Why would a police officer perjure himself? What is the impact of such perjury on the criminal justice network and other citizens in general?

8. Is psychological brutality an important form of police misconduct? Why and in what ways?

9. Discuss the relationship between police misuse of force and the fact that a number of police officers are killed each year.

10. Do you think police misconduct is as serious a problem now as it was a decade or so ago? Support your answer.

REFERENCES

Annarino, W. (1996). Unpublished survey of police attitudes. Cited in Hyatt, W. D. Parameters of police misconduct. In Palmiotto, M. J. *Police misconduct: Reader for the twenty-first century*. Upper Saddle River, NJ: Prentice-Hall.

Associated Press. (2002, April 12). Chicago cop sentenced in drug-running case.

Associated Press. (2001, November 9). Chicago cops plead guilty in drug-running case.

Barker, T., & Carter, D. L. (1986). *Police deviance*. Cincinnati: Pilgrimage.

Barker, T., & Roebuck, J. B. (1974). *An empirical typology of police corruption: A study in organizational deviance*. Springfield, IL: Charles C. Thomas.

Barker, T., & Wells, R. O. (1982, March). Public administrators' attitudes toward the definition and control of police deviance. *FBI Law Enforcement Bulletin, 51*, 8–16.

Bittner, E. (1970). *The functions of the police in modern society*. Chevy Chase, MD: National Institute of Mental Health Center for Studies of Crime and Delinquency.

Bouza, A. V. (1990). *The police mystique: An insider's look at cops, crime, and the criminal justice system*. New York: Plenum.

Bracey, D. H. (1989). Proactive measures against police corruption: Yesterday's solutions, today's problems. *Police Studies, 12*, 175–179.

Chevigny, P. (1969). *Police power: Police abuses in New York City*. New York: Vintage Press.

Christopher Commission. (1991). Report of the independent commission on the Los Angeles Police Department. Los Angeles: The Commission. p. 74.

Claffey, M., & Weir, R. (2000, March 11). Bust four cops in bribe scheme. *New York Daily News*, p. 5.

Cornwell, L. (2001, October 22). Two more Cincinnati police officers on trial this week. Associated Press.

Cooksey, O. E. (1991, September). Corruption: A continuing challenge for law enforcement. *FBI Law Enforcement Bulletin, 60*, 5–9.

Cox, S. (1996). *Police: Practices, perspectives, problems*. Boston: Allyn & Bacon.

Cray, E. (1972). *The enemy in the streets: Police malpractice in America*. Garden City, NY: Anchor Books.

Delattre, E. (1996). *Character and cops*, 3rd ed. Washington, DC: AEI Press.

DeLeon-Granados, W., & Wells, W. (1998). Do you want extra police coverage with those fries? An exploratory analysis of the relationship between patrol practices and the gratuity exchange principle. *Police Quarterly, 1*, 71–85.

Frankel, B. (1993a, September 30). "You'll be in the fold" by breaking law. *USA Today*, p. 1A.

———. (1993b, October 7). For NYC cops, license for crime. *USA Today*, p. 3A.

Glover, S., & Lait, M. (2000, March 31). Public corruption probe spreads to other divisions. *LA Times*, p. A1.

Gorman, J. (1988, November 23). 30 cops charged in funeral payoffs. *Chicago Tribune*, sect. Chicagoland, p. 1.

Hacker, A. (1992). *Two nations: Black and white, separate, hostile, and unequal*. New York: Ballantine Books.

Harrison, B. (1999, August). Noble cause corruption and the police ethic. *FBI Law Enforcement Bulletin, 68*, 1–7.

Hawk, F. (2000, February 6). New twist in Warren probe. *Detroit News*, p. B1.

Human Rights Watch. (1998). Shielded from justice: Police brutality and accountability in the United States. *Los Angeles: The Christopher Commission Report*. Retrieved January 20, 2001 from the World Wide Web: www.hrw.org/reports98/police/uspo73.htm.

Hyatt, W. (2001). Parameters of police misconduct. In Palmiotto, M. (ed.), *Police misconduct* (pp. 75–99). Upper Saddle River, NJ: Prentice-Hall.

Jackson, D. (2000, October 22). Sordid ties tarnishing city police. *Chicago Tribune*, Internet Edition. Retrieved online at chicagotribune.com.

Johnson, D. R. (1981). *American law enforcement: A history*. St. Louis, MO: Forum Press.

Johnson, R. (1998, December). Citizen complaints: What the police should know. *FBI Law Enforcement Bulletin, 67*, 1–5.

Klockars, C. B. (1989). Police ethics. In Bailey, W. G. (ed.), *The encyclopedia of police science* (pp. 427–432). New York: Garland Press.

Knapp Commission. (1973). *The Knapp Commission report on police corruption*. New York: George Braziller.

Lacayo, R. (1993, October 11). Cops and robbers. *Time*, pp. 43–44.

Lynch, G. W. (1989). Police corruption from the United States perspective. *Police Studies, 12*, 165–170.

Main, F., Sadovi, C., & Sweeney, A. (2000, November 22). 4 city cops charged with shakedowns. *Chicago Sun-Times*, p. 1.

Manning, P. K. (1974). Police lying. *Urban Life, 3*, 283–306.

National Advisory Commission on Civil Disorders. (1968). *Report*. Washington, DC: U.S. Government Printing Office.

National Institute of Justice. (2000). *Public attitudes toward abuse of authority: Findings from a national study*. Washington DC: U.S. Government Printing Office.

National Institute of Justice. (1999). *Use of force by police: Overview of national and local data*. Washington DC: U.S. Government Printing Office.

National Institute of Justice. (1997). *Police integrity: Public service with honor*. Washington DC: U.S. Government Printing Office.

Reiss, A. J. (1968). Police brutality . . . answers to key questions. In Lipsky, M. (ed.), *Police encounters*. Chicago: Aldine.

———. (1971). *The police and the public*. New Haven, CT: Yale University Press.

Richardson, J. F. (1974). *Urban police in the United States*. Port Washington, NY: Kennikat Press.

Roberg, R. R., & Kuykendall, J. (1993). *Police in society*. Belmont, CA: Wadsworth.

Rosoff, S., Pontell, H., & Tillman, R. (1998). *Profit without honor: White collar crime and the looting of America*. Upper Saddle River, NJ: Prentice-Hall.

Rubinstein, J. (1973). *City police*. New York: Farrar, Straus and Giroux.

Sadivo, C. (2001, August 14). Cops plead guilty to extortion of immigrants. *Chicago Sun-Times*, p. 8.

Skolnick, J. H. (1966). *Justice without trial*. New York: John Wiley.

Slater, E. (2000, March 30). Scandal forces Chicago police to overhaul anti-gang unit. *LA Times*, p. 5A.

Stoddard, E. R. (1968, June). The informal code of police deviance: A group approach to "blue-coat crime." *Journal of Criminal Law, Criminology and Police Science, 59*, 201–213.

Sykes, G. (1999). NYPD blues. *Ethics Corner, 6* (1). Southwestern Law Enforcement Institute, Center for Law Enforcement Ethics. Available online at: http://web2.airmail.net/slf/clee.html.

Tran, M. (1994, July 8). Corruption riddles New York police: Inquiry says drug dealing rogue cops acted like gangs. *The Gazette* (Montreal), p. A9.

Treaster, J. (1994, July 10). Mollen Panel says buck stops with top officers. *New York Times*, sect. 1, p. 21, col. 2.

Trojanowicz, R. (1992). Preventing individual and systemic corruption. *Footprints, 4*, 1–3.

U.S. Department of Justice. (2001). *Principles for promoting police integrity: Examples of promising police practices and policies*. Washington DC: U.S. Government Printing Office.

U.S. General Accounting Office. (1998). *Drug-related police corruption*. Washington DC: U.S. Government Printing Office.

Walker, S. (2001). *Police accountability*. Belmont, CA: Wadsworth/Thomson Learning.

Warmbir, S. (2001, April 25). Cop's bragging was his downfall. *Chicago Sun-Times*, p. 6.

CHAPTER ELEVEN

COMMUNITY POLICING

It is apparent that American municipal police are far better staffed, educated, trained, and equipped than ever before. Yet examples of excessive force, police corruption, and inefficiency appear frequently in the media. And, as indicated in Chapter 1, the police are unable to prevent most crimes or to apprehend most offenders. For these and other reasons, according to Stevens (2001, p. 8), "Policing has attempted to change from a closed, incident-driven and reactive bureaucracy to a more open, dynamic, quality-oriented partnership with the community to safeguard basic human and constitutional rights." Attempts to make these changes have been included under the general heading of community policing. In this chapter we discuss this newest in a series of attempts to deal with problems confronted by the police.

PROBLEMATIC ISSUES FOR THE POLICE

As we have seen, corruption and inefficiency have been problems in American policing from its beginnings, and they continue to tarnish the police image. Scandals involving theft, use and sale of drugs by officers, police brutality, and other serious violations are far too common (Barlow & Barlow, 2000; Palmiotto, 2000; Walker, 2001).

It appears that many of the programs developed by the police in an attempt to adapt to a rapidly changing society have resulted in, or continued, a cycle of isolation and alienation. Specialization, for example, was viewed as one way of providing better service to the public. As a result, numerous specialized units (internal affairs, community relations, juvenile, robbery, homicide, drug, sex crimes, and traffic) were developed. In many cases, the outcome of such development has been little cross-training; an "it's not my job" attitude; tight-knit, highly secretive units; and little effective communication between patrol officers and the officers who staff these specialized units. If and when scandals arise in such units, the confidence of both the general public and noninvolved officers within the police ranks is understandably shaken.

In the past decade, gangs, drugs, race and ethnicity, and increasingly violent encounters involving automatic weapons and the willingness to use them have become focal points. Increasing visibility of immigrants and a small number of terrorist incidents within the borders of our country have led to a rebirth of concern about racial and ethnic differences and the reemergence of extreme right-wing groups. Meanwhile, relationships between the police and members of racial and ethnic minorities continue to be less than civil in many cases, and downright unpleasant in some. All of the new police technology and all of the old police traditions have failed to provide answers to these apparently different but very much related questions. This has led to a search for new ways of addressing these issues and to the emergence (some would argue reemergence) of community-oriented policing. As we look at community policing, we should keep in mind that it does not require that all traditional policing strategies be thrown out. According to the National Institute of Justice, "Traditional police methods are not, as many fear, incompatible with community policing. Community policing is not just a joint problem-solving process. It can also involve arrest-oriented, get-tough solutions. The difference is that under community policing, the 'tough' police action is not a surprise to the law-abiding community. In fact, it may have been requested by residents and citizens working with the police." (*NIJ Research in Brief*, 1992, p. 9). Harpold (Tafoya, 2000, p. 306) states, "Unless we tell people that CP [community policing] is an enhancement to traditional policing, and not merely and addition, it is very difficult for citizens or police officers, for that matter, to accept CP as different because the incomplete explanation does not make CP seem to be REAL police work."

COMMUNITY POLICING

There is a good deal of confusion about what community policing is, what it might be expected to accomplish, and how or why it might be expected to work where other strategies have failed. In fact, many believe community-oriented policing (COP) simply retreads shopworn elements of police community relations programs, that it is little more than the latest buzzword, a passing fad that will soon fade as have many others before it (Trojanowicz, 1990; Tafoya, 2000; Stevens, 2001, pp. 7–8). This is perhaps especially true in traditional police agencies that are highly resistant to change as a result of their paramilitary organizational structures, civil services regulations, and unionization (Skolnick & Bayley, 1986; Tafoya, 2000; Stevens, 2001, p. 11).

Skolnick and Bayley (1986) studied police innovation that focused on involving the public in the police mission in six American cities. They concluded that these innovative programs, designated as community-oriented policing, took a number of different forms. Still, the researchers identified a number of elements common to all of the programs. These elements included police–community reciprocity, areal decentralization of command, reorientation of patrol, and civilianization (Skolnick & Bayley, 1986, pp. 212–220). A brief discussion of each of these elements will help create a foundation for understanding community policing. *Police–community reciprocity* refers to a "genuine feeling" on the part of the police that the public they serve has something to contribute to policing. Further, the police communicate this feeling to the public, learn from public input, and consider themselves accountable to the community in which they serve. The police and the public become "co-producers of crime prevention" (Skolnick & Bayley, 1986, pp. 212–213).

Areal decentralization of command refers to the establishment of substations, ministations, and other attempts to increase interaction between police officers and the public they serve in a particular geographic area. *Reorientation of patrol* involves moving from car to foot patrol in order to increase police interaction with other citizens. This may involve permanently assigning certain officers to walking beats or may be accomplished by having officers park their cars so they can get out and talk to residents. Positive contacts between officers and other citizens are thought to be one result of foot patrol, and crime prevention another. In a study of police officers in Philadelphia, Kane (2000, p. 278) concluded, "At least among Philadelphia public housing police officers, permanent assignment was associated with a higher level of investigative activity at the street level, from which inferences about increased beat guardianship may be drawn." In other words, "These findings indicate that as a result of permanent beat assignment, officers assumed greater responsibility for their beats than before this deployment was established" (p. 273). Whether such effects are long term is a question that must still be addressed, because the officers in this study were observed for a period of weeks rather than months or years.

Civilianization refers to introducing civilians to an increasing number of positions with police agencies. For example, an increasing number of civilians are being employed in research and training divisions, in forensics, and as community service officers who handle many non-crime-related tasks. Skolnick and Bayley (1986, p. 219) concluded that civilianization was related to successfully introducing and carrying out programs and policies related to community mobilization and crime prevention.

In reality, then, COP is much more than community relations. COP requires adopting both philosophical and operational changes and, to a great extent, turns traditional policing practices upside down. It is, after all, "not easy to transform blue knights into community organizers"(Skolnick & Bayley, 1986, p. 211).

Trojanowicz and colleagues (1998, pp. xi–xiii) elaborated some of the principles on which this transformation from traditional to community policing is based. First, community policing is a philosophy based on the belief that law-abiding citizens should have input with respect to policing, provided they are willing to participate in and support the effort. Second, community policing is an organizational strategy requiring that all police personnel (civilian and sworn) explore ways to turn the philosophy into practice. Third, police departments implementing community policing must develop Community Policing Officers (CPOs) to act as links between the police and community residents, and these CPOs must have continuous, sustained contact with law-abiding citizens.

Additionally, community policing implies a contract between the police and other citizens that helps overcome apathy while curbing vigilantism. Further, community policing is proactive, and it helps improve quality of life for those who are most vulnerable (e.g., the poor, elderly, homeless). Although community policing utilizes technology, it relies on human ingenuity and interaction. Finally, community policing must be fully integrated into the department in order to provide personalized police service on a decentralized basis.

Trojanowicz et al. point out what community policing is not (pp. 14–24). Community policing is not a technique to be applied only to specific problems, but is a new way of thinking about the police role in the community. Community policing is not the same as public relations. Community policing is not antitechnology but utilizes technology in a different framework. Community policing is not soft on crime, nor is it an independent program within a police department. It must involve the entire department, and it incorporates traditional policing responses. Community policing is not cosmetic. It requires substantive changes in the relationship between the police and other citizens. Community policing is not a top-down approach, nor is it simply social work renamed. It incorporates traditional policing responses. Finally, community policing requires risk taking and experimentation.

Put in other terms (Overman, 1994, p. 20), "Traditionally, we in law enforcement have set our own priorities with little regard to community input. . . . We must begin to listen to the people we serve and prioritize our efforts based on quality of life issues. This is where community policing begins. . . . We must go beyond the traditional approaches and begin to judge our effectiveness by the condition of the [street] corner rather than by the number of arrests [on it]."

Carey (1994, p. 24) notes that community policing is not solely directed at addressing problems that cannot be addressed by traditional policing methods. Suburban and low-crime communities also can use community policing to address the specific needs and problems of their citizens. In short, community policing philosophy recognizes that patrol officers are the government representatives best positioned to address a number of social problems, and enforcing the law is only one of several strategies the police can employ to cope with such problems (Cardarelli, McDevitt, & Baum, 1998).

The basic concerns of COP are, then, empowerment of police officers and other citizens alike and cooperation between the police and the public in an attempt to solve problems in order to improve the quality of life in a given community (Kane, 1993, p. 1; Stevens, 2001, p. 8). COP requires a philosophical commitment by the police to cooperate with other citizens in the process of controlling crime, drugs, fear of crime, and neighborhood decay. Further, COP mandates that all police personnel, sworn and nonsworn, reevaluate their positions to seek better ways of carrying out their missions. There also is a requirement that at least part of the police force be deployed as community officers who maintain direct, regular ties with the citizens they police. These community officers must provide a full range of services to those in their areas of responsibility, serving as mini-chiefs within these areas (Trojanowicz, 1990, p. 8; Breci, 1997, p. 1). Long-term interaction between police officers and neighborhood residents fosters the development of relationships based on mutual trust and cooperation. It also encourages the exchange of information between citizens and police officers, including mutual input concerning policing priorities and tactics for specific neighborhoods (Walters, 1993, p. 220). Or, as Trojanowicz and Bucqueroux (1992, p. 1) put it, "By challenging people to work as partners in making their communities better and safer places, Community Policing produces a subtle but profound shift in the role and responsibility of the police. No longer are they the experts with all the answers, the 'thin blue line' that protects the good people from the bad—'us' versus 'them.' Community officers are part of the community, generalists who do whatever it takes to help people help themselves."

Kelling and Stewart (1989), Spelman and Eck (2000), and Taylor and Harrell (2000), among others, discuss a number of things that neighborhood residents can do to help the police protect their neighborhoods. First, they can call the police when they see untoward behavior and come forward to testify as witnesses in criminal court. Second, each individual can take actions to help reduce fear, disorder, and crime. Such actions include buying and using locks, assisting neighbors who need help, hiring private security guards to supplement police protection, and avoiding dangerous areas. Third, they can work with the police to organize neighborhood watch groups, patrol their neighborhoods, and organize neighborhood "safe houses" for children. Fourth, those who belong to private organizations can encourage them to implement programs for youth in the neighborhoods in questions. Fifth, commercial firms can hire private security agencies to help protect their businesses. By cooperating with the police and other criminal justice agencies in these ways, citizens can improve the safety of their neighborhoods and fulfill their roles as part of the police–community partnership.

In COP, patrol officers become liaisons, ombudsmen, problem-solvers, and mobilizers of community resources. They seek to obtain community or neighborhood cooperation to identify and resolve problems rather than simply handling incidents. They look for patterns of incidents that are indicative of problems that may best be addressed by resources other than, or in cooperation with, the police. In short, they practice problem-oriented policing as a part of the overall COP strategy.

Community policing may be viewed as addressing the following issues (adapted from Trojanowicz, 1990, p. 10):

1. Goal: Problem solving
2. Line function: Regular contact between officers and other citizens
3. Addressing problems pointed out by citizens who cooperate in setting the police agenda

4. Police accountability to citizens who receive services
5. Managed change and restructuring within the department with respect to selection, training, evaluation, and promotion
6. Department-wide acceptance of COP philosophy
7. Influence from the bottom up: Citizens and patrol personnel help establish priorities and policies.
8. Continuously accessible officers in decentralized offices
9. Police encourage other citizens to solve many of their own problems.
10. Reduction of citizen fear, crime, and neighborhood disorder are determinants of success.

Implementing COP requires a number of concrete changes in most police organizations. Cox (1992, pp. 2–3) indicates that implementation requires redefining the department's role and training all officers in COP. Employees must be evaluated differently. Officers must be assigned specific patrol areas. Calls must be prioritized, and police work must be tailored to community needs. A community police officer might spend her day as illustrated in Highlight 11.1.

■ ■ ■ ■ ■

HIGHLIGHT 11.1

NATIONAL REPORT DETAILS SUCCESSFUL COMMUNITY-CENTERED POLICING; COMMUNITIES AND POLICE WORKING TOGETHER

PolicyLink, in partnership with the Advancement Project, today released a report citing innovative policing practices across the country which are helping communities and police departments unite to make neighborhoods safer in 50 cities, including Boston, Washington, D.C., San Francisco, Seattle, Minneapolis, New York, Chicago, Memphis, Houston, Albuquerque and Pittsburgh.

The report entitled "Community-Centered Policing: A Force for Change," details practices that help hold police accountable to the neighborhoods that they serve and are the foundation for community-centered policing. These efforts are crucial to building strong relationships between police departments and communities and restoring trust and confidence. "Our report shows that joint community and police involvement is not only necessary, but is essential to making neighborhoods safer, and helping police work with communities," said Angela Glover Blackwell, President of PolicyLink. "The report highlights the strategies that have contributed significantly to promising community-centered policing practices ranging from diversity training for officers, to mobilizing communities, to helping change police policies and practices. These elements are essential to building stronger, safer communities."

Specifically, the PolicyLink and Advancement Project report discloses a series of police practices that have strengthened relationships between the communities and police, including:

- Engaging communities as partners with local police departments in problem-solving, including working with community development corporations
- Recruiting and retaining community-oriented people as officers, such as teaching officers problem-solving skills and rewarding them for living in the city in which they serve

- Achieving democratic participation, including creating independent community oversight committees
- Gathering and sharing information with communities, such as educating communities about police policies via the Internet and seeking community input through public surveys

Still, the report notes that much more work must be done. "While there are a number of community-centered policing practices highlighted throughout the report, no one department is doing it all," said Maya Harris West, a Senior Associate at PolicyLink and principal author of this report. "Adopting one or two of these practices will not make a substantial difference," she said. "Police departments, along with local communities, must rethink, reorient and retool themselves to implement change on several fronts, not just a few."

Moreover, Penda Hair, Co-Director of the Washington, D.C., office of the Advancement Project, added, "We wanted to find a way to help community groups translate their anger into positive change. This report shows that communities can have safe neighborhoods without abusive police forces and racial profiling. We plan to widely distribute it as a resource for community groups across the nation."

(2001, May 17) PolicyLink via Ascribe News.

While President Bush's budget makes cuts in the federal COPS program, which has helped some communities implement innovative, community based police tactics, the report makes a strong argument for increasing support for these practices. "The report demonstrates why federal and local governments should be increasing, not cutting funding for innovative, promising work at the local level," said Ms. Harris West. "These practices are making a difference in communities around the country and the goal should be to have them make an even bigger impact."

ABOUT POLICYLINK
PolicyLink is a national nonprofit research, communications, capacity building and advocacy organization advancing a new generation of policies to achieve economic and social equity and build strong, organized communities. The full report and summary document are available on the PolicyLink website. Log on to www.policyhnk.org/publications.html.

ABOUT THE ADVANCEMENT PROJECT
The Advancement Project is a policy and legal action group that creates strategies for achieving universal opportunity and a racially just democracy by providing community-focused legal skills and other resources to communities engaged in racial and social justice work.

The LEMAS Survey

The Law Enforcement Management and Administrative Statistics (LEMAS) survey assessed the community policing practices of state and local police departments in 1997 and 1999. Highlights of the LEMAS survey (Hickman & Reaves, 2001, pp. 1–11) are summarized as follows:

1. State and local police agencies had nearly 113,000 community policing officers in 1999 compared with 21,000 in 1997.

2. In 1999, 87 percent of local police officers were employed by a department that provided community policing training to new recruits.

3. Approximately one-third of local departments, employing about 50 percent of all officers, actively encouraged patrol officers to engage in problem-solving projects on their patrol beats.

4. Approximately 42 percent of local police departments gave patrol officers responsibility for specific geographic areas or beats.

5. Twenty-eight percent of local departments surveyed citizens to gather information in 1999, compared with 30 percent in 1997.

Problem-Oriented Policing as a Component of COP

The concept of problem-oriented policing (POP) originated in 1979 in the works of Herman Goldstein. Goldstein (1979) noted many of the difficulties discussed in the first section of this chapter and added that while many police agencies gave the appearance of being efficient, this appearance failed to translate into benefits for the communities served. He looked carefully at public expectations of the police and determined that they involved problem solving. Goldstein concluded that if the police were expected to solve problems, they could not be accurately evaluated by focusing only on crime statistics. Instead, evaluation would have to focus on the problems encountered and the effectiveness of the police response to such problems.

Problem-oriented police officers, then, need to define the problems they encounter, gather information concerning these problems (frequency, seriousness, duration, location) and develop creative solutions to them. This model of problem solving is known as the SARA model (Eck & Spelman, 1988; Goldstein, 1990; Stevens, 2001). To expand on the previous definition, this four-step approach involves *scanning* (identifying the problem in terms of time, location, and behavior); *analysis* (answering the who, what, where, when, how, and why questions); *response* (development of alternative problem-solving approaches and selection of most appropriate); and *assessment* (evaluating the response selected to determine whether it worked).

Problem-oriented policing represents a dramatic change from traditional policing, which is incident driven, in which the police typically receive a complaint or call, respond to, and then clear the incident. Although the specific situation is addressed, the underlying conditions are not, so more calls are likely to be made, requiring further responses to similar incidents. POP regards these incidents as symptoms of underlying conditions that must be addressed to keep the incidents from proliferating (Toch & Grant, 1991, p. 6; Barlow & Barlow, 2000, p. 44).

Patterns of incidents that are similar, then, represent problems that must be attended to by the police. Problems, rather than crimes, calls, or incidents, become the basic unit of police work (Toch & Grant, 1991, p. 18). Line officers become problem identifiers and solvers. Identifying and solving community problems requires input from those who live in the community, as well as from other service providers. Thus, POP and COP share the same concerns with community involvement, and both focus on conditions underlying crime and disruption of order (Oliver & Bartgis, 1998; Stevens, 2001, pp. 14–15).

Research on Community and Problem-Oriented Policing

Sklonick and Bayley (1986) are not the only researchers to examine community policing. Sadd and Grinc (2000) studied Innovative Neighborhood-Oriented Policing (INOP) in eight American cities. INOP is a variant of community policing based on the premise that crime and drug problems must be addressed by communities, not just by the police. Using a variety of research techniques, these authors found that it was difficult to convince police officers to accept the new roles required for community policing, partly due to poor communications from police administrators concerning these new roles. INOP officers belonged to special units and were often distrusted by officers, especially senior officers, in more traditional assignments. Other officers felt that they had little or no input into the new program and that community residents were not generally excited about being involved in INOP due to fear of retaliation from drug dealers, which was based on the fear that the police would abandon the program and leave them to suffer the consequences. Still, with proper education and training, community residents did come to report better relationships with the police, even when INOPs' effects on drugs and crime were difficult to detect.

Jesilow et al. (1998), using phone interviews in 1990 and again in 1992, studied the residents' opinions of Santa Ana, California, in experimental (POP) and control (no POP) neighborhoods. They found that citizen complaints about gangs, crime, and disorder in POP neighborhoods decreased over the two-year period, while such complaints remained constant or increased in control neighborhoods. Due to limitations in their research design, the authors indicate that they cannot argue definitively that POP caused the changes, but the data are certainly suggestive. The authors also caution about the possibility of violations of civil rights among the powerless in POP programs that address the complaints of the more affluent. Overall, they conclude, POP seems to be a good thing, in that residents involved in the program seem to be happier about their neighborhoods and the police: "The research suggests that law enforcement agencies that take the time to learn and deal with their constituents' irritants and troubles will be perceived in increasingly positive terms" (p. 460).

In their review of twelve studies of community policing, Lurigo and Rosenbaum (1994) found generally encouraging results in terms of the impact of organizational changes on police officer attitudes. Results indicated generally positive effects on job satisfaction, improved relationships with coworkers and citizens, and greater expectations for citizen participation in preventing crimes.

Cardarelli, McDevitt, and Baum (1998) conducted a survey of eighty-two police departments in Massachusetts communities with fewer than 200,000 inhabitants to determine the community policing strategies, if any, employed. They concluded that deployment strategies such as bike patrol and mini-stations may represent new ways for some departments to perform their policing functions, but that most residents do little more than provide information to departments utilizing these strategies. This is also true for departments using a combination of deployment and crime-targeted strategies. The authors found that residents are more likely to participate in the problem identification and problem-solving processes associated with community policing when collaborative strategies such as advisory councils and citizen academies are established.

They also concluded that the police will have to take the initiative for establishing such relationships, particularly in lower socioeconomic neighborhoods.

Breci (1997) surveyed a random sample of Minnesota police officers in an attempt to determine the extent to which Minnesota police agencies sponsored or offered the kinds of training necessary for line officers to develop the skills and knowledge necessary to make the transition to community policing. Fifty-two percent (801) of Breci's surveys were returned. His findings indicated that many Minnesota police agencies had not provided officers with the training or support required for a successful transition. He concluded (p. 774) that "without clear guidelines and leadership from the department, efforts to connect the police with the community through the line officer will have no more success than did the old police-community relations programs of the past."

In his study of community policing, Stevens (2001, pp. 1–2) found few accounts of automatic success in the community policing arena: "In fact, in the nine agencies studied, most of them failed at both their earlier and recent attempts to implement what they thought were solid police strategies guided by idealized versions of community policing prerogatives that allegedly worked in other departments."

Criticisms of Community Policing

While there is little doubt that community policing is heralded as the major trend in American policing—according to the Bureau of Justice Statistics (1999), in 1999 nearly two-thirds of county and municipal police departments with one hundred or more officers had a formally written community policing plan—there are those who have raised questions about its worth. One common criticism is that many police departments embrace the *rhetoric* of community policing rather than the philosophy. Indeed, there are police administrators who institute foot patrol programs or establish neighborhood watch programs and claim to have initiated community policing. As Offer (1993, p. 8) noted, the considerable enthusiasm for community policing has led to its introduction as an organizational objective with little substance in many police departments. Stevens (2001, p. 17; Palmiotto, 2000, p. 218) indicate that this remains the case as we enter the twenty-first century. While these observations are certainly accurate, they are not a criticism of community policing itself, but of those who claim the title without developing the substance.

Another criticism aimed at those who adopt community policing strategies concerns the fact that there is little empirical evidence to suggest that community policing is effective in reducing serious crime. Stevens (2001, p. 5) indicates, "But it has yet to be reliably supported that community policing initiatives are advantageous for all communities and/or can be implemented and operated by all police agencies." Indeed, available evidence seems to indicate that while people involved in community policing efforts feel more secure, crime is not significantly reduced. It may be that people who feel more secure will use the streets and other public places more frequently, thus eventually making it more difficult for criminals to ply their trades. It may also be that people who feel more secure, but are not in fact more secure, are more likely to engage in activities that make them available as victims, thus increasing the risk of crime. Brown (1992b, p. 4), Gardner (2000, pp. 67–74), and Taylor and Harrell (2000, pp. 167–181) indicate that the only way in which the police can have an impact on violent crime is to form partnerships with the residents of high-crime areas by making police officers permanent, highly visible fixtures in the neighborhood. In any case, further and careful evaluation of community policing programs is clearly in order and is ongoing, as we shall see.

The third major criticism of community policing has to do with its costs. Implementing COP may decrease the mobility and availability of the officers involved, because the officers are out of their vehicles a good deal of the time and because they are involved in community organization activities and are sometimes unavailable to respond to calls. In fact, in many programs, COP officers no longer perform routine motorized patrol, and other officers must take over this duty if it is to continue. It has been suggested, in addition, that the money spent on community policing might be better spent on improving social and economic conditions (Pisani, 1992). In fairness, it must be noted that community policing is seldom touted as a money-saving approach. While it does cost money to implement any new program, there are various ways of measuring costs. Departmental budgets may have to be increased initially to support COP (Palmiotto, 2000, p. 211; Sadd & Grinc, 2000, p. 116). If the strategy succeeds in improving cooperation between the police and other citizens, however, how do we measure the savings in crimes prevented or solved as a result of this increased cooperation? Further, some departments have found that by rearranging priorities, eliminating services for non-emergency calls, and providing reporting alternatives (telephone, fax, letters) for the public, costs can be managed (Burgreen & McPherson, 1992).

A fourth criticism of community policing focuses on the possibility that permanent assignment of police officers who have a good deal of independence in operations enhances the possibility of corruption. This criticism is based primarily on historical accounts of corruption by police officers who walked beats, who were not subject to routine supervision, and who frightened neighborhood business persons (legitimate and illegitimate) into paying them for not enforcing the law and/or for protecting them from other predators. Trojanowicz and Bucqueroux (1992, p. 2) argued, however, that the very nature of COP works against such corruption. That is, COP officers are known by name to everyone in the neighborhood and have every reason to believe that they cannot "cross the lined undetected."

Fifth, some critics argue that the time is simply not right to change from traditional policing strategies to COP. There are always crises to be faced and numerous reasons for not changing strategies now. Burgreen and McPherson (1992, p. 31) recognized this fact: ". . . if we don't risk changing when the time is right, we will be forced to change when we are not prepared. If we are afraid to change because we are comfortable, we may be holding on just to prove that certainty is better than taking a risk. No one benefits in this scenario. Not the police, and certainly not the community."

Finally, there has been major criticism of the Justice Department's Community Oriented Policing Services (COPS) program at the federal level. In 1994, President Clinton pledged to put 100,000 new police officers on the street under this program. Yet in 2000, the program remained some 40,000 officers short of fulfilling the promise, and former government officials involved in passing the funding legislation are questioning whether it will ever measure up. According to Glasser (2000, p. 22), "Critics,

DARE programs may be incorporated into community policing efforts.

including architects of the federal cash-for-cops program, say this is a classic case of politics trumping reality and lofty promises built on false premises."

Some Examples of Community Policing

Community Policing in Seattle.   Beginning in 1987, citizens living in South Seattle began expressing concerns over police services. After meeting with police and elected officials, the community group decided they would have to supply the "vision and imagination" necessary to solve a number of problems. The group was viewed as advisory by the police, but members saw themselves as involved in a partnership with the police. In 1988, the South Seattle Crime Prevention Council (SSCPC) was formed, and the members met regularly with police officials, who discussed police plans and tactics with them. SSCPC served as an umbrella group, bringing other neighborhood groups into cooperative efforts with the police and increasing the geographic area covered (*NIJ Research in Brief*, 1992).

Other city agencies, such as the housing authority, soon became involved in the program. These agencies involved citizen groups, and the police worked together to define problems, select targets, and develop strategies to deal with existing problems. Shared responsibility became a guiding principle, and all parties experienced benefits. Police experienced more community support and other citizens felt more secure: "Over time the partnership has developed into an effective means of increasing community security by expanding its focus to encompass a range of issues that affect the quality of neighborhood life. It has demonstrated that crime prevention, broadly defined, benefits from the joint attention of police and community" (*NIJ Research in Brief,* 1992, p. 11).

Neighborhood Oriented Policing (NOP) in Joliet, Illinois.

Joliet's program began in 1992 with the development of specialized units consisting of volunteers assigned full-time to NOP (Vlasak, 1992). Initially, these officers went door to door introducing themselves, passing out information about the program, and providing residents with cellular phone numbers where they could be reached while on duty.

Officers attended neighborhood watch meetings and promoted after-school opportunities for young people. They spent time with school children during recess and on their lunch hours and served as guest readers for younger children.

Signs of success have begun to appear. Some new businesses have been established in the NOP area and graffiti is less prevalent than it was before the program began. Calls for service and reported crime have decreased, as have complaints against the police. Local media have also been supportive. There have been some setbacks related to a death sentence handed down for a gang member who murdered a police officer, but overall, Chief Nowicki of the Joliet Police Department believes that "Joliet's citizens are reacting positively and starting to treat the officers as a part of, and a partner of, their communities" (Vlasak, 1992, p. 15).

Operation CLEAN.

Operation CLEAN (Community and Law Enforcement Against Narcotics) was initiated by the Dallas Police Department in 1989 to help citizens reclaim their neighborhoods from drug dealers (Hatler, 1990). The series of programs involves concerned citizens and numerous city departments, including the police, fire, streets and sanitation, housing and neighborhood services, and the city attorney.

Each operation involves a number of phases, beginning with target-area selection, moving to intensive police involvement in investigation and arrests, and finally, to reducing the level of police services from its peak and returning control of the neighborhood to residents.

Results of CLEAN operations show a reduction in calls for police services in the target areas, decreases in serious crime, the establishment of citizen crime-watch programs, and improved fire safety and sanitation. Police planners in Dallas conclude that local law enforcement agencies can work with other city departments and concerned citizens to improve quality of life (Hatler, 1990, p. 25).

Community Policing: The Houston Experience.

Brown, in implementing COP in Houston, found that programs are roughly divided into two phases (Brown, 1989). In phase I, programs are implemented that provide the public with meaningful opportunities to participate in police efforts. Phase II involves changing the style, organization, and mission of the police department and other city agencies.

Brown reports that in Houston, the evolution from phase I to phase II took five years. During this evolution, several things occurred. Barriers to change were broken down, and leaders and rank-and-file officers were educated as to the merits of community policing. Department personnel were encouraged to get involved in the change so that they would view community policing as their creation, not something imported from the outside. Training in community policing strategies and techniques was instituted, and the benefits of community policing were discussed with and demonstrated to the public and elected officials (Brown, 1989, p. 5).

CAPS: Chicago Alternative Policing Strategy.   Community policing in Chicago is known as CAPS (Chicago Alternative Policing Strategy). The program had its origins at the time of rising crime rates in the early 1990s and was in planning stages for more than a year before it was officially instituted in 1993 in five of the city's twenty-five police districts (Hartnett & Skogan, 1999). During initial phases, officers were permanently assigned to beats and trained in problem-solving techniques. Citizen committees were formed in the various neighborhoods, and police and area residents began to meet on a regular basis. Police and residents work together to identify and prioritize problems, develop ways of addressing them and bringing community resources to bear on them.

By the spring of 1998, almost 805 of the city's residents were aware of CAPS, over 60 percent knew about beat meetings in their neighborhoods, and about 15 percent had attended such meetings. Support for the program has grown among line officers.

Still, not all has gone smoothly with CAPS. Within the police department, CAPS challenged the "business as usual" mentality of officers and created initial pessimism among officers who did not care to take on non-crime problems. Development of workable performance measures and incentives has been problematic. And "there are no measures of the extent to which officers are involved in problem solving and no indicators of their success" (Hartnett & Skogan, 1999, p. 10).

STOP: San Diego, California.   The San Diego, California, Police Department established neighborhood policing through the development of STOP: Selected Tactics for Policing (Peak & Glensor, 1999, p. 330). Ten patrol officers formed a team to combine traditional policing with Community Oriented Policing and Problem Solving (COPPS) to target criminal activity. Additional examples of neighborhood policing in San Diego include the following:

> Revitalized neighborhood watch program
>
> Citizen patrol groups
>
> Safe Streets Now!—reduction of nuisance properties through civil law actions
>
> Drug Abatement Response Team—Identification of properties with a history of drug activity

Neighborhood-Level Networking: Buffalo, New York.   Buffalo has instituted a community-based initiative that engages city government, the business community, and law enforcement to improve the quality of life on the west side of the city (Community Policing Exchange, 2000, p. 4). The Neighborhood Initiative program had three primary objectives: strict enforcement, high visibility, and increased communication and coordination with the community and other city agencies (Trojanowicz et al., 1998, pp. 307–308). The "Save Our Streets" initiative identified "the dirty dozen" of suspected drug houses in the neighborhood and used housing laws to alter drug activities. These initiatives, along with the deterrent effect of microwave-based surveillance cameras, have reduced crime 25 to 50 percent over a six-month period (Community Policing Exchange, 2000, p. 4).

Community-Oriented Policing Plus: Reno, Nevada. The Reno, Nevada, Police Department adopted a department-wide strategy labeled Community Policing Plus (COP+) (Trojanowicz et al., 1998, p. 315). Major changes were made in recruiting, testing, hiring, performance evaluations, promotions, awards, honors, discipline, and reorganization of the geographic districts. In addition, the department implemented a problem-solving approach using the SARA model and implemented the following programs: "Taking Back the Park," reduction of drug traffic, and social service assistance for youth at risk (Trojanowicz et al., 1998, pp. 318–319).

Community Policing, Department of Public Safety, Saginaw Valley State University. A final example of community policing comes from Saginaw Valley State University, an institution experiencing rapid growth in the number of residential students served. The Department of Public Safety's plans included a retreat to discuss community policing with officers, training sessions for residential assistants, and development of working relationships between officers and assistants. Police officers became more involved in the campus community by sponsoring Monday night football parties, attending residential assistants' meetings, and meeting with administrative and counseling staff. Officers helped students move in, and they set up a tent featuring materials on safety and other campus issues. Throughout the year, officers provided domestic violence, alcohol, and self-defense programs, as well as sponsored two fun nights. As Rusch (2001, p. 35) states, "The community policing program allowed officers to become more user friendly and to challenge the traditional style of policing" (see Highlight 11.2).

CONCLUSIONS

Based on his experiences, Brown (1989, p. 10) concluded,

> Because community policing is a relatively new style of policing, questions have been raised about its effectiveness. Any doubts, however, should be put to rest. Experience has shown that community policing as a dominant policing style is a better, more efficient, and more cost-effective means of using police resources. In the final analysis, community policing is emerging as the most appropriate means of using police resources to improve the quality of life in neighborhoods throughout the *country*.

Dolan (1994, p. 28) puts it in somewhat different terms, stating that community policing makes sense today. Over the years, the police have lost touch with their communities and now find they primarily interact with criminals or people in crisis.

■ ■ ■ ■ ■

HIGHLIGHT 11.2

HOW ARE WE DOING?:
POLICE TO HAND OUT COMMENT CARDS

This summer, being pulled over for a traffic violation in Springfield may have at least one similarity with eating at a fast-food restaurant or staying at a chain hotel.

Police will be handing out comment cards to everyone they come into contact with—from those who get traffic tickets to those whose homes have been burglarized.

Conducted by the Regional Institute for Community Policing, the survey is believed to be the first widespread effort of its kind in Illinois to get feedback from the community on the job police officers are doing. "This gives us an opportunity to get a response on every contact we have with the public," Police Chief John Harris said Friday. "Most of the time, I think, we do an outstanding job. But this will give us an opportunity to measure good service and bad service."

When police officers are dispatched to a call, they will handle it in the normal fashion. Afterward, the officer will provide a comment card to be mailed back to the Regional Institute for Community Policing. That organization will then compile the responses and report back to the city.

"This is not a reaction to anything bad that's happened. It's pro-action," said Mayor Karen Hasara in announcing the initiative. "It's a real opportunity for residents to communicate with us and will be used on every call."

The idea came from Hasara's Springfield Strategy 2020, a 39-page plan that took more than a year and more than 100 people to compile. It is an attempt at identifying a list of goals that will improve Springfield during the next two decades.

Strategy 2020 participants urged the continued implementation of community policing, in which police officers and residents work together to eliminate problems. The philosophy already is widely used within the Springfield Police Department, and the comment cards are an extension of the concept, said Bill Doster, director of the community policing institute.

"This is the heart and soul of community policing," he said. "It's a measure of the quality of service.

"We will get feedback on how the citizens view this department. It's an integrity issue we're heavily involved with."

The institute will oversee implementation of the initiative in order to keep it at "an arm's length" from the police department administration.

About 60 local residents will participate in sessions to determine what questions will be asked on the cards. The first meeting is set for May 24. Anyone who would like to participate can contact the mayor's office.

Harris said the comment cards are not designed to deter people from contacting the department's internal affairs division with concerns about incidents. In fact, he said, there will be a space on the card that instructs people on how to contact internal affairs if they feel their problems are more serious than can be addressed by a comment card.

"We're trying to become a pilot for positive things in community policing around the country," Harris said. "We also want officers to be part of the development of the program.

"Our intention is not just to catch them doing something wrong, but to catch them doing something right."

Antonacci, Sarah. (2001, May 5). *The State Journal-Register,* p. 6.

Burnout and frustration are results of these interactions. Community policing, however, offers the police a means to become professionally healthy. Officers of all ranks are encouraged to spend time outside the patrol car, interacting with law-abiding citizens. The end result should be a greater sense of accomplishment for the officers and greater appreciation from the community.

In spite of the numerous endorsements, not all departments have embraced community policing. Dolan (1994) discusses the nature of resistance to community policing among officers who have come to consider themselves the experts in crime control and order maintenance. Those who have found their niches in specialty areas are also often resistant to the idea that they may be back on the streets as generalists or that others may be permitted to utilize some of "their" techniques. This resistance must be overcome through recruiting and training techniques, managerial demonstration of long-term commitment to COP, proceeding slowly to "sell" the philosophy to all levels of the department, and involving all concerned parties from the initial stages of development. In addition, Overman states, "We must open up the police fraternity for scrutiny and help shed the mystique surrounding law enforcement" (1994, p. 20).

Stevens (2001, p. 271) concludes,

> While police agencies need to control the root causes of crime, the problem is that if real crime is ignored, it will escalate in both frequency and intensity. Because crime is a response in most cases to living conditions, relationship expectations, and pure selfishness, most of these issues are not police business. Therefore, finding the balance between professional intervention for purposes of prevention, crime escalation, and police responsibility is the community policing task. Yet, officers, virtually at every rank, cannot make decisions about professional intervention if policy, regulations, and employment expectations dictate otherwise. The traditional, incident-driven police organization (and policing as an institution) must alter policy, regulations and expectations to fit within a contemporary framework of policing strategies in the twenty-first century.

Overcoming the obstacles to community policing will not be an easy task. Zhao, Thurman, and Lovrich (2000, pp. 234–235) found that many departments continue to face significant impediments to the implementation of community policing and that many police agencies "do not appear to know what it is that they should be doing next" in this regard. Nonetheless, the effort appears to be worthwhile when we consider the lack of success of traditional policing in many areas. According to Overman (1994, p. 20), "The arguments for change are obviously to our past. The first question we must ask ourselves is, 'Are the streets safer than they were 20 years ago?' The obvious answer to this question is 'No.' 'Have we won the war on drugs?' Again the answer is 'No.' It is clearly time, then, to carefully consider alternatives to our traditional efforts."

It appears that the momentum associated with community policing in the 1980s and early 1990s has waned. Internal resistance continues, crime rates have dropped dramatically, and the economy has slowed. As indicated previously, many departments seem lost as to what steps they need to take to further community policing efforts. And yet, there can be little doubt that the basic premises of problem- and community-oriented policing are solid. While community policing is certainly not the panacea many had hoped for, it has directed attention toward the public as the most critical element of any policing system. Organizing and directing community members in the fight against disorder and crime are clearly worthwhile goals for the police as they strive to become better partners in improving quality of life in communities. Perhaps Kappeler and Kraska (1998, p. 308) put it best:

> The police (and criminal justice system) have become the premiere problem-solvers for some of society's most complex difficulties. Politicians and the bulk of the public fall back on juvenile curfews, increasing regulations, order enforcement, and target-hardening as a means to solve social problems rooted in gender, economic, and racial inequity. By staging its own death, the strong arm of the government is emerging rapidly in these times of high-modernity as our helping hand, promising us salvation from the irrationality of crime in an increasingly rationalized society.

Or, as Rusch (2001, p. 35) puts it, "Community policing is not a panacea but it is a tool to provide better relationship building, communication, and cooperation."

DISCUSSION QUESTIONS

1. List and discuss some of the problems characterizing traditional policing. Do you believe community policing can successfully address these problems? Why or why not?

2. What is community policing? Why is it believed to be a better approach than traditional policing?

3. Discuss problem-oriented policing and its relationship with community policing.

4. What are some of the criticisms of community policing? In your opinion, are these criticisms justified? Why or why not?

5. Are there any COP programs in your area? If so, discuss them. If not, why do you think they are not being attempted?

6. Why is there often resistance to community policing within police departments? How can such resistance be overcome?

7. What evidence exists that we need to consider alternatives to traditional policing? Is it reasonable to expect that community policing will solve all quality-of-life issues in the short-term? Why or why not?

REFERENCES

Barlow, D. E., & Barlow, M. H. (2000). *Policing in multicultural society: An American story.* Prospect Heights, IL: Waveland.

Breci, M. G. (1997). The transition to community policing: The department's role in upgrading officers' skills. *Policing, 20,* 766–776.

Brown, L. (1989, September). Community policing: A practical guide for police officials. In *Perspectives on policing.* Washington, DC: U.S. Department of Justice.

————. (1992a). An interview with Commissioner Lee P. Brown of New York. *Law Enforcement News*, *18*, 10–14.

————. (1992b, May). Violent crime and community involvement. *FBI Law Enforcement Bulletin*, *61*, 2–5.

Bureau of Justice Statistics. (1999). State and local law enforcement statistics. Available online at: http://www.ojp.usdoj.gov/bjs/sandlle.htm.

Burgreen, B., & McPherson, N. (1992). Neighborhood policing without a budget increase. *The Police Chief*, *59*, 31–33.

Cardarelli, A. P., McDevitt, J., & Baum, K. (1998). The rhetoric and reality of community policing in small and medium-sized cities and towns. *Policing*, *21*, 397–415.

Carey, L. R. (1994). Community policing for the suburban department. *Police Chief*, *61*, 24–26.

Community policing consortium. (2000, Sept.–Oct.). Community policing in review—successful strategies from around the nation. *Community Policing Exchange*. Washington, DC: Community Policing Consortium, 7, 4–5.

Cox, J. F. (1992). Small departments and community policing. *FBI Law Enforcement Bulletin*, *61*, 1–4.

Dolan, H. P. (1994). Community policing: Coping with internal backlash. *The Police Chief*, *61*, 28–32.

Eck, J. E., & Spelman, W. (1988). *Problem-solving: Problem-oriented policing in Newport News*. Washington, DC: National Institute of Justice.

Gardner, J. (2000). Building a responsive community. In Glensor, R. W., Correria, M. E., & Peak, K. J. (eds.), *Policing communities: Understanding crime and solving problems* (pp. 67–74). Los Angeles: Roxbury.

Glasser, J. (2000). The case of the missing cops. *U.S. News & World Report*, *129*, p. 22.

Goldstein, H. (1990). *Problem-oriented policing*. New York: McGraw-Hill.

————. (1979). Improving policing: A problem oriented approach. *Crime and Delinquency*, *25*, 236–258.

Hartnett, S. M., & Skogan, W. G. (1999, April). Community policing: Chicago's experience. In *National Institute of Justice Journal*. Washington, DC: National Institute of Justice.

Hatler, R. W. (1990, October). Operation CLEAN: Reclaiming City Neighborhoods. *FBI Law Enforcement Bulletin*, *59*, 23–25.

Hickman, M. J., & Reeves, B. A. (2001). *Community policing in local police departments, 1997 and 1999*. Washington, DC: Bureau of Justice Statistics.

Jesilow, P., Meyer, J., Parsons, D., & Tegler, W. (1998). Evaluating problem-oriented policing: A quasi-experiment. *Policing*, *21*, 449–464.

Kane, C. (1993). Community policing: Forging police-citizen partnerships. *The Compiler*, *13*, 1.

Kane, R. J. (2000). Permanent beat assignments in association with community policing: Assessing the impact on police officers' field activity. *Justice Quarterly*, *17*, 259–278.

Kappeler, V. E., & Kraska, P. B. (1998). A textual critique of community policing: Police adaption to high modernity. *Policing*, *21*, 293–313.

Kelling, G. L., & Stewart, J. K. (1989, May). Neighborhoods and police: The maintenance of civil authority. In *Perspective on the Police*. Washington, DC: U.S. Department of Justice.

Lurigo, A. J., & Rosenbaum, D. P. (1994). The impact of community policing on police personnel: A review of the literature. In Rosenbaum, D. P. (ed.), *The challenge of community policing: Testing the promises* (pp. 147–163). Thousand Oaks, CA: Sage.

NIJ Research in Brief. (1992, August). Community policing in Seattle: A model partnership between citizens and the police. Washington, DC: National Institute of Justice.

Offer, C. (1993). C-OP fads and emperors without clothes. *Law Enforcement News*, *19*, 8.

Oliver, W. M., & Bartgis, E. (1998). Community policing: A conceptual frame work. *Policing*, *21*, 490–509.

Overman, R. (1994). The case for community policing. *Police Chief*, *61*, 20–23.

Palmiotto, M. J. (2000). *Police misconduct: A reader for the 21st century*. Upper Saddle River, NJ: Prentice-Hall.

Peak, K. J., & Glensor, R. W. (1999). *Community policing and problem solving: Strategies and practices*. Upper Saddle River, NJ: Prentice-Hall.

Pisani, A. L. (1992). Dissecting community policing—Part 1. *Law Enforcement News*, *18*, 13.

Rusch, B. K. (2001). Community policing: Preparing for the new millennium. *Campus Law Enforcement Journal, 31*, 35.

Sadd, S., & Grinc, R. M. (2000). Implementation challenges in community policing. In Glensor, R. W., Correia, M. E., & Peak, K. J. (eds.), *Policing communities: Understanding crime and solving problems* (pp. 97–116). Los Angeles: Roxbury.

Skolnick, J. H., & Bayley, D. H. (1986). *The new blue line: Police innovation in six American cities.* New York: Free Press.

Spelman, W., & Eck, J. E. (2000). In Glensor, R. W., Correia, M. E., & Peak, K. J. (eds.), *Policing communities: Understanding crime and solving problems* (pp. 125–137). Los Angeles: Roxbury.

Stevens, D. J. (2001). *Case studies in community policing.* Upper Saddle River, NJ: Prentice-Hall.

Tafoya, W. L. (2000). The current and future state of community policing. In Glensor, R. W., Correia, M. E., & Peak, K. J. (eds.), *Policing communities: Understanding crime and solving problems* (pp. 304–314). Los Angeles: Roxbury.

Taylor, R. B., & Harrell, A. V. (2000). Physical environment and crime. In Glensor, R. W., Correia, M. E., & Peak, K. J. (eds.), *Policing communities: Understanding crime and solving problems* (pp. 167–181). Los Angeles: Roxbury.

Toch, H., & Grant, J. D. (1991). *Police as problem solvers.* Newark: Plenum.

Trojanowicz, R. C. (1990). Community policing is not police-community relations. *FBI Law Enforcement Bulletin, 59*, 6–11.

Trojanowicz, R. C., & Bucqueroux, B. (1992). Preventing individual and systemic corruption. *Footprints, 4*, 1–3.

Trojanowicz, R. C., Kappeler, V. E., Gaines, L. K., & Bucqueroux, B. (1998) *Community policing: A contemporary perspective,* 2nd ed. Cincinnati, OH: Anderson.

Vlasak, T. (1992). Walking the beat in Joliet, Illinois. *The Complier, 11*, 13–15.

Walker. S. (2001). *Police accountability.* Belmont, CA: Wadsworth/Thompson.

Walters, P. M. (1993). Community-oriented policing: A blend of strategies. *FBI Law Enforcement Bulletin, 62*, 20–23.

Zhao, J., Thurman, Q. C., & Lovrich, N. P. (2000). Community-oriented policing across the U.S. In Glensor, R. W., Correia, M. E., & Peak, K. J. (eds.), *Policing communities: Understanding crime and solving problems* (pp. 229–238). Los Angeles: Roxbury.

CHAPTER TWELVE

THE FUTURE OF POLICING IN THE UNITED STATES

Changing Images, Technology, and Terrorism

Although it is risky to make projections for the future, it is clear that a vision of where one is going is an important part of getting there. The following discussion of the future of policing in the United States is based on an analysis of current trends, projected demographic changes, and, in some instances, pure speculation. As Crank (1995, p. 107) noted with respect to divining the future of policing, "Any such effort is self-evidently preposterous, and therein lies the sheer delight of it. The notion that anyone can hope to predict the future of his or her own life for even the proximate moment, let alone the future of a social institution over the next eighteen years is pretentious."

THE PUBLIC AND THEIR POLICE

As we have shown, police strategies do not exist in a vacuum. Legislation, political attitudes, and local resources shape these strategies. Still, there is room for change in the attitudes and resources, and change must be regarded as a critical ingredient in effective policing. New police strategies are being, and must be, adopted to meet the changing needs of communities over time. According to Bayley and Shearing (1996, pp. 585–606), policing is experiencing a process of "restructuring that is being driven by the fear of crime, the inability of the government to satisfy society's desire for security, the co-modification of security, the increase in mass private property, and cultural individualism."

Future police organizations may or may not resemble today's police. According to Holden (1994, p. 344), "The emerging police organization is one that will retain some vestiges of traditional policing but will be completely different in other areas. The emphasis will be on identifying community problems and solving those problems in cooperation with various community organizations. The new police officer must be educated, better trained, and have a more thorough understanding of the police role within a multifaceted society." Thibault, Lynch, and McBride (2001, p. 434) recently extrapolated current trends in policing to develop the following future strategies.

1. Deployment of community policing, including more authority for remote supervisors and human service/communications training for officers

2. Proactive planning, including critical incident management, centralized rapid response teams

3. Greater dependence on private police, auxiliary police, and community volunteers; major corporation private police begin to have more public police powers

4. Police executives are highly educated, professionalized, and move between major police departments.

Palmiotto (1999, p. 138) notes, "American society exists in a changing world. The society in which we live in the early twenty-first century will be different from what it has been in the late twentieth century. The age of information will have taken hold. We will be able to communicate visually and orally with anyone in the world instantaneously." According to Carter and Radelet (1999, p. 488), "Visions of the future conjure illusions of streamlined, high-technology devices, which can help us perform tasks at high speed with great efficacy." They envision problem solving simplified, job performance increasing, and a higher quality of life as a result of the implementation of these innovations.

Jurkanin, Bender, and Fischer (2000, pp. 31–32) predict that in the year 2017, the major focus for law enforcement will be in the following areas:

1. Youth-oriented issues: Youth will be involved in gangs that will be better organized and more capable of recruiting and retaining members. In addition, with the decrease in the prominence of family-based structure and values, more youth will be attracted to fringe activities such as cults and hate groups.

2. Multijurisdictional and technologically oriented crime: The potential for criminal activity in this arena ranges from child pornography and solicitation to finance-based crime to international terrorism.

3. Conflict between the rich and poor: It is anticipated the gulf between the "haves" and "have-nots" will widen. On one hand, enclaves of poor will require police to deal with the maladies of the poor—drugs, violence, abuse, and neglect. Police will, at the same time, be required to address criminal activities of those with substantial incomes—computer crimes, embezzlement, and child molestation. This will require a great diversity of talent and capability by individual police agencies.

A number of demographic, economic, and workforce changes will affect the future of policing. For example, the U.S. population is expected to increase to 402 million by 2050 and to 572 million people by 2101 (U.S. Census Bureau, 2000). The Hispanic population will approach 30 percent of the population, while Asians and blacks will each constitute about 12 percent of the population. The United States will be a more culturally diverse society (Palmiotto, 1990, p. 138). In the twenty-first century, race again will become more prevalent in the administration of justice. The current regressive state of the criminal justice system represents a shift from the rehabilitative model of treating offenders to one of increased incarceration due in part to society's low-level tolerance for any type of offender. Those persons most affected during increased periods of protecting society from criminal elements are blacks, the poor, and the legally underrepresented. We will see an increase in arrest, conviction, and incarceration of blacks and other minorities, because prosecutors will revert to scare tactics to encourage cooperation and admission of guilt (Morgan-Sharp, 1999, p. 389).

In the future, elderly persons will present a significant challenge to health care, police, and local government organizations. Senior citizens will pay lower taxes yet require increased levels of service from these organizations (Jurkanin, Bender, & Fischer, 2000). In particular, senior citizens are expected to migrate to rural areas and present substantial challenges for county sheriff's departments and small rural law enforcement agencies. According to Bennett (1993, p. 86), "We cannot simply continue with business as usual. Since most agencies are not equipped with crystal balls, true progress comes from trying something new, seeing if it works, making changes and trying it again. If the organization and its leaders are afraid to fail, stagnation quickly sets in."

A survey of police chiefs (Dale, 2000, pp. 117–122) identified six important concerns for the next decade:

1. Employment—Hiring, and retaining, professional, ethical, educated, culturally diverse personnel
2. Budget—Competitive salary, unions, grants, taxes
3. Technology—Internal/external communication, training, managing technology
4. Crime—Juvenile, elderly, white-collar computer, drugs

5. Growth—Population, diversity, geographic, build-out
6. Quality-of-life issues—Effective community policing, strategic management planning

Consider this scenario from the study by Sparrow, Moore, and Kennedy (1992, p. 228):

Imagine what would happen if a beat officer, during his or her first week on the beat, could be presented with an analysis of all the calls for service received from the area in the previous six months. And imagine he or she was then told that a significant performance measure would be the *decrease* in calls over the next six months. Naturally there would be occasional emergencies out of the beat officer's control. But the officer's attention would immediately be focused on repeat callers, sources of danger and anxiety in the community, and the identification and solution of underlying problems—exactly the commission a beat officer needs.

According to Couper and Lobitz (1993, p. 16),

The shift from time to turf is an absolute organizational necessity for the future of policing. Being shift-driven has had a destructive influence on the ability of the police to listen, relate to and effectively act on community-identified police problems.

Policing has come full circle. We are once again in the position of having to admit that the police cannot be all things to all people and that the police can be effective only when they have widespread community support. This is not at all surprising when we realize that municipal police emerged as a result of citizen needs. (The formation of the London Metropolitan Police is perhaps the most striking, but certainly not the only example.) Citizen need, however, changes at a sometimes frightening pace, depending on economics, demographics, and social policies. To continue to meet the changing demands of citizens, police agencies must first have a realistic view of these needs and, second, invite citizen input as to how best to meet them. A full partnership between the police and other citizens is necessary because the "police themselves are not to blame for the fact that crimes are so common, neighborhoods so frightened, and civility so fragile. And more police, with more technology, will not be enough to remove crime, calm neighborhoods, and promote civility"(William O. Douglass Institute, 1984, p. 9).

Assessing community needs on a continuing basis is the only way in which a realistic understanding of them can be attained; this requires research efforts sponsored by the police.

RESEARCH AND PLANNING AS POLICE FUNCTIONS

"In a society such as ours," state Alpert and Dunham (1992, p. 195), "there are bound to be different priorities placed on the police by different people who live in different communities. In addition, police officers are not all the same, do not have similar opinions or expectations, do not perform at the same level, and do not operate with the same style." How are the police to respond to these differing public priorities, in what ways will different types of officers respond, and what styles of policing are best suited to particular communities? These and other questions relating to areas such as crime and traffic management, level of satisfaction with supervisors, amount of perceived stress among officers, civil and criminal liability of police personnel, and dozens of other areas can best be addressed through the implementation of proper research and planning techniques.

In the research area, projects may be as simple as surveying community residents to determine their priorities, fears, satisfaction with police services, and perceptions of police misconduct, or as complex as attempting to measure the relationships among education, training, job performance, and supervisory evaluations. We might want to assess the impact of combined enforcement groups on drug trafficking or to develop a profile of a specific type of offender. Or we might want to evaluate officer productivity in terms of certain criteria. All of these projects require a certain degree of expertise in research (and, for that matter, a good deal of planning).

Police administrators could, of course, contract for such projects, but the potential for miscommunication in "hired hand" research is considerable, and research funds and grants are not always available for projects when they need to be completed (Fitzgerald & Cox, 1994, pp. 7–10). Thus, greater reliance on in-house research and evaluation is desirable for a number of reasons. The conduct of in-house research requires that at least some staff members have the training and expertise necessary to design and implement scientific inquiries. The value and ease of conduct of such inquiries is increased considerably when an evaluation component is built into new initiatives from the start. According to Fitzgerald and Cox (1994, p. 2),

> In order to understand the nature and current state of affairs in criminal justice, practitioners and students alike must be able to read and comprehend research reports and must know when and how to apply the results of such research. Many will also find it necessary or advantageous to conduct research themselves to do their jobs as effectively and efficiently as possible. It is quite true that any in-depth study of research methods and statistical analysis would take years, but it is equally true that a student can achieve a basic understanding in a relatively short period of time. Complicated research designs and sophisticated statistical procedures do not necessarily result in better or more useful research, and often, useful insights can be gained through relatively simple research designs and elementary statistical analyses.

Conducting such research, of course, requires considerable planning, both short and long range. For a variety of reasons, police administrators have regularly demonstrated their abilities to engage in the former, but rarely in the latter. This might have been true in part because of a public service mentality that characterized not only police chiefs, but also other chief executive officers in the public sector. This mentality was, for years, based on the premise that last year's budget plus 10 percent was a safe bet in most fiscal years. In the public sector, planning for no increases in funding, or for budgetary cutbacks, was unheard of, and the assumptions appeared to be (1) that evaluation of programs was beyond the responsibility of the public-sector executives and (2) that fiscal responsibility was less important than in the private sector, as funds, especially for emergency services, would always be made available.

As we have seen, in the past, several dramatic changes occurred in the public sector. First, taxpayer revolts made it clear that zero-based budgeting and budget cutbacks were not only possible, but also likely alternatives to the automatic 10 percent increase. Second, the demand for accountability in the public sector increased. The need for full-time fire departments was questioned in some small communities; public safety officers who would perform both police and fire-fighting functions were hired in some areas; and police departments began to lose positions through attrition. Third, women and minorities were hired in greater numbers, and the issue of their performance on the job led to a number of evaluation studies.

Fourth, the Kansas City Preventive Patrol Experiment (Kelling et al., 1974) demonstrated the ability of police agencies to participate in the design and evaluation of responsible research. Fifth, the number of well-educated police officers (at all levels) increased, making possible the formation and utilization of research and planning units along with other specialized units. Sixth, personal computers became available at reasonable cost, their capabilities were considerably improved, and police personnel became acquainted with and accustomed to them. Designing, implementing, and evaluating research within police departments is now a real possibility.

It appears unlikely that these trends will be reversed in the decade ahead. In fact, Sherman (1990, p. 9) indicates that over the past twenty years, the "difference in the willingness of police agencies to cooperate with research is astounding. The police are right out front with the medical community in doing the best possible kinds of research to evaluate what they're doing." The number of police personnel with knowledge of basic research and statistical techniques is increasing as the number of college-educated officers increases and as the quality of college programs in criminal justice curriculums improves.

All of the factors outlined thus far make it likely that research and planning will become increasingly important to and utilized by police administrators seeking to justify new programs and demonstrate the value of existing efforts.

CHANGING THE IMAGE OF PATROL OFFICERS

In spite of the fact that specialization is likely to continue to characterize police in the twenty-first century, patrol officers will remain the backbone of policing as a result of their sheer numbers, frequency of contact with the public, and the shift to community policing. Patrol officers, as the eyes, ears, arms, and legs of the police organization, need to be competent, well informed, concerned, and self-confident. Yet patrol officers of the twenty-first century have often been those who could not progress to other specializations or supervisory roles. Many, if not most, young officers cannot wait to put in their time on patrol in order to be promoted to a supervisory position or transferred to the investigative division. College students in criminal justice programs frequently ask, "Do I have to start as a patrol officer? Isn't there some way I can go directly into investigations or supervision?" To a great extent, those who remain in patrol are those who have been unsuccessful in demonstrating the qualities required for these other positions. When referring to a twenty-year veteran of the streets, it is not uncommon to hear, "He's just a patrol officer" or "She's still on patrol." In fact, many veteran patrol officers think of themselves in these terms, and some regard themselves as failures because of their inability to progress to so-called bigger and better things.

Patrol is seldom recognized as a specialization within police agencies, and being a member of the patrol division is somehow often regarded as being less glamorous than being an investigator or a supervisor. Yet extremely capable patrol officers are not all that common, and the function does require special skills. In short, those who perform the patrol function well are specialists in their own right and should be recognized and rewarded as such. They are specialists in handling whatever types of calls come their way and whatever types of encounters in which they become involved. Not everyone can perform these tasks well. Yet there has seldom been an effort made to recognize and reward those who perform well. In fact, young officers are encouraged to leave the patrol ranks as soon as possible. According to Nowicki (1997, p. 370), "Patrol is often a punitive assignment for those officers who have incurred our displeasure. You rarely see an officer who gets into trouble and is taken off patrol and put into investigation or administration, but you often see the reverse."

This strategy makes little sense when we stop to consider that the reputation of any police agency depends greatly on the daily encounters between patrol personnel and other citizens. If we are truly interested in good community relations, we need to reward those officers who interact both frequently and civilly with other citizens. According to Nowicki (1997, p. 370), "If we really believe that patrol is the backbone of a police department, we must find a better and more tangible way of delivering that message to our officers." Some programs, such as the "dual career ladder system" as well as other "progressive salary schedule" systems, encourage productive officers to stay in patrol by rewarding their efforts monetarily. Such efforts need to be expanded if patrol personnel are to regard themselves, and be regarded by the public, positively. The importance of retaining competent patrol officers becomes increasingly apparent as community-oriented police programs spread, as officers become less isolated from the public, and as cooperative efforts between the police and other citizens expand (Grossman & Doherty, 1994).

EXPANDING THE CONCEPTS OF COMMUNITY-ORIENTED AND PROBLEM-ORIENTED POLICING

There is little doubt that the wave of the future in policing will involve expanded involvement of civilians in police work as employees in police agencies, as members of advisory and planning groups, as members of direct support groups (such as neighborhood watch and neighborhood patrol groups), and as critics and reviewers of police activities. The message at last appears to have become clear: The police cannot control crime or maintain order by themselves. The involvement of citizens other than police officers in crime prevention, apprehension of offenders, and order maintenance is absolutely essential. A partnership is required, but the partnership must be a real one. In the past, police partnerships with other citizens meant the police allowing these citizens to be minimally involved in police activities in which the police served as the experts, in which citizen input was sought in certain areas but denied in others, and in which policy making remained the exclusive right of the police. Consider this assessment by Greene (1989, p. 365):

> The importance of citizen involvement in providing public safety and security cannot be overstated. Resources for crime control have dwindled over the years. At the same time public demand for police services has increased. While citizen involvement in community-police programs is no cure-all for the problems of crime and social disorder, it is essential for the maintenance of democratic values. Furthermore, law enforcement agencies can hardly continue to exclude the clients and producers of police service from the policies and decisions affecting the "quality of life" in American communities.

According to Zhao (2001, pp. 191–203), four forces favor a change in the future to community policing.

1. Community policing programs are popular with police executives, the public, and community leaders.
2. The federal government has endorsed the institutionalization of community policing under the Federal Violent Crime Control and Law Enforcement Act.
3. Advanced technology has enhanced the objectives and operations of community policing. (i.e., computerized statistics, automated mapping of crime locations)
4. The crime rate has declined under the progressive implementation of community policing.

In keeping with the trend toward more community involvement in policing, we are likely to see increasing efforts on behalf of the police to improve citizen cooperation in high-crime areas (see Highlight 12.1). While many of these areas have traditionally been written off by the police (as well as by the larger society) simply because they are high-crime areas, the reality is that most of the people living in such areas are not criminals but victims. They continue to be victims because the streets and dwellings do not belong to them, but to gangs and other less well organized but equally predatory criminals. The police patrol these areas and maintain a semblance of order, but the overwhelming evidence is that, by themselves, they have little impact on crime. In spite of gang crimes units, gang intelligence, and the use of informants, the police cannot, nor are they ever likely to, obtain enough information to prevent crimes in these areas or to apprehend the majority of offenders.

Preliminary evidence from community and problem-oriented policing strategies suggests that their chief benefit may be in making area residents feel safer, although these strategies may have little direct impact on crime rates. If, however, neighborhood residents feel safer, they may make greater use of the streets, which, over the long term, may make the streets less accessible to criminal elements. If well-planned, coordinated

■ ■ ■ ■ ■

HIGHLIGHT 12.1
GIVING CITIZENS A VOICE IN POLICING POLICY

Getting out of patrol cars, walking the beat, knowing all the stakeholders in one's patrol sector—these strategies are widely recognized as part and parcel of the community policing philosophy. However, actually soliciting input from the citizenry about the way you are providing policing is a strategy that is perhaps not as widely applied in community policing circles. A minority of departments have established citizen groups, even though they may have embraced many of the other recognized community policing practices.

Why are otherwise progressive departments hesitant to bring the community truly "inside?" For some, the community represents "naysayers," "police bashers," "busybodies," "vigilantes" or "police wannabes." Many departments seem to believe that the community should only have its say via the block club or neighborhood organization with all the associated bureaucracy.

The city of Buffalo, however, offers a model for more meaningful and sustained citizen involvement. In spite of (or maybe because of) its economic, racial and social diversity, Buffalo has historically pulled together in times of need. Time and again Buffalo has lived up to its reputation as the "City of Good Neighbors." When a progressive administration took office in 1994, it was elected largely on a platform of bringing the city out of the "dark ages" and making smarter use of this particular asset.

The new regime made a concerted effort to seek out the city's "good neighbors" and invite these average citizens to assist the police department—but in a way that went beyond just being the law enforcement agency's "extra eyes and ears." The police commissioner's new Citizen Advisory Group (CAG) would bring a new perspective into policing.

To build membership, the city reached out to Buffalo's numerous community-based, commercial and faith-based organizations and asked them to nominate representatives. This strategy ensured that the entity would not be seen as

"handpicked" by the commissioner or as being used as a "rubber stamp" for departmental decisions. The roughly 40 members represented a cross-section of the city's population and closely reflected Buffalo's diversity.

Two CAG committees were developed after polling the membership to prioritize pressing issues. The Planning, Programming and Operations Committee (PP&O) studies the department's inner workings to see what is needed in terms of computer technology, staffing, recruitment policies, officer qualifications, diversity training, budget, managerial rights, equipment and police morale. Committee members interviewed command staff and rank-and-file officers while participating in ride-alongs.

Following each committee meeting, the group reports its recommendations to the commissioner along with supporting published information. The PP&O Committee also produces an annual position paper citing the committee's proposals, "Critical Needs for the Buffalo Police Department," which is forwarded to the city government.

A glaring need to improve relations between youth and the police prompted the CAG to form a second committee, the Youth and Police Committee (Y&P). The Y&P members worked on strategies for bringing the police and youth together in positive situations. For example, the Y&P members sponsored high school summits in which student and police panelists addressed questions from the students and engaged in dialogue. Often the dialogue was heated, but common ground was usually found.

The Y&P committee decided to reach out to seventh- and eighth-graders by offering one-day youth-police learning labs at the Buffalo Police Department headquarters. More than 500 students have come together with the police in a classroom setting to learn to recognize and prevent crime. Juvenile officers, family and city court judges, detectives from the Narcotics and Burglary units, school security officers, transit police

(continued)

HIGHLIGHT 12.1 Continued

and a halfway house graduate have been among the scheduled speakers. Students are shown the lockup and line-up rooms and participate in hands-on activities, such as self-defense demonstrations and role-playing. The 1999 academy promoted an anti-violence theme. One of the highlights was a hands-on demonstration of the effects of violence on the body conducted by a local hospital trauma nurse.

CITIZEN INPUT
ON DIVERSITY ISSUES INVITED

The police commissioner recently called the CAG together to explore the diversity issues that affect police departments internally and externally, such as racial hiring quotas, public discrimination, police behavior and attitudes, and public perception. Buffalo, and indeed the police department itself, is experiencing cultural and racial change. With a growing Hispanic and Asian population, Buffalo continues to evolve beyond the traditional mix of blacks and whites. For this reason, it made sense to expand cultural diversity training for recruits and for the rank-and-file accompanied by a strong message from command staff that racial, ethnic and cultural discrimination will not be tolerated. The CAG diversity committee's goal is to support a consistent, proactive and professional department in dealing with diversity issues. A positively focused citizen advisory group can become ambassadors for a police department. They can provide advocacy, ideas, advice and feedback, and formulate successful strategies that enhance the image of policing. A law enforcement agency will benefit from talent that is given freely through volunteer hours, shared expertise, partnerships and the forward-thinking individuals committed to doing things better.

Graves, Michele. Community Policing Consortium, 1726 M. St., N.W., Suite 801, Washington, DC 20036.

programs between the police and other citizens are initiated and implemented in such a way that more offenders are apprehended, or their fear of being apprehended increases to the extent that they move their activities elsewhere, the sense of territoriality may reemerge, even in high-crime areas. Once this happens, residents and the police together can take back the streets and dwellings from criminal elements. Such efforts will be successful, however, only when area residents are involved in the planning and implementation of policies and programs. Examples of the kinds of changes that can occur exist in several Chicago housing projects where tenant management has been initiated and supported by residents and housing authorities.

Long-term solutions to the problems of high-crime areas depend on the mutual respect and understanding of the police and neighborhood residents. Police officers who continue to serve, and are perceived, as soldiers of occupation in minority neighborhoods are unlikely to be effective in either crime control or order maintenance. They are very likely to continue to regard assignment to such areas as dangerous and unpleasant and to participate in perpetuating the isolation and alienation that exists for them and the other citizens they police. This increases the likelihood that what now appear to be separate incidents involving protests by citizens in the "underclass" against government policies and practices will once again become part of a nationwide protest with the police as targets, unable to maintain order, prevent crime, or apprehend offenders. Only real partnerships between the police and other citizens in general, and citizens in high-crime areas in particular, are likely to be successful in preventing the police from playing a major, undesirable, and unpleasant role in such protests. According to Bobinsky, 1994, p. 19),

> Community-oriented policing does not transform police officers into social workers. It does, however, empower officers to connect individuals with problems to agencies that can help them. COP does involve a few extra minutes handling each call, but this time is well-spent. Most importantly, community-oriented policing recognizes the value of the police and the community working together to reduce crime. A more involved community translates into a community more willing to cooperate with its police department.

According to Cronkhite (2001, p. 35), an emerging trend emanating from community and problem oriented policing might be "community accountability policing" (CAP). This approach involves an effort to enlist the public in determining problems to be solved but holds the police responsible for solving these problems.

In spite of the enthusiasm for community policing, there is reason to be cautious as well. While the approach seems, on the face, to make sense, evidence of success is sketchy at best. This may be because community policing efforts are still in their infancy, but it also may be that the promise exceeds the practice. According to Carter and Radelet (1999, p. 513), the future of community policing is "precarious"; it has a number of debilitating elements:

1. Community policing is difficult to test and measure, so its complete effects are unknown.
2. It is conceptual, thus difficult to understand.
3. It is philosophical, thus difficult to "transplant" between departments.
4. It is nontraditional, thus it does not look like "real police work" and requires organizational change.
5. It is not "flashy," thus diminishing its political appeal.

Can police officers help solve social problems that lead to crime more effectively than others who have tried before them? Will such attempts, even if successful, lead to reduction in crime and improvement in the quality of life? Only careful evaluation and assessment can provide answers to these questions (Joseph, 1994).

CHANGING THE IMAGE OF THE POLICE

Gender and Race

An important part of the community-oriented policing concept involves making the police as representative of the community as possible. Over the next few years we can expect to see continued research on police performance by gender and race. And, if the results of such research follow already established patterns, few if any significant differences in the performance of police officers will be accounted for by gender or race. The rationales for excluding women and minorities from policing will no longer be accepted, and the benefits of hiring police officers from culturally diverse backgrounds will become increasingly apparent.

There are, however, some difficulties in changing the police image with respect to gender and race. Foremost among these are affirmative action programs based on consent decrees that lead to the hiring and/or promotion of unqualified women and minorities (Alpert & Dunham, 1997, p. 47). Hiring and/or promoting police officers of either gender or any race simply to meet quotas and without regard to qualifications is detrimental to the officers hired, their police colleagues, the citizenry at large, and other members of the same gender and/or race for most of the same reasons that discrimination in terms of gender and race are detrimental. To avoid the negative consequences of discriminatory hiring of either variety in the future, race and gender of applicants should be considered only after the issue of proper qualification has been decided. This was always, and remains, the intent of the Equal Employment Opportunity Act and the Americans with Disabilities Act. Court-mandated programs, however, have not infrequently contradicted this intent, resulting in lawsuits based on allegations of reverse discrimination, increasingly bitter feelings on behalf of qualified candidates and practitioners toward those unqualified recruits, serious difficulties for the department in terms of the performance of the latter, and poor service to the community in general.

According to research, the number of female police officers is increasing and will probably continue to increase in the future. However, a study of International Association of Chiefs of Police members concluded the following (IACP, 1998, pp. 1–35):

1. Many departments lack strategies for recruiting women.
2. Female officers face gender discrimination and a "glass ceiling" that inhibits promotion.
3. Sexual harassment occurs in many departments.
4. Few mentoring programs exist for female officers.

Only when all new police recruits meet the same basic qualifications will there be any chance that race and gender will cease to be the controversial issues they have traditionally been in American law enforcement (which simply reflects the larger society). Only if this happens will the difficulties in recruiting qualified women and minorities be eased, and the goal of a community–police partnership, which includes all segments of the community, be achievable.

Civilianization

In keeping with community-oriented policing efforts, increasing numbers of civilians are likely to become involved in policing as employees of police agencies and as volunteers. This trend is beneficial in that it helps to break down barriers between the police and other citizens, often frees police officers to concentrate more of their time on matters for which they have been specifically trained, and fosters the belief that civilians play an important role in both order maintenance and law enforcement.

Accreditation

The image of the police is slowly being changed as a result of the incorporation of high standards of performance and conduct by many departments through the process of accreditation. A growing number of police agencies have demonstrated their desire to be considered among the best in the profession by undergoing the painstaking, lengthy process of accreditation by the Commission on Accreditation for Law Enforcement Agencies. Already more than four hundred police agencies have demonstrated their ability to comply with the majority of the 439 standards utilized by the Commission, with another five hundred or so awaiting accreditation (CALEA Online, 2000). Agencies originally accredited have now been through the reaccreditation process (see Highlight 12.2).

Many other agencies are doing self-evaluations to determine whether to pursue accreditation. Even for those who decide not to apply for accreditation, there is, for the first time, a set of standards that allows police personnel to examine the extent to which they are operating according to the recognized standards of the profession. Some states have formed associations that help individual agencies prepare for accreditation, and this has fostered improved communications among agencies. Additionally, accreditation now requires the use of community surveys on a regular basis, thereby enhancing the police–community partnership and the use of research techniques by police personnel. The trend toward accreditation and the accompanying benefits seems well established.

Lateral Entry

The concept of lateral entry, or movement from one geographic location to enter employment in another area, has been around for some time but is still resisted by a majority of police agencies. Acceptance of the concept would allow police agencies to recruit from other agencies personnel for various supervisory as well as line positions and would allow officers from one department to apply for comparable positions in other departments. As it is, most police officers wishing to transfer from one area or department to another have to start as entry-level officers, even though they may have attained higher rank. While we are willing to accept lateral entry at the level of police chief, we have been far more hesitant to do so at other levels, limiting the pool of applicants for supervisory positions to those inside the department.

Although this strategy does protect insiders from competition from the outside, it is based on the assumption that there are always individuals qualified for promotion inside the department. This assumption, however, does not always hold true. Further, refusal to accept lateral entry at entry-level positions deprives police departments of the pool of already trained applicants seeking to leave their current positions and/or

■ ■ ■ ■ ■

HIGHLIGHT 12.2
THE ACCREDITATION PROCESS

The voluntary accreditation program can generally be divided to two parts: the standards and the process. The standards, discussed in the Standards Manual (Standards for Law Enforcement Agencies), are the building blocks from which everything else evolves. Left to themselves, however, the standards, as with all of the previous law enforcement standard-setting endeavors, would be nothing more than a pile of bricks. The process provides the blueprint and mortar to shape the standards into forms that are sturdy, useful, and lasting for the agency. The process provides order, guidance, and stability to those going through the program and ensures that the Commission can recognize professional achievement in a consistent, uniform manner.

There are five phases in the accreditation process:

1. Application
2. Self-assessment
3. On-site Assessment
4. Commission Review and Decision
5. Maintaining Compliance and Reaccreditation

APPLICATION PHASE

Agencies usually begin with a simple request for information. Staff will provide a free Information Package to the agency. The contents give descriptive information about the standards and program as well as explain how to get involved and order CALEA manuals and products.

The next step is to purchase an Application Package for $250. This package contains everything necessary to study and enroll in the program. The price of the package will be applied to the agency's accreditation fee if the agency signs an Accreditation Agreement within six months. While not officially working on accreditation, an agency is listed in Commission records as being "in the process" once it purchases an Application Package. Staff is available to answer questions or provide general assistance.

The accreditation process begins formally when an agency executes an Accreditation Agreement, which specifies the obligations of the agency and the Commission. Entry into the program is voluntary but requires the commitment of the agency's Chief Executive Officer, who signs the Agreement on behalf of the agency. Along with its signed Agreement, the agency submits a completed Application Form, Legal Basis and Eligibility Statement, and its accreditation fee, which is based on the agency's size.

After reviewing the agency's application materials, the Commission makes a preliminary determination of its eligibility to participate in the accreditation program. The Commission's Executive Director then signs the Accreditation Agreement, which is returned to the agency with an Agency Profile Questionnaire (APQ). The agency has thirty-six months from the date the Commission's Executive Director signs the Accreditation Agreement to perform its self-assessment.

The agency sends to staff the completed APQ containing agency-specific information to facilitate interaction with the accreditation manager to determine applicability of standards, interpret standards, and provide program-related assistance. The APQ is generally completed by the accreditation manager and is forwarded over the signature of the CEO. The information requested is for staff use only. Answers should be provided as conveniently as possible and "best estimate" may supersede research for precise accuracy in all cases.

SELF-ASSESSMENT PHASE

The return of the APQ triggers the delivery of all necessary materials for the accreditation manager to use in conducting the agency's self-assessment. The manager initiates agency self-assessment, which involves a thorough examination by the agency to determine whether it complies with all applicable standards (see Self-assessment Manual).

The agency prepares forms and develops "proofs of compliance" for applicable standards (including brief explanations for not complying with other standards) and assembles the forms and "proofs" in a manner that will facilitate a review by Commission assessors. The agency also develops plans for accomplishing its public information requirements and on-site assessment, which pertain to activities for the next phase.

When the agency is satisfied that it has completed all compliance, preparation, and planning tasks, it notifies the Commission that it is ready to become a candidate for accreditation. The Commission approves the agency's candidate status, requests public information and on-site plans, and invoices the agency for its estimated on-site costs.

ON-SITE ASSESSMENT PHASE

The agency pays its on-site fees and submits its public information and on-site plans. The Commission selects a team of trained assessors, free of conflict with the candidate agency, and schedules all activities for the assessment team's travel, accommodations, and on-site review of the agency during a period mutually agreeable to all parties.

During the on-site visit, the assessors, acting as representatives of the Commission, review all standards and, in particular, verify the agency's compliance with all applicable standards. The assessors' relationship with the candidate agency is nonadversarial. Assessors provide the agency with verbal feedback on their progress during, and at the conclusion of, the assessment.

Later, the assessors submit a formal, written report of their on-site activities and findings through staff; a copy is forwarded to the agency. If the final report reflects compliance with all applicable standards and with required on-site activities, the agency is scheduled for a Commission review. If compliance issues remain unresolved, the agency may return to the self-assessment phase to complete unfinished work, or it may choose other options, e.g., appeal or voluntary withdrawal. A final assessment report is forwarded to the Commission when all applicable standards and required activities have been complied with. The Commission schedules a hearing at one of its meetings, usually the meeting immediately following the on-site assessment. The agency and its Chief Executive Officer are invited to attend, although attendance is not required.

COMMISSION REVIEW AND DECISION PHASE

The agency makes plans (optional) to attend the scheduled hearing. At the hearing, the Commission reviews the final report and receives testimony from agency personnel, assessors, staff, or others. If satisfied that the agency has met all compliance requirements, the Commission awards the agency accredited status. Accreditation is for a period of three years. The agency is given an opportunity to critique the entire process following the award of accredited status.

The Commission furnishes the agency with a certificate of accreditation and encourages the agency to make arrangements for a formal presentation ceremony in its community.

MAINTAINING COMPLIANCE AND REACCREDITATION PHASE

To maintain accredited status, the accredited agency must remain in compliance with applicable standards. The agency submits Annual Reports to the Commission attesting to continued compliance and reporting changes or difficulties experienced during the year, including actions taken to resolve noncompliance. If necessary, the Commission reserves the right to schedule interim hearings to consider continuing accredited status if noncompliance becomes a serious issue. At the conclusion of the three-year period, the Commission offers the agency an opportunity to repeat the process and continue accredited status into the future.

Commission on Accreditation for Law Enforcement Agencies, Inc., 10306 Eaton Place, Suite 320, Fairfax, VA 22303. www.calea.org.

locations in search of better opportunities. While lateral entry may not become commonplace during the next decade, there is little doubt that its benefits outweigh the objections raised against it, and more and more police administrators, city managers, and personnel directors are likely to recognize this fact.

Training

Police personnel will have increasing opportunities to participate in training offered by a variety of training institutes. Among the more popular of these training groups are the Northwestern University Center for Public Safety, the Southern Police Institute, the Institute of Police Technology and Management, and the FBI National Academy, all of which offer courses ranging in length from a week to several months. Courses offered by these institutes cover topics ranging from traffic investigation to executive management. At California's Command College, future concerns of police officers and agencies are addressed. The College covers topics such as "Defining the Future," "Human Resource Management," and "Handling Conflict." Controversial topics and ideas are discussed and alternatives to traditional policing are outlined (Lieberman, 1990).

All training is, or should be, interrelated. The special skills learned at institutes such as those mentioned need to be updated on a continuing basis and can be shared with others through in-service training by those who have attended the institutes. Such sharing is both cost effective and rewarding to those who have received the training and should be encouraged on a widespread basis. In the past, the effects of training have infrequently been properly assessed by police agencies because of the assumptions that the information provided is understandable and absorbed. Increasingly, routine evaluations, which include a pretest of attendees' knowledge of the material to be presented and a post-test of such knowledge, are being employed. This trend should continue, because failure to evaluate training may lead to a waste of training resources. The content of police training, of course, varies with time, place, type of personnel involved, subject matter, and training goals. In general, however, it may be said that the content should be relevant to the needs of trainees, timely, well organized, and clearly presented. When these requirements are met, trainees can best appreciate the value of the training. It is imperative that the information conveyed in training sessions be current and accurately conveyed. The range of subjects, which may be covered in training sessions, is limited only by the imagination of planners and presenters.

A basic purpose of training is to keep police personnel up to date with respect to important changes in the profession. In a larger sense, however, the purposes of training depend on the way in which the role of the police is defined. As indicated throughout this book, in the 1960s and 1970s, crime fighting and law enforcement were emphasized, and, to some extent, many officers still view these aspects of the police role as the most important part of police work. As a result, training courses dealing with survival techniques, patrol techniques, criminal investigation, use of force, and the law are among the most popular courses. It is typically easy to recruit officers for courses dealing with these issues.

According to Kelling (1999, p. 4),

> We now understand that telling officers only what they cannot do, which is so typical of police manuals and rules and regulations, has not improved the quality of policing. We know as well that the work world of police is too complex to tell officers exactly what they should do in every circumstance. The only alternative left for the management of most police work is to teach officers how to think about what they should do, do it, and then talk about it, so that they improve their practice over time and share their emerging values, knowledge, and skills with their colleagues and the profession.

Today we recognize that while law enforcement and crime fighting are critical parts of the police role, they are not the most important in terms of time spent or citizen satisfaction. The fact that today's police personnel spend the majority of their time negotiating settlements between spouses or lovers or neighbors and providing other services that have little or nothing to do with law enforcement will become increasingly apparent. Successful intervention into the daily lives of citizens requires such skills as well as cooperation on the part of the non-police citizens involved. Increasingly then, communications skills (both verbal and nonverbal) and human/community/minority relations skills are emerging as among the most important assets of a competent, effective police officer. According to Birzer (1999, pp. 16–19), police training must focus on issues related to conflict resolution and quality of life rather than on the mechanical and technical aspects of policing. He concluded that police officers should receive training in interpersonal skills, ethnic diversity, drug and alcohol awareness, and domestic violence.

But where are these skills to be learned? A look at basic training curriculums indicates that little emphasis is placed on these skills in that setting. Yet communicating with others in the process of negotiating is what police officers do most often. Some police officers have excellent skills in these areas, and others, practically none. The importance of these skills is most clearly illustrated by focusing on those officers who lack them. Such officers are unlikely to get cooperation from diverse segments of the public, either because they alienate other citizens by assuming an authority figure stance as a defense for their poor communications skills or because they cannot express clearly and convincingly what they want or need the public to do. They receive little input from the public about crime or their own performances. They routinely enforce the law in an attempt to maintain order when their more skilled colleagues could have maintained order without resorting to arrest. They become unnecessarily involved in physical encounters. They create numerous and constant headaches for their superiors or, if they are supervisors, for those who work for them.

Training in communications, human relations, minority relations, analysis of encounters, and negotiation is available, but while the sessions are more popular than they were a decade or two ago, such training sessions are often not well attended unless officers are required to be present. Better educated officers should appreciate the benefits that may accrue from such training; training in these areas, both at basic training institutes and other forms of police training, will increase and improve in the coming decade. Currently, training is available in a self-study format and by distance learning via the Internet, television, CD-ROM, DVD, and videotapes. However, Birzer (1999, pp. 16–19) concluded that most police academies still conduct police training through a lecture format. He found that this approach does not encourage effective learning and called for the implementation of "self-directed learning to foster the community policing culture." Such skills are at a premium when the police are trying to educate the public, whether about a crime prevention program, new police policies, proper complaint procedures, or other issues. Increasingly, the public is being recognized as a major aspect of the police role. And, not least important, communications skills are critical when the police are training their own.

One of the major purposes of future police training, then, is, or should be, to make better communicators of the public servants responsible for maintaining order. Courses dealing with social skills and, more specifically, both verbal and nonverbal communications should be required of all police personnel. Police officers who are trained to express themselves clearly and to be good listeners are likely to be better at both order maintenance and law enforcement. We should also see increasing standardization of training requirements during the next decade. It is likely that minimum training requirements will be established and applied to all police personnel whether full- or part-time, private or public.

Education

One of the most popular proposals for improving the quality of policing has focused on better educated officers. In the United States in the 1970s and 1980s, the idea that a college-educated police officer is a better police officer spawned a federal program (LEAA) that provided millions of dollars annually in support of such education, a dramatic increase in the numbers of college programs related to policing, and a sharp increase in the number of police officers with at least some college education. The debate over the importance of police education continued, federal funding for such education diminished, and there were continuing concerns over the content and quality of police education. However, in 1994 the Omnibus Crime Bill began to provide funding to states for the Police Corps. The Police Corps is a federal program designed to address violent crime by increasing the number of patrol officers with advanced education and training. Typically, these officers serve in low-income, high-crime urban areas or isolated rural areas (U.S. Department of Justice, 2000). Funding allows the officers to complete a baccalaureate degree and up to twenty-four weeks of academy training.

Many of the current concerns surrounding police education result from our inability or unwillingness to decide exactly what we want the police to be and do in our society. It is extremely difficult to develop courses and curriculums for the police under these circumstances. Some believe that liberal arts courses provide the best background for police officers in a multiethnic, multicultural society; others are convinced that specialized courses in criminal justice are preferable, while still others question the value of college education for police officers. Broderick (1987, p. 218) states, "As late as 1985, data were still being gathered which indicated that many in academia, for example advisors of undergraduate pre-law students, still perceived criminal justice education to be too heavily weighted toward technical and vocational training and too often taught by faculty which did not have the proper credentials."

One survey of police departments serving cities with populations of 50,000 or more found that about half of all police executives who responded preferred to hire officers who have majored in criminal justice (Sapp & Carter, 1988). A similar number indicated no preference in college degrees or majors. Those who preferred criminal justice majors did so because of the graduates' knowledge of policing and criminal justice, while those stating no preference indicated they preferred a broader education to prepare officers to deal with a wide variety of situations, including those not dealing with law enforcement.

The same study indicated a general perception among police executives that colleges and universities do not have curriculums that meet the contemporary needs of law enforcement agencies (Sapp, Carter, & Stephens, 1989). The respondents found that criminal justice graduates are very knowledgeable about the criminal justice system and policing in general but are often "narrow in ideology" and lack the broader understanding of divergent cultures and social issues confronting the police. These executives do not want colleges and universities to teach police skills but are seeking graduates who can integrate the duties of a police officer with an understanding of democratic values.

Shernock (1992) argues that many students seeking college degrees in criminal justice and law enforcement are interested only in being credentialed. Being credentialed does not lead to more professional behavior or change police perspectives toward their clients, and thus fails to fulfill the hope that college education will help police understand and deal more effectively with the human aspects of their work. To be effective, college education must not be associated simply with expectations for career advancement and pay increments, but must first become "a requirement for all who enter policing so that it does not become a source of differentiation within policing. In addition, police officials and educators must place less emphasis on mere college credits or a degree for police officers, and much more on receiving the kind of broad-based liberal arts education . . . that Vollmer, the National Advisory Commission on Higher Education for Police Officers, and others have associated with professionalism" (Shernock, 1992, p. 88). The consensus appears to be that liberal arts curriculums should be part and parcel of college and university criminal justice programs in the future.

Police Leadership

As we have seen, the quality of leadership in police organizations has varied tremendously. Some carefully select entry-level personnel, carefully evaluate their potential for promotion, promote based on merit, and prepare those who are to be promoted by sending them to appropriate training and/or educational programs. Other police organizations do none of these things. Many, perhaps most, departments have a difficult time deciding what types of leaders or supervisors they want. Should leadership positions be filled by those with skills in communicating with and supervising personnel? Should they be filled by personnel with extensive street experience? Are policing skills or management skills more important? Answers to these questions are crucial in determining the criteria for promotion to leadership positions. The issue is further complicated by the fact that, at the level of the chief at least, political savvy and the ability to cooperate as an agency representative with respect to other public service agencies sometimes conflict with expectations of agency personnel.

Couper and Lobitz (1993) identified a number of behaviors that they believe are essential for effective police leadership. The leader must create and nurture a vision of the future, and must live according to set of values that can be shared with others. The leader must be a good listener, must hire for the future, and must be more concerned with "turf" (geographic areas) than with "time" (shifts or watches). Good leaders pay as much attention to perceptions as to reality, and they continually strive to improve the quality of their organizations. To bring about positive change within the organization, Couper and Lobitz (1993) believe police leaders must develop the following:

1. A clear, shared vision of where the organization is going
2. A personal commitment to maintaining high standards
3. A system that empowers people to participate
4. A method that develops and rewards people
5. The ability to think and live in the long term

Developing such leaders in policing has not been easy. Germann (1993, p. 10) indicates that the current role model for the traditional police department consists of an administrator who believes that all crime-related problems can be solved by the use of force. There are police leaders with a very different view, however. These leaders see police personnel as community helpers rather than as force-oriented lethal weapons. For them, officers should be engaged in working closely with citizens and develop pride and trust in the department and in fellow professional officers. The actions of these officers show respect for human dignity, human rights, and human values. Germann (1993, p. 10) concludes,

> People like these—professional, well educated, highly motivated, with keen minds, social sensitivity, strength of character, and the courage to tell the king he is naked—are the pride of the American police service. They need to be encouraged, supported, and given access to the authority and power that are needed for immediate implementation of necessary changes of policy and procedure.

Private and Contract Police

For a variety of reasons, we are likely to see a considerable increase in the use of private and contract police officers over the next several years. Policing in rural areas is becoming an increasingly expensive proposition as standards for police officers improve, as gangs and predatory criminals become more mobile and recognize that small-city and -town police are ill prepared to deal with either swift hit-and-run crimes or more long-term invasions, and as the technology of policing becomes more sophisticated and more costly while the willingness and ability of taxpayers to fund public services diminishes.

In many areas in the United States, people living in townhouses, apartments, and condominiums have banded together to employ private protection agents. In numerous housing projects, largely independent police personnel are now responsible for security. According to Nasser (1993, p. 9A),

> In some low-income housing projects here [Los Angeles], the U.S. Department of Housing and Urban Development pays for security guards to protect residents from gang warfare. New York City uses private guards to police schools. Miami hires rent-a-cops to patrol its metro-rail system. . . . In Kansas City, MO, police want to contract private companies to pick up 22 jobs done by the department. Already they've replaced civilian officers at school crossings and may soon be hired to respond to security alarm calls.

Cronkhite (2001, p. 10) reported that there are currently twice as many private police as public police. Furthermore, Bennett and Hess (2001, p. 549) concluded that by the year 2000, 75 percent of the protection will be provided by the private sector. This trend indicates both a desire and a need for improved communication and cooperation between the police, private security, and business communities. As Sherman (1990, p. 11) indicated, one problem with the hiring of private security officers to protect private space and property is a "disinvestment in public safety and the increased investment in private safety (which) raises issues of class, equality, and the increasing gap between the rich and the poor."

Technological Changes in Policing

No discussion of the future of policing would be complete without at least a brief look at the impact of advancing technology on the field. The computerized innovations of the past decade have left us on the threshold of challenging and sometimes controversial possibilities. For example, many police departments are implementing portable/mobile computing to achieve paperless reporting. Portable/mobile computing refers to laptop or notebook computers, mobile digital terminals (MDTs), mobile computer terminals (MCTs), and voice-based computer terminals (VCTs) (Drescher, 2000).

Peak (1995, p. 71) concluded that police in the future will use "electric and methane-fueled scooters and bubble-topped tricycles for densely populated areas; steamwagons and diesel superchargers for police in rural and suburban areas; and methane-filled helium dirigibles, equipped with infrared night goggles and sophisticated communications and lighting devices, for patrol and assistance in planning barricades to trap high-speed drivers and search and rescue operations." DNA fingerprinting and other forms of genetic testing, as well as the use of automated fingerprint identification and optical disk imaging, make it possible to solve crimes that were once thought to be unsolvable (Arkenau, 1990). Facial recognition software is another recent investigative tool. Facial recognition software creates a map of a person's face and compares it with thousands of pictures in a database using eighty distinctive points (Associated Press, 2001).

According to Crank (1998, pp. 268–278), policing in the future will include a return to foot patrol, a shift from 911 systems to penalty fees for bogus calls, the decentralization of police command structures, and the increased use of personal video recording devices. In addition, police will continue to make use of the Global Positioning System (GPS) and the Geographic Information System (GIS). According to Clede (1994, pp. 1–6), "The potential of GPS/GIS ranges from pinpointing the location of evidence in the desert to analyzing data to show where crimes will be occurring in the future." Ryder (1990, p. vii) concludes, "Clearly, advances in technology will affect intergovernmental relations and the whole of society, and will require a commitment from criminal justice practitioners to develop responsible information management policies appropriate for the decade ahead."

The opportunities presented by "on-board" computers and instantaneous communication among police agencies at all levels and in diverse geographic areas are indeed exciting. Yet the challenges of developing a criminal justice system in which information flows freely among agencies, and at the same time, reconciling the right to privacy with police needs to know will not be easily met. Nonetheless, the gap between technology available to industry and that available to the police will surely narrow, raising the possibility of an electronic "Big Brother" society and the subsequent erosion of personal privacy rights (Gitenstein, 1990).

Clarifying the Police Role

The impact of the changes discussed in this chapter on the nature of the police role will be considerable. Although economic circumstances will fluctuate with the times, doing more with less is likely to remain the guiding principle for most police agencies. Crank (1998, p. 124) believes that police officers of the twenty-first century will be doing basically what they are doing today and have been doing for the past one hundred years: "The institution of policing swirls around them in constant change and variation, yet what they do on a day-to-day basis on the street is largely unaffected." This is especially true in policing, in which internal change comes slowly and generally meets with stiff resistance, while the external environment changes at an increasingly rapid pace (Brown, 1999, pp. 10–12). However, the affects of shrinking government resources and increasing community demands will increase the call for consolidation of police services. The costs of fighting crime will be too great for many small and lower income communities to face alone (Jurkanin, Bender, & Fischer, 2000).

According to Meadows (1999, p. 145), "Policing in the twenty-first century will be a more demanding and delicate process. The police and the community will share the crime control function. Private security services will continue to assist the police in meeting community protection needs. The police will be given more legal freedom mandates, but will continually be held accountable for mistakes."

The role of the police as negotiators and educators should become increasingly clear in the decade ahead. Communications skills and the ability to resolve disputes through mediation without resorting to arbitration (arrest) have become increasingly important. For example, a recent police employment listing cited the required qualifications as follows: "Candidates must have the ability to learn public speaking, facilitate meetings, conflict resolution, problem solving; possess good verbal communications skills; ability to read, understand, and apply department policies, rules and regulations, law and instructions; ability to analyze situations and quickly adopt and effect reasonable course of action; ability to write clear and accurate reports; understand and follow oral/written directions" (City of Longmont, 2001, p. 2).

The police cannot be all things to all people. Only by educating the public with respect to crime prevention, their rights and duties as citizens to help maintain order and enforce the law, and understanding the needs of the police can we protect democratic values in a setting that encourages dissent while discouraging violence and destruction. Only through a meaningful partnership between the police and the public will we achieve this goal.

TERRORISM

No discussion of the future of policing would be complete without consideration of terrorism—a phenomenon that has plagued numerous societies throughout the world for many years. Only recently, however, have the effects of these violent and cowardly acts been felt here in the United States of America. Even before the acts of terrorism on September 11, 2001 (9/11), we endured others of significance, such as the bombing of the federal building in Oklahoma City 1995 and the first attack on the World Trade Center in 1993.

The American law enforcement community has not been very proactive with respect to counterterrorism activities, particularly at the state and local levels. For the most part, the burden of counterterrorism has been placed squarely on the shoulders of federal law enforcement agencies. Now, however, it is clear that policing at all levels must assume some responsibility for and commitment to the containment of domestic terrorism. This new priority has created a number of concerns for criminal justice administrators, ranging from budgetary deficiencies and training issues to investigative techniques and expanded police powers, which may be subject to constitutional abuse in the name of national defense.

The Proliferation of Domestic Terrorism

Before proceeding to a discussion of variables that have had an impact on the recent growth in terrorism, we must first define the term *terrorism*, for which there are numerous definitions. The one that best suits our needs is the definition espoused by the Federal Bureau of Investigation (FBI), as cited in Simonsen and Spindlove (2000, p. 19): "Terrorism is the unlawful use of force or threat of violence against persons or property to intimidate or coerce a government, the civilian population, or any segment thereof, in furtherance of political or social objectives." It should be noted that terrorism takes many forms, all of which are serious and few of which are obvious. In addition to the bombings, which are commonplace, emergency service personnel also must be able to respond to biological, chemical, and technological or cyberterrorism. Recent incidents of mail that was contaminated with the deadly anthrax virus (Hu, 2001) and the increased potential for "tampering with data and software in the virtual system [which] could have major repercussions in the physical world, involving such things as disruption of air traffic control systems and tampering with automated pharmaceutical or food production" (Williams, 1998, p. 18) are realities that now must be dealt with and prepared for.

Terrorism, as a criminal activity, was identified as the second most prevalent form of transnational crime by a United Nations report entitled *Fourth United Nations Survey of Crime Trends and Operations of Criminal Justice Systems* (Mueller, 1999). The increase in terrorism is underscored by many factors, the most significant of which is globalization. As stated by Williams (1999),

> . . . the threats to national and international security posed by transnational . . . terrorist groups . . . can be understood as a result of two processes—globalization (the emergence of a variety of systems or activities that are global rather than national or regional in scope and that are generally not controlled by states [p. 62] and the crisis of state authority— both of which contribute to a contraction of the domain of state authority. (p. 19)

Other factors directly related to globalization that have contributed to the rise in terrorism are as follows: the current unprecedented *mobility of people*, as it is estimated that there are currently over 100 million migrants worldwide; *increased trade flows* spurred by the lowering of tariffs, the creation of free trade agreements, and the relatively recent democratization of eastern Europe; the establishment of a *global financial system*, which has enabled countries and financial institutions throughout the world to exchange with one another on a twenty-four-hour-per-day basis; and the *rise of mega-cities*, cities with a population of more than eight million inhabitants, which are linked to one another by advanced telecommunication systems. According to Williams, "Such cities are excellent incubators for . . . terrorist groups. They provide anonymity and encourage the kinds of survival skills and bonding mechanisms that underpin all successful criminal enterprises" (1999, p. 34); *the growth of transnational networks* or "cellular structures adopted by many terrorist organizations . . . in which there is sufficient duplication and redundancy that the elimination of particular cells can have only a modest impact" (p. 39); and the *growth of global communication systems and/or telecommunication capabilities* that have created never-before-seen opportunities for cross-border contacts and the subsequent development of more sophisticated networks, which will more than likely improve the success of recruitment efforts on behalf of terrorist organizations (pp. 24–41).

Many of these same issues emerged as central themes at an international criminal justice conference that focused on global changes in organized crime and terrorism. As stated by one conference speaker and FBI agent, "Undoubtedly, terrorism is here to stay and it is the greatest threat to national security. Increased mobility, improved communication, and the potential use of weapons of mass destruction, such as biological threats, will be major challenges for investigators" (Levinson, 1999, p. 9).

The Law Enforcement Response

Prior to 9/11, many in the law enforcement community predicted that acts of terrorism would proliferate if authorities did not begin to focus on the "front end" of the terrorist problem, in other words, focus on the situation from a "proactive and preventive organizational dynamics perspective" (McHugh, 1998, p. 57). The problem with the traditional American response to terrorism, according to McHugh (pp. 57–58),

> is that the terrorists are always one attack ahead of the law enforcement and security professionals, and as a result of this advantage, are frequently successful. This advantage can be neutralized by reinforcing our government's counter-terrorist information collection, management and analysis methods and integrating threat analysis and threat based security countermeasures tailored to law enforcement interdiction operations.

Shortly after 9/11, and in response to the warnings from the law enforcement community, President George W. Bush and the U.S. Congress passed two key pieces of legislation that, if carried out as intended, should forever change the way the United States deals with terrorism. First, the Office of Homeland Security was formed, the mission of which is

> . . . to develop and coordinate the implementation of a comprehensive national strategy to secure the United States from terrorist threats or attacks. The Office will coordinate the executive branch's efforts to detect, prepare for, prevent, protect against, respond to, and recover from terrorist attacks within the United States. (White House, 2001a)

According to a 2001 report by the U.S. General Accounting Office (GAO), these executive-level mandates are to be accomplished by implementing a risk management approach so as to reduce the risk and mitigate the consequences of future terrorist attacks. This will be accomplished by conducting threat assessments "to evaluate the likelihood of terrorist activity against a given asset or location . . . [which] helps to establish and prioritize security program requirements, planning, and resource allocation" (p. 3); by conducting vulnerability assessments to identify and respond to "weaknesses in physical structures, personnel protection systems, processes, or other areas that may be exploited by terrorists" (p. 5); and by performing criticality assessments "designed to systematically identify and evaluate important assets and infrastructure in terms of various factors, such as the mission and significance of a target" (p. 6).

The other piece of legislation passed into law and viewed as necessary by many in the law enforcement community to effectively conduct counterterrorism operations is known as the Patriot Act, an antiterrorism law designed to dramatically expand federal law enforcement and intelligence-gathering authority (White House, 2001b). Specifically, this new law expands federal police powers in the following ways (Bash, 2001):

- The authorization of "roving wiretaps" or the need for just one court order to tap multiple phone numbers, including cell phones, fax machines, and pagers
- Allowing for the detention of non–U.S. citizens suspected of terrorist activity for up to seven days without formal charges
- Giving law enforcement officials greater subpoena power for e-mail records of suspected terrorists

- Relaxing of restrictions on information sharing between U.S. law enforcement and intelligence-gathering agencies
- Expanding current money laundering statutes by requiring more record keeping and account holder information
- Lengthening the statute of limitations for prosecuting acts of terrorism described as being "egregious"

Probably the most significant component of this new law for municipal police agencies is the one that pertains to the relaxing of restrictions on inter- and intraagency sharing of valuable intelligence between law enforcement organizations at all levels of government. There is perhaps no greater obstacle to effective criminal investigation than the lack of intelligence sharing between law enforcement agencies. This phenomenon sometimes occurs because of bureaucratic disclosure restrictions, on occasion so as to not compromise the integrity of an investigation, but more often than not because of petty jealousies and/or the fear of being upstaged by a different agency. Speaking to this very issue in a speech to the U.S. Conference of Mayors, FBI Director Robert Mueller III (2001, pp. 13–14), said, in part,

> . . . that no one agency or entity at any level, whether it be federal, state or local, has the length or the breadth of talent and expertise. We must work together. Law enforcement, quite simply, is only as good as its relationships. . . . I have asked the special agents in charge in cities where we do not already have a joint terrorism task force to get one up and running quickly . . . they do break down stereotypes and communications barriers, more effectively coordinate leads, and help get the resources in the right places. In short, they are an excellent tool for melding us together in ways that make information sharing a non-issue.

While these new laws are applauded by many, they are not without critics. Probably the most serious criticism is that the expansion of these police powers may be abused or not applied as Congress intended. Worries concerning potential constitutional abuses in the name of national security and patriotism are not without substance, particularly when viewed in light of past abuses by many U.S. law enforcement agencies (see Highlight 12.3).

It is interesting to note that during past national crises (i.e., wars and conflicts with other nations), Congress had almost always expanded the powers of federal law enforcement agencies, perhaps because the vast public relations campaigns that accompanied our nation's efforts allowed for easy passage of such legislation. Whatever the reason, what almost always followed, however, were law enforcement and intelligence-gathering operations that seemed to follow hidden agendas, many times violating the constitutional rights of U.S. citizens. For example, from 1953 to 1973, covering much of the Korean conflict and the Vietnam War, the Central Intelligence Agency intercepted, opened, and photographed more than 250,000 personal letters; collected the names (from arrest reports) of over 300,000 persons arrested for homosexual acts; and regularly monitored the activities of persons whom they identified as political dissidents,

■ ■ ■ ■ ■

HIGHLIGHT 12.3

LOCAL POLICE HAVE ROLE TO PLAY IN NATION'S EFFORT ON TERRORISM

President Bush and Congress have acted quickly and decisively to repair the physical and psychological damage caused by the terrible events of Sept. 11 and to minimize the chances of such acts of terror recurring.

I welcome and endorse these actions, particularly the appointment of Gov. Ridge to head the country's antiterrorist activity as director of the Office of Homeland Security. The full extent of Ridge's responsibilities has not yet been defined, but among them will be coordinating the efforts of the more than 40 federal agencies or elements of agencies—including the Coast Guard, FBI, INS, and Customs Service—responsible for protecting this country and its citizens against terrorists.

Putting all these separate agencies under the control of a single commander who can develop a comprehensive strategy is surely right. But it won't be easy. On the basis of over 33 years of experience in law enforcement in two of the country's largest police departments, and as a consultant to police agencies around the world, I have no hesitation in saying that probably the most difficult aspect of law enforcement is getting independent agencies to work together. Even getting separate units in a single agency to work together can be difficult.

Jack Maple, a former NYPD deputy commissioner who was probably the most innovative thinker on policing that this country has ever produced, used to say that the biggest lie in law enforcement was, "We work well together." Maple therefore developed the COMPSTAT process for managing police departments. COMPSTAT forces individual units to work together. The heads of each unit are required to meet regularly with the top management of the agency to account for their performance. An important measure of their performance is the extent of their cooperation.

If anyone can make 40 or so federal agencies pull together, Ridge can. But to succeed, he will have to introduce a COMPSTAT-like approach to ensure that it happens.

I also welcome the federal government's decision to spend significant amounts of new money on the antiterrorism effort. The State Department, for example, is to get nearly $5 million, half of it for rewards to people who provide information that leads to apprehending terrorists. The FBI is to get $36 million toward the costs of investigating the events of Sept. 11.

In addition, the Federal Aviation Administration will be getting $123 million to pay for federal law enforcement officers to serve as sky marshals and to increase airport security. This will permit the FAA to buy the latest security equipment, including body X-rays that can, employing very low dosage rates of radiation, detect weapons hidden under clothing, or walk-through "sniffers" that, simply by subjecting someone to a puff of air, can tell whether that person has been in contact with explosives by detecting minute traces of explosive adhering to clothing or hands. Such equipment must be deployed as a matter of urgency.

I am concerned, however, about what I did not hear last week. Virtually nothing was said about the role local law enforcement agencies, like the Philadelphia Police Department, can play in our country's antiterrorism effort. Local police know their communities far better than federal or state agencies do and can therefore play a vital role in the collection and analysis of antiterrorism intelligence. We are better placed to advise local businesses and schools and others on how to protect themselves. Because it is our job to deal with the first effects of terrorist activity, we have the greatest interest in preventing it.

We therefore need to be brought into Ridge's planning processes and given the resources to buy the equipment needed to thwart terrorist activity and to train our officers in its use. We cannot rely on federal agencies to lend us this equipment whenever we need it.

(continued)

HIGHLIGHT 12.3   Continued

I am not advocating an anti-terrorism role for every local police department. Most are far too small to take on this added responsibility. But the 52 largest police departments around the country are fully capable of playing this role for their regions. And they would welcome the challenge.

Experience around the country has shown that a regional approach is essential in fighting crime of all kinds. For this reason, the Philadelphia Police Department has been working with colleagues in the rest of the Philadelphia area to establish a regional crime-mapping center that will enable all of us to share information on crime and criminals. We have already begun to have COMPSTAT meetings at which crime is mapped across jurisdictional boundaries.

I believe strongly that such regional collaboration should be an important part of our national antiterrorism program. The Philadelphia Police Department is ready to do its part. I hope that we will be asked to do so.

John F. Timoney is former police commissioner of Philadelphia.
Timoney, John F. (2001, September 26). *The Philadelphia Inquirer.* Reprinted with permission of the author.

including keeping them under surveillance, burglarizing their homes, and eavesdropping on their telephone conversations (Rosoff, Pontell, & Tillman, 1998, pp. 249–250).

From the period extending from World War I through the Vietnam War, the FBI, the most prestigious of all American law enforcement agencies, spied on people who opposed the draft and/or engaged in labor organizing efforts; conducted warrantless searches and wiretapped communications of persons suspected of communist activities; infiltrated the American Civil Liberties Union, numerous peace organizations, and various professional coalitions; and more or less targeted anyone who advocated for social change or reform (Rosoff, Pontell, & Tillman, 1998, pp. 251–256).

In similar fashion, during the 1960s, military intelligence agencies collected and maintained information on the financial affairs, sex lives, and psychiatric histories of persons whom they felt were engaged in "domestic unrest" or those who sought to change existing government policies (Rosoff, Pontell, & Tilman, 1998, p. 250). If there is any credence to the age-old adage that history tends to repeat itself, the most recent expansion of federal police powers is likely to become subject to abuse.

Another area of great public concern regarding the new police response to terrorism is the issue of racial profiling or biased enforcement, discussed at length in Chapter 8. Because of the events that occurred on 9/11, should persons of Middle Eastern ancestry be targeted by various police initiatives simply because of this status? Clearly, the answer is "No," and we must emphasize that recently expanded police powers be tempered by the responsible exercise of discretionary authority and that the actions of the police community be closely monitored.

Recommendations for Improvement

One would be naive to believe, even with the creation of the Office of Homeland Security, the expansion of powers given to law enforcement, and the public's heightened awareness, that we have seen the last of domestic terrorism. The best we can hope for and focus on is preparedness and the mitigation of similar acts in the future. In this regard, there a few things we can do to accomplish these objectives. First, we must be sure not to make the same mistake as before—placing all of the responsibility for counterterrorism on the shoulders of the federal government. For obvious reasons, the federal government must assume the lead role in this endeavor, but our nation's response to terrorism must be a concerted effort on behalf of the police at all levels.

Accordingly, there are strategies and plans that can be implemented and performed at the state and local levels that can assist in this regard. One is for states and municipalities with sufficient resources to cooperate with the various joint task forces about which FBI Director Mueller spoke. The advantages are obvious, and the benefits in terms of preparedness are significant.

Smaller communities with limited budgets also must assist. Police departments, fire departments, social service agencies, health care professionals, and volunteer organizations must work together to increase their level of preparedness in response to the varied threats that acts of terrorism pose. A good example of this new spirit of cooperation was exemplified at a disaster planning conference sponsored by the Casualty Care Research Center. The Center lent their medical expertise to a variety of local emergency service personnel by helping them plan and prepare for emergency procedures following a possible chemical or biological attack (Seaton, 2001).

Another more grassroots approach to assisting in this regard lies within the field of academia. Since 9/11, universities and other institutions of higher education are increasingly beginning to offer courses pertaining to terrorism; world politics; religion; war; race, ethnicity, gender, and class; and foreign policy (Simmons, 2001). It is important to note that all of these offerings have one central theme—to make students begin to think globally in order to put world events into the proper perspective. As one professor stated, "We have a tendency to be very critical of the Taliban and bin Laden . . . and rightfully so. They did attack us . . . [but] we're remiss for not trying to get a little deeper and find out where they're coming from. They didn't attack us just because they hate Americans" (p. 1D).

It is disturbing to think that it took the catastrophic events of 9/11 to persuade many in academia to incorporate internationally based course offerings into their curriculums—this trend or movement should have occurred decades ago. In reference to this very point, we can remember during the months preceding the events of 9/11, a proposal for the creation of an academic center or institute designed to focus primarily on the international issues facing our global criminal justice community, terrorism being targeted as a central issue. Various governing authorities rejected the proposal because of its international emphasis, alluding to their belief that international issues are of no consequence for regional universities. For obvious reasons, this sort of short-sighted decision making must cease if academia is to responsibly react to and assist our nation's efforts to combat terrorism.

Another obvious component of our local response to terrorism should be to provide state and local emergency service personnel with meaningful continuing professional education and training activities. The content of such training, in addition to focusing on terrorism, should stress the topics of ethics, professionalism, and the judicious exercise of discretionary authority. These efforts should assist in mitigating potential abuses that may arise during the efforts of our law enforcement communities to combat terrorism successfully.

If we, as a nation, are to respond to terrorism effectively, we must do so justly, lawfully, and responsibly, and perhaps most important of all, be guided by the spirit of interagency and interdisciplinary cooperation.

DISCUSSION QUESTIONS

1. What is the role of community policing in the future of American policing?

2. Discuss the current relationship between the private security industry and public policing. Is that relationship likely to change in the next few years? If so, in what ways?

3. What qualifications should we look for in tomorrow's police leaders?

4. Will the emphases on police education and training remain the same in the years to come? If not, what changes do you anticipate?

5. Discuss some technological changes that are likely to have a major impact on policing for the rest of this century.

6. What do you see as the future for accreditation? What do you see as the future for lateral entry?

7. Discuss the role of the municipal police in dealing with terrorism. What recommendations can you make as to how this role could best be fulfilled?

REFERENCES

Alpert, G. P., & Dunham, R. G. (1997). *Policing urban America*, 3rd ed. Prospect Heights, IL: Waveland.

Arkenau, D. L. (1990). Records management in the 1990s. *FBI Law Enforcement Bulletin, 59,* 16–18.

Associated Press. (2001). Police receive grant for facial recognition software. In *Law Enforcement and Corrections Technology News Summary*. National Law Enforcement and Corrections Technology Center, National Institute of Justice. Available online at: http://www.nlectc.org/inthenews/newssummary/weeklynews.html.

Bash, D. (2001, October 12). Senate passes anti-terrorism legislation. *CNN.com*. Retrieved January 8, 2002 from the World Wide Web: http://www.cnn.com/2001/ALLPOLITICS/10/12/ret.senate.antiterror/.

Bayley, D. H., & Shearing, C. D. (1996). The future of policing. *Law and Society Review, 30,* 585–606.

Bennett, C. W. (1993). The last taboo of community policing. *Police Chief, 60,* 86.

Bennett, W. W., & Hess, K. M. (2001). *Management and supervision in law enforcement*, 3rd ed. Belmont, CA: Wadsworth/Thomson Learning.

Birzer, M. L. (1999). Police training in the 21st century. *FBI Law Enforcement Bulletin, 68,* 16–19.

Bobinsky, R. (1994). Reflections on community-oriented policing. *FBI Law Enforcement Bulletin, 63,* 15–19.

Broderick, J. J. (1987). *Police in a time of change*. Prospect Heights, IL: Waveland.

Brown, J. M. (1999). Traffic safety in the future. *Sheriff, 51,* 10–12.

CALEA Online. (2000). Commission on Accreditation for Law Enforcement Agencies. Available online at: http://www.calea.org/newweb/accreditation%20Info/standards.htm.

Carter, D. L., & Radelet, L. A. (1999). *The police and the community*, 6th ed. Upper Saddle River, NJ: Prentice-Hall.

City of Longmont. (1992). Employment listings, Longmont, Colorado. Available online at: http://www.ci.Longmont.co.us/police/geninfo/recruit.htm.

Clede, B. (1994). Radio computers locate places, and plot them on a map, too. Available online at: http://www.clede.com/Articles/Police/gps.htm.

Couper, D., & Lobitz, S. (1993). Leadership for change: A national agenda. *Police Chief, 60,* 15–19.

Crank, J. (1998). Policing in the 21st century. In Reichel, P. L. (ed.), *Selected readings in criminal justice.* San Diego: Greenhaven Press.

——— . (1995). The community-policing movement of the early twenty-first century. In Klofas, J., & Stojkovic, S. (eds.), *Crime and justice in the year 2010* (pp. 107–125). Belmont, CA: Wadsworth.

Cromwell, P. F., & Dunham, R. D. (eds.), *Crime and justice in America: Present realities and future prospects,* 2nd ed. (pp. 191–204). Upper Saddle River, NJ: Prentice-Hall.

Cronkhite, C. L. (2001). American criminal justice trends for the 21st century. *Crime and Justice International, 16,* 9–35.

Dale, N. (2000). Survival strategies for the next decade. *Law and Order, 48,* 117–122.

Drescher, C. (2000). LEIM guideline for: Mobile/portable computer technology. Technology Clearinghouse, International Association of Chiefs of Police. Available online at: http://www.iacptechnology.org/LEIM/MobComp.htm.

Fitzgerald, J. D., & Cox, S. M. (1994). *Research methods in criminal justice: An introduction,* 2nd ed. Chicago: Nelson-Hall.

Germann, A. C. (1993). Changing the police: An impossible dream? *Law Enforcement News, 19,* 6, 10.

Gitenstein, M. H. (1990, April). Integrating technology and human values through responsible law and policy (pp. 51–53). In *Criminal justice in the 1990's: The future of information management.* Proceedings of a BJS/SEARCH Conference. Washington, DC: U.S. Department of Justice.

Greene, J. R. (1989). Police and community relations: Where have we been and where are we going? In Dunham, R. G., & Alpert, G. P. (eds.), *Critical issues in law enforcement: Contemporary readings* (pp. 349–368). Prospect Heights, IL: Waveland.

Grossman, I., & Doherty, J. (1994). On troubled waters: Promotion and advancement in the 1990s. *FBI Law Enforcement Bulletin 63,* 10.

Hu, W. (2001, November 14). A nation challenged: The suburbs; small towns find their ingenuity tested by terrorist threat. *New York Times,* p. B6.

Holden, R. N. (1994). *Modern police management,* 2nd ed. Englewood Cliffs, NJ: Prentice-Hall.

International Association of Chiefs of Police. (1998). *Future of women in policing: Mandates for action.* Alexandria, VA: International Association of Chiefs of Police.

Joseph, T. M. (1994). Walking the minefields of community-oriented policing. *FBI Law Enforcement Bulletin, 63,* 8–12.

Jurkanin, T., Bender, L., & Fischer, R. (2000). Identifying the future of law enforcement. *Illinois Law Enforcement Executive Forum, 1,* 29–33.

Kelling, G. L. (1999). *Broken windows and police discretion.* National Institute of Justice. Washington, DC: U.S. Department of Justice.

Kelling, G. L., et al. (1974). The Kansas City preventative patrol experiment: A summary report. Washington, DC: The Police Foundation.

Levinson, A. (1999). Twenty-first century crime goes global. *Crime & Justice International, 15,* 9–10, 33.

Lieberman, P. (1990). Facing the future. *Police, 14,* 44–71.

McHugh, S. (1998). Intelligence, terrorism, and the new world disorder. In Moors, C., & Ward, R. (eds.), *Terrorism and the new world disorder* (pp. 57–59). Chicago: Office of International Criminal Justice.

Meadows, R. J. (1999). Legal issues in policing. In Muraskin, R., & Edwards, A. R. (eds.), *Visions for change: Crime and justice in the twenty-first century,* 2nd ed. (pp. 145–163). Upper Saddle River, NJ: Prentice-Hall.

Morgan-Sharp, E. F. (1999). The administration of justice based on gender and race. In Muraskin, R., & Roberts, A. R. (eds.), *Vision for change: Crime and justice in the twenty-first century,* 2nd ed. (pp. 379–393). Upper Saddle River, NJ: Prentice-Hall.

Mueller, G. (1999). Transnational crime: An experience in uncertainties. In Einstein, S., & Amir, M. (eds.), *Organized crime: Uncertainties and dilemmas* (pp. 1–18). Chicago: Office of International Criminal Justice.

Mueller, R. III. (2001, December). Responding to terrorism. *FBI Law Enforcement Bulletin, 70*, 12–14.

Nasser, H. F. (1993). Private security has become police backup. *USA Today*, p. A9.

Nowicki, D. E. (1997). Speech presented at Police Executive Research Forum. In Alpert, G. P., & Piquero, A. R. (eds.), *Community policing*, 2nd ed. (pp. 265–274). Prospect Heights, IL: Waveland.

Palmiotto, M. J. (1999). The influence of community in community policing in the twenty-first century. In Muraskin, R., & Roberts, A. R. (eds.), *Visions for change: Crime and justice in the twenty-first century*, 2nd ed. (pp. 133–144). Upper Saddle River, NJ: Prentice-Hall.

Peak, K. J. (1995). Peeking over the rim, what lies ahead. In Palacios, W. R., Cromwell, P. F., & Dunham, R. G. (eds.), *Crime and justice in America*, 2nd ed. (p. 71). Upper Saddle River, NJ: Prentice-Hall.

Rosoff, S., Pontell, H., & Tillman, R. (1998). *Profit without honor: White collar crime and the looting of America*. Upper Saddle River, NJ: Prentice-Hall.

Ryder, J. (1990, April). Introduction. *Criminal justice in the 1990's: The future of information management*. Proceedings of a BJS/SEARCH Conference. Washington, DC: U.S. Department of Justice.

Sapp, A. D., & Carter, D. (1988). Factors in the choice of an educational institution and police executive college degree preferences. *ACJS Today, 7*, 1.

Sapp, A. D., Carter, D., & Stephens, D. (1989). Police chiefs: CJ curricula inconsistent with contemporary police needs. *ACJS Today, 7*, 1, 5.

Seaton, R. (2001, November 28). Federal research center is helping: County workers prepare for disaster. *St. Louis Post-Dispatch*, p. 2.

Sherman, L. T. (1990, March 31). LEN interview: Lawrence Sherman. *Law Enforcement News, 16*, 9–12.

Shernock, S. K. (1992). The effects of college education on professional attitudes among police. *Journal of Criminal Justice Education, 3*, 71–92.

Simmons, K. (2001, December 11). Plotting a new course; Sept. 11 prompts some state colleges to tailor studies of world issues. *Atlanta Journal and Constitution*, p. 1D.

Simonsen, C., & Spindlove, J. (2000). *Terrorism today: The past, the players, the future*. Upper Saddle River, NJ: Prentice-Hall.

Sparrow, M. K., Moore, M. H., & Kennedy, D. M. (1992). *Beyond 911: A new era for policing*. New York: Basic Books.

Thibault, E. A., Lynch, L. M., & McBride, R. B. (2001). *Proactive police management*, 5th ed. Upper Saddle River, NJ: Prentice-Hall.

U.S. Census Bureau. (2000). Statistical information staff, population division. Washington, DC. Available online at: http://www.census.gov/population/projections/nation/summary/np-t2.txt.

U.S. Department of Justice. (2000). Office of the police corps and law enforcement education. Available online at: http://www.ojp.usdoj.gov/opclee.

U.S. General Accounting Office. (2001). *Homeland security: Key elements of a risk management approach*. Washington, DC: U.S. Government Printing Office.

White House (2001a, October 8). President establishes Office of Homeland Security. Retrieved January 8, 2002, from the World Wide Web: http://www.whitehouse.gov/news/releases/2001/10/20011008.html.

White House (2001b, October 26). President signs anti-terrorism bill. Retrieved January 8, 2002, from the World Wide Web: http://www.whitehouse.gov/news/releases/2001/10/print/20011026-5.html.

William O. Douglass Institute. (1984). *The future of policing*. Seattle: William O. Douglass Institute.

Williams, P. (1999). Getting rich and getting even: Transnational threats in the twenty-first century. In Einstein, S., & Amir, M. (eds.), *Organized crime: Uncertainties and dilemmas (pp. 19–63)*. Chicago: *Office of International Criminal Justice*.

———. (1998). Transnational threats. In Moors, C., & Ward, R. (eds.), *Terrorism and the new world disorder* (pp. 1–39). Chicago: Office of International Criminal Justice.

Zhao, J. (2001). Future of community policing in community era. In Palacios, W. R., Cromwell, P. F., & Dunham, R. G. (eds.), *Crime and justice in America: Present realities and future prospects*, 2nd ed. (pp. 131–204). Upper Saddle River, NJ: Prentice-Hall.

PUBLIC INFORMATION POLICY: RIVER FOREST POLICE DEPARTMENT

INDEX AS

PURPOSE

The purpose of this order is to establish procedures for releasing information to the public and the news media.

ORDER

Public Information Policy (54.1.1)

Law enforcement operations in a free society must not be shrouded in secrecy; there must be full public disclosure of policies, and an openness in matters of public interest.

Both to protect individual rights and to maintain the confidentiality of records, the Department will release accurate and factual accounts of events of public interest, and strive to make its objectives and policies known to and accepted by the public.

Public Information Function (54.1.2)

A. The Crime Prevention Officer's (CPO) duties include to act as the Public Information Officer and:
1. to help members of the news media gather information about cases investigated by the Department
   a. to prepare a weekly summary for the local press
   b. to prepare special news releases for the regional or national news media when a major case focuses attention on the Village
2. to publicize special Department programs
3. to act as the general liaison person with the media
B. Other responsibilities of the CPO include:
1. to serve as the central source of information about the Department, and to respond to requests by members of the news media (including on-scene responses, when necessary)
2. to be available for on-call response to the news media for major newsworthy incidents
3. to prepare and disseminate news releases
4. to arrange press conferences and to help the press when directed to do so by the Chief of Police
5. to coordinate the release of information regarding victims, offenders, witnesses and suspects, in accordance with Department practice
6. to act as media liaison during crisis situations
7. to coordinate and authorize the release of information about confidential Department investigations and operations, as permissible
8. to arrange interviews with Department members at the request (for good cause) of news media representatives
9. to maintain files of press releases issued by the Department and/or Department supervisors
10. to confer regularly with unit supervisors to keep abreast of cases which may be of interest to the news media
11. to assume a proactive role (at the direction of the Chief of Police) in contacting the news media with information that might not otherwise come to their attention
12. to work closely with the Village Administrator or his designee to promote Village concerns, through the use of means such as cable TV announcements

News Release Procedures (54.1.3)

A. Press summaries are designed to provide accurate, useful information to the public in a timely manner so that the residents of River Forest are aware of incidents in their community and are alert to any possible threat to their security.

B. Generally, release of information to the news media will be governed by the following procedures as they may relate to frequency, content and media recipients:

    1. Frequency. Weekly press summaries are provided each Monday morning by 10:00 A.M. to reporters from the *Forest Leaves* and the *Wednesday Journal*. Early releases are occasionally requested (usually 9:00 A.M. on Fridays) to accommodate early deadlines for holiday weekends. Under normal circumstances, a listing of regional press contacts appears in a file named NEWSCONT.ACT

    2. Content. Generally, media personnel may review only those reports which have been approved and made available to them by the PIO.

    3. Media recipients. The Department will furnish information to the news media in a manner designed to ensure its equal availability to all. When a public news "briefing" or conference is to be held, the Department will notify all local news media representatives. Routine, weekly news releases will be provided to local and regional print media.

    4. Also see section 5 of this directive.

Press Summary Preparation (54.1.4)

A. The CPO will prepare the press summary from original reports under the following categories:

    1. Arrests. Provide details of significant arrests, and indicate the first court date. Minor offenses such as most traffic violations should not be included in this category; such offenses are simply tallied, and the total is inserted into the summary paragraph.

    2. Accidents. Provide details of serious accidents—those resulting in serious injuries or fatalities. Include the following in the Accident summary:

        a. the total number of accidents

        b. the number of accidents involving the citing of one or more drivers

        c. the number of accidents involving injuries

        d. the number of hit-and-run accidents

    3. Offenses. Provide details of significant incidents. However, note the exceptions under (54.1.5, *Press Summary Style*)

    4. Investigations. Provide details of new reports initiated by Detectives, and of newsworthy progress on follow-ups of previous cases. Maintain close contact with the Detectives to keep abreast of developments in cases.

B. Data: While preparing the Press Summary, the CPO will include specific data in several reports and files.

    1. Photocopy the Offense and Arrest reports of any case involving a vehicle pursuit, and place the stapled copy in the *Vehicle Pursuit Survey* folder.

    2. Record all arrests on an "Arrest Worksheet." Each arrest for the purposes of these reports, is credited to a single officer. Arrests may include non-custodial arrests (e.g., capturing a suspect being sought by another agency, and then releasing him to that agency on the street) recorded on an Offense or Incident report, providing the credited officer documented the arrest and was materially responsible for the apprehension.

3. Transcribe information from the "Arrest Worksheet" into the Paradox SE file named "Arrest" followed by the last two digits of the year.
4. Log information from any report involving the underage consumption or possession of alcohol, in two places:
   a. the "Juvenile Alcohol" worksheet (tally sheet) located in the folder of the same name
   b. In the case of an arrest, insert the name, DOB and LO-ticket number in the Word file named Alcohol.Juv (for use by the Village Prosecutor)
5. Constantly scan crime reports to identify significant similarities or patterns between incidents, and report any to the Detectives.
C. Copies: Make four copies of the completed summary. File the original in the Weekly Press Summary folder, and distribute the copies as follows:
   1. Two copies for the local press
   2. A copy for the Chief (placed in his "In" basket)
   3. A copy for the Village Administrator (placed in his "in" basket)

Press Summary Style (54.1.5)

A. Prepare the press summary in chronological order within the four categories identified in (54.1.4A), using hanging paragraphs headed by the case number.
B. Spell out numbers one through ten, and use arabic script for all others.
C. Write the full day and date (e.g., Tuesday, April 3) at the first appearance of the date. Then, in subsequent, consecutive references to the same date, write only the name of the day.
D. Identify incident locations by the block only (e.g, "the 600 block of Forest," or "the zero-hundred block of Ashland"), unless the location is a business or public institution (e.g., "at the Jewel Food Store, 7525 Lake Street"). Identify victims in general terms only (e.g, "a resident of the 7800 block of Oak Street").
E. Identify River Forest Police Employees by position, not by name (e.g., "an officer on routine patrol . . . ," "a tactical officer on assignment in the area . . . ," or "detectives investigating the crime . . ."). Generally, identify officers from other jurisdictions by name (e.g., "Oak Park police officer Jerry Sullivan . . .").
F. Identify adult arrestees who have been charged with a crime by their age, name and home town (e.g., "27 year old Lawrence Fry of Bellwood). Include the first assigned court date in the summary so that reporters can follow-up on the court proceedings.
G. Identify suspects by their physical description, including their race, gender and age (e.g., "a white female in her mid-20's"), unless the description is unique or identifiable enough that the published information might bring additional witnesses forward (e.g., "the victim described the suspect as a black male in his early 30's, 5'9", 175 pounds, with close-cropped hair, a severely pock-marked face, and wearing a blue and white plaid shirt and dark pants").
H. Never identify those under the age of 17 (whether victim, arrestee or witness) by name; instead use their age, home town and gender (e.g., "a nine-year-old Oak Park boy").

I. Release photographs only at the direction of the detectives, and with the approval of the Chief of Police.

J. Generally, include a description and value of property losses (e.g., "a Toro snowblower valued at $360"). However, do not include a description and value of major property losses (over $3,000), in order to prevent the victim from being targeted again (e.g., if a ring valued at $50,000 is lost, report it as "jewelry valued in excess of $1,000"). If the media requests more specific information, consult with the detectives and the Chief of Police first.

K. Parties or other incidents involving underage drinking, by past practice and agreement with the press, should be identified by address, provided the host or homeowner has been cited (e.g., "Officers responding to reports of a teenager party at 603 Quick, charged a 15 year old resident with serving alcohol to minors. He is scheduled to appear in court on June 15 . . .").

L. Several categories of incidents should not be reported in the press summary because their appearance might inspire similar incidents. Reporters have been informed of these omissions. They include:

  1. reports of the loss or theft of license plates or license plate stickers

  2. reports of harassing telephone calls

  3. most animal complaints, unless a severe injury or serious property damage occurs

  4. property losses and minor injuries involving Village vehicles, property or employees

Press Summary Word Usage (54.1.6)

A. Avoid using police jargon, including the following words phrases, in press releases:

  1. "Officers responded to . . . *reference a . . .*"
    Instead: "after a man reported that . . ."

  2. "Officers *cleared the scene.*"
    Instead: "No further police service was required."

  3. "*Plate* entered into the computer"
    Instead: "**The** plate . . ."; use articles as in common speech.

  4. "Plate entered as missing"
    Instead: use the verb: "The plate **was** entered as missing."

  5. "*A resident of the 200 block of Forest came into the station to report . . .*"
    Instead: Walk-in reports should not identify the complainant's address.

  6. ". . . *with negative results.*"
    Instead: use "unsuccessfully," as in "The area was searched unsuccessfully."

  7. "The man *was sent on his way.*"
    Instead: "The man was released at the scene."

  8. "7201 *W.* North Avenue"
    Instead: Do not use directions in River Forest addresses—all addresses are either north or west

  9. "Canvassed" [when referring to an area that was searched]
    Instead: Use "searched."

10. "Officers responded to *the lot* at . . ."
Instead: Use "the parking lot"—do not assume reporters will understand the terminology.

11. "*Auto*"
Instead: Use "vehicle" rather than an abbreviation for the word "automobile."

12. "*$30.00 or $29.60*"
Instead: Round losses to the nearest dollar and do not use decimal points.

13. "*USC*"
Instead: Do not abbreviate United States Currency. A dollar value will imply U.S. dollars. The country of origin should be identified only if the loss is foreign currency.

14. "The house *checked secure*."
Instead: "The exterior of the house was checked, and no sign of forced entry, loss or damage was found."

B. Phrases and styles that should be used in press releases:

1. *Theft (of wallet).* In the case of theft and burglary, the heading should identify what was taken or what was burglarized (e.g., "Burglary [garage]" or "Residential Burglary").

2. *Officer, Theft, Security Agent.* Capitalize official titles (e.g., "Officer Jones"), and formal charges (e.g., "Criminal Trespass to Property"). Do not capitalize when using the word as a noun rather than as a title (e.g., "The man left before the officer arrived"). Capitalize "Department" in formal reference.

3. *Black male . . . , white male teenager.* To maintain consistency, use race before gender when both are to be used in a description.

4. *One, two, eight, ten, 11, 13, 125 . . .* To maintain consistency, spell numbers one through ten, and use numerals for numbers eleven and higher.

5. *Twenties, thirties . . .* Spell out such numbers used in descriptions, rather than using "20's" or "30's."

6. *Both parties were advised of their rights under the Illinois Domestic Violence Act . . .* This should be done on all domestic violence and domestic dispute cases; the notification should specifically be included in press releases.

7. *Evidence was recovered . . .* No further description of physical evidence should be provided.

8. *The case was referred to Detectives for follow-up . . .* Use this if detectives are either pursuing leads developed by patrol or conducting a general inquiry.

9. *The case was referred to Detectives for investigation . . .* Use this if detectives will initiate a separate investigation, particularly one involving a major crime.

News Release Authority (54.1.7)

A. On-scene. To avoid confusion, the Department will disseminate accurate and timely information at the scene of an incident. The CPO will be summoned to the scene or to the station without delay. If the CPO is absent, only his designee or a sworn supervisor may release information to the news media.

B. Department files. Information from Department files may be released to the news media, in accordance with Department directives and under the supervision of the CPO only.

C. Ongoing investigations. Only the CPO, Investigations Unit supervisor, Chief of Police or their designee may release information to the news media regarding an ongoing criminal investigation.

D. CPO unavailable. When the CPO is not available, his duties may be assumed by the appropriate Division Commander, or in his absence the highest ranking sworn supervisor on duty, or his designee. Nominal work hours for the CPO will be 8:00 A.M. to 5:00 P.M., Monday through Friday.

News Media Representatives (54.1.8)

A. The Department does not issue press credentials, but it does recognize official press identification of persons who represent recognized public news services.

1. The Department will demand proper identification before permitting entry to the police station for the purpose of gaining information.

2. The Department will also require proper identification before permitting the news media to enter crime, accident, or disaster scenes.

B. The Department will deny access to an incident scene or to its files to any news media representative who:

1. interferes in an investigation while at an incident scene

2. interferes with the effective operation of the Department or any of its members

3. obtains or publishes restricted information

4. violates these established media relations procedures

C. When a telephone caller identifying himself as a media representative asks for information, his identification should be verified by the Department member before any information is released. Verification can be made by obtaining the caller's name, title, employer, and phone number, and then making an appropriate inquiry.

On-Scene Access by Media Personnel (54.1.9)

A. News media requests for information at an incident scene should be referred to the ranking officer in charge of the investigation. The ranking officer may, at his discretion, refer the media to the CPO. Also see section 5 of this directive.

B. Officers at the scene of a serious incident may establish perimeters/barriers to prevent persons from entering the area. Media members may be allowed access, depending upon the situation. However, the rights of owners of private property must be safeguarded. Normally, a specific area for media access and meeting should be established to provide a cooperative and accurate flow of information concerning the incident. If possible, media personnel should be restricted to public property.

News Media Input into Department Policy (54.1.10)

When the Department is considering modifying policies and procedures dealing with news media relations, it will try to involve media representatives, if possible. The CPO will arrange a meeting with media representatives to discuss the proposed modifications and to obtain their input.

Release of Information (54.1.11)

A. General guidelines and restrictions:
1. Any information to be released will be done in accordance with Illinois Statutes and the Illinois Freedom of Information Act (5 ILCS 140/1, et seq.)
2. The Illinois Freedom of Information Act lists 26 specific exemptions to the release of information. The act places the burden of interpreting how to implement the law in the hands of local authorities. The scope and content of each release of information must be determined according to the facts of each case.

B. Specific guidelines:

Some cases, because of their impact on individuals or the community, may have to be handled differently than the guidelines below would indicate. Nevertheless, the following guidelines should generally govern the release of information to the news media:
1. Do not release victim, complainant or witness information (e.g., name, address, phone number, age) for publication, if:
   a. The information is part of an ongoing investigation, and its release may jeopardize the successful resolution and/or prosecution of the case.
   b. The information is part of a sex offense case or sex-related crime report or investigation.
2. Per 705 ILCS 405/1-7, Confidentiality of Law Enforcement Records, inspection and copying of law enforcement records concerning minors who have been arrested or taken into custody before their 17th birthday, will be restricted to the following:
   a. any local, State or Federal law enforcement officers when necessary for the discharge of their official duties during the investigation or prosecution of a crime;
   b. certain prosecutors, probation officers, social workers, and others assigned by the court;
   c. adult and juvenile prisoner review board;
   d. authorized military personnel; and,
   e. authorized persons engaged in bona fide research.
   Inquiries regarding adult charges being filed will be referred to the State's Attorney's Office of the proper county of jurisdiction.
3. Other restrictions/prohibitions:
   a. revealing the identity of informants
   b. revealing the identity of any deceased person, unless:

      1) The identity has been confirmed officially; and,

      2) A concerted effort has been made to notify the decedent's immediate family.

  c. releasing the exact details of evidence or statements (e.g., a confession, admissions, excuses, or refusals) made by the accused, without the authorization of the Chief of Police

  d. referring to results of investigative procedures (e.g., fingerprints, polygraphs, ballistics, or other tests), or references to the refusal of the accused to submit to such tests

  e. making statements about the testimony or credibility of prospective witnesses

  f. discussing the possibility of either a plea of guilty or a plea to a lesser offense

  g. offering personal opinions as to the accused's guilt or innocence, or to the evidence or merits of the case.

4. Victim information in most all other police reports will be available for publication.

5. Generally, information available for publication should include the following:

  a. the name, age, home town, and occupation of the accused

  b. the nature of the offense, the time and place of the offense, and an account of the arrest, including whether it involved resistance, pursuit and/or use of weapons

  c. the duration of the investigation

  d. any information that would help to capture the accused, or to warn the public of any dangers posed by the accused

  e. a brief description of the incident

  f. the nature or substance of the charge(s)

  g. any bail information

  h. the scheduling or result of any step in the judicial process

6. In order to ensure that the Department's specific guidelines for information release are met, the CPO will work closely with representatives of the news media, regarding daily and routine matters. The news media *will not* be allowed unrestricted review of all police incident reports.

7. If the Department determines that some information should be withheld from the news media, the CPO will carefully explain the reasons for doing so, and attempt to obtain their understanding and cooperation.

8. Generally, information should be disclosed through personal contact, rather than telephone contact. However, information may be disclosed by phone if the caller's identity is known and the guidelines previously cited are followed.

Notification of the CPO (54.1.12)

The CPO should be abreast of all significant events involving the Department. When a press release is formulated at the watch, section or division level, the CPO will be notified in a timely manner and provided with a copy of the information released.

Joint Agency News Releases (54.1.13)

For incidents involving multiple public service agencies (e.g., other police departments, fire departments, the coroner's office, the state's attorney's office), the agency having primary jurisdiction will coordinate the release of information.

By Order of:

_____

MICHAEL HOLUB, CHIEF OF POLICE

NAME INDEX

SUBJECT INDEX